The Remarkable Past

The Remarkable Past

Tales from *My Country* and *The Wild Frontier*

selected by the author

Pierre Berton

Canadian Cataloguing in Publication Data

Berton, Pierre, 1920–
The remarkable past: tales from My country and The wild frontier
ISBN 0-7710-1357-4

1. Canada – History. 2. Canada – Biography. 3. Frontier and pioneer life – Canada. 4. Pioneers – Canada – Biography. I. Title. II. Title: My country: the remarkable past. III. Title: The wild frontier: more tales from the remarkable past.

FC163.B47 1995 971 C93-095372-X
F1026.B47 1995

We acknowledge the courtesy of the following individuals and institutions in supplying photographs:

p. 65 Metropolitan Toronto Library Board (M.T.L.B.) / p. 103 photo by Bill Lingard. Courtesy A. Graham Thomson Memorial Museum, Alexandria Bay, N.Y. Inset: M.T.L.B. / p. 139 M.T.L.B. / p. 198 bottom: M.T.L.B. / p. 200 M.T.L.B. / p. 218 D. Frane / p. 290 Provincial Archives, Victoria (P.A.V.) / p. 318 Rhoda Hirtle / p. 335 Vancouver *Sun* / p. 343 Glenbow-Alberta Institute (G.-A.) / p. 346 top: Public Archives of Canada; bottom: G.-A. / p. 347 G.-A. / p. 349 G.-A. / p. 365 P.A.V.

Maps by Jack McMaster

Printed and bound in Canada

McClelland & Stewart Inc.
The Canadian Publishers
481 University Avenue
Toronto, Ontario
M5G 2E9

1 2 3 4 5 99 98 97 96 95

Contents

Books by Pierre Berton

The Royal Family
The Mysterious North
Klondike
Just Add Water and Stir
Adventures of a Columnist
Fast, Fast, Fast Relief
The Big Sell
The Comfortable Pew
The Cool, Crazy, Committed
 World of the Sixties
The Smug Minority
The National Dream
The Last Spike
Drifting Home
Hollywood's Canada
My Country
The Dionne Years
The Wild Frontier
The Invasion of Canada
Flames Across the Border
Why We Act Like Canadians
The Promised Land
Vimy
Starting Out
The Arctic Grail
The Great Depression
Niagara

PICTURE BOOKS
The New City (with Henri Rossier)
Remember Yesterday
The Great Railway
The Klondike Quest
Pierre Berton's Picture Book
 of Niagara Falls

ANTHOLOGIES
Great Canadians
Pierre and Janet Berton's Canadian
 Food Guide
Historic Headlines

FICTION
Masquerade (pseudonym
 Lisa Kroniuk)

FOR YOUNGER READERS
The Golden Trail
The Secret World of Og

Adventures in Canadian History
The Capture of Detroit
The Death of Isaac Brock
Revenge of the Tribes
Canada Under Siege
Bonanza Gold
The Klondike Stampede
Parry of the Arctic
Jane Franklin's Obsession
The Railway Pathfinders
The Men in Sheepskin Coats
A Prairie Nightmare
Steel Across the Plains
Trails of '98
Dr. Kane of the Arctic Seas
Trapped in the Arctic
Kings of the Klondike
Before the Gold Rush
The Battle of Lake Erie

List of Maps

Preface

This is not a book about Canadian heroes, at least not in the classical sense. In my terms, a hero is somebody who is prepared to give his life for a cause, which narrows things down to martyrs, warriors, and saints (there are no saints in this book – they are boring to write about). By my definition, Isaac Jogues, Billy Bishop, and Pierre, Chevalier de Troyes are the only real heroes in this collection.

However, many of the other characters in these stories do display their own peculiar brand of heroism. Certainly Mina Hubbard, who trekked across unexplored Labrador to restore her husband's reputation, and also François Xavier Prieur, my favourite character in the book. Prieur was not a hero; like John Jewitt, he was a victim. Ned Hanlan, the sculler, and Joshua Slocum, the sailor, were what we today call "sports heroes" – not heroes at all, but celebrities. Samuel Hearne, another favourite of mine, was an anti-hero. He stubbornly refused to sacrifice himself and his followers in a silly war; as a result, we are today able to enjoy his journals of exploration.

Most of the people I've written about are interesting because of their imperfections. Wilfred Grenfell and Cariboo Cameron had flaws of character that make them fascinating. Charles Chiniquy, temperance crusader, Bill Johnston, the pirate, and Charles Bedaux, part-time Fascist, are all entertaining, but I wouldn't want to have any of them to dinner.

Of the eighteen central figures in this book, I've known only one personally, and he would have been the last to call himself a hero. Robert Service didn't even admit to being a poet, only a "versifier." Nor did he remain true to *The Spell of the Yukon*, in which he announced that he intended to go back to the wild that he loved so much. But he reneged.

Why? I asked him, one afternoon at his villa in Monte Carlo.

"It was just too cold," said the Bard of the North.

No hero he.

Pierre Berton
Kleinburg
October 1994

1
The Martyrdom of Isaac Jogues

It is not easy for the twentieth-century mind to come to terms with Isaac Jogues's zeal for martyrdom. To others of his faith, death by torture in the name of their God was certainly an occupational hazard, but to Jogues it was much more: it was a dream to be cherished, a goal to be fulfilled, a sublime climax to a life of sacrifice. The evidence suggests that Jogues longed to be a martyr and that he sought out that fate as fervently as medieval knights pursued the Grail. He revelled in discomfort, welcomed pain, endured the most dreadful torments, and went off to what he knew was certain death on a forbidding frontier with an enthusiasm that today would be equated with lunacy.

But Jogues was no madman, nor was he a witch, as the Indians with whom he lived tended to suppose. He was a seventeenth-century Jesuit priest who believed with absolute conviction in a literal Heaven and an actual Hell – a Hell in which every unbaptized adult, be he Frenchman, Iroquois, or Hottentot, was doomed to suffer eternally the torments of the damned.

To Jogues, one of the greatest services he could render God and man was the hasty and often secret baptism of a dying Huron baby – wiping its brow with a handkerchief dipped in water hurriedly made sacred while feeding it raisins and pretending to take its pulse. Without that act of absolution Jogues was convinced (as were his fellow priests) that the infant would be confined to limbo, denied forever the presence of God. That was a circumstance almost as horrifying as the one which awaited those adult Indians who refused the sacrament and who were thus condemned to be roasted forever over a slow fire or parboiled through all eternity in a lake of molten brimstone. Jogues was better able than most to understand the horror of that fate, for he had himself seen humans roasted alive; indeed, he half hoped that his own life would end in the same fashion. He did not fear the flames, for he knew they would not be eternal; his earthly life was brief and transitory, the pain of his passing momentary. What did a few years of hardship matter when at the end lay the delights of Holy Paradise?

Such convictions are as foreign to us today as were those of the Hurons whom Jogues was trying, without much success, to convert to his way of thinking. Indeed, it has been said that in terms of their beliefs in supernatural forces, the Jesuit and the Huron had more in common than either does with modern man. But that does not mean they were on the same wavelength. The Indians were mystified by Jogues and his black-robed colleagues: what on earth were these bizarre celibates doing among them? They did not even want to trade! And they seemed obsessed by the idea of death. The priests, for their part, were confused by the Huron lifestyle, which they never did understand. The sexual licence common among the unmarried natives appalled them; they were themselves so modest that they shrank from undressing in front of one another. But another aspect of the Huron behaviour shocked them even more – the refusal of the Indians to use physical punishment to discipline their children. These mutual gaps in understanding were exacerbated by the conviction on each side of its own social, spiritual, and intellectual superiority.

Jogues was born in Orléans, France, the middle child of nine in a prosperous merchant family. At the age of ten he was accepted for instruction by the Jesuit order. He was a willing pupil. He seems, in fact, to have been almost *too* devout, for by the time he was a novice at seventeen, he had to be restrained from over-meticulous observation of the most trivial rules. He was a small, agile youth, not strong but wiry, a good swimmer and runner, an excellent scholar and an adequate poet. The contemporary portraits, which are, of course, idealized (for Jogues eventually became a saint), show him in later life as a slight figure, thin-faced and hollow-cheeked, with downcast eyes and a somewhat ragged beard. His ambition was to be a missionary in one of the far corners of the earth – he had thought of Constantinople, but his superior made a more accurate prediction. "Father Jogues," he told him, "you will not die anywhere but in Canada."

His choice of a patron provides a clue to his ambitions. He selected Father Charles Spinola, martyred in Japan in 1622; he carried a picture of that unfortunate priest being burned at the stake. He prayed to him, we are told, "and envisioned a similarly glorious ending for his own life."

He was ordained at the age of twenty-nine and ordered at once to Canada. The year was 1636; Louis XIII was on the throne of France; Richelieu, his first minister, had just four years before given the Society of Jesus exclusive missionary rights in the New World. The Thirty Years War had been raging for a generation; the citadel of Québec, a pawn in the struggle, had changed hands twice – from France to England and back to France again. In Europe, the Renaissance had reached the period of high baroque; Rembrandt in Holland, Velázquez in Spain, Rubens in the Low Countries, were at the peak of their talents. Paris, applauding the work of its rising new playwright, Pierre Corneille (himself a product of Jesuit education), thought itself exquisitely civilized.

On the far side of the ocean barrier – eight weeks' sail for the handful who attempted the journey – lay New France, a vast, virgin wilderness, stretching west from the Atlantic to the unknown shores of Lake Superior and south from Hudson Bay to Lake Erie, a domain far larger than the parent land and scarcely explored. Only one white man, Jean Nicollet, had actually seen Superior and then only its eastern tip near the present site of Sault Ste. Marie. Two pinpoints of civilization, Trois-Rivières and Québec, existed on the St. Lawrence. The rest belonged to the Indians – to the nomadic Algonkins and their relatives, the Montagnais, who roamed the Precambrian forests between the St. Lawrence and James Bay, and to the sedentary Hurons, who occupied the agricultural lands in the neighbourhood of what is now Lake Simcoe. To the south of the Great Lakes lay Dutch territory and the five nations of the Iroquois League, whose language and culture were similar to those of their enemies, the Hurons.

To many on arrival from Paris or Rouen, the culture shock of this wilderness world must have been numbing; to Jogues it acted as a tonic. From Québec he wrote to his mother: "I do not know what it is to enter paradise, but this I know, that it would be difficult to experience in this world a joy more excessive and more overflowing than what I felt when I first set foot in New France and celebrated my first mass here . . . I felt as if it were a Christmas day for me, and that I was to be born again to a new life, and a life in God."

This super-enthusiasm would never be quenched in spite of the dreadful ordeals that lay ahead. One hardly knows whether to pity Jogues, even in his moments of greatest anguish, for he continually gives the impression that he is in a state of ecstasy.

He did not want to stay in Québec; he hungered to be sent to the farthest reaches of New France, to the pagan realm of the Hurons. Since a Huron trading party was due at Trois-Rivières, his superiors dispatched him to meet it. And there the little priest encountered his first example of the Indian lifestyle: he witnessed the torture and death of an Iroquois brave at the hands of a group of Algonkin women and children. This grisly spectacle would have deterred most newcomers, but it merely strengthened Jogues's resolve to "soften their hearts and tame their wild savagery."

A second shock lay in store. Accompanying the Huron trading party was an old acquaintance, Father Antoine Daniel, a skeletal figure, barely recognizable, body wasted, skin leathered and wrinkled, eyes sunk deep in their sockets, cheeks hollowed, beard and hair ragged and matted, cassock in shreds. To Jogues, the other priest was a saint and a hero; he begged to be allowed to return with the Hurons in Daniel's place and, after some palaver, the Indians agreed.

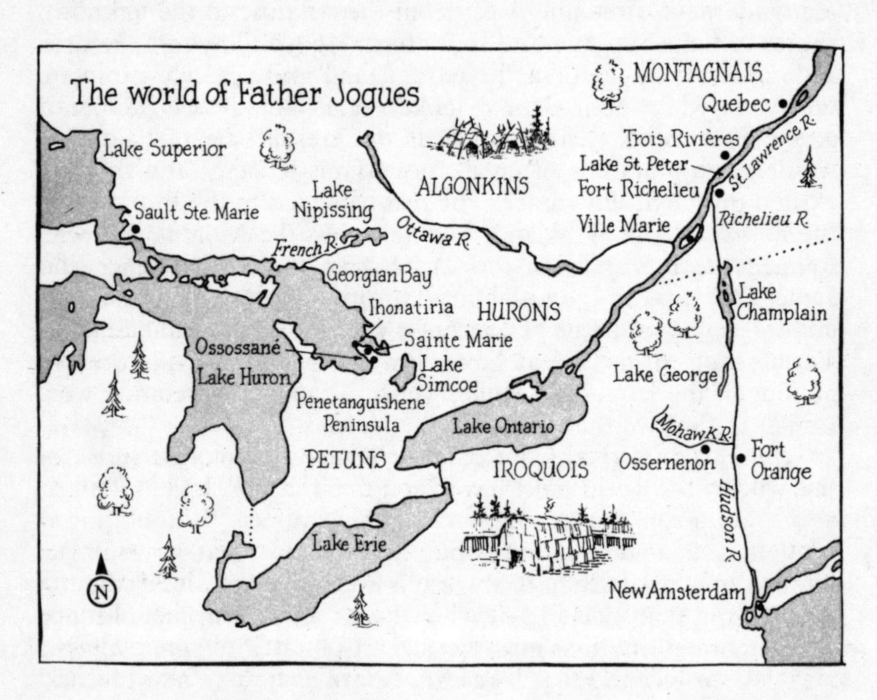

The land of the Hurons lay some eight hundred miles to the west; that meant at least a month of hard travel by canoe and portage, a gruelling experience for a young missionary fresh from France. Jogues was forced to sit motionless in the canoe, his knees drawn up to his chin, afraid to move lest he disturb the balance. His food consisted of a little corn, pounded between two stones and boiled in water without seasoning. At night he slept on the hard ground "or the frightful rocks lining the great river," suffering the torment of mosquitoes and black flies. On the portages – there were more than forty – he scrambled over huge boulders and crawled along slippery ledges, burdened for much of the journey with an eleven-year-old boy who was too exhausted to struggle on his own. Yet, for Isaac Jogues, all this was bliss because "the love of God, who calls us to these missions, and our desire of contributing something to the conversion of these poor savages, renders this so sweet, that we would not exchange these pains for all the joys on earth."

The route led up the St. Lawrence to the Ottawa River, through Lake Nipissing, and along the French River until Georgian Bay was reached and finally the Huron village of Ihonatiria on the Penetanguishene peninsula. Like everybody else who visited the Georgian Bay country in that century, Jogues could not help but be struck by the contrast between the funereal Precambrian land through which he had just passed – a wilderness of sombre conifers and rubbled gneiss – and the luxuriant domain that now greeted him. Verdant with stands of oak and pine, the land rolled gently toward the water, rendered pastoral by small plots of cultivated maize, the Indian corn that was basic to the Huron culture. The forests were alive with deer, beaver, and bear; the surfaces of the lakes dark with wildfowl; the waters beneath teeming with trout, pike, and sturgeon. Unlike the nomadic Algonkins, the Hurons had no need to roam the Shield. Provender lay at their doorsteps. They occupied two dozen semi-permanent villages, located near streams and fertile soil and connected by some two hundred miles of narrow trails. Upwards of eighteen thousand persons lived and lived well in the seven-hundred-square-mile strip between Lake Simcoe and Georgian Bay. It was the most populous wedge of land in eastern North America.

For the missionary, however, life was not easy. Father Jean de Brébeuf, who had been the superior since 1634, warned Jogues that first evening what to expect: six months of continual discomfort and cold during the winter, confined to a draughty cabin constantly crowded with Indians, with whom they must share their food. The hovel in which the six priests and their five helpers would live was, in fact, a smaller version of the traditional Huron longhouse. This windowless structure ("no Louvre, no palace" as Brébeuf warned) was fifty feet long and eighteen feet wide. The smoke from the open cooking fires that ran down the centre of the building was so thick that it was impossible to read. It would be hard, Brébeuf told Jogues, to find in France a hut so wretched.

Worse, he explained, they would live under the shadow of death: "A malcontent may burn you down or cleave your head open in some lonely spot. Then, too, we are responsible for the sterility or fecundity of the earth, under the penalty of our lives. We are the cause of droughts; if we cannot make rain they speak of nothing less than murdering us." There was, of course, from the Jesuit viewpoint, a positive side: the hardships and enforced poverty provided a glorious opportunity to deepen their devotion to God.

Jogues arrived at the Huron village brimming with enthusiasm but broken physically by the hardships of the trail. He was shortly felled by a serious attack of influenza, one of a series of epidemics which, between the years 1634 and 1640, reduced the Indian population by half and turned them against the white men, whom they believed, not without cause, to have spread the sickness among them. Most of the French were stricken by the disease from which they recovered only with difficulty, partly because they could get no peace from the Indians who crowded around their sickbeds from sunrise to dusk. They had never seen white men sick before and could not understand why they lay prostrate rather than sitting, Indian style, with knees drawn up to chin. The priests did their best to keep the cabins quiet, but the Hurons thought it preferable to chant, dance, and feast about the sick in order to drive off evil demons. The cabins were jammed with men, women, and dogs, in a continual uproar.

The French recovered. The priests saw this as a sign of the power of prayer, but the reason was more likely their acquired resistance to a disease unknown to the natives. While the epidemic spread across the whole northern section of the peninsula, each side remained arrogant in the assumption that its remedies – and its alone – were the cure for the affliction. The Hurons turned to their medicine men, one of whom offered to cure the Blackrobes with roots, herbs, and potions, all for the price of ten glass beads; Brébeuf dismissed him as a charlatan. The priests preferred to bleed their patients, a treatment equally superstitious.

Jogues, the first to recover, helped minister to the sick. He was more concerned, however, with their spiritual welfare. Regardless, they stubbornly resisted his attempts to baptize them. It was most puzzling, not to say annoying. These primitive creatures did not seem to comprehend the delights of Heaven or the agonies of Hell. "I have no desire to go to Heaven," one man said, "for I have no acquaintances there, and the French would give me nothing to eat." Another said he would not go to Heaven because his relatives would not be there. Another refused because he understood there were no fields, no corn, no trading, fishing, hunting, or marriages in Heaven.

These responses, which ought to have given the Fathers an insight into Huron values, were lost on them. The Hurons rejected conversion because it would cut them off from their culture and their friends, and, to a Huron, everyone was either friend or enemy. The basic unit of friendship and co-operation was the extended family. Friends shared everything; from an enemy one could expect only hostility, injury, or death. Death was something the Hurons did not care to contemplate, yet it seemed that these peculiar white men in their outlandish dress were obsessed by it. They did not appear to care much about life; they seemed to talk of nothing but the hereafter. Nor were the Hurons immune to the flawed logic of cause and effect. They noticed – how could they not? – that when a priest sprinkled water on somebody, that somebody almost invariably died. From the priests' point of view, it was better for the Indians if they died as soon after baptism as possible, for death prevented them from sliding back into heresy.

The Jesuits had taken pains to learn the native tongue. Brébeuf spoke it fluently and so, eventually, did Jogues and the others. They could speak, but they could not communicate, nor could the Indians with them. Yet both were united in a common belief in the supernatural – in demons who could control human lives. Brébeuf was convinced that the Indians were guided by Satan and his attendant devils whose presence was as real as the maple trees. (Some priests actually "saw" these evil spirits and banished them by making the sign of the cross.) The Hurons were divided about the Blackrobes: one faction believed them to be witches, responsible for the influenza epidemic; another held that they were powerful shamans who could drive off the demons of illness.

Witches, in Huron society, were considered the most dangerous of enemies. Anyone could slay a proven witch with impunity, for his relatives were not permitted the usual practice of seeking compensation or blood revenge. And how was a witch to be identified? By a process not unlike the one then being practised in civilized Europe and white America: any deviation from the accepted social norms was sufficient to arouse the suspicion, especially in times of crisis. A failure to be polite, a tendency to speak harshly, a refusal to be generous with presents or feasts, an unusual desire for privacy – these were seen as un-Huron activities. This was exactly the way the Jesuits behaved, albeit unwittingly, among a people they thought stubborn and ungrateful. Little wonder then that, during the six years he lived and travelled among the Hurons, Jogues and his fellow priests laboured under the menace of execution and torture.

In spite of threats and plots to massacre them, the Blackrobes travelled from village to village, often in waist-deep snow, seeking to baptize the Indians. Jogues had never felt such fulfilment. In June, 1637, with his usual enthusiasm, he wrote to his mother that he and his fellows had managed to baptize two hundred and forty Hurons: "The life of a man, could it be better employed than in this noble work?" he asked. "All the labours of a million persons, would they not be well compensated for the conversion of one single soul, gained for Jesus Christ?" It did not in the least concern him that all but one of these two hundred and forty had been baptized on their deathbeds, often not comprehending the rite. To Jogues, this was irrelevant; he had snatched them from the pit – literally at the eleventh hour. Of all that number, only one healthy adult had voluntarily accepted the Christian faith.

The Hurons believed that the Jesuits were trying to destroy their society and their culture. This was not the intention of the priests, who had specifically learned the language and gone out to the villages to preserve the Indian culture, or so they thought. It did not occur to them that in accepting Christianity, an Indian was rejecting his own lifestyle. For among the Hurons, religion and culture were indivisible; they could not comprehend the European attitude in which the two were conceived of as separate. The blindness on both sides can be seen in the impressive ceremony and feast that marked the baptism of the one healthy Indian. The priests, with a singular myopia, thought it salutary to exhibit a large and grisly painting of the Last Judgment, depicting serpents and dragons tearing out the entrails of the damned. The Hurons completely missed the point. They were convinced that the victims were Indians like themselves whom the Blackrobes had caused to die the previous winter.

By the end of October, 1637, the sporadic voices demanding the execution of the priests had developed into a unanimous chorus. The Huron council, convening after dark on the twenty-eighth, blamed the pestilence on the Blackrobes. No one defended them. So convinced were the Fathers that they were going to die that they adopted the Huron custom of holding a ritual farewell feast in which friends and enemies alike were invited to their cabin and offered prodigious supplies of fish and corn. Yet they were not killed, in spite of continued threats, largely because of the Hurons' greed for European trade goods. They feared, with good reason, that any harm done the Jesuits would result in a break with New France.

Each side continued to misunderstand the other's motives, beliefs, and customs. The priests thought the Indians fickle and inconstant because those who accepted Christianity continued to practise the old rites. The Jesuits could not understand the Indians' ability to borrow from various religions. As far as the Hurons were concerned, Christianity was another healing society; it did not occur to them that membership in one group precluded membership in another. Moreover, the priests failed to realize that politeness was part of the Huron code of behaviour; in dealing with others, a Huron was expected to be gentle and considerate and to repress feelings of frustration or hostility, which were reserved for the common enemy. These are also Christian virtues, but the Christian priests were confused by the Indians' apparent friendliness, by their readiness to accept and to listen, which went hand in hand with an inability to assimilate the truths of Christian teachings. The Hurons, on the other hand, were greatly offended when the priests censured or ridiculed their own explanations of their customs and culture. More than once they gently reminded the strangers that each side had different customs and should respect the other's beliefs. But the Jesuits could not bend.

In the summer of 1638, the Hurons were plunged into a savage war with the Iroquois who, short of European goods, were bent on plundering trading parties in New France. Captured Iroquois were burned, mutilated, scalped, and sometimes eaten by their captors, who, in spite of their paganism, engaging in double-think, became enraged when the captives were baptized by the Jesuits before their ordeal. The Hurons did not think it proper that their enemies should be granted the happiness of paradise – in the event that paradise actually existed. They tossed the bones of their victims into the Blackrobes' cabins. The priests responded with a Christian burial.

The ritualized torture of prisoners of war by all the Iroquoian peoples, which reached its apogee in 1649 with the death of Brébeuf and others, has fostered an image of these Indians as unspeakable savages given to orgiastic excesses. Yet to what degree did their customs differ from similar practices in Renaissance Europe? Pain is pain; horror is horror. Was the mutilation and burning of Spanish heretics, the roasting alive of witches (common to most European nations) and the public disembowelling of living traitors in England less reprehensible than the gauntlet and the stake of the Iroquois? What seemed to horrify Jogues as much as the torture itself was that it was practised not by official executioners but by women and children. But this was as much a part of Indian tradition as the public slaughter for sport of bulls in Spain.

By 1639 there were ten priests in Huronia as well as a number of French workmen, some engaged in building a central mission,

Sainte-Marie (near the modern town of Midland, Ontario) which would be independent of the Indian villages. Father Jérôme Lalemant had replaced Brébeuf as superintendent at the latter's request; Brébeuf felt (quite correctly) that his own abrasive temperament was not conducive to treating with the Indians. A new epidemic, smallpox, was sweeping the country and again the Hurons were blaming the priests – and why not? They seemed to pay attention only to the cabins of the sick, ignoring the living; it seemed obvious that they had a close connection with the disease.

At this time Jogues and a colleague, Father Garnier, were sent on a dangerous evangelical mission to the Tobacco Nation, or Petuns, who derived from the same stock as the Hurons and the Iroquois. These people lived forty miles from Sainte-Marie in the modern day counties of Simcoe, Grey, and Bruce. The two priests went alone, without any idea of the route they were travelling, because no Huron was willing to guide them. The hardships they suffered – they slept out in howling blizzards with only blankets for covering and no fire to warm them – were mild compared to the tensions engendered by their arrival in the Tobacco country. The Petuns turned ugly when a group of Hurons arrived to report that their nation was being ravaged by the white man's disease. The newcomers urged the Petuns to kill the priests. Jogues wrote:

"This whole country is filled with evil reports which are current about us. The children, when they see us arrive at any place, cry out that famine and disease are coming. Some women flee. Others hide their children from us. Almost all refuse us the hospitality which they grant even to the most unknown tribes. We have not been able to find a house for our Lord, nor any place where we can say Mass . . . . They treat us wretchedly in order to oblige us to leave. Truly we have nothing more than what suffices to keep us alive; our hunger usually accompanies us from morning till night. But these poor people do not understand that what keeps us here is more precious than all they can conceive in the way of [the] pleasures of this world . . . "

As they moved deeper into Petun country, the reception became more hostile. Every cabin was closed to them. A screaming, threatening mob followed them from door to door. The chiefs announced that anyone who killed a Blackrobe would be doing a service to his people. The wonder is that they were not murdered; the Indians, who thought nothing of torturing the captives of battle to death, seemed to shrink from cold-blooded assassination.

The two priests toughed it out for three months and then departed, pronouncing the mission a triumph. Why? Mostly because they had suffered so: suffering was their index of success;

suffering was noble; suffering was joy; the path of suffering led directly to the gates of paradise: "This mission to the Petuns has been the richest of all, since the crosses and the sufferings have been most abundant in it."

That spring – the year was 1640 – the missionaries gathered at their new base at Sainte-Marie to calculate their achievements. On paper, they were impressive. They had succeeded in baptizing one thousand Hurons, although more than a third of these were children under the age of seven. The victory was illusory. The smallpox had so terrified the Indians that by early summer fewer than thirty still called themselves Christians. Most of these were traders who saw substantial benefits in professing the white man's religion because it was noticed that those who were baptized got higher prices for their furs in addition to presents. The Hurons were pragmatic; they judged all charms and rites by their effectiveness. Theological argument did not interest them; they considered the French an inferior race intellectually. If they could benefit from their magic, fine; if not, they would seek to neutralize it.

In the summer of 1641, Jogues was put in charge of turning Sainte-Marie into a redoubt against both the Hurons and the marauding Iroquois, who had launched another violent offensive. The work was interrupted by an apostolic mission to one of the Algonkin nations far to the west. Jogues and another priest, Father Charles Raymbaut, made the three-hundred-and-fifty-mile journey in seventeen days, travelling as far as Lake Superior – farther west than any white man had ventured.

Jogues should have been ecstatic; everything he had worked for seemed to be coming true. The Hurons, freed at last from epidemics, were more friendly. New France stood behind the Jesuits. The governor of New France, Charles Huault de Montmagny, who was as pragmatic as the Indians, showered their emissaries with gifts, explaining that these were tokens of the Blackrobes' truths. By Easter of 1642, the missionaries had baptized one hundred and twenty Hurons, all adults in good health – a significant advance.

Yet these successes did nothing to hearten the little priest. He grew impatient, restless, out of sorts. It was almost as if things were going *too* well. The long voyages, the harsh conditions seemed no longer a sacrifice for he had been toughened by the environment. He was now a seasoned woodsman, a veteran of wilderness travel, his muscles as hard as iron, able to digest any kind of food and capable also of bearing up under long fasts. Life had become, well, *normal*, and blessed martyrdom seemed further away than ever! He longed to suffer for his faith, to do battle physically with Satan, but Satan seemed to have been routed or, at least, slowed down. Jogues could not sleep for the agony of it. While his fellow priests slumbered in the smoky cabin, he would rise from his mattress, fall on his knees, prostrate himself before his Maker, and plead for a chance to suffer, to endure pain and fatigue, to face dangers, to be subjected to extraordinary tribulations. He wanted nothing so much as to be "sacrificed as a victim of Divine Love."

Then one afternoon, while on his knees on the hard boards of the chapel, he heard, or thought he heard, God speak: "Thy prayer is heard. Be it done to thee as thou hast asked. Be comforted, be of strong heart." At that moment, Isaac Jogues knew that the martyrdom he longed for would eventually be his.

His prayers were answered with miraculous speed. Lalemant asked him to undertake a journey so hazardous that it came close to being a death mission. Each year it was necessary for a priest to accompany Huron traders down the St. Lawrence to the heart of New France to deliver letters and to fetch reports and supplies. Now, with the Iroquois in full cry against the Algonkins, the Hurons, and the French, this hazardous journey seemed certain to be fatal. Lalemant made it clear to Jogues that the request was not a command; Jogues was free to refuse. *Refuse*! It was exactly the test for which he had been hoping – the beginning of the fulfilment of his prayers.

Father Raymbaut, who was ill, was to accompany him to seek medical attention in Québec. Jogues would have three other white companions – two workmen and a *donné* or lay helper, a carpenter named Guillaume Couture. Eighteen Christian Hurons completed the party.

Even without the threat of Iroquois attacks it was a dangerous journey. Eight hundred miles of wilderness separated Sainte-Marie from Québec, yet the party arrived some forty days later, in the midsummer of 1642, without incident. Ten days later, Jogues, with Couture and another *donné*, René Goupil, headed back, their twelve canoes loaded with a variety of goods ranging from blankets and seeds to chalices and dried fruit. There were more than forty in the group, including some Huron children whom the priests had sent to school in Québec.

The brigade reached the western end of Lake St. Peter, a maze of small islands. The current was stiff, and the canoes held close to shore. To their right, the dense mattress of the forest reached to the water's edge; ahead, in the shallows, the bulrushes grew tall. Suddenly, there arose from the rushes the dread war whoops of the Iroquois. Thirty painted Indians sprang from the weeds and turned their muskets on the flotilla; the Hurons replied with a volley of arrows. Jogues, rising to his knees, made the sign of the cross and shouted words of absolution. When the pilot of his canoe, a non-Christian, was shot through the hand, the priest baptized him on the spot. Then, as more shots rattled around them, the canoe was smashed against the shore and Jogues was thrown into the weeds.

The Hurons in the following canoes turned and fled. Those left to fight were outnumbered two to one: forty more of the enemy appeared; the fighting was hand to hand. It is difficult not to admire Jogues at this moment; hidden in the weeds, he could have made his escape, for the fighting had moved more than one hundred yards away. But he could not abandon his people, especially those that had not been baptized. He stood up and asked to be taken prisoner.

What followed was pure horror. Jogues was knocked down, stripped, and beaten. Goupil, the *donné*, who had also been captured, was tied so tightly with leather thongs that he could not move. The two comforted themselves with the thought that their misfortunes were the will of God, but that did not make the coming torment easier to bear. Couture meanwhile had fought off the Iroquois, killing one of their chiefs, and had fled to the protection of the forest. He, too, decided that he could not abandon his comrades. He was captured, stripped, beaten senseless, and then revived by having his fingernails torn out and a knife jammed through his hand. Jogues did not at first recognize the blood-smeared *donné*, but when he did he threw his arms around him and kissed him. The action bewildered the Iroquois, who thought that the priest was congratulating Couture for killing their chief. Infuriated, they beat Jogues unconscious with clubs, muskets, and kicks. Two grasped his arms, clenched the nails of his forefingers with their teeth, and tore the nails from their roots. They then took each forefinger in their teeth and crushed them to a jelly. This grisly performance, common among all Iroquoian tribes, had a practical origin: it was designed to make escape difficult and to prevent the victim from using any weapon, from musket to bow, against his captors.

Jogues was desolated, not because of his physical condition but because he realized that, with one blow, the Iroquois had devastated the Huron Christian church. Almost all of its leaders had been captured. Paradoxically, his spirit was at peace. The torment that he had sought to suffer for his faith had begun. It would continue unabated for weeks.

The horror began eight days after the battle when the party came upon a camp of two hundred Mohawks. These warriors, armed with clubs and thorn switches, formed two parallel columns, a few feet apart, upon a slope. The prisoners, naked, were formed into a file, the older men at the head to keep the pace slow, and forced to run the gauntlet. Jogues was placed last so that his punishment would be the greatest. Before he had gone a hundred paces he was tripped, beaten unconscious, dragged to the top, revived, and beaten again. The Indians dug into his flesh with their fingernails and thrust burning faggots against his arms and thighs. One bit and crunched into his thumb until the bone was exposed, causing the priest to faint. He regained consciousness but did not rise, for he expected to die. He was exalted; the God "for whose love and sake it is delightful and glorious thus to suffer" had fulfilled his most cherished hopes.

The Iroquois, however, intended to keep him alive. Jogues was hauled to his feet and forced to witness the torture of his comrades, including Eustache Ahatsistari, a Huron warrior who had become a Christian. The priest, tears streaming down his cheeks, tried to intervene but was thrust away. The torture continued into the evening until, at last, the captives were left to sleep on the ground, their bodies a mass of festering flesh, caked with blood, dirt, and cinders.

The following day, the Indians and their prisoners moved off, heading for their home villages. Jogues might now have escaped. He was unfettered; he was at the end of the column; there was no guard; he could easily have slipped into the protection of the forest. But he could not: "I wished rather to suffer the most extreme tortures than to abandon the French and Christian Hurons in their death and to deprive them of that consolation which a priest is able to impart." In Jogues's creed, his comrades would be consigned to the eternal fires if they did not receive the last rites of the church while suffering the temporal flames of the Iroquois.

A march of thirteen days followed. "By the favour of God our sufferings on that march . . . were indeed great," Jogues wrote; "hunger and heat and menaces, the savage fury of the Indians, the intense pain of our untended and always putrefying wounds, which actually swarmed with worms . . . " On their arrival, the tortures grew more hideous. At one point a Christianized Algonkin woman was forced on pain of death to cut off Jogues's thumb. She took the knife in a trembling hand and slashed and tore until she had cut the tendon and pulled the thumb free. Throughout the ordeal, the priest remained silent. He looked at the thumb, which lay at his feet where the woman had dropped it and came to the odd conclusion that his Maker was punishing him for not loving him enough, a divine vengeance for which, as he later wrote, he was profoundly grateful:

"Picking up the severed thumb with my right hand, I offered it to You, my living and true God, for I remembered the Holy Sacrifice which I had offered to you on the altar of your Church through seven years. I accepted this torture, O my God, as a loving vengeance for the want of love and respect that I had shown in touching your Holy Body. You heard the cries of my soul."

Jogues was still struggling with this inverted reasoning when Couture called to him to throw the thumb away; if he didn't, he would be forced to eat it. God surely had not intended any act of cannibalism; Jogues did as he was bidden.

It would be pointless to detail the continued tortures to which these three devout and gentle men and their Huron comrades were subjected. But it is necessary to reiterate that they were scarcely more hideous than those visited upon heretics, traitors, and accused sorcerers in contemporary Europe. In each culture, religion was at the root of the savagery. The torment of captives by the Iroquoian tribes was a sacred ritual, the eating of parts of their bodies an act of religious significance. In Europe, heretics were disembowelled, broken on wheel or rack, roasted over slow fires, confined in iron maidens, gnawed to death by rats or torn to pieces by swine, all in the name of religion. The Iroquois were not the only people who mangled fingers; the Inquisition's thumbscrew was just as painful and mechanically more efficient.

The Mohawks who tortured Jogues and who seem in the Jesuit accounts to be little removed from animals were, in fact, among the most sagacious and civilized of the North American Indians. They belonged to the Five Nations Confederacy, the most sophisticated political alliance on the continent, stretching from the valley of the Hudson to the western end of the Finger Lakes. This league of mutual peace was a creation of genuine political genius. It survived the advent of white settlers and, centuries later, was used as one of the models on which the charter of the United Nations was based after the Second World War. Although the Iroquois often tortured captives, they spared far more, adopting them into their own culture, so that long after the Huron nation was decimated, many of its former members lived on as Iroquois.

Adoption was to be Jogues's fate and that of all but three of his fellow captives. He had been told that he was to die at the stake and had prepared himself, with his usual optimism, for the end: "Sooth to say, this last act was not without its horrors, yet the good pleasure of God, and the hope of a better life, where sin should have no place, rendered it rather one of joy." Again the delights of martyrdom were denied him. Conciliatory members of the Mohawk council argued for the life of the white men, hoping by that action to wean the French from their support of the Hurons and Algonkins.

But conciliation proved illusory. At Fort Richelieu on the St. Lawrence, three hundred Iroquois were driven away by the cannons of the French. The defeated natives returned, eager to put their captives to death. The Dutch, who lived peacefully among the Mohawks – and with reason, because they supplied them with the weapons to do battle with their trade rivals, the French – pleaded for the prisoners' release, offering gifts worth six hundred florins in exchange. The Indians vacillated.

Couture had been adopted by a family in another village. Jogues and Goupil, too weak to escape, were permitted to wander freely about Ossernenon, a community of some forty cabins and garden plots surrounded by a strong palisade. Jogues adapted easily; Goupil, unused to Indian life, was horrified by the filth and the savagery. The Mohawks despised him for his gentleness and feared his devotions, convinced that in making the sign of the cross he was weaving an evil spell. His death was foreordained.

It came one afternoon on a hillside above a brook, while he and Jogues were praying. Two Indians appeared; one produced a tomahawk from beneath his blanket and struck Goupil on the head. The *donné* called out the name of Jesus, staggered, and fell. Jogues knelt to give absolution, then presented himself for execution. The expected blow did not fall. The priest was later to learn that his friend's death had been ordered by an old chief who had seen him make the sign of the cross over his baby grandson.

For the next two months, Jogues was hidden in the home of the family that had adopted him. He was convinced he would soon die and made sure that he was never without a copy of St. Paul's Epistle to the Hebrews and a crude wooden cross he had made, so that when the end came he would have the cross and the scriptures in his hand and be spared damnation.

With autumn came the hunt. Jogues was lent to another family to help carry supplies. With winter approaching, his only clothing was a thin shirt, torn breeches, and a cloak. His stockings were in shreds, his moccasins almost worn through. In spite of his emaciated condition he was expected to carry a crushing load. Soon his legs were torn and bloodied by sword grass and rushes. He could scarcely walk with the pain, but he did not complain.

At first his new family treated him kindly: he was a novelty, docile and eager to help, amusing in his efforts to master the language. But once the hunt began, they lost interest. Jogues remained blind to Indian customs. He was offended when the choicest part of the first animal killed was offered to the Mohawk god. This was superstition: the priest would not, *could* not be a party to it. He was ravenous; his wasted body cried out for nourishment; there was plenty of venison, but he refused to eat a scrap of the heathen meat. His sole food would be corn.

After a week or two the game became scarce. The pagan Mohawks turned out to be as blind as the Christian priest. A sorcerer convinced them that Jogues, by his refusal to eat and his contempt for their god, had driven off the animals. They beat the Jesuit unmercifully, convinced that his prayers were demonic incantations.

The return trip to the village, in December, was an eight-day nightmare, first through tangled underbrush and thorny vines and then through bitter snowstorms. Jogues arrived back at Ossernenon, exhausted and frostbitten, his arms and legs cracked from the cold and running with blood. Now his adopted family, especially his master's wife, whom Jogues learned to call aunt, began to treat him with kindness, nursing him, feeding him, giving him two new deerskins, one to wear and another to use as a blanket. Her motive at the outset was pity; later she grew to like the priest, who was slowly becoming a second son. For the first time since his capture, Isaac Jogues no longer felt under sentence of death.

Forty miles to the east of Ossernenon, white civilization flourished after a fashion at Fort Orange and the surrounding settlement of Rensselaerswyck, the site of Albany, the present capital of New York. The Dutch existed among the Mohawks on sufferance; though they knew that white priests had been enslaved and tortured by the Indians, there was little they could do apart from offering money for their release. In May, Jogues and Couture actually appeared at the settlement but under heavy guard. In New France they were believed to be dead.

Once again the opportunity for escape arose. Jogues's "aunt" told him that if he slipped away during a trading expedition she would not sound a warning. But Jogues had no intention of escaping, for, as he asked himself, who in his absence would console the French captives, "who absolve the penitent? who remind the christened Huron of his duty? who instruct the prisoners constantly brought in? who baptize them dying, encourage them in their torments? who cleanse the infants in the saving water? who provide for the salvation of the dying adult?" Divine Providence had placed him in the hands of the savages for these specific purposes; who was he to shirk God's work? Without him, potential believers would be denied eternal life.

Arent Van Corlaer, the leader of the Dutch community, was irritated by the priest's attitude. Here he was, a Protestant, bending every effort, perhaps at the risk of his own safety, to ransom a Papist (or to connive at his escape), only to be met with a stubbornness he could not fathom. This wretched Jesuit in his tattered cassock seemed determined to remain among the very people who had mutilated him and who still spoke of killing him! Jogues, on his part, seemed to believe that any attempt to liberate him was the work, if not of Satan himself, then of some minor devil. Daily, he wrote, he bowed his knee to his Lord "that if it be for his glory, he may confound all the designs of the Europeans and savages for ransoming me and sending me back to the whites."

At Fort Orange, Jogues was able to pen a long and detailed letter to his superior in France, relating all that had happened. Written in Latin, the report ran to fifteen thousand words – a considerable feat for a man whose hands were so crippled he could hardly hold a pen and whose familiarity with that ancient language had been blurred by long disuse.

Then, once again, the Mohawks turned ugly, cursing him as an evil sorcerer and demanding his death. Some time before, Jogues had taken the risk of trying to smuggle a letter through to New France; a member of the Mohawk war party had taken it, thinking it might be used to entrap the French at Fort Richelieu. But on reading the letter the French had turned their cannon on the Mohawk warriors. The Indians were furious. It was clear now to everyone that Jogues's days were numbered.

Van Corlaer could not stand by and see a white man, albeit a Catholic, tortured to death. He sought out Jogues, who was being held in the Indian camp outside Fort Orange, and pleaded with him to try to escape. A Dutch ship, due to leave shortly for England, lay anchored in the harbour. If Jogues could reach it and hide in the hold until the ship sailed, he would be safe.

Jogues astounded the Dutch leader by asking for time to think the proposal over. Was he out of his mind to consider any other course? No; he was simply being true to his own concept of duty; with Jogues, personal comfort was never a consideration. All that night, surrounded by Indians in a stuffy barn, he wrestled with his conscience and came, at last, to the realization that there was no longer any compelling reason for him to stay. Couture, the only other white prisoner, was safe, adopted into a family. The best of the Huron Christians had managed to escape; the rest avoided his ministrations, believing that he was marked for death. On the other hand, he possessed a fund of Indian lore that would be extremely useful to his superiors in France. Again he weighed the pros and cons: what did the Lord want him to do? He concluded that the Lord "would be more pleased with my taking the opportunity to escape."

The following morning, he informed Van Corlaer of his decision. The Dutch leader called in the ship's captain, who assured the priest that he would be safe aboard ship. The plan was for Jogues to slip out of the barn during the night and to make his way to the river bank, where a rowboat would be concealed to get him to the ship.

The escape had all the elements of a scene from a suspense novel. The barn in which Jogues and his Indian captors were lodged was one hundred feet long, without partitions. It was owned by a Dutch farmer who kept his cattle at one end and slept with his Mohawk wife and children at the other. The Indians sprawled in the middle. When Jogues slipped out of the barn to reconnoitre his escape route, he was set upon by a watchdog that sank its teeth into his bare leg, all but crippling him. The outcry roused his captors, who brought him back, barred the door, and made him lie between two of them. There he remained until dawn, when a Dutch servant came to his rescue, tied the dog, and helped him to limp from the barn without waking the Mohawks. But when the priest reached the river bank, several hours after the appointed time, he discovered to his dismay the tide had gone out, leaving the rowboat stuck fast in the mud. He struggled but it would not budge. The sky had lightened, and he was now in full view of the Mohawk huts. He made one last superhuman effort to loose the rowboat and was successful. A short time later he reached the ship and was hidden in the hold.

The Indians were furious. They threatened to slaughter all the Dutch cattle and burn down the houses. Van Corlaer tried to calm them, offering a present of three hundred guilders; this they refused. The settlers were greatly alarmed. The natives were in a savage mood. Prudence won out over humanity. What was the life of one Catholic against those of a hundred Protestants? One man was deputized to go to the ship to persuade Jogues to return to prevent a massacre. The priest proved himself a more admirable human being than the wavering Dutch. Although in terrible pain from his leg wounds and nearly suffocated from the stench in the ship's hold, where he lay prostrate and half-conscious, he gave no thought to his condition. He was ready, he said, to return to captivity if it would save the Dutch settlement.

The ship's captain, however, had given his word that Jogues would be safe, and he did not intend to go back on it. Jogues remonstrated with him: "If this trouble has been caused by me, I am ready to appease it at the loss of my life." With that, he fainted and fell to the deck.

The Dutch delegate argued with the captain: the settlement did not want to surrender the priest and would do so only in the last extremity. He would be hidden among the Dutch and handed over only if the Indians threatened a massacre. The captain allowed himself to be persuaded. Jogues was rowed to land and hidden for twelve days in Van Corlaer's house. His condition was pathetic; one of the wounds inflicted by the watchdog turned gangrenous. The local surgeon prepared to amputate his leg but fortunately this proved unnecessary. Jogues was moved to another house owned by a miserly old trader who hid him in his attic. While accepting food and drink for the priest, he appropriated most of it, leaving the fugitive half-starved and cramped, crouched among a pile of barrels for hours while, on the floor below, the Mohawks traded with his host.

Meanwhile the Queen Regent of France, Anne of Austria, acting for the new child-king, Louis XIV, heard of Jogues's imprisonment and appealed to the Netherlands government to secure his release. The order came to Van Corlaer: Jogues was to be freed at once and sent to New Amsterdam. The Dutch leader stopped his vacillation. He bluntly told the Mohawks that Jogues was under his protection; if they refused his present of three hundred guilders, all trading would cease.

Why had he not used that threat before? Trade was the key to the matter. The Dutch had temporized because they dreaded the loss of trade as much as they feared the savage tomahawks. But the Indians, too, were unwilling to put an end to barter. On both sides trade was seen to be more important than a human life. That, of course, was not new. Trade was at the root of the bloody war between the Iroquois and the Hurons who were surrogates for the two commercial rivals, the Dutch and the French. It could not be helped that white Europeans were sometimes caught in the middle and condemned to agonizing death.

After much haggling, the Indians capitulated, and the priest was taken aboard a schooner bound for New Amsterdam. He was thirty-six years old but looked closer to fifty, his face drawn and deeply lined, his skin as rough and dark as an Indian's, his beard greying, his hair sparse. He waited until November 5 in the tiny settlement of New Amsterdam on the island of Manhattan until a small barque was ready to take him to England. The Atlantic crossing was stormy, but it did not matter to Jogues that his bed was a coil of rope on the top deck and that he was nightly drenched by the salt waves that rolled across him. He was inured to hardship.

His reception in England was anything but friendly. Civil war was raging between Oliver Cromwell's Roundheads and the Cavaliers of Charles I. Four Roman Catholic priests had already been executed. Jogues was forced to discard his cassock and to travel incognito until he secured passage to Brittany on a collier. It put him ashore on Christmas Day, 1643. The local inhabitants must have found him grotesque, a scarecrow of a man in a sailor's battered cap and an oversize greatcoat, speaking French with a strange accent as he asked the way to the nearest church. But for Jogues it was a moment to be savoured. He lost no time in confessing all the sins he could remember since the previous July – it is intriguing to wonder what these were – and then, on receiving communion, he "tasted the sweetness of . . . deliverance."

He made his way to Rennes and presented himself at the Jesuit college as a traveller from Canada. The rector hurried to greet the stranger. Did he happen to know Father Jogues?

"I know him well," came the reply.

"We have heard of his capture by the Iroquois and his horrible sufferings. What has become of him? Is he still alive?"

"He is alive," cried Jogues, "he is free, he is now speaking to you!" and he threw himself at the feet of his astonished superior, asking his blessing.

He became an instant celebrity. The *Jesuit Relations*, read throughout the nation, had announced his capture and probable death; now he had miraculously reappeared. His fellow Jesuits treated him with awe and reverence, but this was the last thing that Father Jogues wanted. He disliked talking about his adventures; he resisted showing his mutilated hands and his scars; he was concerned that people might think him a martyr, for he knew that he was not. That fate, he was convinced, was yet to come.

He did not want praise and recoiled from recognition but could escape neither. The next edition of the *Relations*, telling the full story of his experiences, was read eagerly. The Queen Regent commanded him to visit her. Alarmed, he tried to avoid the audience but of course could not. Feeling ill at ease, he was presented in the hall of the Palais Royal, where the Queen, examining his mangled hands, kissed them and wept. The publicity made him quail. He had only one ambition: to return to the frontier of New France and to the glory of martyrdom.

His contemporaries in France thought him mad to go back. Surely, it was said, he had done enough. Why expose his mutilated body to further hardships and almost certain death? But perhaps, having come to know something of Jogues's character, we can understand how he felt. For one thing, he felt guilty. Was he truly serving his God in the mirrored, marble halls of Paris? For another, he was genuinely homesick – homesick for the pine forests, the leaping cataracts, the winding trails of New France; homesick for the Indians with whom he had lived, for the smoky, suffocating lodges, and for those magic moments when, often with nothing more than a few drops of dew, he was able to dispatch a dying child to paradise; homesick even for Ossernenon and the verdant valley of the Mohawk, the scene of his greatest trials. Jogues had become a creature of the frontier. But there was something more: this humble and dedicated man had another frontier to cross – the frontier of the soul. He would not rest until he had conquered it.

He was faced with one obstacle – his mutilated hands could no longer hold the sacrament; how could he officiate at the Mass? The reigning pope, Urban VIII, was noted for his strict observance of ritual; would this stickler for rules grant a dispensation? The pope would and did – with dispatch. Jogues left France on the first ship to cross the Atlantic in the new year of 1644, a vessel so old and leaky that the passengers threatened to mutiny until the priest placated them.

At Quebec, Jogues learned that the Five Nations were again on the warpath, rapidly destroying their enemies, the Hurons and Algonkins, already ravaged by disease and famine. To the astonishment and admiration of his superiors, the priest begged to be allowed to work among the Iroquois should the opportunity arise; meanwhile he was sent to the far outpost of Ville-Marie on the island of Montreal, a settlement of fifty colonists then only two years old. Jogues was satisfied: the new community offered an ideal base from which to evangelize the Iroquois, should peace come.

All parties wanted peace, or said they did. Between July and the following May, the French, the Hurons, the Algonkins, and the Iroquois held three councils at which they all pledged themselves to end hostilities. Jogues attended the first of these, at Trois-Rivières, where the brilliant Iroquois orator, Kiotseaeton, spoke with such eloquence that the French suspected he was being more than a little devious. And so he was: officially peace would reign, but at a private meeting with the governor, Huault de Montmagny, Kiotseaeton shifted ground. The Iroquois would make peace with the French and the Hurons but not with their traditional enemies, the hated Algonkins. A compromise was reached, also in secret: there would be two kinds of Algonkins: Christian and non-Christian. The peace would apply to the Christians only; open season would prevail on the heathen. Nobody bothered to ask how an Iroquois war party, falling on an unsuspecting enemy, would be able to separate believers from infidels.

The shakiness of the peace was further demonstrated at council in September. The governor was vaguely disturbed by the fact that the Iroquois spoke only for the Mohawks and not for the other nations of the confederacy; he had indicated, in fact, that the Oneidas in particular were not satisfied. Further, as Jogues himself took pains to explain, even the Mohawks were divided. The Wolf and Turtle clans wanted peace; the Bears were for war.

In spite of the danger Jogues was desperate to return to the land of his tormentors. In April, 1645, he undertook a retreat, praying that he be allowed to go while steeling himself against disappointment. No man, surely, ever sought his own destruction so tenaciously. At this juncture, a letter arrived from his superior, Lalemant. Jogues described his reaction:

" . . . would you believe me that when I first opened the letter of your reverence, my heart at first was seized as if with dread; for I feared that which I desired might actually come to pass. My poor nature, which remembered all that has gone, trembled. But Our Lord in his goodness bestowed calm on it, and will calm it some more . . . . Ah, with what regret should I be filled if I lost such a wonderful occasion, one on which it might depend only on me that some souls were not saved . . . ."

On May 7, the third peace council was held. Again, the Mohawks pledged peace but warned that the Oneidas had refused to join with them. Jogues was appointed to return to the Mohawk nation as an ambassador. The journey was expected to be a brief one, but the little priest had other ideas: he would be more than an ambassador; he would become a permanent missionary to the Iroquois. Accordingly he packed a large box with everything he would need for the task: chalice, candles, wafers, sacramental wine, together with winter clothing and gifts.

He took the advice of a friendly Algonkin and packed his cassock also; he would travel as a civilian, not as a priest. The Indian warned him not to speak too freely of Heaven and Hell for "there is nothing so repulsive to us at the beginning as is your doctrine. For your teaching seems to destroy completely everything that men hold dear. Your long robe preaches as well as your lips. Hence, it would be better for you to walk in clothes which are shorter." Accordingly, Jogues set off in high-topped boots, pantaloons, a cloak, and a broad-brimmed hat.

His task was to confirm the goodwill of the French toward the Iroquois. Arriving at Ossernenon after an uneventful trip, the new ambassador was welcomed by the same people who had once used him so badly. The Mohawks were impressed by the new Jogues: his authority and his bearing contrasted vividly with his former docility and mildness. The one-time slave had become a figure of power.

The Mohawks unanimously pledged peace with the French and, though with more restraint, with the Algonkins. But there was resistance to Jogues's demands that the other four nations make similar pledges. There was only one disturbing incident: the black box containing the priest's possessions – strongly bound and locked and kept in the cabin of his Indian aunt – was causing difficulties. The Mohawks were afraid that it might contain demons – malicious spirits known to live in such things as boxes, hollow trees, caves, and holes in the earth. Jogues did his best to allay these suspicions, opening the box, removing its contents, and explaining that these were only personal effects. The Indians appeared to accept the explanation but were not entirely convinced. Jogues left the box behind and set off for Trois-Rivières, where he was greeted with a salute of cannon and the congratulations of the French officials.

He wanted to return at once, but his superiors demurred. The peace was untried. He must remain at Trois-Rivières unless an exceptional opportunity arose. The exceptional opportunity presented itself in September when the Huron plenipotentiaries arrived. If they decided the time was ripe to treat with their enemies, Jogues could accompany them.

He prayed that he might be permitted to go, even though he had a premonition that the journey would be his last. "If I shall be employed on this mission," he wrote to a friend, "my heart tells me . . . I shall go but I shall not return. In very truth it will be well for me, it will be happiness for me, if God will be pleased to complete the sacrifice where he began it, if the little blood which I shed there in that land will be accepted by Him as a pledge that I would willingly shed all the blood which I bear in all the veins of my body and of my heart . . . ."

He was determined that this time he would go back to the Iroquois as a priest and missionary first and an ambassador second. When the Hurons formally requested that he accompany them on the peace mission, he decided that once again he would wear the black robe.

The party set off from Trois-Rivières on September 24, 1646, in three canoes. Jogues and a young lay assistant, Jean de La Lande together with the Huron ambassador, Otrihouré, and another brave, occupied the lead canoe; a group of Hurons followed in the second; the third carried Mohawks returning home for the winter.

From the start, a sense of uneasiness hung over the convoy. At the site of Fort Richelieu, now abandoned by the French as unnecessary, a tense discussion took place. The Hurons sensed that something was wrong; they were about to enter Mohawk territory and their intuition told them that danger lay ahead. Only Otrihouré could be persuaded to continue the journey; his comrades retreated to the St. Lawrence. Then, suddenly, all the Mohawks vanished.

The three men continued alone up the Richelieu to its source and then, leaving the canoes, followed the mountain trail to Ossernenon. On October 14, they spotted a file of Mohawks coming toward them. Jogues halted and called out a greeting, but the newcomers melted into the forest. Jogues called out again, identifying himself. At this the Indians sprang from the trees, uttering war whoops, and surrounded the little party. Jogues went rigid with shock. La Lande froze beside him. Otrihouré was terrified.

The priest could not grasp what was happening. This was supposed to be a peace mission, but the Indians, brandishing muskets and knives, fell upon the three men, knocking them to the ground, beating them and ripping off their clothes. At last Jogues understood: this was a war party; the Mohawks had repudiated the peace. Dragged to the village and lodged again in the cabin of his Mohawk aunt, he learned what had happened. The Bear clan, always in favour of war, had gained the support of the other four nations in the confederacy as the result of events that took place after Jogues left Ossernenon earlier that summer.

Following his departure several people had fallen ill. The sickness spread; the people grew frantic. Pestilence, the greatest of their enemies, was threatening again to destroy them. Who or what could have caused it? A group of Hurons, adopted into the Iroquois nation, remembered that six or seven years earlier, their people had been similarly affected. It was the Blackrobes who brought the disease, they said; the Blackrobes wished to destroy all native people and have the land for themselves.

To make matters worse, in September, the corn began to wither, eaten by worms. Suddenly somebody remembered the box that Jogues had left behind. *The black box!* Might it not contain a blacker demon, who by sorcery was killing both the people and the corn? Was not the priest himself, robed in black, a harbinger of death? Now everybody recalled how he had fashioned a cross and uttered strange words over people who had subsequently died. Clearly he was a man who worked evil spells. He had come to them that summer in disguise; obviously this was designed to deceive them. He did not really want peace – he wanted to exterminate them. He was a witch, a sorcerer.

They dared not smash that terrible box, for that would release the demon. Instead, they drowned it in the river. With the sorcerer's creature destroyed, all that remained to be done was to destroy the sorcerer.

The object of this witch hunt and his companion were considered public hostages until a council could decide their fate. The priest had friends in the village who advised him never to venture beyond the stockade. As long as he remained in the house of his Mohawk aunt, a member of the conciliatory Wolf clan, he was safe.

But events which could not be reversed were now set in motion. On the evening of October 18, a young brave came to the cabin and invited Jogues to visit another lodge where there were people who, he said, wished to talk to him and eat with him. Jogues was in a dilemma; what was he to do? The invitation was highly suspicious because it came from a member of the war party – the Bear clan. Yet to refuse would be considered a deadly insult; no matter which course he took, he would be in peril. He did not wish to appear cowardly; what, he asked his aunt, should he do? She, too, feared treachery, but felt that he had to respond to the invitation. He went, accompanied by her grandson, Honatteniaté.

The two followed their guide through the village to a longhouse with Bear symbols carved on the doorpost. Realizing that the slightest hesitation, the smallest sign of suspicion or fear would give the Indians advantage over him, Jogues moved on, casually pushing the skin covering aside and bending to pass through the low doorway. A warrior stood behind the door, tomahawk raised, and as the priest entered brought it down on his head. Honatteniaté thrust his arm forward to deflect the blow, but the tomahawk slashed through the young man's flesh and thudded into the priest's skull. The guide sent the youth reeling as, with a second blow, the murderer dispatched Isaac Jogues. Screaming curses, Honatteniaté roused the villagers, who flocked to the cabin as the members of the Bear clan dragged the corpse into the street, dancing and chanting in triumph. In spite of the protests of Jogues's aunt, they scalped the corpse, cut off the head, and after parading it through the streets, impaled it on a sharpened pole at the northeast corner of the palisade. Later that night, they also ambushed and beheaded young Jean de La Lande.

Thus abruptly ended the mission of Father Isaac Jogues to the Iroquoian peoples. But why did he leave the safety of his friends' house for what he must have known was almost certain death? Is the usual explanation, that he did not wish to insult the members of the Bear clan, really valid? Had he chosen not to go he would have been safe, for the council, meeting that very day in a neighbouring village, had decided that both men were to be returned alive to Trois-Rivières. The young Bear hotheads were roundly condemned (though not otherwise punished) for their impulsiveness and the Huron chief, Otrihouré, was sent back to governor Huault de Montmagny to explain what had happened – a mission he could not complete, for he was killed en route. Jogues's actions, then, seem incomprehensible unless one has regard for his absolute faith in an all-wise Deity. Jogues was convinced that God was guiding his steps; if he was meant to die that night, so be it. As we have seen, he expected and even welcomed his own doom.

In a sense – an ironic sense – it may be said that he was fortunate. It is probable that sooner or later a more brutal and painful martyrdom would have been his. The shaky peace was shattered by his murder, though it was not until the following June that the French learned of his death. By that time the Iroquois nation was on the warpath, massacring and ravaging Hurons, Algonkins, and French. Three years after Jogues's swift dispatch, his former comrades, Jean de Brébeuf and Gabriel Lalemant suffered at their hands the ghastly tortures that the little priest firmly believed had been in store for him.

The tomahawk of the Bear murderer may have saved Isaac Jogues from the long torment of the stake. There were those, no doubt, who believed that he had already suffered enough and that Divine Providence had dictated a sudden and painless end. But would Jogues have wanted it that way? Knowing something of the workings of that zealous and passionate mind, knowing, too, the constancy of his aspirations which, in a more worldly or self-seeking man could be dismissed as vaulting ambition, one may be permitted to speculate that Jogues himself might have felt that the ending of his life had been unnecessarily swift, unnecessarily anticlimactic, even a little – dare one say it? – disappointing. But if so, that, too, was God's will.

2 The First Commando Raid

The story of Pierre, Chevalier de Troyes and his successful guerrilla attack on three English forts on James Bay has all the qualities of a bad movie – one of those gaudy, swashbuckling adventures that Hollywood churned out in the forties. In the saga of de Troyes, the good guys (the noble, daring French) always win; the bad guys (the dumb, incompetent English) always lose. One longs for some setback: a blunder, possibly, by a flawed lieutenant, which almost loses the day; an act of treachery by a turncoat in the French camp; the tragic death, perhaps, of one of de Troyes' trusted comrades. But there is none of this. De Troyes' saga is just too pat; it could only happen in the movies.

Still, it *did* happen. In 1686 the governor of New France sent this consummate soldier and a hundred men on a twelve-week canoe trip into totally unknown country with the task of capturing three supposedly impregnable forts, bristling with cannon. No riskier or more reckless venture can be imagined. A few dozen men – half-starved, living on weeds part of the time, armed only with muskets, swords and pikes – out-manoeuvred their foes, subdued all three strongholds, and captured an armed naval vessel without losing a single man in battle.

We have no idea what de Troyes looked like. His incandescent appearance on the Canadian scene was too brief for any painter to capture his likeness. But we know what he *ought* to have looked like: a lithe, tough soldier with the eyes of a rogue, flashing teeth and a mustache turned into a smile to match the *mouche* on his lower lip – Errol Flynn, in short, got up as d'Artagnan. A good deal of de Troyes' heroics are pure Dumas, and there are, of course, the three dauntless Le Moyne brothers by his side to sustain the comparison. The rest is pure de Mille. The story can almost be told in press agent superlatives: *See the mighty Canadian forest in flames! See the incredible dash through the foaming rapids! See the battering ram attack on the fort, the capture of the armed ship, the molten lead raining down on Fort Albany! See the flashing swordplay as determined men redden the soil of the Northwoods in a savage battle to wrest control of the fur country for New France!* A box office smasheroo.

It is necessary to get the history out of the way before beginning the adventure. In the latter half of the seventeenth century, the fur trade had become the single most important factor in the Canadian economy. The English, with their prior claims to Hudson Bay, controlled it. The French, through the newly formed Compagnie du Nord, were struggling to expand but could not get a foothold in the north. At this point the ragged figure of Pierre Radisson enters the story. As every schoolchild knows, it was Radisson and his brother-in-law, the Sieur des Groseilliers, whose explorations led to the founding of the Hudson's Bay Company. It is doubtful, however, if a more untrustworthy *coureur de bois* ever existed. Having set himself up as a kind of marketing consultant for a gigantic English enterprise, Radisson switched sides, gained a pardon from the French king, Louis XIV, and helped establish a rival firm in French Canada. He and Groseilliers went on to build a fort deep in Hudson's Bay territory (Fort Bourbon they called it) at the mouth of the Bourbon (or Nelson) River. Skirmishes followed with the rival Hudson's Bay post just four miles away – skirmishes which Radisson won. Now perfidy was piled upon perfidy. Taxed out of his profits, Radisson again turned his coat. He rejoined the Hudson's Bay Company, attacked Fort Bourbon and, in 1684, captured it from his own nephew. He renamed it Fort Nelson and successfully barred his former compatriots from trading on Hudson Bay.

It was Radisson's treachery that gave the incoming governor of New France, Jacques de Brisay, Marquis de Denonville, an excuse to mount an attack that he hoped would drive the English out of James Bay. It is a principle of guerrilla warfare that unorthodox methods are often successful, that deception is the best weapon and surprise essential for victory. It was these commando tactics that were first used on the North American continent by the man charged with harassing the English: Pierre, Chevalier de Troyes.

Denonville was circumspect in the orders he issued de Troyes. The expedition was to "occupy posts on the shores of the bay of the North" and to bring back Radisson and his adherents to face charges of desertion and treason.

The governor was careful not to order the capture of any English or to name specifically any posts except Fort Bourbon-Nelson which had, of course, originally been French. Thus his official orders could not be construed as a declaration of war against the English. What de Troyes did was de Troyes' affair. Like many politicians before and since, Denonville did not want to know the sordid details. De Troyes did not have to be told, at least in writing, what was expected of him. He had no intention of going after Fort Bourbon: it was far away on the west shore of Hudson Bay, unreachable by land. His objectives from the outset were the three Hudson's Bay forts on the southern shores of James Bay: Albany, Moose and Rupert.

Denonville's machinations were Machiavellian, to say the least. England and France were not at war. There was a live-and-let-live understanding between the two nations over their respective trading zones. The Hudson's Bay forts were manned not by soldiers but by traders and clerks recruited in London. Denonville, pretending to get a trading foothold in the north, was sending an armed expedition to do the job. It was scarcely sporting; but then, there is very little that is sporting in the long, and often grisly, history of fur trade rivalry in Canada.

The Chevalier was newly arrived from France, the son of a Paris attorney, and a former captain in the French regulars: tough, competent, totally professional. He had no experience at all in the Canadian wilderness, and knew none of the men who would go with him on the adventure. But he knew how to lead, how to organize, how to delegate. The governor gave him thirty marines; the rest of the force consisted of seventy Canadian canoemen with Canadian officers. The total cost was underwritten by the Compagnie du Nord, one of whose founders had been Charles Le Moyne, the Montreal merchant who sired the most famous family in French Canada. Three of Le Moyne's remarkable sons took part in the expedition. Jacques, Sieur de Ste. Hélène, aged twenty-seven, was de Troyes' second-in-command. Pierre, Sieur d'Iberville, was his second lieutenant. This would be his first encounter with the English, but by no means his last – he would wage sea war against them from Newfoundland to the Gulf of Mexico; at the moment, however, he was glad to leave Montreal to evade a paternity suit brought against him by the father of a teenage girl he had seduced. A third Le Moyne brother, Paul, Sieur de Maricourt, was de Troyes' adjutant. In addition, de Troyes took along an experienced navigator, Pierre Allemand, to command the English ships he hoped to capture; a scout, St. Germain, who knew the route; and a Jesuit chaplain, Father Antoine Silvy, whose years as a missionary among the Indians made him invaluable.

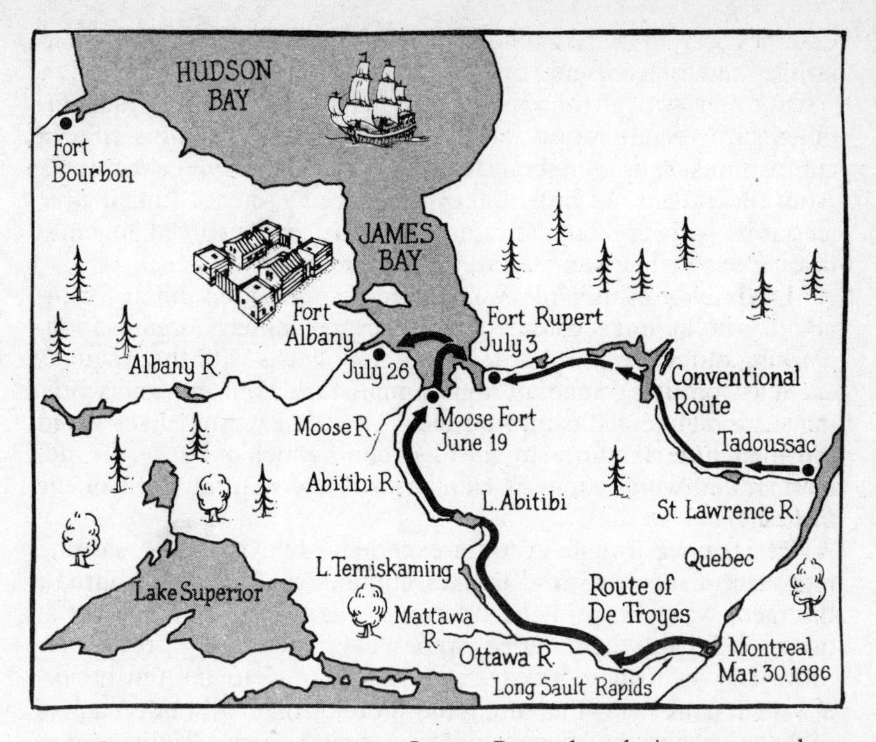

There were two routes to James Bay: the obvious one, taken by earlier expeditions, from Tadoussac through northern Quebec to Rupert House, and a less obvious one much farther to the west leading up the Ottawa River. De Troyes chose the Ottawa route, first because the English would not expect an attack from the west, and secondly, because the waters to the west, unlike the others, were navigable in mid-April. He wanted to reach James Bay just at spring breakup, weeks before ships from England could arrive from the north.

Although he intended to attack forts protected by cannon, de Troyes carried no weapons heavier than muskets: cannon could not be loaded into canoes. He was gambling that he could capture one fort by surprise and use its own cannon and ships to attack the others. His canoeists, all seasoned voyageurs, included tradesmen who would be useful after the capture: a carpenter, a blacksmith and a gunner, for example. By the time they reached their objective, they were burned so deeply by the sun that the local Indians thought they were Iroquois.

The expedition set off on March 30, 1686. The ice was so soft that two oxen pulling a sledload of baggage broke through and had to be hauled out. The following day they broke through again; de Troyes, in exasperation, sent the oxen back to Montreal. But his men were also breaking through the ice. On the second day they moved scarcely more than two miles because they spent most of the time rescuing one another.

But they struggled on, lining and poling their canoes up the famous Long Sault rapids, where Adam Dollard and his sixteen companions had been besieged and killed by Iroquois in 1660. After several days of travail, they next faced a series of impassable ice jams, with crevasses so wide that they were forced to build bridges to get their canoes and supplies across.

De Troyes, meanwhile, was hammering his undisciplined Canadians into an unaccustomed but necessary military organization, working out a marching order of three brigades with three squads each, appointing Canadian non-commissioned officers, and working out a regimented camp routine. "Thus," he wrote, "I subjected the men little by little to the discipline which military life demands, and which alone is lacking from the natural merit of the Canadians."

The trip was rough, even for experienced voyageurs. A shifting montage of incidents and images illuminates de Troyes' journal: the men, waist deep in the freezing waters, and sometimes neck deep, hauling on their loaded canoes like pack beasts; three nearly drowned when one craft strikes a rock in midstream and breaks up; de Troyes struggling along the shore through a braided tangle of fallen timber, thick brush and gigantic boulders, "frightening in its loneliness." A series of personal close-ups punctuates the montage: a man burns his hand in a fire, another cuts off his finger with a hatchet, several others sicken and come close to death from exposure.

In such conditions, discipline was all-important. When one Canadian made an insulting remark, de Troyes forestalled the incipient mutiny by tying him to a tree; in the regular army he would have been flogged, but the commander was too wise for that. "The character of Canadians," he wrote, ironically, "hardly accords with submission...."

Two hundred and fifty miles out of Montreal the expedition reached the Mattawa and paddled and portaged its way up the right branch, sometimes smashing their canoes in the vicious rapids. On reaching Lake Temiskaming, they encountered, on an island, one of the Compagnie's trading posts. De Troyes left four of his men behind to augment its numbers and continued on north.

Forest fire! It is late in the afternoon of May 30; the weary expedition has covered twelve miles and made eight portages since morning. But somebody has left the breakfast fire burning. Racing round the lakeshore on a strong wind, it catches up with the rearguard just as it reaches the last portage, a fifteen-hundred-foot strip of land between two lakes. The men at the rear fling their gunpowder and themselves into canoes to escape the flames; but the lake is so narrow that they are still in danger of being roasted. They cover themselves with soaking blankets and are saved.

The fire races on across the portage, pursuing more fleeing men. De Troyes and Father Silvy are caught three-quarters of the way across, running with all their strength, the flames pressing so closely that the sleeves of the commander's shirt are singed. At the lake ahead, the advance party is already hurling supplies and equipment into canoes, but de Troyes isn't safe yet. The clearing is only twenty feet wide and so soggy that he and his companions sink to their knees in the mud. They clamber, dishevelled, into the canoes and paddle desperately to the centre of the lake. Here the water is only thirty feet wide and the flames sweep like a torrent over their heads, igniting the bush on the opposite side. The canoes, made of birchbark and cedar strips, seem ready to burst into flames. There is only one way out – to flee back the way they have come, into the scorched and blackened forest through which the fire has already passed. This action probably saves their lives.

After the fire, the way led upward toward the height of land that divides the James Bay watershed from that of the St. Lawrence. Here the rapids and waterfalls climb the Precambrian shield like steps, acting as natural locks. On May 31, de Troyes stood on the divide and looked down on the rocky, beautiful countryside stretching off to the north, mantled in its spring mist of larch green and speckled by a thousand little lakes, glistening in the sunlight between the sombre ridges of gneiss and granite: English territory, all of it – enemy territory.

De Troyes' orders were to build a new trading post for the Compagnie du Nord on the English side of the divide. The site he chose, on Lake Abitibi, was so suitable that the post has been maintained ever since, first by the French, then by the North West Company and, since 1821, by the Hudson's Bay Company.

While his men were constructing the fort – the task took three days – their commander busied himself by laying out, with stakes and string, models of the English forts he intended to attack. One marvels at his sense of organization and even more at his conceit: he had to make do with models, he wrote blandly, "because I had not been able to find a suitable open clearing for building full-size replicas"! Now, he was able to show his officers exactly what part each man would play in the coming battle. "Subsequent events," he commented dryly, "showed me that this exercise was far from useless."

De Troyes left four more men in charge of the new post and paddled north on Lake Abitibi and down the Abitibi River into the Moose River. On June 10, one of his voyageurs, Noel Leblanc, an expert canoeist, was lost trying to shoot a series of rapids with Iberville. Like most of his comrades, Leblanc couldn't swim. Iberville was saved but lost most of his provisions, as well as his guns and clothes. Since it was standard on such expeditions for each man to carry his own rations, de Troyes shared his own with his second officer.

The way grew wearier. The men, slogging across gullies cluttered with falling timber, began to drop from exhaustion. De Troyes' two Indian guides deserted. Hardened though they were to forest travel, some of the voyageurs could not negotiate the final portage at day's end.

On June 19, they reached the junction of the Abitibi and the Moose rivers. Where, exactly, was Moose Fort? De Troyes questioned local Indians and sent Iberville and St. Germain to reconnoitre ahead. The following night, Iberville was able to lead the party to an island a little more than a mile from the Hudson's Bay post at the mouth of the Moose.

At daybreak, St. Germain rejoined the party. Going without food for twenty-four hours, he had found out how the fort was constructed and what the English were up to. He reported that the English had a ship, the *Craven*, anchored about four miles below the fort. De Troyes sent a detachment to guard the canoes, set up another as a rearguard and began, methodically, to plan the coming attack.

Moose Fort, a log castle standing on an island at the river's mouth, seemed impregnable. The thick palisades were eighteen feet high. The walls, each one hundred and thirty feet long, were guarded at the four corners by bastions, strongly constructed of earth, stakes and planks. Each bastion was armed with three seven-pound cannon that fired through slits which could be closed by sliding panels. Inside the walls was a three-storey redoubt (a strongpoint armed with three two-pounder cannon and one eight-pounder) towering above the walls of the fort so that its cannon could fire into the country beyond from all sides. The main door of the fort faced the river; it was six inches thick, reinforced by nails, strap hinges and iron bars. There was a similar door in the rear wall. Such was the stronghold that de Troyes intended to subdue with a force of about seventy men armed only with muskets and swords.

But de Troyes knew exactly what he was doing. First he sent for two canoes, one of which he loaded with picks, shovels, spades, ladders and planks. On the other he placed a newly constructed battering ram. The canoes were to follow de Troyes and his men who would march along the foreshore of the fortress island to their objective.

Ste. Hélène and Iberville, with eighteen men, were ordered to attack the two bastions that protected the rear wall, while the Sieur de la Liberté with six men was to make a diversionary attack on the bastions protecting the right wall. De Troyes' orders to La Liberté were explicit: three men were to attack each bastion, two of them firing continuously at the slits to neutralize the cannon, while the third hacked away at the palisade. The remainder of the party was grouped in three detachments for the major assault. Two of these detachments were ordered to keep up the hottest possible fire on the forward walls and bastions in order to interfere with the accuracy of the cannon, while the third would smash down the main gate with the battering ram.

Ste. Hélène immediately asked permission to leap over the palisade at the rear. De Troyes replied that when one gave orders to capture a fortress it did not matter how one entered it. Ste. Hélène took him literally and when the attack came, he and his two brothers and half a dozen others, swords in hand, climbed the palisade, seized several cannon and opened the rear door.

Meanwhile, de Troyes' orders were being carried out to the letter. The fire was so brutal, the fighting so confused that some of the attackers mistook Ste. Hélène's men on the inside for defending Englishmen and actually shot one in the loins. Shortly after, the battering ram smashed the main gate and de Troyes entered the fort at the head of his men, ordering them to keep up a withering fire on the gun ports, windows and other openings in the redoubt. While this was going on, de Troyes managed to turn one of the cannon against the interior stronghold, only to find that it was empty, with no balls available.

It did not matter. The others had smashed in the door of the redoubt and the English within were already asking for quarter. De Troyes had some difficulty dampening down his Canadian voyageurs who were whooping like Indians and wielding knives. Finally, he managed to have his interpreter call out that if the enemy surrendered they would be given quarter. One Englishman shouted that he wished to fight, but in doing so revealed his position; Ste. Hélène shot him dead.

With that the attack resumed. Again the English asked for quarter. The battering ram at that moment smashed in the door of the redoubt and Iberville was through in an instant, a sword in one hand, a musket in the other. The door was still on its hinges, however, and the English managed to slam it shut again. Iberville found himself alone with the enemy who swarmed over him. He fought back, wounding several in the face with his sword, until the battering ram completed its work and his comrades poured through the ruined door, ending the battle. De Troyes had taken the fortress with its seventeen defenders in exactly half an hour.

The English, still in their nightshirts, had been totally unprepared for any attack. The governor, John Bridgar, and all his officers had gone to Fort Rupert, leaving Moose virtually unguarded. Even sentinels had not been considered necessary. Now with his prisoners safely locked away in the hold of an abandoned ship and the fort guarded by his own men, de Troyes could turn his attention to the capture of the other two Hudson's Bay posts on southern James Bay: Forts Albany and Rupert.

The prisoners told him there was no watch or guard on Rupert, but it was a hundred miles to the east over a bad route and almost empty of supplies. Albany, on the other hand, seventy-five miles to the west, was well guarded and supplied, fortified with twenty-five cannon and manned by thirty men. Clearly de Troyes could not capture it without artillery. However, he could not convey cannon in his canoes, and so made his decision to attack Rupert first. He had learned that the *Craven*, which St. Germain had earlier observed a few miles away, had sailed for Rupert. De Troyes' plan was to seize the ship before it proceeded on to its next stop at Albany. Then he could use it to carry the cannon.

He took sixty men with him, leaving the others at Moose Fort under St. Germain. Ste. Hélène and Iberville commanded an advance party, taking along an Indian guide, some food, tools and two small cannon removed from their carriages. A passing canoe party of Indians confirmed that the *Craven* was anchored offshore from Rupert.

De Troyes knew that he must move in stealth. He and the main party crept towards the fort in darkness, concealing their canoes in a small bay. Ste. Hélène returned to report that their objective was a copy of the fortress at Moose. No cannon were visible in the bastions and no sentinels. The ship was moored where the Indians had spotted it – directly in front of the fort.

De Troyes again laid out his plan. Iberville was given thirteen men and ordered to capture the ship. Another detachment, under a sergeant, would provide covering fire from the shore. Ste. Hélène would attack the main gate with the battering ram. Once the door was down, de Troyes would lead the main force into the compound.

Slipping silently along the shoreline in their canoes in the early light of July 3, the men moved into the attack. The battering ram did its work. De Troyes led his followers into the courtyard, the men firing steadily at all the slits and openings in the redoubt. Ste.

Hélène, the best shot in the party, put a ball between the eyes of one of the gunners as he tried to load a cannon with glass shards.

As the musket fire grew hotter, the English within could be heard crying out for quarter. De Troyes accepted their surrender, whereupon the commander, Hugh Verner, "approached me in fear and trembling, clutching me by the arm as though he would be safe in my presence." (Again, a cheap adventure film comes to mind; even the ship, be it noted, was called the *Craven*.) "In this posture," wrote de Troyes, "I dragged him to the gate of the fort, where I asked him everything that I needed to know." Verner warned him against musket fire from the ship and was astonished to find that the *Craven* was already in French hands.

Iberville had boarded the vessel from a canoe on the starboard side while the crew and one sentry were snoring peacefully on the deck. The French stamped their feet to wake them up, then shot the sentry. A man charged out of the cabin; Iberville slashed him across the head with a sabre. The Englishman plunged on; Iberville gave him a second cut across the body. Meanwhile his followers had chopped holes in the cabin with their axes and were pouring musket balls through the opening. This brought a speedy surrender. Iberville locked his prisoners in the hold. De Troyes' captives, who included the newly appointed governor of James Bay, John Bridgar, were locked away in the hold of another abandoned ship, aground near the fort.

The men loaded five iron cannon and a good deal of loot from the fort aboard the captured ship. De Troyes then ordered one of his captives, a shipwrecked captain named Outlaw, to sail the prize back to Moose, while he and some of his men returned by canoe. It was a hellish journey. The fog was so thick that the canoes lost contact with each other. De Troyes, caught in "an abyss of waves," had no idea where he was. Reaching an unknown shore, exhausted and half-starved, the company lived on weeds to keep alive. One man, sent off to hunt for game, was never seen again. Finally, much weakened, the party reached Moose Fort.

There de Troyes turned his attention to his third objective, Fort Albany, which lay in the opposite direction from Fort Rupert. The journey by canoe along the shoreline was complicated by the fact that no one knew exactly where the fort was. Fortunately, the English had the habit of firing off their cannon at sundown and these muffled reports, carried over the waters, told de Troyes when he was nearing the mouth of the Albany River. He brought his canoes into shore and sent Ste. Hélène with twenty men to reconnoitre. Shortly after this, the captured ship, loaded with cannon, arrived with Iberville in command.

The next day, following Ste. Hélène s directions, the party

moved up to a position not far from Fort Albany, which lay beyond the woods across the marshy river. De Troyes and ten men crept closer until they were a musket-shot away. Here the commander found a spot where he could set up his cannon. By this time his men were worn out and famished. Worse, the fort was aware of his presence and had fired off a warning shot; de Troyes would no longer enjoy the advantage of surprise.

He sent an interpreter to treat with the enemy. The French demanded the release of three prisoners captured the previous year (they had long since been freed) and the surrender of the fort. The governor equivocated. De Troyes called for the cannon to be unloaded, but unfortunately the sea was too rough to make that possible. There was some sporadic shooting: musket fire came from de Troyes' guerrillas concealed in the bush; in reply cannon balls from the fort whistled harmlessly over their heads. Stalemate.

At this point, de Troyes and his men were running out of food. Every hour now was precious. Fortunately the wind died down and he managed at last to unload eight cannon. On July 25, he fired his first volley at the governor's house, which had been identified for him by his English captives. It was the dinner hour, and the governor was at table with his wife and a clergyman. The governor's lady was reaching for a glass of wine when two cannon balls whizzed past her face. She fainted dead away. A servant leaned forward to pour more wine; a third cannonball passed just under his arm. He dropped his pitcher in terror. The man of the cloth dropped his glass. The entire dinner company hastily left the room.

The following day de Troyes, now in a desperate situation himself, turned all his light cannon on the fort. In less than an hour he had fired more than one hundred and forty cannon balls "which roasted the place on all sides." He was running short of ammunition. To keep up their sagging spirits, his men began to shout "Vive le Roi!" The English shouted the same phrase back, indicating that they no longer had the stomach to fight. However, none was prepared to brave the cannon long enough to climb out of the redoubt and strike the flag. One who attempted the feat was forced to dart back quickly.

De Troyes was out of food. To keep alive, his exhausted followers were gathering and eating Macedonian parsley, a weed resembling Queen Anne's Lace. It was their only food. At the same time de Troyes was attempting to make more cannon balls from a wooden mould. The fort, he knew, must be taken quickly if it was to be taken at all; and it must be taken by bluff rather than force of arms.

One of his scouts returned to report that a party with a white flag was setting out from the opposite shore. De Troyes hastily lined up sixty armed men on the shoreline to greet them. The others were ordered to bustle around the camp in the rear, making noises as of a large force.

He and Father Silvy went out to meet the English party. At its head was the Reverend John French, the first clergyman sent to James Bay by the Hudson's Bay Company. French informed de Troyes that the governor wished to speak to him. With magnificent aplomb, de Troyes replied that the governor could come to his camp in perfect safety – something he secretly hoped to avoid, as "I was scarcely anxious to receive him there for fear he would discover our sorry state." As expected, French suggested a compromise: why not meet halfway in boats in the centre of the river? De Troyes pretended to consider the matter, shrugged and, at length, agreed. The clergyman bowed deeply and replied that the governor would be ready in an hour. De Troyes retorted that he had better be ready in half an hour, or his men would root him out. The shaken envoy replied that the governor would come at once.

De Troyes left a few men to guard the base camp and marched the remainder to the battery of cannon he had assembled on the shoreline. He marshalled his men under arms in full view of the fort, with two cannon loaded and aimed directly at the redoubt and the rest ready with short matches lit to fire. Then, observing the articles of war to the letter, he picked the same number of men as were embarking from the far shore and set out to parley with the enemy.

The two boats met in mid-stream and cast anchors. Governor John Sergeant came aboard the French craft and, with great ceremony, opened a bottle of Spanish wine to toast the health of the kings of France and England. De Troyes and Iberville responded. The governor, who had brought several more bottles with him, wished to continue the ceremony, but de Troyes told him bluntly that he had not come to carouse, that he was not short of refreshments and that if the governor so wished he might come to the French camp where he would be offered much better wine! In truth, all de Troyes had was a half-litre of brandy, saved for an emergency.

The parley immediately got down to business. The governor agreed to surrender the fort "under suitable articles of capitulation," meaning that the prisoners would be well-treated. The capture was effected with much pomp and ceremony and beating of drums. De Troyes immediately razed all four of the fort's bastions, rendering it militarily ineffective. He and his men were now in charge of the three English strongholds in the area and James Bay, for the moment at least, was a French lake.

Various arrangements, not all of them satisfactory or even humane, were made for the prisoners. (The wretched governor, Sergeant, was eventually charged with cowardice in London and dismissed from the service of the Company.) Iberville and Ste. Hélène were left to hold the Bay with forty men. De Troyes and the others returned to Montreal almost immediately and arrived without incident.

The commander's victory had been total and it was due largely to his own brilliance and organizational ability. New to the country, unfamiliar with the terrain, knowing nothing of the perils and limitations of canoe travel, he had picked good men, and organized them into a strongly disciplined force. Thus did the Chevalier de Troyes set the pattern of warfare in Canada for the next half century, until the Seven Years' War brought European generals and troops and more formal methods of conflict to the New World. Until the mid-1750s, both the French and the English were to use de Troyes' guerrilla tactics of "le petite guerre," in which lightly equipped troops moved through the wilderness, using surprise and ambush as their basic strategy – an Indian pattern that later helped give the North West Company an advantage over its rival in the struggle for the fur trade.

The forts on James Bay continued to change hands by treaty and cannon fire in the years that followed. De Troyes had no part in this long wrangle between England and France. Sent to command the garrison at Fort Niagara, he was doomed by the problem that had almost ruined him at James Bay – a lack of provisions. It is possible that he never understood the stringency of a Canadian winter. Whatever the reason, his garrison was isolated during the 1687–88 season without fresh vegetables. All but a handful of men perished from scurvy or starvation. De Troyes himself died on May 8, 1688, not much more than two years after he had set off into the north to humble the English.

Some of his comrades in arms fared better, notably Pierre Le Moyne d'Iberville, the most famous son of New France, the man who established the first French colony in Louisiana, who founded the modern city of Mobile, Alabama, and captured the island of Guadaloupe from the English. Part colonizer, part explorer, part pirate, part smuggler – seducer, entrepreneur, naval genius, adventurer – Iberville was the quintessential swashbuckler and his story is one of the gaudiest in all Canadian history.

But that, of course, is a different movie.

3
Samuel Hearne's Epic Trek

In the crowded pantheon of early explorers there are only a few whom I would care to invite to dinner. Cartier and Champlain are admirable historical figures, no doubt, but both were hard cases: the former was a kidnapper, the latter an assassin; in each instance their victims were unsuspecting Indians. Radisson, Groseilliers, Brûlé and their ilk are intriguing forest creatures, viewed from a distance, but all were out-and-out rascals. One would be unwise to trust them with either wife or pocketbook. The Scots – the Simpsons, Mackenzies, Frasers *et al* – are certainly indomitable, but they would make dour companions, I suspect, for they were single-minded men and not a little frightening. Nor can I warm to the Arctic adventurers of the nineteenth century – Franklin, Rae, Belcher and their kind – ambitious certainly, brave, foolhardy and sometimes foolish, but not really engaging company.

Samuel Hearne is an exception. I would dearly love to have spent an evening with that uncommonly sensitive and sensible man, a week or so, say, after the completion of his five-thousand-mile trek across the bleak desert that he named the Barren Ground. *Five thousand miles*, almost all of it on foot, in just two years, seven months and twenty-four days in a land that no white man had ever visited! The mind boggles.

The idea of anybody actually *walking* five thousand miles is almost incomprehensible to us. And we must remember that Hearne did not travel, as the Cross-Canada hikers did in 1921, on well-defined railway embankments. He stumbled in his moccasins over miles of rubbled glacial moraine; he waded through acres of cheerless swamp; he trudged on home-made snowshoes through leagues of drifting snow. In the summer he was beset by swarms of insects that all but blotted out the sun; in the winter he set his face into shrieking gales and raging blizzards. Much of the time he was hungry; often he went without food for three days or even a week. The wonder isn't that he thrived, which he did; it is that he survived at all.

Surely a more unlikely explorer never existed. It was not Hearne's ambition to conquer new worlds as it was Fraser's or Franklin's. He was a seaman, not a landlubber. He had only elementary surveying experience and his arithmetic was abysmal. He hadn't a scrap of geological training, knew scarcely anything about Indians and very little about northern land travel. Yet his masters sent him off without any sensible direction to find a mysterious Indian chief and an equally mysterious treasure of copper somewhere – no one was terribly sure where – on the Arctic's rim. The remarkable thing is that at the third attempt Hearne succeeded, perhaps because, not being a professional explorer, he approached his task without preconceived ideas.

Yet it is not the great feat of discovery that sets Hearne apart from your run-of-the-mill pedlar, voyageur, coureur de bois or map-maker. Certainly he demonstrated all the adaptability and common sense of the best of these. His other qualities I find even more engaging and, considering the time and place, more remarkable. His curiosity was boundless. Everything he saw intrigued him: animals, people, customs, food, environment; and he was patient enough and prescient enough to record all his observations in detail. This is not as easy as it sounds. A man who has struggled for twelve hours, heavy-laden, over broken country, wants to put his feet up at the end of the day and swallow a brandy and some hot food before collapsing in his tent. He does not want to scribble endless descriptions in his notebook or make pencil drawings of what he has encountered. But Hearne, scarcely educated and ashamed of his deficient grammar, managed to produce, en route, a journal that has become a literary classic.

There was no side to him and no bigotry; he accepted his Indian companions for what they were and made no attempt to impose upon them or upon his view of them any of the values of Christian Europe. He was remarkably sensitive; his famous account of the massacre at Bloody Falls shows that the incident left him permanently horrified. He was also fastidious; robbed by the Chipewyans of almost everything he possessed in the summer of 1770, he asked, and was allowed to take, as much soap as he felt he would need on the long retreat back to his post. He loved animals. He kept two housebroken beavers as pets and fed them on plum pudding, and he also tamed mink, lemming, foxes, eagles, buntings and horned larks. A self-taught naturalist, he left behind accurate descriptions of creatures no European had ever heard of, much less seen: musk-oxen, wood bison, whooping crane. He was a great reader; Voltaire was a favourite. One night, driven to despair by the failure of an expedition and unable to sleep, he tells us how he repeated "above an hundred times the following beautiful lines of Dr. Young: 'Tired Nature's sweet restorer, balmy sleep. . . .'" All in all an adaptable, agreeable fellow, brave and stubborn as we shall see, but never prey to ego or to the kind of false heroics or foolish impetuosities that characterized so many of his contemporaries.

One might easily wonder why the Hudson's Bay Company would send a seaman like Hearne on a journey which no other white man had attempted, from Fort Prince of Wales (the present site of Churchill, Manitoba) on Hudson Bay to the shores of the western Arctic in search of copper. But one must consider the curious fashion in which that great business enterprise was managed. In 1769, the year in which Hearne was first launched on his expedition, the gap of understanding between the absentee landlords of the Honourable Company and its post managers was at least as wide as the Atlantic. No London official had ever set foot on the shores of the Bay, let alone in the Arctic desert or tundra that stretched off, treeless and forlorn, into the fog of the northwest.

It is true that the London Committee was well supplied with maps and reports on sub-Arctic Canada from their representatives in the field. But it is also true that as late as 1784, long after Hearne had returned from the Arctic, officials in the London office actually dispatched one hundred and fifty copies of *The Country Clergyman's Advice to Parishioners*, to be distributed among the traders and the Indians who, apparently, were held to be panting for this form of salvation. The noble Governors, enjoying the music of Mozart and Haydn, the tabletalk of Samuel Johnson, the plays of Goldsmith and Sheridan, the parliamentary oratory of William Pitt and the iconoclasm of Hearne's favourite, Voltaire, could not comprehend the kind of journey that lay before him.

Nor could they have really understood the strange, terrible creature who was Governor of Fort Prince of Wales. Moses Norton is simply too much: he could scarcely survive as a believable villain in the most macabre melodrama. The half-breed son of a previous governor, brutal and semi-literate, he had had the advantage of nine years in England. But this veneer of civilization peeled off him easily on the shores of Hudson Bay, where he lived like an Oriental potentate and acted like one, abusing all those beneath him, especially his white employees. Although he prevented any European from attempting sexual relations with any Indian woman, he himself kept a veritable harem of them – five or six of the most comely girls that he could select from the available crop. And select he did in the most savage fashion. He kept a box of poison about him to administer to those wretched natives who refused him the pleasure of their wives and daughters. The poisoning was not confined to the menfolk. When two members of his harem were observed to fancy younger men, Moses Norton calmly poisoned *them*.

This was the man who convinced the Governors in England to send Hearne on a voyage of discovery to seek the fabled coppermines of the Arctic. No one had the slightest idea where the mines were. Indians had been bringing copper samples into the post for more than half a century, but none had ever seen the legendary trove. Thus Hearne's instructions from the villainous Norton were vague: to find the "Far Off Metal River" with the help of an Indian Chief in the Athupuscow country, one "Captain" Matonabbee, and trace that river to its mouth. It was Matonabbee who had originally brought some crude maps of the copper country to the fort, but exactly where the river was and where the chief was, and why the Indian would agree to go anywhere without formal instruction or reward – these important pieces of information were never spelled out. In Hearne's description, Moses Norton seems to have been as incompetent as he was unscrupulous. Hearne says he was a notorious smuggler, but adds that he never made any money at it.

At this point, Hearne was twenty-four years old and had been a seaman since the age of eleven, having served at one point under that Captain Samuel Hood who, as Lord Hood, was to merit Nelson's accolade as "the best officer ... that England has to boast of." He had seen action throughout the Seven Years' War and then, when the war ended, had joined the Hudson's Bay Company, serving for two years as the mate of a sloop and two more as the mate of a brigantine sailing out of Fort Prince of Wales. His ambitions were nautical: he wanted to be captain of his own ship. He applied to the company for such a post. Instead they decided to turn him into an explorer overnight.

In addition to the instruction to find the river of copper, Hearne was given two other tasks. He was to arrange for more tribes to bring in furs to the post and he was to find the North West Passage – that elusive waterway said to lead directly to the jewels and spices of fabled Cathay, and which had captured the imagination of every explorer. There was also a hard political objective to Hearne's journey. On originally receiving its charter, the Hudson's Bay Company had promised to explore and develop the

Hudson Bay watershed, an immense area embodying about two-fifths of present-day Canada. It had done nothing of the sort. Company men sat on their rumps on the margin of the Bay while their rivals, the "pedlars" who later formed the Montreal-based North West Company, ranged far into the hinterland. Now, with questions being asked in the British Parliament, the Company finally decided it was time to thrust inland. Samuel Hearne would form the spearhead of that thrust.

"The continent of America is much wider than many people imagine," Hearne was to write. It was the understatement of the century. Clearly, Norton himself, let alone his masters in London, had no idea what their servant was in for. More than half of Canada was then a blank spot on the crude maps of the day. The Rockies had been seen from a distance but no white man had ever set foot in them. The first tentative Spanish discoveries on the Canadian west coast were five years into the future. The gargantuan fresh-water seas of the north – Great Bear, and Great Slave lakes – were as unknown as the Mackenzie River.

The Barrens were a mystery. Hearne could not know that his goal lay a thousand miles to the northwest and that everything between Fort Prince of Wales and that far-off river of metal was treeless desert. To reach it he would be subjected to unknown terrors and unbelievable horrors; he would eat the most exotic of foods (the carcasses of unborn animals, for example) and witness customs no man could imagine. For more than two years he would live a life so far removed from that of the ordinary Englishman that few could give it credence.

Physically, the tundra has scarcely changed since Hearne's day. It rolls on for hundreds of miles, a cold, forsaken land, carpetted by a thin mattress of moss and lichen and scoured by the bulldozer action of the great Keewatin ice sheet, two miles thick, the relics of whose passage may still be seen in the form of vast rubbles of broken rock, and the serpentine embankments called eskers, which are the silted remains of sub-glacial rivers.

The tundra is a canoeist's nightmare. The inexorable glacier disrupted the ancient drainage pattern so that the few remaining rivers run every which-way and the myriad of little lakes (more than one can count in all the rest of the world) are joined only by spasmodic stretches of white water. For an untried traveller the country can, and has, meant terrible death. In the summer, the swarms of mosquitoes and black flies can drive men and animals into imbecility. In the winter, the cold is so savage that, in Hearne's day, it sometimes caused the thin gun barrels to burst apart on being fired.

There is a worse obstacle to sustained travel – one that strangers to the tundra have difficulty in comprehending. In all this empty thousand-mile expanse there is scarcely a sliver of timber: no twigs with which to kindle a fire, no poles with which to erect a shelter, no wood to repair a broken paddle; nothing but caribou moss and sedges and small trailing vines which, in microscopic examination, are seen to be willows and birches, some of them more than half a century old.

This was the desert that Hearne set out to conquer. The marvel is that after two setbacks that could have driven a lesser man into a permanent funk, he actually set out again.

His first expedition began on November 6, 1769. Hearne and his two white companions were given as a guide, a singularly untrustworthy Indian chieftain named Chawchinahaw. His main purpose appears to have been to steal everything Hearne owned and then leave him and his comrades to starve on the Barrens. He very nearly accomplished that purpose. Two hundred miles from his base, the tyro explorer found himself without food, and forced to subsist on his hunting ability and the largesse of some friendly Indians whom he fortunately encountered in his humiliating retreat back to the fort. He reached it on December 11, "to my great mortification."

Undeterred by this setback, Hearne tried again on February 23, 1770. He had already learned one valuable lesson: travel with the Indians only and with no other white companions. Outside the Company factories, the natives' loyalty to one another gave them an advantage over any Englishman. Hearne determined to become like a native: to move with the tribes, allowing them to set the pace and the patterns; to adopt native customs and eat native foods, and to follow, as much as possible, native folkways. This simple acceptance of the natives' superiority in their own environment – it seems so obvious now – tells us a great deal about Samuel Hearne. He was totally unaffected by the egotism and snobbery that was to bedevil some later English explorers. He was perfectly prepared to eat raw whitefish and beavers' wombs, food that would have nauseated most white adventurers. Moreover, he had the patience to follow wherever the Indians led, even when the trail seemed to lead in circles. Franklin's seamen, almost two centuries later, had still not grasped the truths that Hearne absorbed after a month on the tundra. Had they done so, they might have returned safely to the warmth of their English beds.

Hearne had learned a second lesson: to take women along on any expedition. They were needed, he realized, to haul baggage, dress skins, pitch tents and cook food while the men did the hunting – a practical division of labour which the natives had relied on for centuries. But Moses Norton would have none of this, claiming that there would be too many extra mouths to feed. In spite of his Indian blood, Norton showed himself to be remarkably obtuse in his judgment of people, customs and geography. He saddled Hearne with an even more incompetent guide, one Conne-e-quese, who had no real idea of where the Coppermine country was, though he pretended to know. He led the expedition in a desultory fashion through the *taiga*, the thin forest that borders the tundra; then, in springtime, he guided them out onto the Barrens, feasting one day and starving the next and gathering about him an ever-increasing gaggle of hangers-on, until by the end of July the party of six had become an army of six hundred.

Hearne felt himself constantly cheated by these Indians, who made continual demands upon him for ammunition, guns, tobacco, medicine and clothes, "as if I had brought the Company's warehouse with me." Finally, on August 12, after his quadrant was broken, he knew that he must return to the fort.

There followed an appalling ordeal. The Indians stole almost everything Hearne owned, including his ammunition and most of his tools. With winter approaching, lacking both warm clothes and a tent, the young explorer fell behind the main party and must surely have frozen or starved to death if, by a stunning stroke of luck, he had not run into the very man he had originally set out to find, Chief Matonabbee.

This handsome, six-foot native, agreeable and modest, had lived for several years at Fort Prince of Wales, as the adopted son of Richard Norton, Moses' father. He was a Northern Indian (Chipewyan) but could speak the dialect of the Southern Indians (Crees) and also a few words of English. He is as important to Hearne's journey, and hence to history, as Hearne himself, for it is quite clear that, without him, the white man would never have accomplished his objective. Thus Matonabbee takes his place with the large and noble band of intelligent native leaders whom history has largely neglected. He was to Hearne what Donnaconna was to Jacques Cartier or the English Chief to Alexander Mackenzie: absolutely essential.

This remarkable Indian immediately took Hearne under his wing, rustled up some food and warm clothes, and offered to guide him on another expedition to the Coppermine. Hearne could have been pardoned if, after all his travail, he had rejected the offer, but, "as I had already experienced every hardship that was likely to accompany any future trial, I was determined to complete the discovery even at the risque of life itself."

First, however, he and his guide had to make their way back to home base. It took them two gruelling months. Hearne had no ammunition to hunt game and had to make do by chopping up his ice chisel into square lumps to use for ball – a dangerous experiment. Pickings were very slim. During one seven-day stretch he lived on a diet of water, burnt bones, cranberries and scraps of leather. The blizzards were so bad that his only dog froze to death and he was obliged to pull his own sledge. He and Matonabbee finally made it back on November 25, having been absent for eight months and twenty-two days on a fruitless journey.

The wonder of it is that he was chafing to return and, indeed, could scarcely contain himself waiting for Norton to give him the go-ahead. Just twelve days later he set off again with Matonabbee, "the most sociable, kind and sensitive Indian I have ever met with." This time they took women with them because, as the chief explained, "women were made for labour." They could carry burdens "as much as two men can do," pitch tents, mend clothing and keep the men warm at night. They were cheap to feed, too, since they could lick enough food off their fingers as they did the cooking to keep themselves alive. They did not eat until the men had eaten, on pain of a beating, and if the men ate everything then they did not eat at all.

Hearne's account of the journey that followed is a chronicle of marvels intermingled with tales of hardship and flashes of horror. His dispirited diary entry, on December 27, 1770, noted that nothing had passed his lips for the previous three days except a pipe of tobacco, and a swallow of snow water. Already his strength was failing, and "I must confess that I never spent so dull a Christmas."

But he and Matonabbee pressed on until they reached the camp of women and children who were waiting for their chief's return from the fort. Hearne discovered that his guide rejoiced in five wives, seven children and two adopted orphans. These formed part of the entourage that now moved slowly westward through the thin *taiga* forest in the bitter cold of January and February.

"It is impossible to describe the intenseness of the cold we experienced this day," Hearne wrote on February 7 as the party crossed Partridge Lake. It was so cold that one of Matonabbee's wives, who belted her clothes up high for easier walking, froze her thighs and buttocks. "I must acknowledge that I was not in the number who pitied her," Hearne wrote, "as I thought she took too much pains to shew a clean heel and good leg, her garters being always in sight, which, though by no means considered here as bordering on indecency, is by far too airy to withstand the rigorous cold of a severe winter in a high Northern latitude."

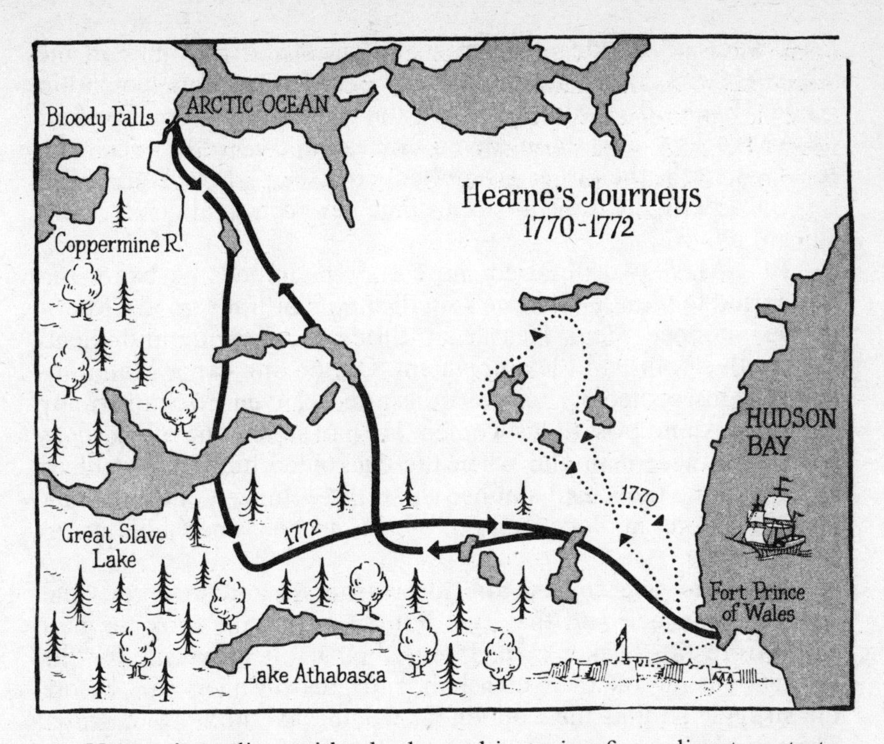

Hearne's earlier guides had erred in trying for a direct route to the copper country in the dead of winter. Matonabbee did not make that mistake. The party crept west in the shelter of the *taiga* and it was not until April, when the numbers had been swelled to some seventy persons, that they began to ready themselves for the Barrens, gathering birchbark with which to fashion canoes and cutting tent poles that could be converted into snowshoe frames in the winter. Here Matonabbee bought himself a sixth wife from a party of passing Indians. She was a strapping woman, built like a grenadier, in Hearne's phrase, and a commonsense choice, as he acknowledged, considering the rigours of the impending journey. Hearne had already grasped something of the practicality of Indian existence on the Barrens. If an Indian fell sick (as one was to do with consumption) and could not keep up with the main band, he or she was simply left behind. Hearne himself recognized the necessity of this custom, cruel though it sounds. There was no use everyone sitting down and dying with the invalid.

The party was about to move on but was delayed for two days by a woman in a difficult condition of labour. Once the child was born, however, she set out with the rest carrying the infant on her back. For the first day, some one else pulled her sledge, but after that she was on her own, carrying the baby as well as the heavy load, wading knee-deep in water and snow and moaning all the while. Hearne noted that the Indians gave no help to a woman in labour. Even other women refused to serve as midwives. For four or five weeks she was considered unclean and forced to stay in a tent by herself, the father prohibited from seeing his offspring lest he take a permanent dislike to it, since newborn infants were considered ugly.

That May, two hundred more Indians joined the band and these tried to plunder Hearne's small supply of trade goods. Matonabbee stopped them. Hearne's attitude to his guide and friend was, at this point, a little ambivalent. On the one hand, Matonabbee was his protector; on the other, he behaved atrociously, by European standards, to his women. He had stolen one of his wives from a younger man and when the cuckolded husband ventured to complain, the chief stabbed him three times. The incident, Hearne wrote apologetically, "by no means does honour to Matonabbee."

It was, however, the custom, as Hearne was at pains to explain. The stronger men and the good hunters habitually took the best wives from the weaker men. It was their habit to wrestle for the women, cutting off their own hair and greasing their ears before the struggle so that their opponent would have nothing to grasp. They did not, however, punch or kick each other. The prize was stripped and borne off to the victor's tent, often against her will. It is well to note that these practices were not greatly different from the treatment of women in many parts of the seventeenth-century world, where men were not only predominant but also held the power of life and death over their female chattels. The Indians sometimes beat their wives but rarely killed them, as the Japanese samurai often did in that same era, with a single, unpredictable sword stroke.

Hearne accepted these customs philosophically. To him the Indian was neither a noble savage nor a sub-human. As for Matonabbee, he got his come-uppance, after a fashion, when the man who had sold him his sixth wife returned and demanded further payment for her. Since his opponent was bigger and stronger, the chief had to give in; but he was angered and humiliated and Hearne had great difficulty persuading him to continue the journey north to the copper country.

On May 31, the men left the women and children camped on the edge of the tundra and headed merrily into the north while their families wailed their goodbyes. They were soon joined by another band of Indians whose intention was to go to the Coppermine on an Eskimo-murdering expedition. Hearne was horrified by this turn of events, but the Indians scoffed at what they considered his cowardice. Knowing that his life depended on their good humour, the explorer told them that he would not interfere but would help them only if the Eskimos themselves actually attacked. "This declaration was received with great satisfaction, and I never afterwards ventured to interfere with any of their war-plans."

They were now so far removed from civilization that the people they encountered had never seen a white skin. A group of Copper Indians, who had joined the party, circled the explorer with great curiosity, pronouncing him a perfect human being except for the colour of his hair and eyes. The former they likened to the stained hair of a buffalo's tail and the latter, being light, to those of a gull. As for his skin, they thought it looked like meat that had been sodden in water until all the blood was extracted. All the combings from the stranger's hair were carefully collected and hoarded as souvenirs.

And then, just after midnight on July 16, in the gloomiest corner of the Canadian mainland, near a series of cataracts that bear to this day the name of Bloody Falls, there occurred the incident that was to overshadow all of Hearne's other adventures and discoveries.

The Indians lay camped in some scrub brush near the Coppermine River, which was only 180 yards wide at this point and totally unnavigable. Three spies returned from a reconnaissance and reported five tents of Eskimos pitched on the west side. One can imagine the air of expectancy and tension that fell over the party. Hearne's companions painted their faces and picked up wooden shields which they had emblazoned with representations of their guardian spirits. They had all tied up their hair or cut it off and now, to make themselves light for running, they removed their stockings, rolled up or cut off the sleeves of their jackets and, in some cases, stripped down to breechcloths and shoes in spite of the maddening hordes of mosquitoes. Hearne, who refused to stay behind lest he be slaughtered by an escaping Eskimo, took off his own stockings and cap and tied his hair. But he told the Indians that he would not join in the killing except in self-defence.

Then, in the bright rays of the midnight sun, the Indians mounted the attack on their defenceless and unsuspecting prey while Hearne stood by and watched in horror. No writer can improve on his own account of what happened in that bloody midnight hour so long ago:

"Men, women and children, in all upward of twenty, ran out of their tents stark naked, and endeavoured to make their escape, but the Indians having possession of all the landside, to no place could they fly for shelter. One alternative only remained, that of jumping into the river; but, as none of them attempted it, they all fell sacrifice to Indian barbarity!

"The shrieks and groans of the poor expiring wretches were truly dreadful; and my horror was much increased at seeing a young girl, seemingly about eighteen years of age, killed so near me, that when the first spear was stuck into her side she fell down at my feet, and twisted round my legs, so that it was with difficulty that I could disengage myself from her dying grasps. As two Indian men pursued this unfortunate victim, I solicited very hard for her life; but the murderers made no reply till they had stuck both their spears through her body, and transfixed her to the ground. They then looked me sternly in the face, and began to ridicule me, by asking if I wanted an Esquimaux wife; and paid not the smallest regard to the shrieks and agony of the poor wretch, who was twining round their spears like an eel! Indeed, after receiving much abusive language from them ... I was at length obliged to desire that they would be more expeditious in dispatching their victim out of her misery.... One of the Indians hastily drew his spear from the place where it was first lodged, and pierced it through her breast near the heart. The love of life, however, even in this most miserable state, was so predominant, that though this might justly be called the most merciful act that could be done for the poor creature, it seemed to be unwelcome, for though much exhausted by pain and loss of blood, she made several attempts to ward off the friendly blow. My situation and the terror of my mind at beholding this butchery, cannot easily be conceived, much less described; though I summed up all the fortitude I was master of on the occasion, it was with difficulty that I could refrain from tears; ... Even at this hour I cannot reflect on the transactions of that horrid day without shedding tears."

This slaughter was scarcely concluded when the Indians spotted seven more Eskimo tents on the east side of the river. They could not cross, having left their canoes upstream, but opened fire on these new targets. Now an odd thing occurred. As each bullet struck the ground, crowds of curious Eskimos would run forward to see what the Indians were sending them and to examine the pieces of lead that ricocheted off the rocks. Only when one man was shot in the leg did the whole multitude tumble into canoes and flee.

But one old man fell behind while collecting his belongings and twenty Indians speared him until, in Hearne's grisly phrase, "his whole body was like a cullender." And one old woman, so blind and deaf that she was oblivious to danger, was spotted sitting alone by a waterfall, killing salmon. She, too, was butchered in the most hideous fashion, being stabbed first in the eyes and then in the non-vital parts so that she would die slowly in pain. This was savage treatment, certainly, but no more savage than that visited upon the Aztecs of Mexico about the same time by the Christian conquistadores of Spain or upon heretics and witches of Europe who were consumed by slow fires in full public view. Hearne, who missed nothing even in moments of high emotion, noted that the river, which must have been running red with blood, was also clogged with an incredible number of salmon, heading for the spawning grounds.

Now, at last, the young explorer was able to fulfill his mission. He erected a mark and took possession of the bleak coast in the name of the Hudson's Bay Company "for the sake of form," as he put it. After the events of that night and in those dismal surroundings there could be no joy in such an empty gesture. The crooked river, with its banks of solid rock, winding through a dreary region of barren hills and marshes, was of no value as a water highway. And the fabulous mines turned out to be nothing more than a jumble of rock and gravel. Though the Indians had talked about hills of solid copper, Hearne, after four hours' search, found only a single ingot weighing about four pounds. It found its way eventually into the British Museum and is there to this day. Even if there had been copper in quantity, the problems of mining and transporting it south would have been insurmountable.

Hearne's other discoveries were more valuable. It was clear to him by now that the North West Passage, that legendary channel of open water supposedly joining the two great oceans, was a myth; it did not exist in any navigable form. More important were his detailed observations of native customs and habits, which he continued to set down in great detail and in spite of incredible hardships as the party moved south again. His feet and legs were swollen, his toenails had dropped off and all the skin between his toes had been chafed away by the constant sandpaper action of the terrain. "I left the print of my feet in blood almost at every step I took," he recorded.

But when they reached the camp of the women and children these afflictions soon abated and the entire party, reunited, arrived at last at Athapuscow Lake, which we know as Great Slave. Hearne, the first white man to see this immense stretch of slate-grey water, must have been impressed. Lashed by storms as wicked as those on the ocean, the lake is so huge that no shoreline can be seen from its waters. Here, on its margin, Hearne made his sketches and observed and recorded the native rites.

He was particularly intrigued by the rituals of the medicine men, all of them expert conjurers, who pretended to swallow and disgorge knives, hatchets and other tools in an attempt to cure their patients. Specially built conjuring houses were constructed for the sick and in these the naked doctors would suck and blow on the afflicted parts, administering charms, singing and talking to spirits as they worked their legerdemain. Hearne saw one medicine man devour a bayonet in an attempt to succour a sick man and confessed that, although he did not believe the conjurer had actually swallowed it, he could not see how he managed to hide it. The man then feigned great pains in his stomach and eventually appeared to vomit the bayonet out again, "a very nice piece of deception, especially as it was performed by a man quite naked." The patient recovered.

On another occasion, one man fell dangerously ill, his whole side paralysed. The medicine man pretended to swallow a large board and all the men who administered to the invalid fasted for several days until they, too, fell ill. All recovered, including the paralysed man who was able to walk within three weeks and go hunting in six.

What Hearne was observing, no doubt, was a primitive form of psychosomatic medicine. So strong was the faith of the Indians that it was believed, with considerable evidence, that if a medicine man cursed somebody, death was inevitable. Matonabbee believed that Hearne himself had the power to curse his enemies and at one point persuaded him to put a hex on an Indian who had treated him badly. Hearne obligingly drew a rough sketch of two figures representing himself and Matonabbee's enemy. Opposite the figures he drew a pine tree with a large human eye over it and a hand projecting from it. He gave this paper to the chief. When the enemy heard of the curse he sickened and died. Hearne was careful not to repeat this mumbo-jumbo and so preserved his reputation.

He was now eating almost everything the Indians ate and enjoying it. He became so used to eating his food raw that for the rest of his life he preferred his fish undercooked. He was especially fond of a dish made of half-digested food from a deer stomach and mixed with blood and fat first chewed by men and boys and then heated and cooked for several days in the deer's paunch. Wombs and genitals became normal fare and unborn calves, fawns and beavers, taken from their mothers' wombs, he pronounced "the greatest delicacies that can be eaten." The Indians also enjoyed eating the lice that crawled through their long hair and deerskin garments and the warble flies that settled on fresh meat, but these Hearne refused – not through any sense of disgust, he hastens to tell us, but because he did not want to become ad-

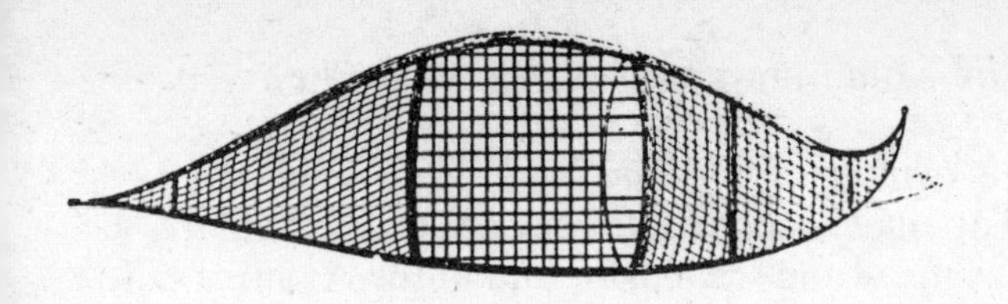

Hearne's drawings, taken from his journal, show his eye for detail. At left: *Indian snow-shoes, a skin kettle and,* below, *a bark canoe.* Bottom: *Great Slave Lake as it looked to Hearne, the first white man to gaze upon its slate-grey waters.*

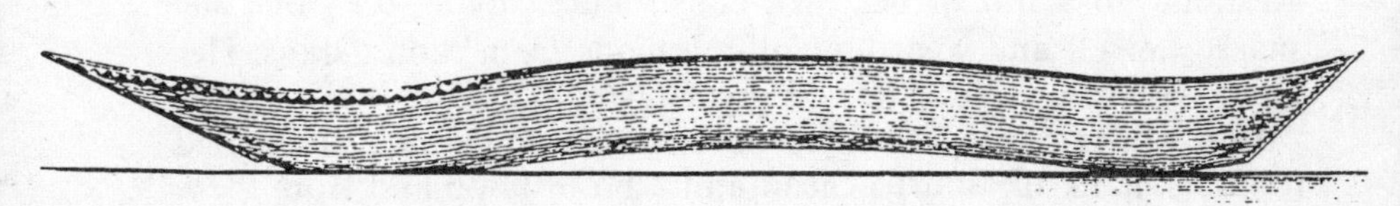

dicted to delicacies that he would not be able to get when he returned to his own world!

His own world in that winter of 1771–72 must have seemed very far away. James Watt had just invented steam power; the Russians had seized the Crimea from the Turks; and in the American colonies the first rumblings of revolution were being felt – a revolution which would have a glancing effect on Hearne's own future. Hearne knew nothing of these events. The slow progress of the Indians, who moved this way and that, following the game or meeting up with other tribes, might have maddened a less patient man but does not seem to have concerned him. He had reached the Arctic in July of 1771. The following January found him moving even farther to the west, somewhere between Great Slave and Athabasca Lake.

It was in these environs that he had another remarkable encounter, this time with a young Dogrib woman who had been taken prisoner by the Athupuscows eighteen months before. She had escaped and had managed to survive for seven winter months, all alone, in a hut of her own construction, living on game she snared herself and wearing clothing made from rabbit skins. Her attire, Hearne noted "shewed great taste, and exhibited no little variety of ornament." She had never seen iron before but she had found a shank of an arrowhead and a bit of hoop and from these she had made a knife and an awl with which to construct a crude pair of snowshoes. Her fire, which she managed to keep alive for the entire winter, she had first kindled by rubbing two stones together.

This resourceful creature was clearly an uncommon prize for any man and the strongest began to wrestle each other to see who would have her. "The poor girl," Hearne wrote, "was actually won and lost at wrestling by near half a score of different men the same evening." Matonabbee was intent on entering the fray until one of his own women told him, dryly, that he already had more wives than he needed, a remark that so infuriated the sensitive chief that he beat her unmercifully; she died of her injuries.

The party moved on in its wayward fashion. Whenever the Indians encountered a poorer tribe, they fell upon them, plundering their luckless victims of goods and women. On April 14, they robbed a community of strange Indians of all their belongings and gang-raped the younger women. They were heading east again but we cannot be sure of the exact route because Hearne's quadrant had been broken the year before and his watch had also stopped. It was no longer possible for him to measure distances or fix his position.

Finally they encountered another party of Indians who were bound for Fort Prince of Wales with a load of furs. They joined them and on June 30, 1772, Hearne at last reached his home base after an absence of eighteen months and twenty-three days.

What had he accomplished? His chief findings, as we have seen, were negative ones. He was right about the North West Passage but old myths die hard; the Royal Navy, twenty years later, was still instructing Captain George Vancouver to search for one. He was right about the impracticability of mining copper on the Arctic's shore, a judgment confirmed by Franklin in 1821; but such is the optimism of the treasure-seeker that hundreds of claims were filed in the very same region between 1913 and 1954. All were allowed to lapse. Hearne's maps, inaccurate though they were, remained in use for half a century. And nothing approaching his feat of crossing the Barren Ground was attempted until the Geological Survey of Canada sent J.B. Tyrrell there in 1893–94. But Hearne's real contribution was his close and accurate descriptions of the Chipewyan and Dogrib Indians, the flora and fauna of the country through which he travelled, and his willingness to adapt to native ways, which set the pattern of Arctic survival for generations.

Hearne had one more significant feat before him; the establishment of Cumberland House north of The Pas, which marked the first move of the Hudson's Bay Company into the interior in direct competition with the more adventurous Nor'westers. It was here that Hearne, in effect, invented the York boat, the light skiff used for more than a century to convey shipments of furs across the continent.

And now we come to the odd coda to Samuel Hearne's story – one that has caused controversy for two centuries. He was made governor of Fort Prince of Wales in 1776, the year of the outbreak of the American Revolution. The fort itself was a monstrous battlement, constructed of gigantic blocks of granite. It had taken thirty-eight years to complete and was considered to be one of the most impregnable strongholds on the continent. But in 1782, when a French admiral, Le Comte de la Pérouse, sailed into the harbour (the Revolution had once again pitted Britain against France), Hearne calmly surrendered the fort to him without a shot being fired.

Why? Certainly not through cowardice, Hearne's bravery was never in dispute. But as we have seen, he was also a man of prudence and common sense; false bravado was not part of his makeup. Certainly he could have invited a siege and, had he done so, it is quite likely that Fort Prince of Wales would have been memorialized in song and story as an early Alamo, and Hearne and his men hailed as martyr-heroes, of the order of Adam Dollard and Davey Crockett. But Hearne was having none of that. La Pérouse had three ships, mounting a total of 146 guns and he landed four hundred men at arms before the British realized who they were. Hearne, with a mere thirty-nine men, bowed gracefully to the inevitable. Since fortresses were traded back and forth between warring nations as part of armistice documents (Louisburg was a good example), Hearne obviously saw no reason why he should sacrifice a single life for no clear gain. The French could not destroy the fort, only its guns and wooden buildings. Those massive battlements can still be seen, towering above the cold waters of Hudson Bay, a few miles from the modern town of Churchill.

As for Samuel Hearne, he was made a prisoner and taken back to Europe, not to durance vile, but to his native England by the chivalrous La Pérouse, who, having devoured that fascinating journal en route, made Hearne promise that he would have it published. Hearne agreed, but before that was possible the war ended and the Company sent Hearne back again to Hudson Bay, where he built a new fort on the site of modern-day Churchill. He retired in 1787 and it is ironic to report that he quickly frittered away his savings because he did not understand the value of money, having lived for most of his life in a land where it was of no use. Then, in 1792 he sold the manuscript of his northern journey to a publisher for two hundred pounds, a handsome enough sum in those days when you compare it with the eighteen pounds that John Milton got for *Paradise Lost*. Alas, Hearne did not live to witness the birth of his literary progeny; a month after the sale he died of dropsy at what, in those times, was the ripe age of forty-seven.

And Matonabbee, the chief who had befriended him and led him on the greatest journey of his life – what of him? He had prospered after Hearne's return, achieving the leadership of all the Northern Indians and continuing "to render great service to the Company...by bringing a greater quantity of furs to their Factory at Churchill River, than any other Indian did, or ever will do."

It would be pleasant to report that Matonabbee, having achieved fame and greatness, died in bed surrounded by his many wives. Alas, his end was as tragic as it was remarkable. When he learned in 1783 that Hearne had surrendered to the French without a shot he could not bear the shame. He hanged himself, leaving six of his wives and four of his children to starve to death in the biting cold of the winter that followed.

In death, Matonabbee was unique, as he had been in life. For this is the only record we have of a Northern Indian putting an end to his own existence.

4
The Slavery of John Jewitt

John Jewitt, the armourer, was cleaning muskets at his bench in the steerage of the trading ship *Boston* when he became aware of a commotion on the deck above – a running and a thumping, the sound of blows, harsh human cries, alarming splashes, whistles and rattles and all manner of pagan outburst. He seized his musket and scrambled up the steerage companionway. As he lifted the hatch, a brown hand smeared with red paint poked through the opening and grasped at his head. Jewitt's short hair saved his life; the ribbon slipped off; he fell backward, trying to ward off the axe blow that gashed his skull and sent him reeling into the hold as the hatch slammed shut. There he lay, stunned and senseless, for the next four hours, regaining consciousness occasionally, struggling to stand upright, toppling and fainting from loss of blood, while the war cries and triumphant songs of the Nootka echoed above and his shipmates died and were decapitated with their own knives.

The date was March 22, 1803. The place was Nootka Sound on the sodden western shore of Vancouver Island, as isolated from European civilization then as the coasts of Hokkaido or Togoland. Some three hundred miles to the north, Russian territory began; some six hundred miles to the south, the Spanish domain ended. The islands between, and the mainland drained by those two great rivers, the Fraser and the Columbia, yet unnamed, were the realm of the Indians. Only one white man, Alexander Mackenzie, had managed to force his way through the mountains from the interior plains to the Pacific Coast. The expeditions of Fraser, Thompson, and Lewis and Clark lay in the future. The wilderness stretched unbroken from the beaches of the Pacific to the shores of Lake Ontario.

And yet for a quarter of a century the white man's ships had been anchoring in Nootka Sound. At one time Spanish officers had feasted there from silver plates, proposed toasts from crystal goblets, and organized displays of fireworks. The natives were so friendly that James Cook named the little bay on whose shores their village stood, Friendly Cove. Now, deserted for a decade by the white man, it was friendly no longer.

In the dark of the hold, some time during that brutal March afternoon, John Jewitt regained his senses. He was a young man, barely twenty, with a long solemn face and full, sensitive lips. Above him he could hear the Indians yelling and chanting; were they saving him for torture? For a long time he remained in "this horrid state of suspense" until at last the hatch opened and a familiar face peered down – a noble face with an unmistakable Roman nose, smeared with black and red paint, belonging to a man Jewitt called king: Maquinna, the head chief of the village of Yuquot. At the Indian's bidding, Jewitt climbed to the deck and listened to his proposal.

"John – I speak," Maquinna said. "You no say no. You say no – daggers come!"

Jewitt did not say no. His life had been saved by the chief himself, who had ordered the hatch closed and had called off his assailants, not for reasons of compassion or prudence, but because he needed a man with a blacksmith's skills. His proposal was that Jewitt be his slave for life, work for him, repair his muskets and daggers, and fight for him in battles. Jewitt, drenched in his own blood, one eye swollen shut, surrounded by naked Indians clamouring for his death, their daggers raised to strike, had no choice. On Maquinna's order, he signalled his submission by kneeling before his captor and kissing his hands and feet.

In various corners of the globe at that time, white men were making slaves of aborigines. But here, against the dank backdrop of the rain forest, the position was reversed. For more than two years John Jewitt would be the personal property of Maquinna, accorded the status of a dog, a canoe, or a cedar-bark robe.

He was shivering uncontrollably from a combination of cold, weakness, and plain terror. Maquinna went to the captain's cabin and returned with a greatcoat, which he threw over the blacksmith's shoulders. He allowed his captive a swallow of rum, then led him by the hand to the quarter-deck, "where the most horrid sight presented itself that my eyes have ever witnessed." Arranged in a row were the decapitated heads of the crew, twenty-five in all. Maquinna ordered one of his people to bring a head to Jewitt to identify. It was the captain's. He was then forced to identify each head that was not too badly mangled to be unrecognizable. Jewitt now realized that every one of his shipmates had been massacred.

Maquinna continued his solicitude. He bound Jewitt's head wound with the blacksmith's silk kerchief and, at Jewitt's suggestion, dressed it with a tobacco leaf from the ship's stores. Then he ordered his new slave to set sail for Friendly Cove. Jewitt cut the cables and sent some natives aloft to loose the sails "which they did in a very bungling manner." Nonetheless, with a fair wind, he managed to get the ship to the cove where, on Maquinna's order, he beached her.

Here, at the village of Yuquot, the head chief was greeted with the hammering of sticks on the houses and blazing torches. Women and children ran out of the cedar lodges to hail him. Maquinna's own lodge was enormous – one hundred and fifty feet long and forty feet wide; it housed one hundred persons, half of them members of his extended family and half of them slaves. Five hundred warriors arrived to celebrate the capture of the *Boston*, but when it was suggested that Jewitt be put to death, the chief drove the visitors from his house.

Jewitt was young in the ways of the world, but he had a great deal of common sense. He understood (far better than most young men of that age) that it was foolhardy to battle overwhelming odds. He must make the best of things, and if that meant placating his captors, so be it. They had murdered his comrades, men who had slung their hammocks next to his on the long voyage round the Horn and up the coastline of the two Americas, but he put the memory out of his mind. He set out to ingratiate himself with his new master, charming Maquinna by taking his young son on his knee and stringing a necklace from the metal buttons on his coat as an impromptu gift.

But he could not sleep that night because of the pain of his wound and the anxiety he felt for his life. Maquinna had warned him that some of his people might try to stab him in the dark. He had never before felt so alone. Then, at midnight, an Indian rushed in to inform the chief that another survivor was on the beached ship – a white man who had knocked him down.

Lying in the dark, the captive allowed himself a glimmer of hope. A Christian companion! But who could it be? After some thought he concluded that the other survivor was John Thompson, a tough, surly sailmaker from Philadelphia who had been at work between decks before the massacre. There could be no doubt that the Indians intended to kill him. How might he be saved? Jewitt worked out a deception: Thompson was about forty and looked older; he would convince Maquinna that this man was his father and ask that his life be spared.

As dawn broke, he dozed off, only to be wakened by the chief who informed him that the man on the ship was to be killed. Jewitt followed the chief to the boat, taking Maquinna's young son by the hand. A palaver followed: did the men of the tribe wish to spare the life of the second survivor? With one voice they shouted for his blood.

Now Jewitt acted out his scheme. He pointed to Maquinna's son, still clutching his hand, and asked the chief if he loved him. Maquinna replied that he did. Jewitt asked the boy if he loved his father; the boy nodded. Whereupon the blacksmith cried, "And I also love mine!" With that he threw himself at his master's feet and, with tears in his eyes, begged him to spare his father's life. If his father died, Jewitt declared, then he too wished to be killed.

Maquinna was moved by this piece of theatre; moreover, as the blacksmith had shrewdly concluded, he was reluctant to lose his valuable new slave. The chief agreed that if the man on board should prove to be Jewitt's father, his life would be spared. He ordered Jewitt to find and bring the man to him. Jewitt climbed into the hold and was overjoyed to find that it was indeed Thompson, unharmed except for a slight wound on the nose. He outlined his charade to the older man explaining that his safety would depend on his playing the role of parent. Thompson's skill with a needle was also an asset. Maquinna realized that he would be useful making sails for the great forty-foot dugouts, which his people took to sea.

The following day, the Indians stripped the ship of everything movable – of arms, powder, sails, and masts. Jewitt managed to filch the captain's records and writing desk together with a Bible, a prayer book, and an account book in which he determined to keep a running chronicle of his captivity.

The Indians set up the ship's cannon on the beach, and when, three days later, two American vessels sailed into the sound, they were driven off, an incident that the impetuous Maquinna immediately regretted, knowing it would frighten other traders away. That was the last thing he wanted. His people were consummate traders, their shrewdness honed by twenty-five years of barter with English and Yankee seamen. The prize the visitors sought was the skin of the sea otter, a pelt that could fetch sums ranging from thirty to more than one hundred dollars. The day was long gone when a skin could be purchased for a dozen glass beads. Inflation had come to the Pacific Coast. The Indians wanted iron utensils, guns, metal jewellery, and, above all, the thick sheets of copper that were highly prized as gifts to be dispensed at the potlatch. Possessions in Nootka society signified status, and if Maquinna possessed more status than any other household chief at Friendly Cove, it was not only because of his inherited rank but also because of what he owned.

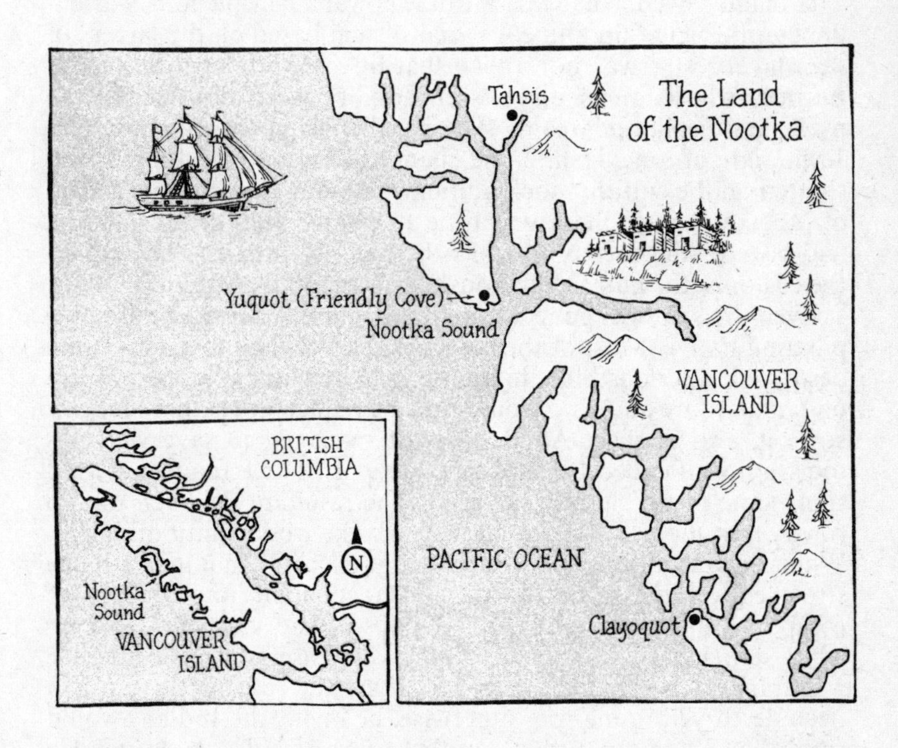

Now he was eager to show off his newest chattels to his peers. In the week that followed, people from twenty neighbouring bands poured into Yuquot to view the captives. Maquinna and Jewitt climbed to the roof of the lodge and drummed with sticks. Thompson was detailed to show off the plundered firearms. These the visitors examined with great curiosity, running up and down the beach, some carrying as many as eight muskets upside down. A feast of whale blubber and herring roe followed. Maquinna's son, wearing a wolf-mask, executed a spirited dance, followed by the chief himself in his sea otter robe, a whistle in his mouth, a rattle in his hand. For two hours Maquinna danced with enormous vigour, springing into the air from a squatting position and constantly turning on his heels as he landed to the insistent thrum of his fellow chiefs' drumming with sticks on hollow logs. There were presents for the visitors: one hundred muskets, one hundred looking glasses, twenty barrels of powder, for the giving of presents among the Nootka Indians, as among all the Pacific Coast tribes, was a means of achieving and maintaining status and the key event in the elaborate potlatch ceremonies, in which every tribe periodically indulged.

It might be said that this attitude toward conspicuous waste – the by-product of an affluent social system based on the largess of sea and forest – was not unlike that of the white civilizations of Europe, whose kings and lesser nobility were devoted to the profligate display of wealth. The parallel is superficial. For John Jewitt, late of Lincolnshire, the change in lifestyle must have been shattering, the culture shock numbing. Among the dripping cedars of Nootka Sound, there was little to remind him of the man he had been or the society in which he had been reared. The ethics, the customs, the human relationships were totally foreign.

Even the ship was gone, destroyed in a fire set accidentally by a pilfering native. Most of the cargo, and all of the provisions, were destroyed, a serious blow to the two slaves who had hoped to live on familiar fare and who would now be reduced to eating blubber, seal oil, and dogfish. All that Jewitt managed to save were his tools, a box of chocolate, and a case of port. The Indians preferred rum, some of which they salvaged. The resultant debauch was so rowdy that the two white men fled into the woods until midnight. When they returned, they found every man in Maquinna's lodge stretched on the floor, drunk. Jewitt thought immediately of escape – but to where? With no ships in the vicinity – and no white settlement of any kind – flight would amount to suicide. He was trapped. He thanked his Maker that the rest of the rum had been destroyed in the fire; otherwise, he knew, the Indians would surely have killed both slaves in the course of a drunken orgy. He found a cask of gin still whole, bored a hole in the side, and drained it on to the ground before the Indians were roused.

A less resourceful man, or a less adaptable one, could scarcely have endured the months that followed. But Jewitt belonged to that breed of men – they are to be found on every frontier – who are best described as "survivors." Thompson was not of this temperament. A rigid and stubborn seaman, consumed by hatred for the people who had massacred his comrades, he could not have lived a day without the steadying influence of his fellow captive. John Jewitt had yet to attain his majority, but it was he, not Thompson, who acted as a wise father toward a stubborn and quixotic child. Maquinna himself noticed it and was puzzled by it, remarking that Thompson had a disagreeable disposition compared to that of his "son"; the chief concluded that the good-tempered Jewitt must have had a very kind mother.

Jewitt's real father, also a blacksmith, had thought him intelligent enough to take him out of the local school in Lincolnshire in favour of an academy in a nearby town, hoping eventually to apprentice him to a surgeon. But young Jewitt preferred his father's trade and excelled at it. Later, when the family moved to the seaport of Hull, he began to yearn for adventure in lands beyond the ocean's rim, devouring books of travel, notably the *Voyages* of Captain James Cook, one of the best-sellers of the day. Cook and his crew were the first white men to enter Nootka Sound and the first to set foot on Vancouver Island. Reading the explorer's account of that incredible realm of gigantic trees, outlandish sea creatures, and bizarre ocean-going natives dressed in bark and skins, Jewitt was fired with a longing as old as time: to see a world that few other men had seen, to witness customs unknown and mysterious, and, of course, to profit from the experience. His chance came when Captain John Salter brought the *Boston* into Hull for repairs. Salter was headed for the northwest coast of North America and the sea otter trade. Jewitt jumped at the offer to sail with her as armourer. Away he went, mindful of his father's counsel to be "honest, industrious, frugal and temperate" and to "let the Bible be your guide" – advice that would serve him well in the travail that was to follow.

From the outset Thompson insisted that Jewitt keep a journal. He was himself illiterate but had been so long at sea that he considered a journal indispensable. He even offered to cut his finger to supply blood with which to write, but the resourceful blacksmith made his own ink by boiling blackberry juice with powdered charcoal. His inkwell was a clamshell; his pens were ravens' quills. The result was an invaluable anthropological document, a detailed account of the customs of a primitive people whose way of life had not changed greatly since the coming of the white man. Without it, our knowledge of early Nootka culture would be fragmentary.

Both men were the personal chattels of their master. This swiftly became obvious when Thompson, after being teased by Maquinna's young son, knocked him to the floor. The chief, entering at that moment, seized a musket. Thompson, who was strong, powerful, and an expert boxer, showed no fear but bared his chest and dared his master to fire. It was a brave but foolhardy gesture, and had Jewitt not entered at that moment, his comrade would have died. Maquinna made it clear that Thompson existed on sufferance; if anything should happen to Jewitt, the sailmaker would be killed at once. A council meeting followed at which Thompson's death was demanded to avenge the insult to the young prince. Again, Jewitt interceded for his "father" and again Maquinna spared the older man's life. Yet this narrow escape in no way curbed the sailmaker's temper. A few weeks later he struck the eldest son of another chief – an eighteen-year-old who had called him a white slave. For the third time, Maquinna saved him.

Jewitt saw no purpose in provoking their captors. He was later to write that he had determined from the first moment of capture to adopt a conciliatory attitude and to conform as far as possible to their customs and manner of thinking, "trusting that the same divine goodness that has rescued me from death would not always suffer me to languish in captivity among these heathen." He maintained a cheerful mien, joined in the sports and tricks of the Indians, made fishhooks and daggers for the men and ornaments for the wives and children. He also picked up some of the Nootka language to reinforce his knowledge of Chinook, the traders' jargon.

Thompson refused to learn a word, saying he hated the heathen and "their cursed lingo." He made no attempt to hide his bitterness, adding that he would destroy the entire race if he had the ships and guns to do so. He had spent almost his entire life at sea, running away from home in Philadelphia at the age of eight to ship across the Atlantic as a cabin boy. Pressed into service in England, he had served in the British Navy for twenty-seven years, being present at the great Channel battle of June 1, 1794, when Lord Howe defeated the French fleet. He was very much the arrogant sailor, taking bitter offence at the slightest insult, real or fancied, and continually bemoaning his lowered status. In this, oddly, he resembled his captors, who were equally obsessed by status and who took immediate and often violent umbrage at the most inconsequential slight. In Thompson's view, "to a brave sailor like him, who had fought the French and Spanish with glory, it was a punishment worse than death to be a slave to such a poor, ignorant, despicable set of beings." Jewitt's attitude was more elastic: life among the Nootka might be harsh, but it was better than the grave.

The people of Yuquot set their faces toward the sea. Behind the village – mysterious and gloomy – rose the green wall of the forest into whose dark recesses the Indians rarely ventured. Who knew what demons lurked among those creeping mosses, what spirits were concealed in that infinity of waist-high bracken? Above the tangle of salal and grape, above the webwork of rotting logs, above the grotesque shapes of plate-sized fungi rose the great trees – the monstrous cedars, the towering firs – blotting out the sun and cloaking the forest in perpetual twilight. The Indians preferred the wide beaches, the open ocean to this ghost world; what little contact they had with their cousins, the Kwakiutls, on the opposite side of the island, was generally made by sea.

The village was not large. It consisted of some twenty houses, most of them in a row, differing in size according to the importance of the chief of each family. The smallest house was forty feet in length; all were forty feet in width. The ridge poles were built of immense cedar logs – Maquinna's was eight feet in circumference. The roofs were lapped cedar shingles, covered by planks held down with heavy stones and extending out to shelter the lodge from the rain. The posts supporting the ridge poles were carved with human heads and painted.

The political structure was loose, its main unit being the extended family, whose members, presided over by a hereditary chief, lived under one roof. Maquinna, whom the white men called king, was in no sense an absolute ruler, being no more than the highest-ranking house chief in the loose confederacy that made up this one village. Twenty-five similar villages, containing perhaps ten thousand persons, were strewn along the western shores of Vancouver Island for two hundred miles.

As slaves, Jewitt and Thompson dined with members of their family, but not from the common tray. They sat on the ground, ate with their fingers, and scooped up soup and oil with clamshells. At feasts, where guests were carefully seated in order of rank, the slaves were allowed the leftovers. As Jewitt described it, this was "a most awkward thing for us, at first, to have to lug home with us, in our hands and arms, the blubber of fish . . . . But we soon became reconciled to it." Their feeding habits were erratic: porpoise meat one day, clams and fermented whale oil the next, boiled salmon the third, and often nothing but nettle stalks gathered in the fields. When there was nothing to eat in his master's house Jewitt would beg for food elsewhere; it was rarely refused.

The two men spent their Sundays in prayer and Bible reading; it helped alleviate their despair, for they felt that no ship would ever come to release them. They would walk to the banks of a freshwater pond about a mile from the village and here, after bathing and putting on clean clothes, Jewitt would read some chapters in the Bible and the prayer appointed for that day by the Church of England. The two men would end with a "fervent prayer to the Almighty that He would deign still to watch over and preserve our lives, rescue us from the hands of the savages and permit us once more to behold a Christian land."

Maquinna, who did not object to these ceremonies, reacted

strongly to Jewitt's keeping a journal. He was convinced that his slave was "writing bad about him." Jewitt made his entries secretly while his master was off fishing. That Maquinna was sensitive to what others thought or said of him is clear from the record. He was a man of mercurial temperament: as Jewitt learned, his touchiness had sparked the massacre aboard the *Boston*.

When the ship had anchored in Nootka Sound, about five miles above the village, on March 12, there had been no hint of hostility or discontent among the Indians. Maquinna came aboard the following day, wearing his knee-length mantle of black sea otter skin, accompanied by several villagers in long cloaks of woven cedar bark. The chief's appearance was extraordinary. His legs, face, and arms were covered with red paint; his eyebrows were painted black in two broad crescent-shaped stripes; his hair, shiny with oil, was fastened in a bun above his head and powdered with white eagle down. He had no difficulty in making himself understood in English.

Captain Salter gave him the obligatory presents of rum, molasses, and ship's biscuit and traded fishhooks and knives for fresh salmon. It was too early to buy otter skins; Salter had put in at Nootka for wood, water, and fresh fish because Maquinna was said to be friendlier than the Indian chiefs farther to the north. And so he appeared to be. He was invited to dine on March 15 and again on March 19, on which occasion the captain made him a gift of a double-barrelled shotgun; it pleased Maquinna greatly.

Two days later he returned with a present of nine pairs of ducks, complaining that the gun was no good. He had broken the lock. Salter was offended by the remark, which he perceived as a mark of contempt for the gift; touchiness, it would appear, was a common failing among whites and Indians alike. He called Maquinna a liar, seized the gun, and flung it into the cabin. He called out to his armourer, "This fellow has broken this beautiful fowling piece; see if you can fix it."

Maquinna understood exactly what Salter had said. To a man of his uncommon sensitivity, it was enraging; but he repressed his anger, repeatedly putting his hand to his throat and rubbing his chest, in order, as he later told Jewitt in a colourful and apt phrase, to keep down his heart, which was rising in his throat and threatening to choke him. In that instant, all the insults, all the demeaning incidents with the white traders over the past quarter of a century crowded in upon him.

Yet when he returned on March 22 to join a group of his fellow tribesmen on board the ship, he appeared good humoured. He was wearing a mask and carrying a whistle, which he blew as he and his men danced around on the deck. This feigned gaiety was a subterfuge; the chief's purpose was calculated and deadly.

As the ship was preparing to sail, Maquinna persuaded the captain to take on a load of fresh salmon. The first mate and nine men were accordingly sent ashore in a longboat on a fishing expedition. Thus was the crew's number depleted. It was at this point that Jewitt was in the steerage working at his bench and Thompson was between decks preparing sails. The steward also was on shore, washing clothes; Salter was on the quarter-deck; the second officer and the rest of the crew were hoisting the launch aboard, preparatory to leaving. Since there were not enough crew to complete this task, some of the Indians were pressed into service. None was armed, all having been carefully searched before boarding the ship. But they outnumbered the seamen four to one, and it was thus a simple matter, on Maquinna's signal, for each to reach into the pocket of the sailor beside him, pull out his knife, and dispatch him.

The signal was clear enough. Maquinna simply pushed Salter into the ocean, where a canoeload of Indian women beat him to death with paddles. With the decks running with blood, Maquinna sent a crew of Indians to kill the men on shore and cut off their heads. The corpses on the deck were also beheaded, the torsos thrown into the sea and the heads arranged in order of status on the foredeck, with the captain's at the top end and the cook's at the bottom. Status in death as in life was important to the Nootka, now capering about in a dance of victory.

How was it possible that a single remark could have had such bloody consequences? Though part of the answer lies in the character of Maquinna, the larger explanation has to do with the fierce competition for the sea otter trade in the sinuous fiords of the north Pacific Coast. It had begun in 1785, some years after Cook's men returned to England with a fortune from the sale of furs in China; it had reached its crest just after the turn of the century. At this time the trade was dominated by Americans, with Boston the leading home port for trading vessels, of which there might be as many as fifteen along the coast in a single season. The British, who had started the trade, melted away in the face of Yankee competition, which was fierce and sometimes bloody. With a single exception all Indian attacks on trading vessels were directed against American ships, whose crews used every artifice to obtain the increasingly scarcer pelts. In the words of the explorer Alexander Mackenzie, the coast trade had been "left to American adventurers, who without regularity or capital, or the desire of conciliating future confidence, look altogether to the interest of the moment

. . . . They, therefore, collect all the skins they can procure and in any manner that suits them." Some skippers thought nothing of kidnapping a chief and holding him hostage to obtain the coveted skins; others used threats, force, even theft. There was one instance of an entire village being destroyed because the natives were reluctant to trade. The British had always bartered at arm's length, avoiding the villages and insisting that the natives remain in their canoes at shipside. But as the competition grew fiercer, American captains began to allow them on to the deck so that the Indians considered it their right to be aboard. It was a classic case of familiarity breeding contempt.

Sporadic attacks on Yankee trading ships, tentative at first, had been occurring since the early 1790s. Revenge was a major motive. The Indians, holding to "a doctrine of vicarious responsibility," as F.W. Howay, the West Coast historian, has called it, made no distinction among sea captains. It was the class that was being attacked, not the individual. As Jewitt was to write, they would "wreak their vengeance upon the first vessel or boat crew that offers, making the innocent too frequently suffer for the wrongs of the guilty." And there was something else that perhaps did not occur to the traders: to the Indians, all white men looked much the same and thus were the same.

Maquinna confirmed much of this to Jewitt. As the chief came to know the armourer better, he regaled him with tales of white men who had shot Indians, specifically condemning Esteban José Martinez, the Spanish don who had established himself at Yuquot in 1789 and taken possession of the surrounding territory in the name of the King of Spain. Martinez was responsible for the murder of Maquinna's brother, Qualicum, and this indicated to Jewitt that a thirst for revenge as much as Salter's insult had driven him to kill the *Boston*'s crew. There was something else: the fierce desire, so deeply ingrained in all the West Coast tribes, to emulate and if possible outstrip their peers in such triumphs. The attack upon the *Boston* was the worst in a decade of sporadic incursions; it gave Maquinna enormous prestige.

The chief was determined not to lose his prize captives. He warned Jewitt that if he tried to escape, he would kill him. The same fate awaited him if he tried to defect to one of the other chiefs who coveted him. To emphasize his point Maquinna cited the case of seven deserters from another ship, the *Manchester* of Philadelphia, who had sought shelter with him and subsequently tried to defect to another chief, Wickinninish, his great rival, on Clayoquot Sound. Maquinna had had them all put to death.

His was no idle warning. The most valuable property among the

Nootka was a slave, and Jewitt was a pearl among slaves. Undercover attempts were made to lure both white men from Maquinna. Neighbouring chiefs secretly offered to help them escape, but Jewitt suspected, rightly, that this was only a ruse to steal them in much the same way that a society woman might steal her hostess's chef. A younger sister of Maquinna's chief wife purposely made Jewitt her favourite; because of a defective eye, injured in an accident, she could not marry. She tried to induce the blacksmith to return with her to the village of her father, the powerful Wickinninish. He refused.

In July a ship appeared on the horizon. It did not stop. "I shall not attempt," Jewitt wrote, "to describe our disappointment – my heart sank within me, and I felt as though it was my destiny never more to behold a Christian face."

Yuquot was the summer village of the Nootka. When September came, the whole tribe moved to winter quarters at Tahsis, about thirty miles up the sound, taking with them in their canoes all their belongings, including the cedar planks from the roofs. This meant there would be no further opportunity that season to spot a ship coming into the sound. At Tahsis, sheltered from the winter storms, the Nootka people could enjoy the harvest of the salmon run, catching as many as twenty-five hundred fish in a single day and feasting on roe, a great delicacy, which Jewitt found loathsome. "Scarcely anything," he wrote, "can be more repugnant to the European palate."

Thompson, who had annoyed many of the tribesmen by his habit of knocking at the stick ornaments projecting from their noses, now proceeded to gain favour by making Maquinna a sail for his canoe and clothes cut from European cloth, in particular a royal mantle of coloured patches sewn together, trimmed with the finest otter skin. On this Joseph's Coat were five or six rows of gilt buttons, closely set around the bottom above the fur. The chief wore it with enormous pride, strutting about as the buttons tinkled and exclaiming that no Nootka could have made such a garment. He was immensely vain and in the fashion of his people would sometimes spend a full hour painting his face, only to rub all the colour off and start afresh when the results failed to please him.

It is a sad commentary on Canadian history that only a handful of Indians stand out from the almost faceless mass of tribesmen as distinct individuals, subject to human strengths and weaknesses, vanities and whims, and all those diverse and contradictory qualities that differentiate real people from plaster saints or dark villains. Tecumseh and Joseph Brant in the East, Big Bear and Crowfoot on the Plains, Mackenzie's "English Chief" and Hearne's

Matonabbee in the North belong to this select few. But Maquinna, perhaps more than any other, comes through in the memoirs of a number of white seamen – the most detailed being Jewitt's – as a fully rounded character: volatile, vain, cowardly, bold, acquisitive, shrewd, passionate, sensitive, proud, vengeful, generous, selfish, sagacious, temperamental, and always fascinating. We may not understand him but, through Jewitt, we can feel we have met him.

The great mystery, which has never been entirely unravelled, is whether or not there were two Maquinnas. Was the Maquinna who, in 1778, spotted the tops of three sticks above the horizon and watched them grow bigger until they took the shape of a great canoe with white wings (it was, in fact, Cook's three-masted *Discovery*), the same Maquinna who, twenty-five years later, destroyed the *Boston*? We cannot be certain, for there is one piece of evidence suggesting that the original Maquinna may have died before Jewitt's day. In September, 1795, Captain Charles Bishop encountered him at Friendly Cove, extremely ill with ague. Some weeks later Maquinna's rival, Wickinninish, told Bishop that his fellow chieftain had died and that he had attended his funeral. In Nootka society a chief's name is not his property; it is passed on to others. (In the early twentieth century there was still a Maquinna living among the Nootka.) Thus it is possible, if Wickinninish spoke the truth (and that is open to question), that the man who enslaved Jewitt was not the one who greeted Cook and his successors.

Yet it is difficult to read Jewitt without coming to the conclusion that his master was the Maquinna of Cook's day. Jewitt does not himself question the assumption. He and the chief had long talks in which Maquinna went over the past and told of Qualicum's death at the hands of Martinez in 1789 and of the arrival of Captain James Hanna, who began the sea otter trade in 1785. Though descriptions of Maquinna differ, Jewitt's Maquinna, with his Roman nose (unique among his tribe) and his pencil moustache, bears an uncanny resemblance to an earlier sketch of Maquinna by a Spanish artist.

There is something more: Jewitt's Maquinna acts and sounds like the Maquinna of an earlier time. It is hard to believe there were two so similar. He came into the chieftainship in 1778, just before Cook's arrival, having avenged his father's death in a war with a neighbouring tribe. Maquinna led his men to the enemy villages, took them by surprise, and massacred the inhabitants. But if he was bold and precipitate he could also be prudent and vacillating. After his brother's death at the hands of Martinez, realizing that the Spaniards were too strong for him, he retired from Yuquot to Clayoquot, allowing the Spanish to occupy his village and make it their headquarters – an action he bitterly resented but was powerless to prevent. His failure to avenge his brother's murder, as he had his father's, rankled. It also lowered his prestige, because any Indian group (and Maquinna was the symbol of his group) that failed to act decisively in response to the injury of one of its members was considered impotent. An English captain, James Colnett, called him "a most miserable, cowardly wretch . . . [who] flies whenever he sees the Spaniards." But Colnett had also been bested by Martinez and driven half mad in the process. It would be just as fair to say that Maquinna preferred to live and fight again.

To be forced to skulk at Clayoquot under the protection of his rival, Wickinninish, was a humiliating experience. His fellow chieftain was as wealthy and as powerful as he – perhaps more powerful, for in the occasional battles between the two villages, the people of Yuquot always lost. When the time came, Maquinna would display his two white slaves before his rival with special glee; he did not like to be second to anyone.

He was touchy about his prerogatives. When the English adventurer John Meares left his village in 1788, the chief arranged a farewell ceremony but learned later that Meares judged this to mean that the Indian acknowledged the white man as his sovereign. The chief was enraged; *no* one was his superior. From that point on he referred to Meares as "Aita-aita Meares," meaning "Liar Meares." The Spanish captain, Pedro Alberni, who was stationed permanently at Friendly Cove, understood this quality in Maquinna. He took advantage of it to help break down Maquinna's suspicions by inducing his seamen to sing a song in Nootka, praising the chief. When Maquinna heard about it he asked that the song be sung to him repeatedly until he had memorized it. Two years later it could still be heard.

The following year, 1790, the Spanish navigator Alejandro Malaspina visited Maquinna at Tahsis, where the chief, "his face revealing both anger and fear," did his best to impress his visitors with his power, showing off his most valued possessions – a chest containing fifteen muskets, a set of elaborately carved boxes, and, of course, the sheets of beaten copper to be used as potlatch gifts. Of him, Malaspina wrote:

"Macuina's character these days is difficult to decipher, his temper seems simultaneously fierce, suspicious and intrepid. The natural course of his inclinations is probably stirred up, on the one hand by desire of the Europeans to capture his friendship, the treasures he has stored up in a few years, discords that have occurred among Europeans, and perhaps suggestion from one side or another to secure a monopoly of pelts; on the other hand consider the weakness of his forces, skirmishes suffered, profit from the traffic and excessive frequent presence of European vessels in these regions."

Because he held the key to the sea otter trade – a trade that was turning the young men from the traditional occupations of salmon fishing and whale hunting – Maquinna was able to pit the trading nations against each other. His one desire was to rid the coast of Europeans and return to his summer village with his personal prestige intact. But he did not reject those aspects of European culture or ingenuity that appealed to him or he found useful. The Nootka were ignorant of sails; Maquinna was quick to adopt them. And when that remarkably civilized Spaniard, Juan Francisco de la Bodega y Quadra, arrived at Friendly Cove in 1792 to negotiate a land settlement with George Vancouver (Spain and England having become allies after the French revolution), Maquinna joined him at his dinner table – a table that often sat more than fifty guests dining from 270 plates of sterling silver. Bodega wrote that "upon hearing the dinner bell, Maquinna comes daily, performs his courtesy with his hat and sits at the Commander's side. He asks for anything he pleases and uses spoon, fork and glass very well. He asks for wine and sherry, coffee upon finishing and if there is any chocolate in the morning . . . ." Though he was fond of wine, the chief was careful not to lose his dignity; he appointed a relative to watch that he did not grow intoxicated in front of the white men. Bodega gave him a steel helmet and a coat of mail and treated him and his followers to displays of fireworks. He was, the Spaniard noted, "endowed with a clear and sagacious talent and knew very well the rights of sovereignty. He complained a great deal about treatment from foreign vessels trafficking on the coast because of some of the outrages his people had received." The Spanish finally departed early in 1795, leaving Vancouver Island technically to the British, who did not occupy it, and the village site to Maquinna, who was given a Union Jack to hoist whenever a trading vessel appeared. All that remained was an excuse for revenge, and that came on the deck of the *Boston* in 1803.

His captives had given him enormous prestige; he delighted in displaying them. In January, when the salmon run ended, the tribe moved from Tahsis to Coptee, sixteen miles down the sound. Here they fished for herring and sprats. Maquinna could scarcely wait to take Jewitt in his canoe to show him off to Chief Upquesta of the Ai-tiz-arts. Few of these people had ever seen a white man; Maquinna's prize, still in European attire, was a fascinating novelty. They crowded about him, plucking at his clothes, peering at his face and hands, and looking into his mouth to see if he had a tongue, for his master had forbidden him to speak unless ordered to. At last he gave the signal: Jewitt might talk. They were astonished. Now, they told Maquinna, they understood that this strange creature was actually a man. But they thought his blue jacket and trousers were ugly and did their best to convince him to disrobe. Their best was not good enough; but they were mollified by Maquinna's spirited description of the massacre aboard the *Boston*.

From the north came a party of Indians to warn the chief that twenty-five ships were on their way to rescue the two slaves. This was probably a ruse to worry Maquinna, but it served only to anger him. If another ship arrived, he warned Jewitt, he would launch a second massacre. He guarded his captives as a miser guards his treasure. "Nothing could be more unpleasant than our present situation," Jewitt wrote. "Our lives were altogether dependant on the will of a savage, on whose caprices and suspicions no rational calculation could be made."

In February, the Indians returned to Yuquot, the summer village at the mouth of Nootka Sound. The following month a singular incident took place: Maquinna's brother-in-law went insane, something that no native had done in anyone's memory. He was a chief, Tootoosch, known as the greatest warrior of the tribe, a leading figure in the incident aboard the *Boston*. His madness was touched off by the death of his eleven-year-old son, a tragedy which he connected, somehow, with the massacre. He began to imagine that he could see the ghosts of two seamen, Hall and Wood, whom he had personally slain.

The tribe was shaken by this development. Maquinna took his two white slaves to see Tootoosch to ask if they had put a curse on him, but the deranged chief told Maquinna they were both good men. When Jewitt tried to persuade him that the ghosts were not there, Tootoosch replied, simply, "I know very well that you do not see them, but I do." Maquinna then asked Jewitt how his own people dealt with madness. The blacksmith replied that in his country lunatics were tied up and whipped. Maquinna tried this but found it too painful to watch and ordered it stopped, "saying that if there was no other way of curing him, he must remain mad."

This sensitivity to torment was curious in a man who had seen twenty-five seamen dispatched with knives, but it was genuine;

Bodega had reported a similar incident in 1792 when Maquinna had ordered the execution of one of his band for seducing a nine-year-old girl. Before the sentence was carried out, the chief arrived at the Spaniard's house "with an expression that betrayed his mental unrest" and told Bodega that "they are now inflicting the punishment, and I have come here in order not to suffer the pain of hearing his laments." As for the unhappy Tootoosch, the whipping drove him madder still, and he set about beating his wife who was forced to flee to Maquinna for protection.

In April, the whaling season began – a time of increasing tension, for the whale hunt was the supreme ritual of the Nootka people, giving enormous prestige to those who were successful and ignominy to those who failed. Only men of the highest rank were permitted to harpoon a whale. In the prow of each of the slim eight-man canoes stood two harpoonists – a head chief and his brother. Traditionally, the chief made the first cast; the final cut to the heart was his prerogative also. This undertaking was preceded by various ceremonies – a ritual cleansing with hemlock twigs, for example – for besides being a difficult and hazardous sport, the whale hunt was a symbolic act designed to ensure the prosperity of the tribe.

Maquinna's attitude at this time was, in Jewitt's words, "thoughtful and gloomy." He scarcely spoke and gave his captives very little to eat. The chief had good reason for this dark mood, for the whaling was not going well. He told Jewitt that if he did not kill a whale his people would kill him, and he ordered the blacksmith to guard him day and night with a brace of pistols and a cutlass.

Danger lurked at the forest's rim. Slave and master were united in a mutual fear of assassination. The Indians, apprehensive that a ship would appear, were determined to kill both white men the moment a sail appeared on the horizon; they wanted no witnesses to the horror of the previous summer. Two canoes arrived from Maquinna's old rival, Wickinninish – their occupants intent on dispatching both the chief and his slaves – but the cutlasses and pistols frightened them off. In his journal on May 16, Jewitt wrote: "We walked all last night before our huts to keep watch, and at twelve o'clock fired one of the great guns off for an alarm in order to terrify the natives who had left us the day before, and as a signal to them that we were on our guard."

Jewitt, meanwhile, had been working on a special harpoon with a steel shaft; perhaps with this his master might kill a whale and ease the tension. To the chief's delight and the blacksmith's relief, Maquinna was successful. He made his two captives a present of blubber, which they boiled in salt water with nettles and other greens – "tolerable food" in Jewitt's description.

May 21 was Jewitt's birthday; he could not foresee another. "I now begin to give up all hope of ever seeing a Christian country or a Christian face," he wrote, "for the season being so far advanced and not hearing of the arrival of any ship on the coast, we feel ourselves very unhappy . . . . We are much cast down at the thought of spending the remainder of our days among these savages."

Worse was to come. On June 5, the Indians took away their greatcoats and other clothing, which had also served as beds. The following week a native stole the canoe that Maquinna had given them to use for fishing. Maquinna retrieved it, confiscated the thief's catch, and gave it to his slave. But the situation was deteriorating. Both men were afraid they would soon be obliged to go naked, if, indeed, they survived at all. The chiefs of the various families continued to meet to decide whether they should both be killed if a ship appeared. Maquinna again held out for sparing their lives.

Their rations grew scarcer. On June 15, Jewitt recorded that they had eaten nothing for the past three days. He was forced to barter a handkerchief for a dried salmon and a little whale oil. On June 19, he wrote: "The natives take our canoe when they please. If we say anything to them they tell us we are slaves and ask us where our captain is, making signs that his head was cut off . . . ."

The Indians, too, were short of food. They blamed the deficiency on Maquinna, saying that the blood of the *Boston* crew had driven away the fish. At one point, Thompson and Jewitt, having managed to acquire some fresh salmon, reversed roles with their master and played hosts to him and his wife at dinner. A curious *rapprochement* was taking place between captor and captives, a kind of vague bond not unlike the so-called Stockholm syndrome of the 1970s, when hostages and terrorists in hijacking incidents found themselves drawn to each other. During the dinner, Jewitt complained that the common people abused and insulted him. Maquinna promised to put a stop to that. He went further, saying that anybody from another tribe who insulted the white men would be killed. And he warned them to go about armed.

A short time later, Thompson was washing his clothes, including a blanket owned by Maquinna. Several members of Wickinninish's tribe arrived to taunt him. One walked over the newly washed blanket. Thompson threatened to kill him. The Indian continued to trample the blanket, whereupon Thompson drew his cutlass and cut off the offender's head. He presented this grisly memento to his master, who professed delight. After this incident the two slaves were treated with some respect.

In July there came a new alarm – a threat of war. A canoe load of Indians arrived from the north telling of a battle in which a hundred men and women had died. The cause of this bloodshed was instructive. "We hear both from the north and south that the natives are massacring one another for want of cloth, muskets, etc.," Jewitt wrote in his journal. "Our chief expects to be obliged to make war with them as they have threatened him on account of destroying the ship, *Boston*, which they say has injured their trade very much, and that no ship will now come to their ports to trade with them."

Thus Maquinna's escapade was revealed as double-edged. It had helped to slake his people's thirst for revenge; it had given him enormous prestige through the possession of two white slaves and a vast quantity of goods and arms; but it was also seen as an impediment to further barter. Contrary to what has become popular cant, not all native peoples in North America lived an idyllic life in which the concept of private property was unknown. The Indians of the Pacific Coast were among the most acquisitive creatures in history. In 1778, Cook observed that he had never come across natives who had such a highly developed sense of proprietary right as these; not even the grasses on which they walked were public property, he reported ruefully. He had sent men ashore to cut forage for the ship's goats, never dreaming that the Indians would object. But object they did, insisting on an immediate and exorbitant payment.

"As soon as I heard of this," Cook wrote, "I went to the place and found about a dozen men who all laid claim to some part of the grass, which I purchased off [*sic*] them and, as I thought, liberty to cut as I pleased, but here again I was mistaken for the liberal manner I had paid the first pretended proprietors brought more upon me and there was not a blade of grass that had not a separate owner, so that I very soon emptied my pockets . . . ."

The beads-and-trinkets explanation of white duplicity among the native tribes tends to crumble a little in the case of the Pacific Coast; within a decade of Cook's arrival, the Indians had become the shrewdest of bargainers. John Meares reported in 1798 that "in all our commercial transaction with these people we were, more or less, the dupes of their cunning; and with such peculiar artifice did they sometimes conduct themselves, that all the precaution we could employ was not sufficient to prevent our being overreached by them. The women, in particular, would play us a thousand tricks, and treat the discovery of their finesses with an arch kind of pleasure that baffled reproach."

Now these people were being denied the pleasure of barter, the joy of possession – and the fault was Maquinna's. Hostilities were imminent. Maquinna would not wait for them to begin; he intended to fight a preventive war. To this end he ordered Jewitt to make daggers for his men and fashion a special weapon for himself – some kind of super-club designed to kill a man with a single blow, preferably when he was asleep. The resourceful blacksmith obliged with a truly fearsome device – a six-inch spike of sharpened steel set in a rough knob at right angles to a fifteen-inch handle of iron, crooked at the end to prevent it from being wrenched from the hand. The back of the knob was ornamented with a man's face, the mouth agape, the eyes of black beads fastened with red sealing wax. Maquinna, of course, was delighted.

The enemy were encamped fifty miles to the south. To prepare for battle, the warriors abstained from sex for several weeks and scrubbed themselves repeatedly with brier brushes. Maquinna urged his two captives to harden their skins in the same way; they refused. Finally, the war party embarked in forty canoes, each containing between ten and twenty men, armed with bows, arrows, and daggers. Jewitt and Thompson preferred cutlasses and pistols.

The battle was bloody and decisive. The attack came at dawn, many of the enemy dying as they slept. Thompson zestfully killed seven men, an act that considerably raised his status. Jewitt, who abhorred killing, took four prisoners. He was allowed to keep them to help him work and fish – slaves to a slave. Few of the enemy escaped; the old and the sick were dispatched on the spot. The slaughter over, the party returned to Yuquot for a victory feast.

Jewitt's value was increasing. Maquinna's old rival, Wickinninish, could hardly contain himself when he saw the club the blacksmith had made for his master. He *must* have him! To that end he made a formal offer to purchase; the price included four young male slaves, two highly ornamented canoes, a parcel of sea otter skins, and a variety of trade goods. It must have given Maquinna great satisfaction to refuse; his own prestige rose with his captive's price.

Another chief, Ulatilla, whom Jewitt considered the most civilized native he had encountered, also tried in vain to buy the blacksmith. Ulatilla, who spoke good English, was fascinated by European customs; when Jewitt satisfied his curiosity on this subject, the chief promised to try to get him aboard the first trading vessel that came to his country, if Maquinna would release him. Jewitt, who wrote sixteen letters begging to be rescued at different times and smuggled them out to various parts of the coast, sent one to Ulatilla, asking that he give it to any passing ship. That letter eventually led to his release.

But at the time there seemed no hope of rescue; Maquinna had no intention of losing his most valuable property. His intention was to turn the white man into an Indian, to marry him off to a local girl, and to convince him to settle down among the Nootka and conform to local customs. Jewitt had no choice; his master made it clear that he must marry or die. Since the blacksmith did not fancy any of the Nootka women, Maquinna agreed that he might marry outside the tribe. Accordingly, in September the chief took his slave and fifty men to Ai-tiz-art with a plenitude of gifts – cloth, muskets, sea otter skins – with which to purchase a bride. Jewitt, having to choose someone, chose the seventeen-year-old daughter of the chief, whereupon Maquinna, in a speech that rolled on for a full half-hour, extolled the blacksmith as a useful and well-tempered prospect. The girl's father replied with an even longer speech, praising his daughter and agreeing, at last, to part with her. Gifts were exchanged; feasting and dancing followed; joy was unconfined save in the heart of the bridegroom, whose diary entry for his wedding day is laconic: "This day our chief bought a wife for me . . . . It is very much against my inclinations to take one of these heathens for a partner, but it will be for my advantage while I am amongst them, for she has a father who always goes fishing, so that I shall live much better than I have at any time heretofore." Jewitt was nothing if not practical.

He now felt more hopelessly bound to the aboriginal life than ever, especially since Maquinna decreed that he must be considered a native and dress the part in a single mantle of red cedar bark. Again he had no choice: "He informed us that we must go naked like themselves, otherwise he should put us to death. As life is sweet, even to the captive . . . we thought it best to submit to their will without murmuring, even though it was a very grievous thing to us."

The two men were now accepted as Nootka and allowed to participate in the winter religious festival, a week-long ceremony from which they had been excluded the previous year. Jewitt scorned the ritual as a "farce"; it appeared to him to consist of continual feasting. "The natives," he wrote, "eat twenty times a day." At that moment, the Church of England, his strength and his comfort, seemed light-years away. It was as if he had been transported, through some warp in time, to an alien cosmos whose order and harmony bore no relation to any he had known. And so, in a sense, he had; adaptable he most certainly was, but after more than a year in captivity he was still not able to come to terms with an environment that was to him always unnatural and often grotesque. About this time he was called upon to perform a particularly distasteful task: Maquinna's older brother asked Jewitt to file his teeth, so that he might disfigure his wife by biting off her nose. She had refused his sexual advances and according to Nootka custom he was allowed to mutilate her so that no one else would wish to wed her.

The two slaves were eating better, thanks to Jewitt's father-in-law, the fisherman. Yet it seemed they had merely exchanged one hardship for another. On December 1, Jewitt wrote in his journal: "Frosty weather. Very hard times. All the European clothes being expended I am obliged to go almost naked like the Indians, with only a kind of garment a fathom long, made of the bark of trees to defend me from the inclemency of the weather. I have suffered more from the cold this winter than I can possibly express. I am afraid it will injure my constitution and make me very weak and feeble during the remainder of my life." Because neither man was allowed to wear shoes or stockings, their feet were cut badly and often frozen. Thompson suffered from rheumatism so severely that he was rarely able to leave the lodge.

In February, Jewitt had all but given up hope of rescue. In March, he was taken seriously ill "with a pain in my bowels, which I presume was occasioned by going naked in the cold." Too weak to stand, he could eat nothing. Soon, he expected, he would share the fate of another slave who had died and was "thrown out of the house as soon as the breath was out of his mouth" and pitched into the ocean.

Maquinna was convinced that the illness was caused by Jewitt's young wife. He offered to return her to her father – a flawed chattel, subject, apparently, to a money-back guarantee. To this Jewitt gratefully agreed. At last, however, the chief was made to realize that his slave's illness was actually caused by the climate, not sex, and he was allowed once more to wear clothes. One cannot read Jewitt's journal without concluding that Maquinna was genuinely fond of him, as a man is fond of a favourite horse or retriever, for he treated him with much greater affection than he did his other slaves.

As May ended Jewitt received news that rekindled an ember of hope: word came that Ulatilla had managed to pass his letter on to the captain of a trading ship, who was planning to come to the sound to rescue the white men.

When this news spread among the natives, it caused a buzz of consternation. What to do? Would the Yankees seek revenge? Would trade be resumed? What should be the Nootka response?

Jewitt and Thompson were the only witnesses to the butchery of 1803; if they were killed and their bodies hidden, who would be left alive to testify concerning that bloody spring afternoon? But perhaps the presence of two hostages might work to the Indians' benefit; perhaps *they* could be bartered, like sea otter skins, in return for a pardon. Some of the tribe began to treat the captives with greater kindness; others argued for their immediate death. The head chiefs of the lodges, in council, decided upon a conciliatory course: Thompson and Jewitt would be sent aboard the ship to mediate on their behalf and to re-establish regular trade.

Everybody waited; nothing happened. A month passed; no sail appeared on the dark ridge of the ocean. On July 2, Jewitt learned why: the ship had been involved in a skirmish with one of the northern tribes, losing ten men including the captain. He gave up hope of rescue. Of all the vessels trading on the Pacific Coast, the *Boston* had been the largest, strongest, and best equipped; hers had also been the most valuable cargo fitted out for the northwest trade. Clearly her destruction had filled all other captains in the area with a dread of Nootka Sound. He was doomed to spend the rest of his life as an Indian.

Deliverance came suddenly, without warning, on July 19, two years and four months after his capture. Jewitt was making chisels at his bench when one of the natives spotted the outline of a vessel on the horizon. Maquinna at once called him out to look. She was the brig *Lydia*, out of Boston. "My heart leapt for joy at the thought of getting my liberty," Jewitt wrote.

Maquinna dispatched a canoe at once with a letter from the blacksmith saying that there was no danger in entering Friendly Cove. The canoe returned with word from the captain, Samuel Hill, that he was coming in. The *Lydia* anchored off the cove about noon.

The Indians were in a quandary; if Maquinna went on board the ship, they reasoned, the captain would certainly put him in irons, at least until the two slaves were released. As one, they urged him not to go. Jewitt, meanwhile, had worked out a deception; he would hide his excitement and pretend that he was not anxious to go aboard. His plan was to have his master precede him and be held as a hostage for the two slaves.

The brig gave a salute of three guns. Jewitt replied, using the cannon from the *Boston*. Roles were now rapidly being reversed. Master turned to slave to ask what he should do. The slave urged his master to go on board the ship; the captain, he promised, "would use him well." But the chief was justifiably suspicious, whereupon his captive – scarcely a captive any more – offered to write a letter of recommendation to the captain, which, he said, would keep the chief from harm. Maquinna gazed at him quizzically, "eyeing me with a look that seemed to read my inmost thoughts."

"John, you no lie?" the chief asked.

Jewitt brazened it out. At Maquinna's request an odd little mime followed. The chief could not read, but he would run his finger across Jewitt's scribble, line by line, and have the blacksmith read out the words as his finger moved. Jewitt complied; the letter, he said, told the captain to treat the great chief kindly and to make him presents of molasses, biscuits, and rum. What it actually said was that Maquinna had been the leader of the attack on the *Boston* and that he should be confined "according to his merits" and not allowed to escape until the two white men were released.

At this moment, Jewitt reaped the harvest of his behaviour over the previous twenty-eight months. Maquinna had come to trust his slave. His wives and fellow chiefs crowded around him, pleading with him not to go to the ship, but Maquinna had decided upon his course. "John no lie," he said firmly. Would John go with him? he asked, tentatively. No, John would not. John made it clear that he had no desire to leave the Nootka.

Thus disarmed, Maquinna set off for the *Lydia* with Jewitt's letter and a present of four sea otter skins. The captain read what Jewitt had written, offered the chief a tot of rum, escorted him to his cabin, locked the windows, clapped Maquinna in irons, and placed him under an armed guard. The chief was surprised and terrified. He sent back a messenger who told the villagers that "John had spoke bad about him in the letter." An incredible scene followed: the villagers rushed up and down the beach, howling and wailing and tearing out their hair. The men ran for their weapons. The women threw themselves on their knees around Jewitt, begging him to save Maquinna's life. Some of the men circled him, brandishing their weapons, threatening torture. They would cut him into pieces no bigger than their thumbnails; they would burn him alive over a slow fire, suspended by his heels; they would – but it was all quite useless; their master was a captive and his captive had become their master.

"Kill me!" cried the blacksmith, dramatically, throwing open his bearskin robe. "Here is my breast . . . I can make no resistance but unless you wish to see your king hanging by his neck to that pole and the sailors firing at him with bullets, you will not do it." He knew they would not.

The chiefs were calmer than their followers. What should be

done? Jewitt assured them that Maquinna was safe and would be returned to Yuquot as soon as the two white men were released.

Thompson was allowed to go on board the ship at once. Jewitt then proposed that three natives should take him to within hailing distance of the brig to arrange an exchange. There was an affecting little scene as Jewitt was about to step into the canoe. Maquinna's young son, who had become very fond of the blacksmith and "could not bear to part," asked him if he would please not kill his father.

Jewitt's plan was to get on board the *Lydia* before Maquinna was released; in that way the chief could be held hostage for the return of the property from the *Boston*, notably the cannon. By threatening the native paddlers with his pistol, which he had been allowed to keep, he forced them to row directly to the ship. He climbed quickly aboard – a grotesque and astonishing figure, painted red and black from head to foot, dressed in a shaggy bearskin wrap-around, his long hair, which he had been forbidden to cut, fastened in a huge knot above his head and tied with a sprig of green spruce. The captain later told him that he had never seen anything in the form of a man, civilized or savage, who looked so wild.

Now the ex-slave faced his former master. Maquinna brightened. "*Wocash*, John!" he exclaimed, using the native word for "good." Captain Hill was intent on executing the chief at once, but Jewitt deterred him, explaining the circumstances of the massacre and all the events leading up to it. His life among the Nootka had made him the world's leading expert on the sociology of the West Coast Indians. He explained to Hill that if he had the chief executed, Maquinna's followers would be duty bound to exact revenge; the crew of the next ship to drop anchor in the sound would surely be massacred.

Maquinna constantly interrupted this discourse to plead with Jewitt to save him. He did not believe, however, that he would be spared, and when at last he learned that he was to be permitted to live, he was incredulous. His own notion of revenge would have called for death.

It was now past five in the afternoon. Jewitt told the Indians waiting in the canoe that their chief would be returned the following day in exchange for the remaining effects from the *Boston*.

He must have felt the strangeness of his new position. All through the night, the man who had been his undisputed master for more than two years, who had forced him into an unwelcome marriage, who had feasted or starved him at his own caprice, now kept him awake pleading for reassurance that his life was to be spared. Proud Maquinna had been reduced to a grovelling suppliant.

The following morning the Indians delivered the *Boston*'s cannon, anchor, sea chests and ship's papers, and – most important – Jewitt's personal journal to the *Lydia*. Maquinna sent for sixty otter skins, which he presented to Captain Hill. Now, he was told, he might return to his village. Ecstatic, he threw off his mantle and presented it to the captain, who, to his delight, gave him a hat and a greatcoat. Hill then asked Jewitt to tell the chief that he would be back in November to trade; Maquinna, in his turn, pledged that he would save for the *Lydia* all the sea otter skins his young men brought in.

There followed an affectionate and touching farewell between the two men whose lives had for twenty-eight months been bound together in such a curious fashion. Maquinna seized Jewitt's hand and told him he hoped he would return in a big ship loaded with blankets, biscuits, molasses, and rum; in return, he said, he would save all the furs he got for his friend. At the same time, he observed, with a shrewdness that was almost comic, that he would never again accept a letter of recommendation from *anyone*. He held no grudge against Jewitt for his deception; he simply said he would never trust himself on board a white man's vessel unless the blacksmith himself were present. Then he took both of Jewitt's hands in his "with much emotion while the tears trickled down his cheeks," and, releasing his grip, stepped into his canoe, waved a final farewell, and was paddled ashore. There is no record of John Thompson's role in the parting.

Jewitt, too, was moved: "I could not avoid experiencing a painful sensation on parting with the savage chief, who had preserved my life, and in general treated me with kindness and, considering their ideas and manners, much better than could have been expected."

He could not, of course, go directly home, for the *Lydia* had only commenced her voyage. She sailed north along the coast to trade with other tribes and then south again to the mouth of the Columbia, where, it was learned, Meriwether Lewis and William Clark had arrived just two weeks before to complete their famous land crossing of America. A good deal had been happening during John Jewitt's captivity; Napoleon had been crowned Emperor of France; the United States had purchased the Louisiana Territory; Beethoven had written the *Eroica* Symphony; Robert Fulton had propelled a boat by steam power.

The *Lydia* returned to Nootka Sound late that fall. The Indians were in winter quarters, but Jewitt, following Maquinna's earlier instructions – "when you come make 'pow' " – fired the brig's cannon, and a canoe shortly appeared with a message: Maquinna would come aboard only if his friend Jewitt would fetch him. Much to Hill's and Thompson's anxiety, the blacksmith agreed to return to the shores where he had been held captive. Maquinna welcomed him with joy and the two paddled to the ship with a small fortune in otter skins.

Maquinna had missed Jewitt; he urged him to return, promising, in the meantime, to look after the five-month-old baby son who had been born to Jewitt's Indian wife. But the armourer had no intention of coming back. The *Lydia* sailed once more up the coast and then, on August 11, 1806, more than a year after his release from captivity, set off for China. As Jewitt stared back at the green curtain of the cedar forest and watched it diminish until it was no more than a blurred line on the horizon, he resolved that "nothing should tempt me to return, and as the tops of the mountains sank in the blue waves of the ocean, I seemed to feel my heart lightened of an oppressive load." But he could not escape the frontier; it had affected him more than he then knew.

The *Lydia* left China in February, 1807, and arrived in Boston 114 days later. There Jewitt found a letter from his mother in England, expressing her joy at his safety.

He was no longer a captive of Chief Maquinna; but for the rest of his days he remained a captive of his experience. He could not put it out of his mind, nor, apparently, did he wish to. It dominated his remaining years, seduced him away from his trade, and turned him into a kind of wandering minstrel, repeating, over and over, the story of his trials on that far off coast.

He was determined to turn his experience to his advantage. The owners of the *Boston* gave him a small reward with which he financed the printing of his journal, of which only a handful of copies survive. Jewitt had intended to open a smithy in Boston but, instead, he spent most of his time moving about, peddling his little book.

He was married on Christmas Day, 1809, to an English immigrant girl from Bristol. They settled in Middletown, Connecticut, and raised a family of five children. But Jewitt remained obsessed by his captivity. After his marriage he encountered a flourishing merchant, Richard Alsop, who was a part-time satirist and poet. The two collaborated on a new version of the tale. Alsop interviewed Jewitt at great length and in 1815 produced *The Adventures and Sufferings of John R. Jewitt, Captive among the Nootka, 1803-1805.* It was an enormous success. For years it was carried in the sea chests of sailors all around the globe. It has since gone into more than twenty editions and several languages, has been bowdlerized in a children's version, and is still in print. But Alsop's nephew thought the book did Jewitt more harm than good, for he "became unsettled in his habits by his wandering life," peddling his books from handcart, wheelbarrow, or one-horse wagon all the way from Nantucket to Baltimore. In addition he hawked a broadsheet of a popular sea shanty, "The Poor Armourer Boy," which retold his saga in verse. In Philadelphia, he went so far as to play himself in a melodrama based on his experiences. Later on he joined a circus of sorts at the Vauxhall Garden, a summer amusement park near Philadelphia, where, dressed in Indian costume, he performed songs. He died in Hartford in 1821 at the age of thirty-eight, his life shortened, as he himself had predicted, by his ordeal in the harsh and distant land of the Nootka.

5
The Pirate of the St. Lawrence

History has an odd way of turning rogues and villains into popular heroes. Blackguards, whose very names were once a stench in the nostrils of upright citizens, become dry-cleaned by the passage of time to emerge, after a century or so, as profiles on bas-reliefs, their exploits honoured by ribbon-cutting aldermen and their reputations scrubbed up by local journalists, brochure-writers, and even historians.

Such has been the fate of William Johnston, a thief, plunderer, vandal, kidnapper and pirate. Pure longevity turned Johnston into an honoured citizen; when he died, respected and even loved at the age of eighty-eight, he had outlived all of his bitterest enemies. Another half-century went by and he was memorialized by the very country he had loathed so much, with the inevitable bronze plaque, unveiled by the inevitable flitch of civic dignitaries.

If, in the words of another Johnson (Samuel), patriotism is the last refuge of the scoundrel, then William was as black a scoundrel as ever mounted a cannon on a longboat; his patriotism seems to have been little more than a front for his own acquisitive interests. He was called every name in the lexicon of villainy: rogue, rascal, traitor, turncoat, rotter and wretch. A renegade Canadian, he pillaged farms, burned ships, chopped off men's fingers and terrorized the border, all in the name of loyalty to his adopted country, the United States. In return for this loyalty he was able to walk the streets of French Creek, New York, heavily armed with knives and pistols, and to carry out snatch-and-grab raids from his fortress in the Thousand Islands without being apprehended or betrayed. But of his main objective there was little doubt; it was booty, and of that he got his share.

Still, it is difficult not to admire him. After all, my country has produced few, if any, pirates and this particular one was everything a pirate should be. He was tough, bold, colourful and dashing – a swarthy, bullet-headed rapscallion, blessed with the traditional pirate's flair for eluding his clumsier pursuers. Again and again, Bill Johnston was able to evade capture. No jail, it seemed, could hold him.

Moreover, to add a touch of spice to his legend, there is a beautiful daughter lurking offstage. She aids him in his escapes. She watches out for his enemies through a telescope from her home in French Creek. She sends him signals in a specially designed Morse-style code. She secretly dispatches food and provisions when he hides out in the watery labyrinth of the Thousand Islands. Small wonder, then, that the saga of Bill Johnston inspired at least two novels, a stage play and a sheaf of popular folk songs.

Bill Johnston was born a Canadian in 1782 at Three Rivers, Quebec, and raised not far from Kingston, the chief naval base for Lake Ontario and later the capital of Upper Canada. There he went into the freighting business, which meant that he was also up to his ears in the smuggling business. Most border freighters in those times were also smugglers, a fairly honourable profession then as it may be still. Protective tariffs on both sides of the border made it profitable. In 1810, Bill Johnston married an American girl, Ann Randolph. According to his later, sardonic account, this caused him to be "looked upon with a jealous eye by the more loyal subjects of His Most Gracious Majesty, George III, and my acts ... closely watched by the slaves of the despot ...."

That's as may be. It is certainly true that after war broke out between Great Britain and the United States in June 1812, he *was* watched carefully by Canadian authorities who felt, not without evidence, that he was more than a little sympathetic to the Yankee cause. He was, after all, consorting with Americans, albeit American smugglers. In November, he was arrested on suspicion, held for twelve hours, and then released for lack of evidence.

The following June, he was clapped in jail again. He had taken an interest in bailing out men who had "rendered themselves obnoxious to the police by their intercourse and conversations with the damned Yankees." In those days, the Yankees were hated by the Canadians as much as the Germans were in two world wars that followed. Johnston's motives here are subject to interpretation. He may well have been a Yankee-lover – he certainly became one; or he may have been a humanitarian, distressed by the conditions in the Kingston prison – conditions so bad that one man, captured with frozen feet, received so little attention that he was later forced to have them amputated.

Johnston was told that he would be held in jail for the duration of the hostilities. Almost immediately he engineered the first of his many jail breaks. In those days, Kingston was encompassed not by fertile farms but by heavy brush, a perfect hiding place for a fugitive. Here Johnston found many like himself, mostly Americans who wanted to get back to their own country and avoid internment. Half a dozen of them came across an old birchbark canoe. In this flimsy craft Johnston determined to escape across Lake Ontario to the American shore. It was a daring and hazardous plan. None was an experienced canoeman and they faced thirty-six miles of open, choppy waters. Fortunately they encountered an American warship, which picked them up and took them to Sackets Harbor, New York.

Bill Johnston arrived on the American side, harbouring an intense hatred of his former countrymen and owning nothing but the clothes he was wearing. He had lost everything – his property was confiscated, his family beggared and his subsequent pleas for reparation ignored. The British government might perhaps have saved itself endless trouble and cost if it had made some restitution to Bill Johnston; it did not do so.

Johnston wanted revenge and he got it; for the duration of the War of 1812, he served as a spy for the Americans. In a fast, six-oared barge, he and his gang darted about the familiar waters of the Thousand Islands, attacking small craft, pillaging farms and intercepting messages. On one occasion, he robbed the mail coach between Kingston and Gananoque, stripping the unfortunate passengers of their clothing and tying the coachman to a tree; he passed the captured military messages on to the American authorities. Another time, he captured a dragoon carrying official papers, shot his horse and drove the man away on foot to wander through the bush. He was far too slippery to be trapped. Once, when he was driven ashore by a gale, his entire crew was apprehended; but Johnston managed to get away and flee across the lake, again by birchbark canoe.

After these depredations, it was not possible for him to return to his native land. He settled down in French Creek (which was to become Clayton, New York), a smugglers' haven directly across the lake from Gananoque. It is likely that in this little lakeside hamlet – it had scarcely more than two streets – every man, woman and child benefitted in some way from smuggling. Certainly Johnston did. At that time, the Thousand Islands were still covered with dense forests and thick underbrush, forming a maze of narrow wriggling channels, tiny hidden coves, protected tree-shaded bays and rocky promontories. No more secure retreat for freebooters could be imagined. By 1838, after the collapse of the Upper Canada Rebellion, the larger islands were inhabited by lawless bands of semi-brigands, their numbers augmented by as many as a thousand rebel refugees. It was said that this group could muster a hundred boats, the swiftest being Johnston's own, so lightly built it could be carried on men's backs across the islands, many of which served as his personal fiefs.

Johnston had one hideout on Wells Island, now known as Wellesley, another on Abel Island and, on the Canadian side, a personal redoubt which he called Fort Wallace on an island now known as Fort Wallace Island.

His daughter Kate became known as the Queen of the Thousand Islands. Still in her teens, she could handle a boat and a rifle as well as any man. As the years went by, her story became romanticized. She was generally referred to as "beautiful" or "handsome," words that journalists tend to apply to any woman under the age of sixty. Perhaps she was at sixteen; but in her later pictures she has the profile of a drill sergeant.

That was the situation on the St. Lawrence in 1838, the year following the abortive attempt by that difficult if dedicated Toronto editor, William Lyon Mackenzie, to overthrow the colonial government of Upper Canada. After Mackenzie's defeat, some of his followers who escaped capture lit out for Navy Island on the Niagara River, just above the Falls, and there helped set up his so-called Provisional Government of Upper Canada. From this island the nucleus of the Patriot Movement, as it was known, was formed in the states adjacent to the Canadian border.

This fascinating underground venture was really a loose group of various secret societies with such names as "Hunters and Chasers on the Eastern Frontier" and "Lodges of Patriotic Masons." The total membership of the Hunters, to use a general appellation, has been variously estimated at anywhere from fifteen thousand to two hundred thousand persons – expatriate Canadians, rebels, Americans who wanted to free Canada from the British yoke, vagabonds, renegades and self-serving adventurers whose main objective was loot.

The Patriots had a flag with two stars, representing Upper and Lower Canada, and they also had an army and navy of sorts; but they lacked any strong unified control. The military commander was a curious American blueblood, Rensselaer Van Rensselaer, described by a contemporary as "a degenerate scion of an old Dutch family . . . a young man of more ambition than brains." Among other things, he was a drunkard. The naval commander, who bore the title of Commodore of the Patriot Army of the East, was made of sterner stuff; he was none other than Bill Johnston, described as a "gentleman of intelligence, equal to fifty ordinary men" who could raise "two hundred bold volunteers as ever drew a trigger."

It soon became clear that if the Patriot Army was going to fight a war it would have to be fought in Bill Johnston's territory. Early in 1838, the British drove the rebels out of their base on Navy Island and the scene shifted to the Thousand Islands. It was from this jumping-off place that Van Rensselaer and Johnston, with their ragtag-and-bobtail crew, set about giving expression to an ambition that seems, at least in retrospect, to have been as harebrained as it was desperate. They planned nothing less than the invasion, capture and subjugation of Upper Canada. They would free it from British rule and transform it into a republic.

The strategy was sound enough, even though the subsequent execution was abominable. The main point of the attack would be Kingston, the key to Upper Canada, and specifically its citadel, Fort Henry, built on a promontory overlooking the river. Apparently impregnable, the great fortress had one weak point: in wintertime it could be attacked from the south by the ice bridge which forms across the St. Lawrence. The tactics called for the Patriots to launch their invasion from nearby Hickory Island, feinting at Gananoque to draw the militia out of Kingston, and then to attack the unguarded Upper Canadian city. Key objectives would include the citadel and the penitentiary, whose prisoners (especially the political ones), it was assumed, would join the revolt on the side of their liberators.

In addition, the Patriots had devised a remarkably modern ploy. A century before the word was coined, they determined that a fifth column of "traders" and "tourists" would enter Kingston in the days before the attack. When the Patriot Army arrived, these strangers would rise up and capture the town.

It is just possible that this plan might have succeeded, at least initially, and that Kingston could have come under rebel rule. Certainly, the Patriots were well armed. On February 19, they broke into the American armoury at Watertown, New York, and seized four hundred weapons. This was followed by successful attacks on two other state armouries. But there was one fatal flaw in the enterprise. To succeed, such an attack must be planned and executed in the utmost secrecy – and of that there was none. A child of ten, seeking his father in any one of the numberless border taverns, would know in the first buzz of overheard conversation that February 22, 1838, was the date planned for the capture of Kingston.

Bill Johnston's "beautiful" daughter, Kate, as portrayed by a contemporary artist, was remarkably hatchet-faced in real life.

Every man, woman and child along the American side of the St. Lawrence apparently knew it, including a young school teacher named Elizabeth Barnett who acted upon the knowledge immediately – thus introducing into an otherwise mediocre affair a dash of genuine romance. Miss Barnett was an American who lived and worked in Kingston. On February 20, while visiting relatives in French Creek she heard the rebels openly discussing the forthcoming adventure. Miss Barnett had no wish to see her Canadian friends murdered in their beds. Accordingly, she cut short her visit, crossed the ice of the St. Lawrence – a remarkable feat of courage and endurance – aroused the community and got word to the military command.

Terror and even panic followed. The militiamen were called up immediately from all neighbouring counties and hastily drilled. Fort Henry, which had been going a little to seed, was spruced up. Arms were polished, ammunition ordered, guns scoured, ovens put into working order. A parade of fearful citizens shortly appeared bearing silver plate and valuable papers for safekeeping. A watch was placed on all suspected traitors. Holes were punched in the ice near Wolfe Island to prevent sleighs from crossing the river. Barricades were erected on country roads. Mohawk Indians were engaged as scouts. Signal rockets were readied. Then, on the fateful night of February 22, the little community waited for the worst: "Never was such a a night known in Kingston. Not a soul slept; fire and sword were momentarily looked for."

Nothing whatsoever happened. On Hickory Island, the mustering point for the great Patriot Army, an ill-clad, ill-disciplined and ill-led shamble of men stood with chattering teeth, answering their names to the roll call. On the first call, only eighty-five answered; on the second, seventy-one; on the third, a mere thirty-five. It was just too cold to fight; besides, General Van Rensselaer was clearly drunk. The troops who had crossed the ice on foot and by sleigh melted away in the dark. When a British cavalry patrol gingerly began to investigate the island early next morning, it found only a few shivering stragglers and several large bags of scrap iron intended for use as shot.

Miss Barnett's warning had been timely and accurate but, because of rebel bungling, totally unnecessary. It is pleasant to report that she met and fell in love with one of the militiamen who had swiftly donned uniforms to repel the attack. Subsequently she married him and presumably lived happily ever after until her death in 1906, in Gananoque, at the age of ninety-two – an unsung Laura Secord.

As for Bill Johnston, he was furious at Van Rensselaer. He

swore then and there that he would never again take part in a formal attack but would fight a guerrilla war of raid and ambush based on secrecy and speed. The key to his purpose would be his famous pirate craft, a gaudy creation, with a black hull, a white top, a broad yellow side stripe and a crimson interior. Two strong men could carry this twenty-eight-foot longboat through the underbrush of the Thousand Islands; its twelve oars made it the fastest of its kind on the lakes. Now Bill Johnston was ready to carry on a one-man war against Canadian shipping – a war that was aided by the complacency of the American authorities, who were still passively hostile to the British.

Johnston's plans were nothing if not grandiose. His private war reached its zenith just after midnight on May 30, 1838. He determined to hijack one of the fastest and largest ships then plying the lakes – the new passenger steamer *Sir Robert Peel.* A narrow vessel, 160 feet long, of light draught, she had been launched the previous year at Brockville for service on the St. Lawrence and Lake Ontario. The attack was later memorialized in song and legend:

> It was on a Thursday morning, the thirtieth of May,
> While quietly at anchor the British steamer lay
> Among the Thousand Islands, nearer to the Yankee shore –
> That land of peace and plenty, which free men all adore.
> That morn no breath of air disturbed the waters round
>   the keel
> Of that fine British steamer, the proud *Sir Robert Peel*;
> Within the arms of slumber her passengers were laid,
> Unconscious of their danger while riding o'er the wave …

The *Peel* was proceeding upriver from Brockville to Kingston when the attack came. She had some twenty-five first-class passengers on board and forty more in steerage, all sound asleep as the poem says. The night was dark and rainswept, exactly the kind of Gothic evening with which readers of the novels of the day were familiar. The ship docked at Wells Island, the largest of all, to take on wood – a pause of two hours during which time the captain should have been thoroughly alerted to the danger. For one thing, one of the passengers had already received warnings of impending violence – warnings which went unheeded. For another, the man in charge of the woodpile, one Ripley, told the captain that he had seen a longboat filled with men running past the island at two or three different times during the night and that when the steamer first appeared someone in the boat had cried: "There she is!" A megaphoned warning could scarcely have made the situation clearer. But when Ripley urged the captain not to tarry, he replied that "if there were not more than 100 or 150 he did not fear them." There were, as it shortly developed, far fewer than that.

The attack came at two in the morning. A group of men burst from the bush, costumed as Indians, complete with feathers and warpaint, but uttering very un-Indian cries, "Revenge for the *Caroline!*" being the main one – a reference to the American-owned ship which the British had shot to pieces on the Niagara River the previous year when she was attempting to run supplies to the rebels holed up on Navy Island.

How many were there? As usual in such cases, the invaders, in order to make the attack seem all the bolder, minimized the number, while their terrified victims inflated it. One of the passengers thought there were one hundred and fifty. The beleaguered captain put the figure between fifty and seventy. Bill Johnston, who planned the attack, reported a modest thirteen: so much for the reliability of eyewitnesses. A later investigation set the figure at twenty-five.

The pirates were armed with muskets, bayonets, swords and pikestaffs. They addressed each other by code names, such as Tecumseh, Nelson, Admiral Benbow, Judge Lynch and Bolivar, but the unmistakeable growl of Bill Johnston could be heard above the din. They ordered the captain and his passengers ashore. One passenger, Colonel Richard Fraser, was almost murdered: hearing a noise on deck, he thought that a quarrel had broken out among the crew. Then he found his cabin door forced open, his windows smashed and five men – four with bayonets and the leader with a sword – towering over his bed. The swordsman spotted the colonel's military tunic hanging on a nail. "He's a British officer. Run him through!" he shouted. The colonel must have had remarkable powers of persuasion. Choosing discretion over valour he disavowed the uniform; the rebels, either through gullibility or compassion, spared his life, merely knocking him to the floor and kicking him several times.

Men and women, many of them half-naked, were herded brusquely onto the deck and refused permission to return to their cabins for warm clothes, trunks or jewelry. There were insults to the ladies: "their cries were truly distressing," to quote a contemporary account. No officer or gentleman could stand for that; a Captain Bullock, taking his life in his hands, "rushed fearlessly among the ruffians to secure the females from insults." Shivering in night attire, the entire company was shoved off the ship and herded into a little shack on the dock where they stayed, embar-

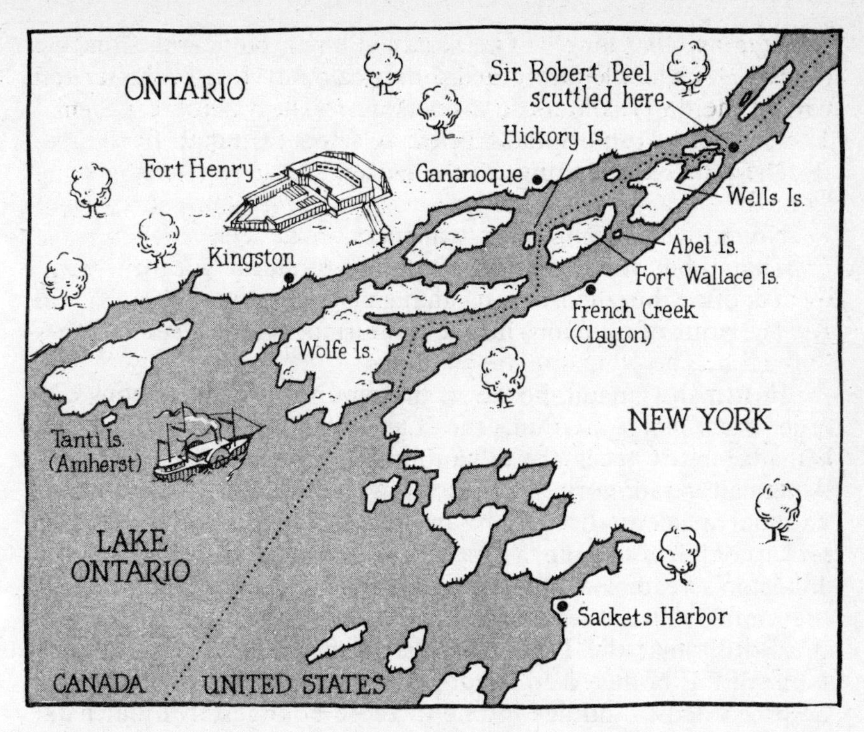

rassed and numb with cold, until five a.m. when the steamer *Oneida* picked them up and took them to Kingston.

Johnston's plan, apparently, was to use the captured ship as the nucleus of a navy with which he hoped to ravage Canada. Transformed into a pirate warship, the *Peel* would mount an attack on a second vessel, the *Great Britain.* That scheme came to nothing because Johnston, who was a good man in a longboat, knew very little about larger craft. He set off in the *Peel* from Wells Island but ran her onto a shoal almost immediately. Unable to dislodge her, he and his men proceeded to pillage her and then put her to the torch, before departing for Abel Island in their small boats. The *Peel* was still burning when the passengers were rescued and her charred hulk was visible at that spot for decades after.

The loss was considerable. Many of the passengers had brought small fortunes in banknotes, jewelry and other valuables – people lugged their silver plate about with them in those days. The estimated personal losses amounted to $75,000, an enormous sum in 1828. In addition, there was another $100,000 intended for the paymasters of the Upper Canadian forces.

This was loot on a grand scale. For many years after, on feast days and special occasions, it was said that members of the Johnston family wore jewelry and gaudy clothing plundered from the *Sir Robert Peel.* Certainly, from that day forward, Bill Johnston carried the ship's colours on his person.

This act of piracy was greeted as a rebel triumph by sympathizers south of the border:

No more upon the waters, will evermore be seen
That noble British steamer, Ontario's proudest Queen;
Yet oft within their bosoms that gallant band shall feel
The pride of righteous justice for burning *Robert Peel.*

In British Canada, however, the sentiment was righteous outrage. Sir George Arthur, the Lieutenant-Governor of Upper Canada, felt it necessary to caution Canadians against any anti-American retaliation; the last thing he wanted was an international incident. Lord Durham, who had just been appointed Governor General, put a price of five thousand dollars on Bill Johnston's head. The Governor of New York, awakened at last to the pirate's lawlessness, added another five hundred to reassure the British that the United States did not condone his actions. None of this bothered Johnston in the slightest. Instead of fleeing, he proceeded to indulge in one of those bold gestures that make men legends in their own time: he issued a public proclamation taking full responsibility for the crime.

To all whom it may concern

I, William Johnston, a natural born citizen of Upper Canada, certify that I hold a commission in the Patriot Service of Upper Canada, as Commander-in-Chief of the naval forces and flotilla. I commanded the expedition that attacked and destroyed the steamer *Sir Robert Peel.* The men under my command in that expedition were nearly all natural born English subjects; the exceptions were volunteers for the expedition.

My headquarters were on an island in the St. Lawrence, without the jurisdiction of the United States, at a place named by me Fort Wallace. I am well acquainted with the boundary line, and know which of the islands do, and do not, belong to the United States; and in the selection of the island I wished to be positive, and not locate within the jurisdiction of the United States ....

I yet hold possession of that station, and we also occupy a station some twenty or more miles from the boundary of the

United States, in what was His Majesty's dominions, until it was occupied by us. The object of my movements is the independence of Canada. I am not at war with the commerce or prosperity of citizens of the United States.

Signed, the tenth day of June, 1838

WILLIAM JOHNSTON

In spite of this bold pronouncement, Johnston was neither discovered nor betrayed. From his lair among the Islands, he managed to create such a sense of menace that the Speaker of the Upper Canadian Assembly, Sir Allan MacNab, an old foe of the rebels, passing through Watertown en route to England, thought it prudent to disguise himself as a common labourer. Twelve of Johnston's men were captured eventually, loaded down with booty from the *Peel,* and one of them was tried on six counts of arson. It could not have been much of a trial; the American jury acquitted him and the others were later released. Meanwhile, President Van Buren ordered U.S. federal troops to Sackets Harbor and armed men placed on lake steamers to prevent further attacks.

This did not faze Bill Johnston. With his sixteen-oared boats, all mounted with cannon, and his parties of armed raiders, he kept the frontier in a continual state of agitation. Sorties of sailors were dispatched from Kingston to capture him; they were driven off by fire from an unseen foe. One adjutant, on a secret expedition, discovered a concealed bivouac on an almost inaccessible islet near the northwest part of a channel close to Fidler's Elbow; here he spotted cleverly constructed inclined planes up on which boats could be drawn. Lieutenant-Colonel Sir Richard Bonnycastle, apprised of this, mounted an expedition to capture Johnston and his men but all he found were the smouldering fires of his quarry. The pirate had a spy in the army's midst, who reported every move the British made.

On June 7, Johnston's gang appeared at Tanti (now Amherst) Island, only a few miles from Kingston, and plundered three farmhouses. One settler, trying to defend himself, was shot in the hand, losing three fingers. A week later, Johnston was reported at Ducks Island at the foot of the lake. Shortly after, he struck terror by appearing in the Brockville area. A second attack on a farmhouse on Tanti Island followed. Another farmer lost part of his hand – Johnston had a habit of maiming men in this way with his 12-inch, ivory-handled Bowie knife so they could no longer pull a trigger – and his son died of wounds. By this time, American sympathizers were referring to him as Sir William, a reference to the fact that the British had knighted MacNab, then commander of the Niagara forces, after the destruction of the *Caroline.*

Again and again Johnston eluded capture. On July 4, 1838, a combined British-American force of eighty men had him surrounded. Johnston and most of his gang gave them the slip, vanishing into the dense brush; only two were captured. At Fort Wallace, he maintained a sort of feudal sovereignty aided by sixteen-year-old Kate, who, from her home in French Creek, kept him informed of the whereabouts of his would-be captors.

In November of that year, there was another abortive attempt by a group of Hunters Lodges to invade Canada by way of Prescott. Again Johnston was involved, this time in charge of a vessel called the *Charlotte of Oswego.* Again his poor seamanship caused the ship to run aground, where she was quickly attacked and captured by the British. And again he escaped into the rainswept dark with thirty men and considerable ammunition.

This time he was at large for only five days. American troops, hot on his trail, seized his son and his boat and then flushed him from the woods. Even then he was able to dictate his own surrender terms, insisting that his son and not the soldiers take his weapons; he was carrying a twelve-shot Cochrane rifle, two large pistols, four small pistols and his Bowie knife. In Auburn he was put on trial for his part in the Prescott raid. The proceedings were casual, and Johnston was released for "lack of evidence." This was too much for the U.S. marshal, a man named Garrow, who had been on his trail for months. Garrow immediately arrested Johnston on earlier charges. But to arrest him was one thing, to hold him, another. Before dawn, Johnston had escaped from jail again and was miles away. But this time he was not close enough to his familiar Thousand Islands to elude capture for long. A few days later he was seized again, jailed and tried once more. He was given a year in prison and fined $250, not a very onerous sentence for a man who had killed, maimed, looted and kidnapped.

This time Johnston stayed in jail – not, apparently, because escape was impossible but rather because jail was pleasantly informal. His daughter Kate was allowed to visit him, to look after him and to share his cell. After a few weeks Johnston was to be observed strolling about the streets of Albany, free as the zephyrs that scud over the lakes. On January 23, 1839, there was an even more remarkable incident. A theatrical benefit was held in Johnston's honour. The play itself, *Bill Johnston, The Hero of the Lakes,* was a highly flattering account of his own derring-do. It was announced that Johnston himself would appear as the patron of the drama; and appear he did, with his daughter, seated prominently in the audience, applauding away, and surrounded by friends and well-wishers.

A few months later, with only half of his sentence served, Bill Johnston, tiring of prison, vanished again. As usual, he hid out in the Thousand Islands, to emerge at length from his redoubt with a petition for his pardon signed by scores of adherents. Off the jailbird went to Washington and presented the petition to the White House. President Van Buren did not sign it, but the incoming chief executive, William Henry Harrison, an implacable foe of the British during the War of 1812, was pleased to grant the pirate his unconditional release.

Not only did Johnston get a government pardon; he was also granted a government job as keeper of the Rock Island lighthouse, ironically located on the very spot where he and his gang of marauders had burned the *Peel.* Later on he became a tavernkeeper at French Creek and returned, so it was said, to his old trade of smuggling. And here, some years later, Sir James Alexander, searching for deserters from the British garrison at Kingston, encountered him and left the following description:

"The veritable Bill Johnston ... now stood before me at the corner of his son's house, which, by the way, contained Bill's very handsome daughter, the Queen of the Thousand Isles, who used intrepidly to row with supplies for her parent, whilst he was dodging the man-of-war's boats.

"Bill, in 1843, was about sixty years of age but he was hale, and straight, and ruddy; his nose was sharp, as were his features generally, and his eyes were keen and piercing; his lips compressed and receding; his height about five feet ten inches; he wore a broad-rimmed black hat, black stock and vest, frock and trousers of dark duffle. His discourse with me was principally about boats; he offered to sell his galley for sixty dollars, "not a cent less." ... He now offered to row or sail against any boat on either side of the St. Lawrence, adding that his galley would not leak a gill, and was altogether 'first rate.'"

It was during this encounter that Sir James was faced with a distressing puzzle: Could all the fooferaw connected with the Johnston nuisance – the border raids, the maimings, the loss of a ship and untold sums in money and goods, the deploying of troops and seamen, the extra guards and posted rewards – could all of that been easily avoided if the British had been less stiff-necked about Johnston at the outset? That was Johnston's contention years after the event. He insisted to Sir James that he could have been bought off early in the game for the sum of fifteen hundred pounds, which was the amount of his claim against the government in 1813, after he fled from Canada.

Did the British, then, pay through their noses for the cavalier treatment of the future pirate? "What has been gained by this rebellion?" someone once asked Johnston with more than a trace of contempt. To which the pirate replied: "Do you call the expenditure of four millions of British cash nothing? That is what our side gained."

A good deal of that, of course, went into Johnston's own pocket, but this only added to the legend that began to flourish during his own lifetime. At least two romantic novels, *The Empress of the Isles* and *The Prisoner of the Border,* were written in the 1850s, based on his exploits. As for the pirate himself, he lived on to the ripe age of eighty-eight, his villainies long forgotten, his offspring respected as "first families." One son, John Johnston, became a prominent banker and New York Assemblyman, with the word "Honorable" in front of his name. Another became the proprietor of the Walton House, then the most popular hostelry in Clayton. Kate, the Queen of the Isles, married the brother-in-law of the Honorable John and had five children of her own. By the time she died, at the age of sixty, Johnston was firmly enshrined as a minor American hero.

The remarkable coda to the story is that in 1958, he became a minor Canadian figure as well. One hundred and twenty years after he burned the *Peel,* the Ontario government put up a plaque to his memory directly across from the site of that malfeasance. Local politicians were delighted to preside at its unveiling.

6
The Ordeal of François Xavier Prieur

Prieur's own account of his seven-year exile to Australia following the abortive rebellion of 1838 is long out of print in Canada; yet it is the most Canadian of tales. I cannot read it without being moved by the intensity of longing that Prieur and his fellow convicts felt for their homeland. One does not encounter that same passion among the rebels from Upper Canada. With a single exception, all the French-Canadian exiles managed to return to Canada following their pardon. But their English-speaking counterparts scattered; some remained in the convict colony; some went to the United States; many more went back to the "old country," Great Britain. But to Prieur, Canada *was* the old country. When he was given a chance to go to France, he rejected it.

Another thread runs through Prieur's narrative – a devout Catholicism that goes deeper than the routine beatitudes of early French-Canadian documents. Prieur's unswerving faith did more than merely sustain him through danger, humiliation, uncertainty and suffering; for he not only survived his ordeal, he also prospered in exile and, when it was over, profited from what he had learned. His story, often hideous in its details, is essentially a love story – love of family, love of country, love of God. There is only one photograph of him extant, a rather muddy picture made in 1871 when Prieur was past middle age. It shows him surrounded by his family, plump, sleepy-eyed, bewhiskered – the typical Quebec bourgeois, by then a Conservative in politics. Nobody could know, gazing on that placid, domestic portrait, the trouble that François Xavier Prieur had seen. Nobody could know the despair he had suffered. Nobody could know the victories that were his.

Prieur was a fresh-faced farm boy in the parish of St. Joseph when the restlessness that led to the troubles of 1837 and 1838 began. At twenty-one, he set up a small store in St. Timothée, west of Beauharnois, on the south shore of the St. Lawrence. Business took him to Montreal and the bookstore of Edouard Fabre, a gathering place for Patriote leaders during the 1830s. There, Prieur met some of the great figures of the coming rebellions, including Louis Joseph Papineau, Louis Hippolyte LaFontaine and George Etienne Cartier. These men were to lead, in Lower Canada, a struggle for a fully democratic government that paralleled that of William Lyon Mackenzie in Upper Canada.

Prieur took no part in the rebellion of 1837, which saw Papineau driven into exile and the Patriote movement suppressed. But in 1838 he was sworn in as a *castor* in the secret society known as the Frères Chasseurs, an underground movement planning a second uprising. A *castor* was an officer commanding a company of ten platoons. Prieur became the rebel leader for his village of St. Timothée, mustering his men and his small hoard of munitions against the day of uprising. A less bloodthirsty youth cannot be imagined.

"I was young and inexperienced," he recalled, "a sincere lover of my homeland; I believed in the existence of all the evils enumerated; in the efficacy of the proposed remedy; I had read something of the heroism of my forefathers; I felt myself of good stock. Enthusiastically, I took part in the general training."

In St. Timothée, as in other parishes scattered throughout Lower Canada, the Patriotes awaited the call to arms. It came on the night of November 3. In the confused struggle that followed – scores of isolated skirmishes – the rebels, with their sporting guns, iron pitchforks and scythes, were no match for the better armed and disciplined British and Scottish regulars. The confusion of the Patriote forces was compounded by a lack of communication between parishes. The members of one community would prepare to resist while others were fleeing in disorder; one leader would be recruited while another was escaping across the border. It is not pertinent to detail Prieur's own tribulations – the early, brief successes; the rumours of defeat elsewhere; the uncertainty, the dissension and the desertions that weakened his own forces to the point where resistance became useless. It is only necessary to sketch in the final picture of the youth and his followers falling to their knees to tell their beads and repeat their litanies, as night falls and the rumbling of heavy gun carriages and cavalry swells in the distance.

All of Prieur's men melted quietly away into the night. Their leader went home, to find it a smoking ruin. Now François Xavier Prieur was a hunted man, hiding out in the haylofts of sympathetic farmers, to be betrayed, eventually, by an old comrade who turned him in to secure a pardon for himself.

The long ordeal began: forty prisoners, shivering in the bitter cold, living on bread and water in a flour mill at St. Timothée, hastily converted to a jail; fifty-two men now, almost all fathers of large families, chained two by two, and marched through the snow to Montreal to the infuriating skirl of bagpipes and the cries of an outraged mob; "Shoot them! Hang them!"; scores more men, jammed for five weeks in the gloomy prison of La-Pointe-à-Callières, watching while their comrades returned from their trials, condemned to die.

On January 9, 1839, Prieur and eleven others were taken in chains before the court martial, forced to walk directly under a scaffold spattered with the blood of two rebels whose hangings had been botched. The proceedings took place in English, a language few of them understood. They were not allowed French-Canadian lawyers because, they were told, this would prejudice the judges against them. The judges were prejudiced anyway: they insulted the prisoners and some amused themselves, during the sittings, by sketching little figures hanging from gibbets.

The case dragged on. Eight times the accused men were dragged into court handcuffed, to be abused and insulted by a rabble along the way. On January 18, as they arrived at the jail they saw the corpses of five of their comrades stretched out on the snow in their convict garb. One of the guards pointed out that all of them would shortly be in the same state.

Prieur's parents arrived to visit him. As he was led from the courtroom his mother rushed toward him, but a soldier thrust her back. Two hours later, when she was allowed to see him, she fainted in his arms: "At this moment," he writes, "I suffered the greatest anguish it has been my lot to endure during the course of a life which has suffered so much."

On the afternoon of January 24, Prieur and all his comrades were sentenced to be hanged. The condemned man told his parents to leave before the execution and to bury his body in the parish of his birth. In adjoining cells there were other tragic visits. Without breadwinners, most of the families of the Patriotes had nowhere to turn. Their homes and farms had been looted and burned; they were destitute.

Coffins were ordered; prisoners were led to the scaffold. Prieur, who knew his name was high on the list, waited for the fatal summons. It did not come. His own humanity had saved him; during the abortive uprising he had treated his captives with kindness. Among these were Jane Ellice and her husband, Edward, who was a nephew of Earl Grey and related to the Governor General, Lord Durham, and had until recently been one of his secretaries. They had successfully petitioned Sir John Colborne, the military commander at Quebec, to spare Prieur's life.

With fifty-seven others, Prieur remained in jail, not knowing from one day to the next what his fate would be.

He endured six months of misery. Then, on the afternoon of September 28, he and his fellow prisoners were told that their sentences had been commuted and that they would be transported the following morning to the penal colony of Australia for life. For many, there was not enough time to inform their families.

At eleven the next morning the fifty-eight men, shackled two by two, were led aboard the steamer *British America.* They were later joined by eighty-three rebel prisoners from Upper Canada and transferred, at Quebec City, to the big prison ship *Buffalo.* All were squeezed together in the unventilated hold, four and a half feet high. Each had about fifty cubic feet of air space. A row of packing cases ran down the length of their floating dungeon; on either side was a three-foot alley along which they could walk bent double. A bench, eighteen inches wide, flanked each walkway. Behind the bench lay a double row of compartments, nine on each side, six feet deep. These were their beds, each one holding four men on coarse mattresses with one blanket shared between two sleepers. Two small hatchways, covered by iron grilles and guarded by sentries, were the only source of light and air. For five months this was to be their home.

The English occupied the starboard side of the hold, the French the port. Prieur in his tiny corner at the far end slept well that first night, for he was exhausted. As he awoke, he heard the rattle of the anchors being raised; as the ship got underway, he realized that "we were leaving our native land without being able to cast a last glance at that beautiful landscape of Canada . . . so lovely; especially in this magnificent seaport of Quebec." With one accord, Prieur and his comrades fell on their knees to say their morning prayers, a ceremony from which they never wavered, morning and evening, throughout the long, distressing voyage.

At seven they were divided into groups of twelve to get rations. Their communal dish was a bucket, their only tableware a cup; there were no other utensils, although Prieur's group had a little pocketknife with which to cut meat. Breakfast was a pint of oatmeal soup; dinner consisted of four ounces of salt meat, a little suet pudding and some biscuit or, on alternate days, a pint of pea soup, three ounces of bacon and a little biscuit; supper was a pint of cocoa. Lest they die in the close atmosphere of the hold, they were allowed a daily two-and-a-half-hour walk on deck; the time was later reduced to one hour as punishment.

Now these men, most of whom had never seen the sea even from a distance, faced the horrors of an ocean voyage. After five days of calm, the waters grew rough and most of the passengers became ill. The decks became slippery with vomit. Forbidden to use the beds by day, the wretched prisoners huddled on the benches. The crew and officers abused them, calling them cut-throats and sons of bitches. Prieur, one of the few who wasn't seasick, busied himself cleaning up after his less fortunate fellows.

When the storm ceased a week later, all were starving. Their clothes were infested with lice, their food buckets unbelievably filthy. They shaved in cold water with razors eaten away by rust. During their hour of freedom on deck they tried to wash their clothes. As the ship neared the tropics, the heat below the water-line became stifling. One man died; others were desperately ill. Everyone suffered from a raging thirst. Two sailors who brought the sick men water and rum were flogged for that act of mercy. Other sailors sold water in return for some of the prisoners' few clothes. A brief respite on deck during a stop at Rio de Janeiro saved many lives. Here their rations were improved by the addition of lime juice; but in spite of this, scurvy was rampant, and the lice unbearable.

On February 13, the Upper Canadians were put off at Van Dieman's Land. Two weeks later, the ship reached Sydney. But Sydney did not want the rebels. Articles from the English-language newspapers in Montreal had arrived, branding them as bandits and roughnecks. They were rumoured to be destined for the hellish Norfolk Island, reserved for the worst criminals, hundreds of miles distant. They were held aboard the ship for two weeks while the Roman Catholic bishop, Monsigneur Polding, petitioned the authorities to allow them to stay, guaranteeing their good conduct. They were released at last from their floating prison, taken to Longbottom on the Paramatta River, eight miles out of Sydney, and marched for a mile inland. It was all they could do to make it.

"We were so weak, so worn out, and shaky on our legs that this short mile walk, taken at a slow pace, made us so tired that it gave us all pains in our limbs, pains that persisted with several of us for a few days...."

The prisoners were lodged in four huts, just fifteen feet long and six feet wide, arranged with some outbuildings and barracks in a square. Anyone crossing the square without permission was subject to fifty lashes. For the first six weeks there were no beds, only bare boards to sleep on. The men awoke in the damp, chilly mornings with aching backs and heavy colds. Their food ration was as bad as that of the prison ship: porridge for breakfast, half a pound of rotting beef and twelve ounces of truly terrible bread per person for the rest of the day. The only available water came from rain holes dug in the ground. Each man's clothing was stencilled with the painted initials LB (for Longbottom) on back, legs, arms and chest. They worked under armed guards from early morning until six at night, smashing stones in a neighbouring quarry. The guards, it appeared, were terrified of them, having heard the rumours from Canada that these were dangerous, desperate men.

But Prieur and his fellow prisoners were determined to justify Bishop Polding's trust in them by maintaining an impeccable behaviour. The prison superintendent, Henry Clinton Baddeley, a coarse and brutal man who had been discharged from the army for misconduct, tried his best to provoke them into open rebellion, which he knew he could quell with bloodshed. He failed. During "those long years of misery," Prieur was to write, ". . . one thing alone has supported me against the agonies of the heart and body, against the outbursts of temper; that thing believers will easily recognize, Religion." In the stable, which also served as a dining room, the prisoners set up a little chapel in which to receive the bishop when he visited them. They cleaned it, decorated it with fern leaves, built an altar out of sticks and covered it with a cotton cloth on which they hung all the little holy pictures their families had given them on departure.

One of the priests who visited them wrote to a local Catholic paper complaining about the food and conditions at the prison and urging that the men be allowed to find jobs for themselves. This only resulted in a vitriolic attack in the Sydney *Herald,* in which the Canadians were called cutthroats whose whole career had been marked by murder, pillage and arson.

But in the prison compound a bizarre turn of events helped alleviate the prisoners' suffering. The Canadians were guarded by one squad of police and one squad of soldiers. One night, the superintendent became involved in a drunken brawl with one of the policemen, whose wife he had insulted. The policeman was arrested and this touched off a wild mêlée, some taking the superintendent's side, others taking the policeman's side. In desperation, Baddeley released the Canadians and ordered them to arrest and lock up all the police and guards, except one sergeant. By obeying him they won his confidence, and completely changed his attitude toward them. After three months the authorities, in a remarkable gesture, removed all the guards and left the superintendent in charge. In effect the prisoners would guard themselves. Baddeley began to give those prisoners least used to manual labour easier jobs as overseers, cooks, servants and watchmen. Prieur became a night sentry.

The food improved slightly. The superintendent now trusted his prisoners, allowing them to leave their hut doors open at nights and to collect shells off the beach to sell to lime-burners to earn a few pennies for rice and sugar. Conditions were still execrable, but to a very real degree the prisoners were themselves given charge of their own prison.

A year passed. Life remained unbearably harsh. One man died of dropsy. Another, of colossal stature, expired from starvation because, though his friends shared their rations with him, he could not get enough to eat. The diminutive Prieur must have considered himself fortunate that he was under five foot five.

Under the Australian penal system convicts progressed by stages to become free citizens. In November 1840, twenty months after their arrival at Longbottom, the Canadians reached stage two of this progression: they were given permission to hire themselves out to residents of the country, a practice that meant they would no longer be a burden on the government. The rules continued to be strict: they were rationed to ten pounds of fresh beef, ten pounds of flour, a pound of sugar and four ounces of tea a week; they were quartered like plantation slaves in little huts adjoining their master's home; they worked a twelve-hour day and cooked their own food; and they could not leave their master's property except on Sundays, without a written permit. Nevertheless it was an improvement and, as Prieur wrote, "the only thing which troubled us . . . was the thought that we were about to be separated from one another."

Man by man they were hired out. When all but one had left, Baddeley, the superintendent, sickened and died in the arms of the last Canadian prisoner. "No other person came to be present with him in his last moments, and not a single friend followed his coffin to the cemetery."

Prieur and a fellow prisoner, Louis Bourdon, were hired out to a Frenchman from Mauritius. They discovered that he had no intention of keeping them but proposed to rent them, at a profit, to another Frenchman and his German partner who had arrived in Sydney to open a confectionery shop. The two Canadians worked and slept in a small shed, making syrups and candy. Compared to prison it was "an earthly paradise."

After three months, Prieur was suddenly denied his Sunday holiday and told he could not longer attend mass. To a devout Catholic this was outrageous. Prieur took the unusual step of striking. It was, he said, against his religion to work on the Lord's Day and also against penal regulations. Unable to get a hearing from his original master, the stubborn Canadian went to the government itself and was taken before the head of the department, a Captain McLean. Prieur attempted to tell his story in the halting English he had picked up in Australia. McLean responded politely that he might speak in French; he understood the language. A long man-to-man talk followed – for Prieur a "truly moral tonic." It was the first time in years that he had felt enough dignity to talk with ease to a man of superior intelligence, education and heart. "The interview reconciled me to my environment, and filled me with hope for the future."

Ordinarily, Prieur would have been sent back to the penal camp until a new master could be found. But McLean knew the difference between Canadian political exiles and criminals. He gave Prieur permission to seek his own job in Sydney and invited him to come back from time to time to let him know how he was getting along. Overcome with gratitude, Prieur felt that he had grown six inches.

But jobs in Australia were almost impossible to find; the colony was in the throes of a financial crisis brought on by land speculation and unhindered immigration. Prieur had a few gold coins from Canada hidden in the cover of a prayer book and a few shillings paid him by the confectioners, which he used to rent lodgings from a man who had once lived in Montreal. Within a fortnight his money was used up and he found himself without a roof over his head. He managed to get a job as an assistant gardener from a man who had once been a convict himself and was now a wealthy merchant. After three months in this job he and the other Canadian exiles were promoted again from the status of assigned convicts to that of ticket-of-leave men. Now, although he must always carry a pass and could be picked up by the police whenever a crime was committed, Prieur could work for himself.

He ran into his former partner, Louis Bourdon, who persuaded him to go with him to a sawmill in the bushland where ten of their comrades were working. They bought some tools and set off a week later, walking the nine miles to the sawmill through dense, snake-infested bush. Their welcome was warm and, in Prieur's account, there is a touching scene in which the dozen exiles, seated at night in their frame hut on mattresses stuffed with fern leaves, sing French-Canadian folk songs and talk among themselves about their wives, children and parents in Quebec. In all this time there had been no word from Canada. Prieur had no idea whether his mother and father, brothers and sisters, were alive or dead; nor would he ever learn of them during all the years of his exile. It was as if he had been transported through a fourth dimension into a shadow world.

Prieur and Bourdon decided to try their hand at making laths. They worked desperately hard, felling and splitting huge trees, their hands covered with blisters and their limbs stiff with fatigue. On a trip into Sydney, Prieur encountered some officers from a French whaling vessel who offered to help him escape to France. He refused: he did not want these men to risk fine and imprisonment for him and, as for France – well, that, too, would be exile. Bourdon, however, sailed on the whaler and eventually made his way back to Canada.

For another year Prieur toiled in the forest, trying to make and sell laths. The work provided him with just enough funds to stay alive. Finally, he moved back to Sydney and went to work as business manager for three Frenchmen who wanted to set up a candle factory. He soon realized the business would fail and after four months resigned, went job-hunting again and finally got work clearing land.

Then a new venture beckoned. Two of the Canadians who had made a profit at the sawmill invited him to help them set up what was, in effect, a primitive shopping centre at a new village called Irish Town, twelve miles from Sydney. They would supply the capital and Prieur the business knowledge. They built their own shops from wood cut in the bush and within three days managed to erect a grocery, a bakery and a smithy. Near the bakery they built a Quebec-style oven, something that immediately drew curious spectators, for it was unknown in Australia. The bakery made money from the start; the shop broke even; the smithy failed and the blacksmith moved away. Prieur and his one remaining partner remained, making just enough to live on. And so another year went by.

In Canada, unknown to Prieur and his fellow exiles, attitudes had been mellowing. A new leader had emerged in Quebec: Louis Hippolyte LaFontaine, who had tried to pursue the French-Canadian cause by constitutional means. LaFontaine doggedly fought for an amnesty for the rebels of 1838. In 1843, Edouard Fabre, in whose bookstore Prieur had first espoused the cause of revolt, was helping to organize L'Association de la Déliverance to raise funds for the passage of the exiles back to Canada once an amnesty was proclaimed. The following year word of the first pardons began to filter to Australia.

Prieur had been at Irish Town for a year when he heard this unbelievable news. Two of the exiles had been pardoned. One of them was a close friend, Charles Huot, a former lawyer now in his fifties; Prieur had worked with him as night sentry in the prison camp. He rushed to see Huot, held the actual document of amnesty in his hand, read and reread it, finding it difficult to believe his eyes. Huot was overjoyed, even though for him the pardon was useless since he had no funds for passage home.

The following month, pardons arrived for half the Canadian exiles. Prieur was one of these. Nothing, he determined, would stop him from getting home again. "We were a-hungered and a-thirst for our homeland, we were consumed with the desire to return to Canada, to see again our families, our friends, our beautiful countryside, to salute the belfries of our parishes, to speak French, and to gaze on the sight of our good French-Canadian customs."

He, too, lacked the money for his passage. His partner in Irish Town, who had worked in the sawmill (which was far more profitable than lath-making) was able to leave. Again, Prieur went to Sydney to look for a job. By this time, the Canadians were in demand because their honesty and hard work were well known. Prieur had no trouble getting employment in a drygoods store; the salary was the highest he had yet known in Australia.

In August, twenty-eight Canadian exiles embarked for England, where money raised in Lower Canada had been banked to pay for their passage home. These men promised to raise more money to pay for the later passage of those left behind. By this time, Prieur was fiercely homesick: "This disease threatened to bring me to my grave. Never, at any period of my exile, had I experienced anything approaching it. The boredom that I suffered is indescribable. I was very soon on the verge of falling into a state of melancholia, and of seeking only solitude, in the depths of which I nourished my sorrow. Every Sunday I spent my afternoon on a rock situated in the recesses of a solitary little bay overlooking Sydney Harbour; there I dreamed of my homeland and my family."

Prieur, who had now passed his thirtieth birthday, imagined he was watching the wake of the ship that had carried his comrades homeward. He saw himself aboard her, sailing home, up the St. Lawrence, finally reaching the parish where he was born – his mother's kisses, his father's joy, his friends' hand clasps. In anguish, he cried out, again and again, to the winds and to the sea: "When, oh when, shall I be able to set out for Canada?"

At this juncture he encountered a French merchant who was

planning to sell his stock and return to Europe. He offered to take Prieur with him and to lend him the funds to go on to Canada. Prieur quit his job to help the Frenchman. In the evenings and on Sundays, he and seventeen other pardoned exiles, who also lacked funds, met and talked together.

More months dragged by. Prieur was summoned to see the Governor, Sir George Gipps, who told him that friends in several Quebec parishes had been requested by the British government to send money collected in Canada to Australia for the exiles' passage. Prieur and his friends were overjoyed. But more time passed and the money did not come.

At the end of January 1846, eighteen months after the first exiles had left Australia, Prieur and the French merchant finished selling all the stock and booked passage for England on the *Saint George*. They left in February. Prieur met one last time with his comrades and enjoined them to have courage: their turn would come. He shook hands with each one, the tears streaming down his face. Four months later (such was the slowness of ocean travel in those times) he reached England.

He began to search for the source of the funds said to be awaiting the return of the exiles. He had no idea where to look but after some days got in touch by letter with John Arthur Roebuck, an English member of Parliament, sympathetic to the cause. Roebuck sent him to see a Mr. Graham, who at once gave him the money to pay his London expenses and his passage home. There wasn't enough on deposit to bring the others back. Prieur was asked to help raise more funds in Canada.

On July 13, 1846, Prieur sailed from England for his homeland. At seven in the morning of September 2 he went on deck to see the Gaspé shores: "The Homeland! After more than seven years of exile!" It was so intoxicating that he reflected that the pleasures of entering Heaven must be beyond imagination. His fellow passengers were moved by his ecstasy. For two days he was too excited to sleep.

On September 10, Prieur touched the soil of Canada for the first time as he stepped off the ship at Quebec City. He took a carriage to his hotel. Every tiny detail moved him. "I cannot express . . . the effect that the sight of this carriage had upon me and the impression that I experienced when I heard French spoken around me . . . especially the simple words that the coachman addressed to his horse."

The news of his arrival spread through the city by a kind of moccasin telegraph. Strangers flooded into his room to congratulate him, to wish him well, to ask for news of those still in exile.

They pressed invitations upon him but these he could not accept. He must go home; he still did not know whether his parents were alive.

He took the steamer to Montreal and there he heard the good news that his family were alive and well and, thanks to a letter from Roebuck, the British MP, expecting him. But before rushing home, he felt he must keep his promise to solicit more funds. He visited Fabre, who told him that sufficient money had been collected but a mistake in the methods used to transmit it to Australia had caused maddening delays. Prieur, with his experience in New South Wales, was able to advise him of better methods. Within sixteen months, fifty-five of the original fifty-eight exiles were back in Quebec: two had died at Longbottom and one had married and stayed in Australia.

The next day, Prieur took the steamer to his home parish. There was a frustrating hold-up in the Beauharnois Canal, which meant that he did not reach his parents' doorstep until two in the morning of September 4, 1846. By then everyone was in bed. It had been eight years since Prieur had stood on this spot: "Reader of my notes, put yourself in my place. Imagine it is you who stands waiting upon this threshold, and you will understand how I felt."

Suddenly the door was flung open. "It is he! It is Xavier!" His parents flung their arms around his neck. He knelt before his father to ask his blessing. Then, on their knees, the reunited family offered up their prayers, thanking their Maker for their son's return.

The word travelled like a fast-burning fuse. Old men in nearby cottages, getting up to light their pipes from the stoves, saw the lights in the Prieur house and woke their families. For miles around, men, women and children tumbled from their beds and set out to greet the returned exile, tapping on windows as they passed down the road, calling out, "Xavier Prieur has arrived. Aren't you coming to see him?" Half an hour after his return, the house was crowded with neighbours, with more arriving by the minute, the men in their caps, the women in their big woollen shawls, shivering in the cold but warmed by the miracle.

It was five in the morning before Prieur ceased shaking hands and even then his story was not told. He promised to relate the rest of it later; now he needed to go to bed – his own bed, which had been held ready for him for all those years. He felt indescribably happy. "It is good to be here, my Canada, parish of my birth. Here I find again my parents, the friends of my childhood and my youth. O God, full of kindness, blessed are Thou!" For François

Xavier Prieur, rebel, patriot, ex-convict, devout Catholic, jack-of-a-dozen-trades, the eight-year ordeal was over.

Prieur settled down as a merchant in Chateauguay and later in Beauharnois. In 1849 he married. All during his exile, even in the Quebec prison "when over me hung the weight of the death sentence; when the dead bodies of some of the companions of my captivity hung suspended from the gibbet," the resourceful young man had recorded his experiences on loose sheets of paper. In 1864, he arranged these notes and published them. "I do not propose," he declared in his introduction, "to write history. . . . I wish to provide, for those who do, my share of the exact information concerning the things that I have seen with my own eyes, touched with my own hands, and suffered in my own person." He had long since begged God's pardon, he said, for disobeying the order of the church and he had long since forgiven all those who had done him wrong. "It is therefore in a spirit of calm that I write . . . without any desire to injure. . . ."

By the time his book appeared, Prieur had taken a new job. Thanks to the influence of his Conservative friends he was appointed Superintendent of the Reformatory at Ile-aux-Noix. One cannot imagine a man better experienced or more humanely equipped to run a jail. In 1875, he was promoted to Superintendent of all Canadian prisons. A man of great energy and perseverance (he lived to the age of seventy-five) he travelled widely across Canada, the United States and throughout Europe, visiting prisons and reform institutions, talking to wardens and jailers, investigating the latest methods of prison administration.

In his new job he saw a good deal of the world and also the inside of a good many prisons. But there was one part of the world he did not need to visit, one example of prison administration he had no further cause to study. There was no need for François Xavier Prieur to go back to the penal colony of Australia.

7

The Zeal of Charles Chiniquy

It is given to few men to be venerated as saints and excoriated as devils in their own lifetime but Charles Paschal Telésphor Chiniquy managed it with ease in the last century. His name is scarcely a household word today but there was a time when the Abbé Chiniquy was successively the best-known Roman Catholic priest in the province of Quebec and the best-known Protestant minister in all of Canada. The emotions he stirred were such that tens of thousands hung his lithographed portrait in their parlours; a decade or so later some of these same people became part of the howling mob that tried to tear him to pieces.

A brilliant temperance fighter who was himself a prey to the sins of the flesh, he caused multitudes of supporters to sign the pledge against strong liquor. A spell-binding orator and best-selling author, he was banished and finally excommunicated by his own church, apparently for sexual peccadillos and heresies. A converted Protestant, he managed to seduce more thousands away from the Catholic fold. As a Catholic he was compared regularly to St. Louis-de-Gonzague, one of the most venerated of modern saints. As a Protestant he was hailed as a modern Martin Luther.

It is not easy today to comprehend the emotions that Chiniquy stirred up a century ago; we tend to forget the enormous power and emotional appeal of the temperance movement in nineteenth-century Canada, just as we tend to forget the almost maniacal bitterness of the Catholic-Protestant division. To comprehend the Chiniquy story, it is necessary to understand these twin emotions. Even then it is difficult to really *know* Chiniquy, for his character was anything but simple. It is not easy to like him, for he was clearly a hypocrite, a liar, a sensualist and an egotist. Yet it is hard not to admire him, for he had courage, charisma, passion and a golden tongue. More than most of his contemporaries, he was a product of his time. In these more tolerant and permissive years, I doubt that he could have made much of an impact.

Chiniquy's father was a mean drunk and that has to be borne in mind when one considers his later temperance crusades. He was also a failed student of the priesthood, having switched from a seminary to the law courts. The well-to-do Chiniquys of Kamouraska (the grandfather was the *seigneur*) were certainly religious but there was a kind of maverick streak operating in the family. Charles' uncle, Martin, was a Trappist monk who later gave up Catholicism for Protestantism only to re-embrace his former faith on his deathbed.

Most of what we know about Charles Chiniquy's childhood comes from his own pen and must be scrutinized with care. He can be believed, however, when he indicates that he was a born orator; later events made that obvious: "We were some distance from the church, and the roads, in the rainy days, were very bad. On the Sabbath days the neighbouring farmers, unable to go to church, were accustomed to gather at our house in the evening. Then my parents used to put me up on a large table in the midst of the assembly, and I delivered to those good people the most beautiful parts of the Old and New Testaments. The breathless attention, the applause of our guests, and – may I tell it – often the tears of joy which my mother tried in vain to conceal, supported my strength and gave me the courage I wanted, to speak when so young before so many people."

The elder Chiniquy died when Charles was twelve and the boy's welfare was taken over by his uncle, Amable Dionne, a wealthy Kamouraska merchant who treated him as his own son and subsidized his education at the Seminary of Nicolet. Three years later, however, there was a complete breach: Dionne suddenly announced that he would no longer support the boy. What had happened? Chiniquy in his memoirs glossed over the incident which, he wrote, was a "misunderstanding." But a Dionne grandson, Bishop Henri Têtu, claimed in a memoir that Chiniquy was banished from his foster-father's favour because he tried to tamper with one of Dionne's daughters. In the light of later revelations, Bishop Têtu's story rings true.

Such was young Chiniquy's scholastic ability, however, that two of his teachers offered to pay his fees. The boy repaid the investment by winning prizes for recitation and rhetoric. For the first time, but not the last, his humility caused him to be compared with (and nicknamed for) Saint Louis-de-Gonzague – known, in the Encyclopaedia Britannica's intriguing phrase, for his "intense love of chastity." Not everybody agreed with this assessment. Bishop Têtu later wrote that some thought Chiniquy was "a hypocrite of the first water."

Chiniquy's mother died when he was twenty-one, after eliciting from him the standard nineteenth-century deathbed promise that he would never drink more than two glasses of wine. Three years later, on the occasion of his ordination as a priest, Chiniquy also abjured tobacco, throwing away his pipe and snuff box forever. Some time during the next four years, while serving as a curate and also as a hospital chaplain, he became interested in the problem of alcohol abuse. As is usual in the Chiniquy story, there are two versions of how this came about.

Chiniquy's version goes this way: He asked, he said, for a glass of brandy – for purely medicinal purposes. The Protestant doctor at the hospital, James Douglas, admonished him, explaining that alcohol was a poison. Chiniquy demanded proof; Douglas convinced him by performing an autopsy on a alcoholic. Fascinated, the young priest took up the study, witnessing some two hundred autopsies over the next four years, and was astonished "to view the damage made even in moderate drinkers."

Douglas, in his memoirs, gave a shorter, blunter version, which did not picture Chiniquy as an avid student priest. The doctor wrote that he caught his chaplain drinking brandy and rebuked him severely for setting such a poor example, whereupon the chaplain stalked angrily out of the room. There was no mention of a later interest in autopsies.

Whatever Chiniquy's interest in the curse of alcohol may have been, it lay dormant for some time. He applied to go as a priest to the Red River country but was rebuffed in a letter. The Bishop of St. Boniface mentioned a "blunder" on Chiniquy's part but did not go into detail. Then, in September 1838, when Chiniquy was thirty-one, he was made curé of Beauport, one of the most important parishes in Quebec.

Beauport was renowned for the amount of liquor its parishioners could put away. It was actually cheaper to drink than to eat. A jug of rum cost a mere twenty-five sous – about twenty cents. There were seven saloons in the town exploiting that fact. Chiniquy was shocked to discover that his parishioners did not buy their rum by the jug; they hauled it home by the cask.

For thousands of farmhands and common labourers in both Canadas, liquor provided the only real respite. Booze was the great lubricant at barn raisings, country bees, sports events and political rallies. Women, banned from the taverns, often sat outside in carts and buggies enduring the freezing cold while their husbands drank themselves into bankruptcy. But the temperance movement, gathering power in Protestant Ontario, sparked by the churches and later by some of these same women, changed all that. By 1831, there were some hundred temperance societies in Upper Canada; thousands, attracted by mass meetings and a snowstorm of anti-liquor pamphlets, were taking the pledge.

Lower Canada was more tolerant. There were only a few temperance societies operating in the early 1830s among the French Canadians – until Chiniquy came along. Almost single-handedly, he changed the Quebecois attitude toward strong drink.

The original spark came from a priest, Pierre Beaumont, in a neighbouring parish, who had been attracted to the fledgling temperance ideal by reading the English-language newspapers. In 1839, he and Chiniquy decided to found twin temperance movements in their two parishes.

Chiniquy began preaching temperance at once. In March, 1840, he founded his Société de Tempérance. No fewer than thirteen hundred of his parishioners took the pledge "to avoid intemperance and never go to cabarets." Then they went on to swear that "I will never use strong drink without an absolute necessity, and if to become temperate I must renounce all kinds of drink, I will so agree; I promise also to do all in my power by my words and my deeds so that my parents and my friends will do as much."

This pledge did not proscribe beer or wine. The following year, however, Chiniquy drew up a new document which demanded total and perfect temperance. More than eight hundred of his flock signed it. The Catholic Church was never as extreme as Chiniquy; it was more concerned with the general virtues of sobriety. (After all, the serving of wine was part of the Mass.) Chiniquy came to regard this tolerant attitude as a personal attack upon himself and he charged, in his memoirs, that the church had actually opposed temperance, which was certainly not true.

Largely because of his rhetoric, the Abbé Chiniquy became the most prominent priest involved in the temperance movement of Lower Canada. "Everywhere his zeal goes, intemperance flies," *Le Canadien* reported. His speeches began modestly; frequently he admitted that he had known drunkenness. Then his tone grew feverish as he recounted horrible tales of the downfall of drunks. He was a slight young man, under five and a half feet, with intense, sympathetic eyes and a shock of soft, dark hair. His followers began to call him "le petit père." Sometime later Bishop Bourget of Montreal was to ask, ruefully: "How could such a little man cause such an uproar?"

Chiniquy's initial moment of triumph came in September

1841, when he organized a grand spectacle around the unveiling of a Temperance Column at Beauport. Ten thousand people, accompanied by seven choirs of women and led by two little girls, dressed in white and carrying white flags, marched from the Seminary of Quebec, after Mass, to dedicate the pillar with its gilded Corinthian base and its cross. The Bishop of Nancy, then touring French Canada, also turned up to bless the column, accompanied by twenty-two horsemen.

Chiniquy's star was rising. The Bishop of Montreal, Ignace Bourget, invited him to preach that October at the cathedral where, in *Le Canadien's* words, he "made a great sensation." His parishioners commissioned one of the province's best portrait artists to render his likeness in oils. He seemed on the verge of greater triumphs when suddenly and without warning, he was gone – flung out of his parish by his bishop and banished to Kamouraska. The bishop acted with so much dispatch that the priest's own parishioners didn't have a chance to bid him goodbye.

What had happened? Clearly, there had been a scandal of some sort. Chiniquy's biographer, Marcel Trudel, mentions a "secret memoire" which describes it, evasively, as "a misadventure which would be comic if the subject were not so lamentable." This titillating remark is reminiscent of Chiniquy's earlier "misunderstanding" in the home of his uncle and the "blunder" to which the Bishop of St. Boniface referred. For all of his years in the Church of Rome, Chiniquy's career followed this topsy-turvy pattern of blinding success followed by "misadventures" hushed up, banishment and then a slow rise to a new pinnacle. The abbé was nothing if not resilient. He bounced from one misadventure to another, blandly dismissing each scandal as a personal and uncalled-for attack visited upon an innocent zealot by dark forces bent upon his destruction.

For the moment Chiniquy was demoted to acting curé of Kamouraska. Some months later, when the ailing priest died, the title was confirmed. Immediately he began to press his temperance campaign.

His attitude to strong drink had hardened. He would have none of the *auberges de tempérance*, which were springing up in Quebec to cater to followers of *la petite tempérance*. These establishments attempted to sell strong drink in a moderate fashion. To Chiniquy they were just as bad as the all-out saloons. By the spring of 1844, when he published his *Manuel de Tempérance*, Chiniquy was accepted as the leading theoretician and preacher of temperance in Quebec. The first edition of four thousand copies sold out quickly. Parish after parish begged to hear him. At St. Gervais, for instance, he persuaded thirteen hundred to take the pledge. His peccadillos, whatever they may have been, were forgotten. And then, once again as he reached for the pinnacle, the weakness of the flesh brought about his downfall.

He had gone to preach in the neighbouring parish of St. Pascal. Here, while he was enrolling abstainers and handing out temperance cards, his eye fell upon a local housewife. Chiniquy started to pay court to her; she tried, not without difficulty, to fend him off. He persisted; at last she fixed a rendezvous. But when the ardent priest arrived at the trysting place it was not a comely woman who came to meet him; it was the local curé. Chiniquy fell to his knees and confessed his sin. Again the scandal was hushed up, but he obviously could not remain in Kamouraska. He asked to enter the novitiate of the Oblate Fathers (an order committed to temperance) at Longueuil near Montreal, and a relieved bishop approved the transfer.

There are always, in the tangled history of Charles Chiniquy, two versions of every one of these intriguing incidents. Years later, when Chiniquy came to write his memoirs, he gave an entirely different account of his sudden switch to the Oblate order. He was so disgusted, he claimed, by the scandals he saw around him among other clergy that he wanted to die. When the head of the Oblates urged him to join, "I fell to my knees and made to God, in the midst of burning tears, the sacrifice of my parish."

En route to the Oblate mission, Chiniquy stopped off at Trois Rivières where he enrolled two thousand persons in total temperance. He had managed by this time to complete a second edition of his *Manuel*, a slicker one than the first, carrying letters of endorsation from four bishops, including one unlikely signator, the Bishop of Walla Walla in the distant territory of Washington. The book, which was published in January 1845, sold ten thousand copies in a few months, became a text in Quebec schools and went into an English-language edition. No book had enjoyed such a success up to that time in French Canada.

As a novice, Chiniquy kept a high profile, continuing to make speeches for temperance and involving himself in the politics of the order to the point where the Superior General called him impertinent. His application for admission was unanimously rejected and Chiniquy, on leaving, wrote to Bishop Bourget of Montreal that "I feel more than ever an invincible repugnance to being an Oblate." Years later, in his memoirs, he took a different tack: "From the first to the last day of my sojourn among the Oblates I was honoured with the esteem and friendship of all, without exception; tears flowed from the eyes of all when I said goodbye." One suspects that, if there were tears, they were tears of relief.

In the spring of 1848, Bishop Bourget assigned Chiniquy to work as a temperance crusader in Montreal. As a result he became more prominent than ever. One religious magazine kept a box score of his converts: by summer it had reached twenty thousand. The mayor and the bishop both turned out to hear him address a crowd of five thousand at the Bonsecours Marketplace in October where Chiniquy made an impassioned speech in favour of drinking water, using himself as a healthy example of total abstinence. The rhetoric made the bishop uneasy. He wrote to Chiniquy suggesting he calm down a bit: "Avoid all kinds of trivialities and unworthy details ... Guard against self-love, which is so subtle and dangerous above all in the midst of great successes." There is no evidence that Chiniquy took this advice. By the end of the year his converts had reached sixty thousand. Bookstores began to sell lithographs of the painting his former parishioners had commissioned and these became standard adornments in the parlours of French Canada.

The following April, in a monumental crusade, Chiniquy signed up eighteen thousand persons. Then, in a two-week crusade in June, he converted twelve thousand more to total abstinence. In Montreal, at the height of a great temperance fête, he was presented with a gold medal inscribed "in homage to his virtue, his zeal and his patriotism." He would wear it all his life. The third edition of his *Manuel* now contained his portrait along with biographical notes comparing him, once again to Saint Louis-de-Gonzague. In 1850, in recognition of his temperance crusade, the LaFontaine-Baldwin government of the United Canadas presented him with a gift of five hundred pounds, the equivalent of twenty-five hundred dollars, a remarkable sum for those days. There seemed no end to the triumphs of the Abbé Chiniquy; and yet, once again, his downfall was imminent.

Bishop Bourget was clearly aware of Chiniquy's weaknesses. In May 1851, when the abbé went to Illinois to investigate the need for a French-speaking priest to minister to the eleven thousand Quebecois who had settled there, Bourget admonished him to take strict precautions in his relationships with "personnes du sexe." In addition, he reproached Chiniquy for eating meat on Friday. The advice went unheeded. En route to Chicago the priest made amorous overtures to a girl of respectable family. He departed in haste when the Bishop of Detroit started to investigate.

On his return to Quebec he plunged into a new crusade, this one designed to boost French-Canadian immigration to what he felt were the greener pastures of Illinois. This did not help his deteriorating position with the Bishop of Montreal. The last thing Bourget wanted was a mass exodus of his flock to a foreign land. The bishop knew, of course, about Chiniquy's indiscretions at St. Pascal. Later on he had discovered that there had been three similar incidents at other parishes. On the heels of this knowledge came evidence of still *another* incident.

"We had had proof of M. Chiniquy's guilt for some time," Bourget was to write, "when a certain girl came to give evidence against him, testifying that she would feel repugnance to be confronted by him . . . ."

On September 28, 1851, Chiniquy was relieved of all his priestly functions. He demanded to know the name of his accuser but Bourget refused to give it. Chiniquy, who apparently knew her identity all along, confronted the girl and pressed her to retract. Instead, she repeated her testimony under oath. For Chiniquy this was the end. "I will hide the disgrace of my position in the farthest and most obscure corner of the U.S.," he wrote to Bourget.

The farthest and most obscure corner of the United States turned out to be the twin parishes of Bourbonnais and St. Anne, two relatively new French-Canadian settlements about fifty miles from Chicago, both badly in need of a French-speaking priest. The Bishop of Chicago, James Van De Velde, was in Montreal at the time searching for just such a man and speedily agreed to give Chiniquy a chance. All suggestion of scandal was hushed up; indeed, Bishop Bourget publicly presented his erring servant with a chalice and thanked him for his work, an action that the embattled abbé made much of. Chiniquy's parishioners, who gave him a moving farewell, believed that his departure for the United States was another example of his self-sacrifice. Soon Chiniquy was saying (and perhaps believing) that Bishop Bourget had offered him a handsome parish to try to prevent him from leaving, but that his resolve had not been shaken.

He was given the parish of St. Anne, a settlement of about a hundred families. And here, Chiniquy threw himself into a new kind of evangelism, and one that brought down anger from his native province. He actively began to persuade immigrants to leave Quebec for the United States. In the summer of 1852, he made a recruiting trip to French Canada and even announced, at Kamouraska, that he would say mass in his old church. But the curé refused him permission and his former neighbours treated him coldly, a considerable rebuke for one who had been raised in the parish.

Back in Illinois, he began to adopt habits that would result in his excommunication. His sexton, Godefroi Lambert, left a memoir, listing some of his transgressions. He ate meat on Friday, for instance, boldly declaring that the Pope would never hear of it. He talked lewdly to women. He even made advances to Lambert's wife and tried to convince her that sexual activities were not forbidden to priests. He consorted with "women of ill repute."

In 1853, a mysterious and disturbing event occurred at the neighbouring parish of Bourbonnais: the chapel, half completed, burned to the ground. There had been a controversy over this edifice. Chiniquy wanted it built of imposing stone; his bishop, Van De Velde, insisted that it be of simpler frame construction. A few days after the bishop visited Bourbonnais and laid down this edict, the wooden chapel was consumed by flames. Oddly, all the consecrated vessels had been removed to the parsonage just before the fire broke out. Suspicion naturally fell on Chiniquy but he claimed that he had actually seen the real arsonist escaping. When his parishioners insisted he name the criminal, Chiniquy backtracked; he had seen him, he explained, but only in his mind's eye. Later on, when he wrote a dramatic appeal to *Le Canadien* for funds to rebuild the chapel, a group of parishioners signed a letter to the paper saying that the donations would be surer of reaching their destination if they were addressed to the bishop and not the priest. Clearly, Chiniquy was on shaky ground; and it was growing shakier.

In 1854 a new bishop, the Irish Anthony O'Regan, replaced Van De Velde. He was not satisfied with the quality of some of the priests in his new charge and determined to weed out the poorest. In the midst of his investigations, which certainly included Chiniquy, the abbé found himself embroiled in a defamation lawsuit brought by a man named Peter Spink with whom Chiniquy had lodged on his first visit to Illinois. The two trials that followed were mainly notable for the fact that Chiniquy was defended by Abraham Lincoln, then a young Illinois lawyer. The first trial ended in a hung jury; during the second Chiniquy backed down completely and apologized. The apology was undoubtedly triggered by the fact that the new bishop had placed him under suspension.

The abbé fought back – and hard. In a letter to his parishioners he denied boldly that he had been suspended. In private letters to the bishop he pleaded for mercy, asked that the interdiction be lifted, and apologized. His public attitude showed no such humility. He told his flock that O'Regan's actions were based on the traditional Irish hatred for French Canadians; as a result the expatriates backed him to a man.

O'Regan's response was excommunication. On September 3, the vicar-general of the diocese arrived at St. Anne with two priests. Their carriage was met by a threatening crowd who hooted when he read the proclamation aloud and fixed it to the door of the church. Chiniquy blandly announced that the document was not legal: it was nothing more than an unsigned translation of the original. "If you think you can deal with me as a carter with his horse . . . you will soon see your error," he wrote to O'Regan.

He had only just begun to fight. A band of devotees, calling themselves the Société de Tondeurs (Shearers) appeared in the two parishes and began to shear the hair of those whom they suspected of disloyalty to their priest. The French-Canadian press rallied to Chiniquy's side, in the belief that O'Regan wanted to turn his church over to the Irish. When Bishop Bourget entered the fray, challenging Chiniquy to reveal the real reason why he left Canada, the priest retorted that a prostitute had been paid one hundred dollars to perjure herself against him. Bourget then sent two priests to Illinois to persuade Chiniquy to submit. They failed. A second delegation was somewhat more successful. They engineered the defection of the sexton, Lambert, and a good many other parishioners. But some two hundred families remained loyal to Chiniquy.

A year went by. Chiniquy continued to say mass in his church at St. Anne. In September 1857, O'Regan, worn out with worry, returned to Rome. Another year passed; Chiniquy was still in business. Then a new bishop, James Duggan, arrived to take over the Chicago diocese, determined to resolve the Chiniquy question once and for all.

On August 3, 1858, Bishop Duggan arrived in St. Anne accompanied by three priests. The quartet approached the public platform in the village square. There was Chiniquy, standing boldly beside the steps, hand out-stretched in greeting. The bishop ignored him, and ascended to the platform. Chiniquy followed and placed himself on Duggan's right. A stack of books containing press clippings favourable to the abbé, was on the platform. Chiniquy picked one up, opened it and attempted to show it to the bishop. Duggan looked at him coldly. "Leave your books," he said. "If you are not under interdiction I am going to place you under interdiction, and excommunicate you according to the rites."

The bishop then made the sign of the cross and pronounced sentence: "I declare to you in virtue of the authority of the Catholic Church invested in me that Mr. Chiniquy is truly and validly interdicted and excommunicated." The crowd booed lustily.

Duggan wanted no ambiguity. He repeated the sentence: "I again place Mr. Chiniquy under interdiction and excommunicate him so that no person here present will be able to pretend ignorance."

Ignoring the tumult that this caused, the bishop then turned and looked directly at Chiniquy: "Wretch, abandon these people you have deceived, go somewhere to make penance; and then I assure you that you will be pardoned and the church will again receive you in her breast."

By this time the crowd was in a perfect fury. Dozens surged forward to prevent the bishop from leaving the platform – the women "howling like mad dogs" and spitting on him, as the sheriff struggled to help him to his carriage.

The resilient Chiniquy was in no way discomfited by the ritual. In fact he allowed the publicity to work in his favour: as an ex-priest he soon became the object of intense interest to Protestants. In a few weeks he had founded a new sect, *L'église catholique chrétienne* with the same chapel of St. Anne as its headquarters. Chiniquy claimed the move had been divinely inspired – that he had decided to cut his own throat when the hand of God knocked the knife from his grasp and, while he was in a trance that followed, "my Saviour showed himself to my amazed eyes." The seeds of what would be a lifelong anti-Catholic crusade were sown at once; the cross and the statue of Mary were removed from the St. Anne chapel, the confession ritual was ended and the dogmas mocked.

Meanwhile another tempest was brewing. A Canadian Oblate father, Augustine-Alexandre Brunet, who had come to preach in the area, accused Chiniquy in the hearing of others of firing the Bourbonnais chapel. Chiniquy sued Brunet for libel. Brunet, who had returned to Canada, was found guilty *in absentia* and sentenced to pay Chiniquy damages of twenty-five hundred dollars or serve a prison term of seventeen years. Alas for Chiniquy, the verdict backfired on him. Brunet returned to Illinois at once, gave himself up, and announced he would serve the entire prison term before he paid a cent to the apostate. This was a financial blow to Chiniquy because, under the law of that time, he himself would have to contribute three dollars a week to the prisoner's upkeep.

Fortunately for Chiniquy a group of parishioners who had grown to like Brunet decided to free him. They got the sheriff drunk and proceeded to attempt to saw through the bars of the Oblate's cell. It was no easy task. They managed to remove one bar only, and, after much tugging and pulling got the plump

Brunet half way through the opening. At that point, the priest stuck fast and it was only with difficulty that he was finally freed and spirited, more than a little bruised and dented, across the Canadian border.

Whatever names one can apply to Chiniquy – hypocrite, publicity seeker, satyr, fanatic – none can deny his personal courage. Who but Chiniquy would have chosen this particular moment in his career to return to Quebec? But return he did, in January 1859, to make a preaching tour funded by Quebec Protestants.

The lions were waiting for their Daniel. He had trouble finding a hotel in Montreal which would accept his custom. No meeting place save one, the Mechanics' Hall, would give him a platform. Bishop Bourget ordered his flock to shun him. Crowds at his meetings chanted: "Go away Judas!" In Quebec City, four hundred angry neighbours surrounded the private home in which he was lodging and forced him to flee by carriage. In St.-Hilaire-de-Rouville his very life was threatened and he had to leave town hurriedly.

All this attention brought invitations to address Protestant gatherings in Boston, Philadelphia, Washington, Pittsburgh, New York, Chicago and Baltimore. Here he told of his battle with the Roman Church and collected money to combat food scarcities, which he claimed were afflicting his parish of St. Anne. The local paper denied there were any shortages but Chiniquy claims to have collected seventy-five thousand dollars and a vast quantity of food anyway. It is unlikely, in the light of later financial discrepancies, that the parish saw all of it.

In February 1860, Chiniquy became, officially, a minister in the Presbyterian Church of the United States. For each new member enrolled, the mother church gave a subsidy of ninety dollars. Chiniquy claimed that he enrolled two thousand members at St. Anne. Considering the size of the community, the figure seems inflated. He was rewarded by a trip to Europe where some saw him as a latter-day Luther. In Scotland, France, Switzerland and Italy, he solicited donations for "the seminary of St. Anne," an imaginary institution which Chiniquy described as having thirty-two dedicated students. He collected ten thousand dollars and returned to the United States where the Presbyterian Synod, puzzled by inquiries about the non-existent seminary, called him to account. Chiniquy refused to appear and once again found himself stripped of his ministry.

He turned now to the Presbyterians of Upper Canada, who welcomed him with open arms, formally attaching his parish to the presbytery of London. The Canadians decided that the affair of the ten thousand dollars was all a misunderstanding based on Chiniquy's unfamiliarity with Presbyterian ways. It was not too difficult for them to gloss over his transgressions since he was a very big catch indeed in a country bitterly divided by religious strife. In the battle with the Papists, Chiniquy was seen as a potential general.

The bitterness of the Protestant feeling against the Catholics in the united Canadas is difficult to grasp today. It had its root, of course, in the binational character of the country; but as Confederation approached, feelings grew more extreme as each side feared the other's interference in its own culture. An important factor in exacerbating the issue was the establishment in Upper Canada, achieved largely through the Lower Canadian vote, of separate schools for Roman Catholics. In addition, there was the growing nativist sentiment against the waves of immigrants arriving from Europe; many of these were Roman Catholics.

The focus for this hatred was the Grand Orange Lodge of British North America, founded at Brockville in 1830. In Orange eyes, the Church of Rome was a sinister and secret international conspiracy, bent on controlling the minds of men through the confessional. Papists in Canada were viewed much as Jews were in Hitler's Germany or communists in McCarthy's America. Orange demonstrations on the Twelfth of July were often violent affairs as Catholics and Protestants clashed in the streets. On July 12, 1843, for instance, men were killed in an attack on the Orange Hall in Kingston. Six years later, on the Twelfth, there were a dozen deaths and countless injuries in street riots in St. John's. The demonstrations on July 12, 1862, just after Chiniquy joined the Canadian Presbyterian Church (he, too, was to become an Orangeman) were said to be the largest on record.

Chiniquy fell enthusiastically in with the church's plan to use him as an effective and energetic weapon against the Romanists. In 1863, he published an inflammatory tract, *The Church of Rome Is the Enemy of the Holy Virgin and Jesus Christ*. In 1864, he married one of his servants, Euphémie Allard; she was to present him with three children. In 1867, he published a brochure attacking the concept of the immaculate conception. In 1869, he mounted a speaking tour of Prince Edward Island on the subject of papal indulgences. The man who had once been the best-known Roman Catholic priest in French Canada was on his way to becoming the best-known Protestant minister in English Canada.

In 1873, the Presbyterian Synod decided to put Chiniquy in charge of a new campaign to undertake the systematic conversion of French Canadians. Before moving to Montreal, the former

Chiniquy's curious career paralleled and was fostered by the twin controversies of the nineteenth century.

Left: *The cover of his book,* The Priest, the Woman and the Confessional, *which played on anti-Catholic prejudices.*

Below: *The temperance campaign he helped mount in 1840 was still going strong almost half a century later as these cartoons from* Grip *(1887) show.*

MISS CANADA, BARMAID.

LET THE PEOPLE UNITE TO SWEEP THIS CURSE FROM OUR COUNTRY.

YES! THEY'D BETTER ATTEMPT A RESCUE!

PUBLIC OPINION HAVING DETERMINED TO "CLEAN OUT" THE LIQUOR TRAFFIC, THE POLITICIANS WILL DO WELL TO HEED THE CRY OF "HANDS OFF," WHEN PROHIBITIONISTS FIND THEM PATCHING THE LAWS IN THE INTERESTS OF THE LIQUOR MEN.

abbé embarked on a six-month speaking tour of England, collecting twenty-five thousand dollars for himself in fees. Protestantism, he was discovering, was more rewarding – at least financially – than Catholicism.

He moved with his family to Montreal at the beginning of 1875 and began preaching on Craig Street, bringing to his evangelism all the zeal which had once marked his temperance crusades. So much violence accompanied his services that, at the beginning, three hundred men were required to protect him from injury. The same year he published a major work, *The Priest, the Woman and the Confessional*. This turned out to be a fairly gamey piece of literature. Chiniquy peppered his polemic with racy accounts of priests who became so aroused by the confessions of their feminine parishioners that they themselves pursued a heady course which brought about their downfall. No doubt Chiniquy was describing his own former condition and, when he said that enforced celibacy contributed to the problem, he was probably right. After his marriage there is no further suggestion that he strayed from the path. As for the book, it was an enormous success, going into fifty editions in two languages by 1892.

The Roman Catholic Church was predictably enraged. Bishop Bourget published a lengthy pastoral letter attacking the author and his work. An anonymous Catholic pamphlet described with relish Chiniquy's future death and even included a deathbed description in which foam issued from the mouth of the dying renegade while a diabolical voice chortled: "Yet another for my kingdom!" But at sixty-six, Chiniquy was very much alive. Between 1875 and 1878 he boasted of having converted seven thousand French Canadians to Protestantism.

In 1878, he began a long series of hugely successful and often tumultuous speaking tours. After a turn around the western United States he travelled to Australia, New Zealand and Tasmania at the invitation of the Orange Society of Australia. His energy was prodigious. He was approaching seventy and yet he managed to give seven hundred speeches over a two-year period and to collect forty thousand dollars. He was nothing if not inflammatory. One town required a full four days of martial law to calm it down after Chiniquy's appearance.

Advancing years did nothing to still those inner fires. Back in Canada, in June 1884, a crowd gathered outside the Protestant church in which he was preaching in Quebec City. Stones began to crash through the windows. Chiniquy escaped by carriage to the railway station. The enraged crowd pursued him, and Chiniquy was forced to hide in a trunk while awaiting the train. The mob tore his carriage to pieces.

Not in the least daunted, the stubborn old man then churned out an eight-hundred-page autobiography. *Fifty Years in the Church of Rome*. It was an enormous bestseller. By 1892 it was in its twentieth edition and had appeared in French, English, Italian, Spanish, Swedish, Czech, Dutch, German and even Chinese. The Protestant world greeted its publication with wild enthusiasm. One leading churchman wrote that "I do not believe there exists in our time a Protestant work more important or more alive with interest."

Chiniquy's own version of his career was not always in accord with the known facts. His treatment of Abraham Lincoln, for instance, suggests how he made free with the truth. Chiniquy implied that the Great Emancipator had sided with him in his struggle with the Catholic Church, writing that Lincoln had acted for him in his victory over Bishop O'Regan. Lincoln, of course, had done nothing of the sort; he had been his lawyer in the two abortive suits involving Spink and there was certainly no victory there.

But this was only the first volume of a longer memoir. At the age of eighty Chiniquy was scribbling away at a second tome, *Forty Years in the Church of Christ*, and continuing to make converts among Quebec Catholics. His most famous convert was Louis-Joseph-Amédée Papineau, the son of the famous rebel of 1837. Papineau insisted that Chiniquy officiate at the conversion ceremony because he considered him "le Luther du Canada."

When this event took place, Chiniquy was eighty-five years old, still energetic, in possession of all his faculties, and, as his photograph shows, remarkably well preserved. (How his religious enemies must have gritted their teeth at this *prima facie* evidence of the fruits of sin!) Eighteen months later he was off on another lecture tour of England. He made eighty-five speeches and would have made more but illness forced a change in his itinerary. Sick or not, however, the old man made a point of visiting Luther's tomb at Wittenburg.

Stubbornly, he refused to die. Returning home he divided his time between his house in Montreal and his country place at St. Louise on the south shore of the St. Lawrence. It was almost three years later, in January 1899, that he fell ill and it became clear that the end was near. Would he, on his deathbed, re-embrace his former faith? There was widespread speculation on that question. The Catholic Church did what it could to encourage a conversion. The Archbishop of Montreal, Paul Bruchési, wrote a letter of encouragement to Chiniquy's son-in-law to which the old man himself replied with unaccustomed gentleness: "I am grateful to the archbishop ... but I have definitely left the church of Rome. I am perfectly happy in the faith of Jesus Christ ... ."

The détente was temporary. In the final days of his life the old fire returned and Chiniquy dictated a religious testament to be sent to the newspapers and to the archbishop after his death, in which he made one last violent attack on the Catholic Church. Even while he was dying there was a brief, inconclusive struggle for his soul. Two nuns sneaked into the house, apparently in a last-ditch attempt at conversion, but were politely shown the door by his family.

Thus expired the Reverend Charles Chiniquy, at the age of eighty-nine. In death as in life he attracted multitudes. His body was laid out in state in his home and more than ten thousand persons filed past the bier. It was a mixed crowd; for once Catholics and Protestants were united in a common obeisance – or was it curiosity? Certainly, the controversy that swirled around him in life followed him to the grave. The Catholic periodical, *L'Evénement*, reserved no niceties for its editorial comment on the deceased. "Chiniquy," it declared, "leaves to history a soiled name."

He was interred in the Protestant Cimitière de la Montagne. Oral tradition has it that he was buried standing up and that his tombstone was cleft in two by a divine curse. With Chiniquy, anything seems possible: but, like so much that was written by and about the embattled former abbé, this, too, must be taken with more than a grain of salt.

8
The Overlanders

The days of the great gold rushes are long gone. One cannot embark on a stampede in a twin-engine Otter or a helicopter. The gold country has been mapped and settled, the free colours are all panned away. There are no mysterious Eldorados left to lure romantics across a wild terrain, no dizzy Chilkoots to test the mettle of the tyro pioneer. Like so many other communicable diseases, gold fever has been wiped out; there is nowhere for the virus to breed.

But there was a time when the slightest whisper of a strike produced in otherwise sensible people a kind of insanity which, in a curious way, was also a kind of high courage. Men and women would dare anything for gold; or at least that was the excuse. Perhaps the real lure was simply the age-old desire for adventure beyond the horizon. No matter how far off the bonanza might be (and it was always desperately far), no matter how weary the route to reach it (and it was always hideously weary), the hordes pushed off, convincing themselves that the wealth of the ages lay just over the next hill. Gold fever produced a kind of mass blindness; its victims were ready to swallow the most preposterous absurdities on pure faith. Like supplicants at a camp meeting, or marks at a carnival, they *wanted* to believe.

Consider, for instance, this advertisement, published in English newspapers in the spring of 1862 at the height of the Cariboo gold rush:

> The British Columbia Overland Transit Company will punctually dispatch ... at 12 noon from Glasgow – in the first class and powerful screw steamship *United Kingdom,* 1,200 tons burden, 300 horsepower, James Clarke commander, a party of first and

second class passengers for Quebec, Canada, and over the Grand Trunk Railway and continuous lines of railway to Chicago and St. Paul and via the Red River Settlements, in covered wagons, to British Columbia.

This is the speediest, safest and most economical route to the gold diggings. The land transit is through a lovely country unequalled for its beauty and salubrity of climate. More than half the distance from Quebec is by railway.

Through fares, £42 from England to British Columbia; saloon berths £5 extra.

Letters received from the agents in Canada announce that a first spring party of 52 in number have left for British Columbia by this route. About 1,000 carts annually travel along this line. There are numerous posts, missions and trading stations from the Red River Settlements along the Saskatchewan, now discovered to abound in vast gold deposits, to the Rocky Mountains. The route is constantly travelled with perfect safety. Full particulars can be had at the offices, 6 Cothall Court....

The enterprise was a hoax. The company, which made one of the harshest of overland adventures seem like a pleasant Sunday outing (it claimed the journey would take only five weeks), welshed on almost all of its promises, as those who were caught up in the scheme discovered as soon as they reached Toronto. The climate might sometimes be salubrious, the scenery might indeed be unequalled; but when the rails ended men and women who had never saddled a horse found themselves on their own, facing a journey of more than four months across empty and often vicious terrain – a thousand miles of friendless prairie, and at the far end the implacable wall of the mountains. But such was the pull of gold that many of those who had fallen for the hoax refused to quit. As the *Globe* reported: "Though not pleased with the conduct of the company, the party now in Toronto are resolved to push on like brave men and we cannot help thinking they are in the right."

One of these Englishmen of whom we have record was a young nineteen-year-old biology student from Cornwall, named Eustace Pattison. His photograph in the Archives of British Columbia shows a Byronic youth, with a pageboy haircut, lidded eyes, sensitive nostrils and full lips. His pose is languorous and unselfconscious; he seems, indeed, to be day dreaming and perhaps he was. Contemporary accounts reinforce the impression left by the portrait: he was described by his friends as refined, shy and not very gregarious. What, then, impelled him to travel almost halfway round the globe in a mad rush for treasure? The gold? Or the romance?

Whatever the reason, young Pattison and his English companions became part of a larger group of Canadians travelling together for mutual protection and convenience who crossed Canada in the summer of 1862 and who are known to history as the Overlanders. Starting in mid-April, they travelled more than thirty-five hundred miles by rail, steamer, Red River cart, horseback, foot, canoe and raft to reach the gateway to the Cariboo goldfields in late September. The wonder is not that so many managed to reach their objective, but that only five perished in the attempt.

It is not possible to follow all of them as they rattle on greaseless axles through the waving buffalo grass. Nine separate parties were organized in the towns of Ontario and Quebec in the spring of '62 when news of the Cariboo strike trickled through to the east. These were joined, in St. Paul and Fort Garry, by other goldseekers, eager to reach British Columbia. Out of Fort Garry, the Overlanders coalesced into three main parties, one of which split in two at Tête Jaune Cache. Before that objective was reached some had defected and a natural leader had emerged, a teacher from Queenston, Ontario, named Thomas McMicking. His party's long odyssey is the best documented of all the Overlanders'; it is also the most eventful.

McMicking's portrait, taken when he was a student at Knox College, also survives in the archives but there is no languor in his pose. He sits bolt upright, gazing directly at the camera, a book on his knee, an academic gown over his shoulders. His Celtic features are marked by a strong jawline, a determined mouth and clear, unwavering eyes. The effect is one of serenity and confidence, twin qualities which were to make McMicking the undisputed leader and hero of the overland expedition. McMicking, who was thirty-three, was accompanied by his nineteen-year-old brother, Robert, who had been working for the Montreal Telegraph Company.

McMicking originally led the Queenston party of twenty-four men, a quasi-military group like all the others, with a tight set of rules and a five-dollar organization fee. Values change; five dollars in those days was for many more than a week's wages. The total per man cost of the 141-day journey across Canada, for McMicking's followers – including supplies and transportation – came to $97.65, all found.

All these men had a strong sense of community. In the 1860s, Canada was not a mobile nation. Men and women were born, schooled, married and buried in the same village; many never travelled more than a few miles from their birthplace. Friendships made as a child lasted for the rest of their lives. It is not surprising that the men from Acton, Huntington, Queenston and the other communities who started off together in April, shared the same rafts in the final dangerous dash down the Fraser and Thompson rivers in September. This kind of teamwork sets the story of the Overlanders apart from most other Canadian adventures, for this was probably the first community enterprise in which men worked in loose coalition, democratically organized for their own ends.

Steam travel, a century ago, was haphazard, uncomfortable and tedious. The McMicking party took more than a month to reach Fort Garry from St. Catharines in fits and starts, using a variety of railroads, steamboats and stagecoaches.

Consider, for instance, the trip to St. Paul, Minnesota. On April 23, at 11:40 a.m., the party left St. Catharines for Detroit by Great Western Railway. They arrived at 9:30 that evening and stayed overnight. On April 24, they boarded another railway, the Detroit and Milwaukee, and travelled 186 miles to Grand Haven on Lake Michigan. There they changed to a steamer, the *Detroit*, which took them 86 miles to Milwaukee, which they reached at two the following morning. At five that afternoon (April 27) they boarded the Milwaukee and LaCrosse Railway for a 201-mile journey to LaCrosse on the Mississippi River. They reached it at 10 p.m. on April 28. Here, after another four-hour wait, they transferred to the steamer *Frank Steele* which took them upriver to St. Paul.

St. Paul, then a town of ten thousand, was at the end of organized transport and also of civilization. Here, the various parties of Overlanders found their number swelled by eighteen young Englishmen, including Eustace Pattison, who had been lured by the B.C. Transit advertisements. There were something like two hundred people moving through St. Paul, heading for Fort Garry, and these all had to be transported, literally by stages, to Georgetown, the frontier village on the Red River, where a steamboat was being readied for them. Since the stagecoach could hold no more than ten at a time, the process went on for days.

In Georgetown there was another maddening wait. The steamboat, *International,* was not completed. Workmen hammered away on her superstructure, while the goldseekers, their numbers swelling daily, hunted, fished, and played ball. Finally, the sternwheeler was ready. There were so many passengers that scores had to sleep on the decks. The ship almost came to grief when, attempting to navigate a tight bend she crashed into the bank, smashed the pilot house and knocked off two funnels. But at last, on May 26, she reached Fort Garry. The McMicking party had been on the road for thirty-three days and the real journey had yet to begin.

Gold fever gripped Fort Garry. Residents and newcomers who had arrived by canoe or on foot clamoured to join one of the parties heading west. One of these was a German immigrant named Augustus Schubert. Schubert had left his native Dresden some years before, emigrated to the United States and married an Irish girl from County Down. Before coming north to Fort Garry, the two had run a beer hall in St. Paul. Now they had three children and Catherine Schubert was again pregnant. But her husband, wandering among the tents of the Overlanders at Long Lake, became obsessed with the idea of trekking to the goldfields. McMicking had no objection to taking him but balked when Mrs. Schubert appeared and insisted that she and the children share the perils of the journey with him. She must have been persuasive because McMicking waived his strict no-woman rule and agreed to take the entire family along. Had he known about Mrs. Schubert's condition he might not have been so accommodating. As it was he never had cause to regret his decision. As one of the members of his group was to write: "Her presence in the company helped to cultivate a kindly and more manly treatment of man to man." Equally important, perhaps, is the fact that the presence of a domestic group may easily have made the Overlanders' passage through Indian country easier; clearly, this was not a war party. The Schuberts packed their belongings in a covered spring democrat, drawn by an ox and a cow, and devised two basket cradles for the older children, Mary and Augustus, Jr. Mrs. Schubert rode horseback with a child in a cradle slung to each side of her saddle. The younger boy, Jimmie, aged three, was carried by his father.

By the time the Overlanders left Fort Garry, the nine groups from the various eastern Canadian communities had become three. McMicking's, with one hundred and thirty-eight men, plus Mrs. Schubert and her three children, was by far the largest. It also included Eustace Pattison, who had joined the Toronto group in St. Paul but switched to McMicking's party at Fort Garry.

A mass meeting, chaired by McMicking, hammered out an organization. Under the captain, there would be a committee of thirteen, each of these a leader of a sub-group. Schedules, starting times, hours and rate of travel, relations with the Indians and the arrangement of the wagon train were all laid down. On June 5, the party set off for Fort Edmonton, nine hundred miles to the west.

Like a great, jointed snake, the train of ninety-seven carts and one hundred and ten animals stretched for half a mile across the prairie, travelling for ten hours a day at a speed of two and a half miles an hour. At nights the carts were drawn up in a triangle,

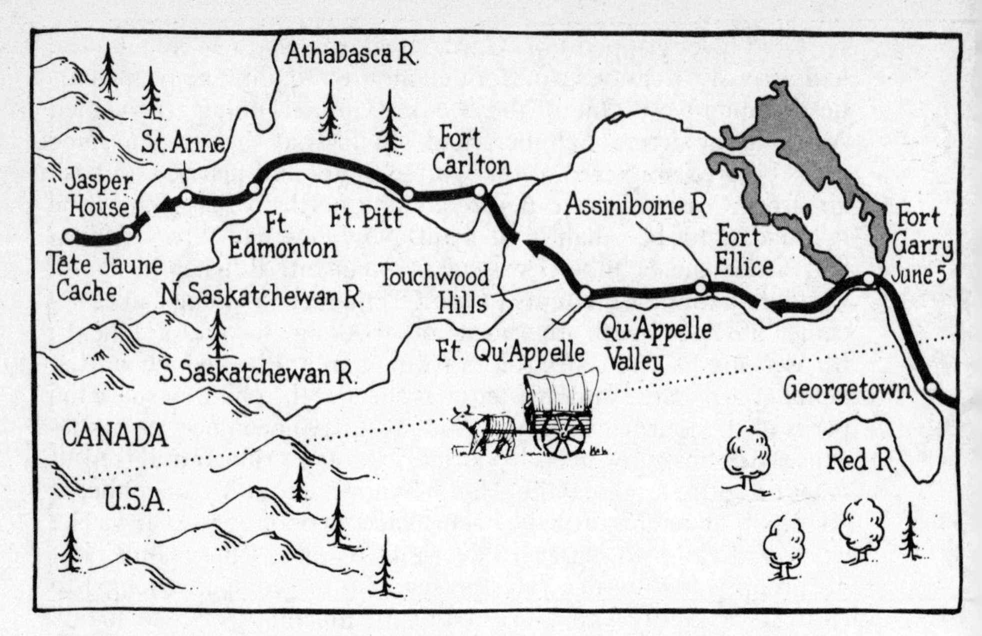

shafts out, animals tethered within the makeshift corral, guards posted. The Overlanders rose at 2:30 each morning, pushed off at three, halted at five for two hours to breakfast and feed the animals, halted again for a lunch break at eleven, and set out again from one until six in the evening. Sundays were sacrosanct, for these men took their religion seriously. On the Sabbath they halted, sang hymns, prayed aloud, listened to the scriptures and appointed one of their number to preach a sermon.

There wasn't a single bridge between the Red River and the Rockies – the Hudson's Bay Company had seen to that; the great fur enterprise did not want settlers moving into its territory and this was one method of dissuading them. To cross the Assiniboine at Fort Ellice, McMicking's people borrowed a crude Hudson's Bay scow attached to a rawhide rope that stretched from bank to bank. It was only large enough to hold a single cart and ox. That meant more than a hundred crossings before the entire party was ferried over: it took six hours.

In the broad valley of the Qu'Appelle the rains had turned the long, steep slopes into greasy slides. Men and animals slipped, slid and were maimed. One unfortunate, W. W. Morrow of Montreal, was dragged downhill by his own ox; at the bottom a cartwheel ran over his head. A doctor patched the unconscious man together and he continued on with the party.

On June 18, the Overlanders awoke to find the prairie white with frost, the ice thick in the waterbuckets, and their guide gone:

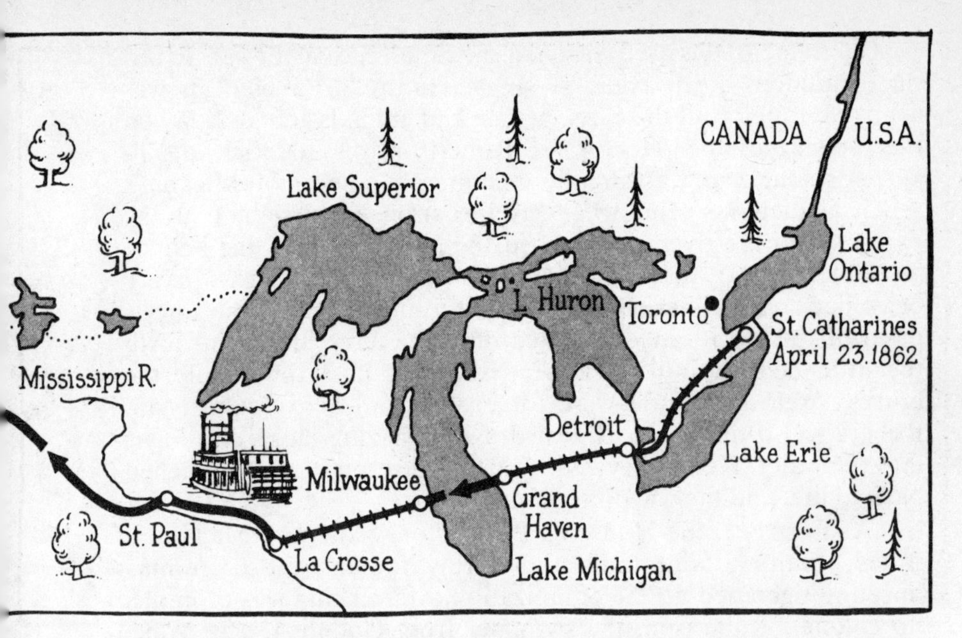

from this point on they would have to find their own way to Edmonton. But spirits remained high. The country was indeed lovely, and in the Touchwood Hills there were wild strawberries.

Then, on June 25, they left the shelter of the woods and burst out onto an immense and trackless plain. Few had thought to husband their fuel supply and not all had brought nets to fight off the torture of the mosquitoes that swarmed over them. In spite of the rules, some groups began to scramble to reach the head of the wagon train: it was the last ones to cross a ford or a mudhole who had the most trouble. Some even abandoned their meals and rushed for the carts with cups of tea or pancakes still in their hands. Tempers began to fray; small, ignoble quarrels flared. Sunday could not come soon enough; the day of rest served a healing purpose. McMicking wrote that "the vigour with which our journey would be prosecuted, and the cordiality and good feeling that characterized our intercourse after our accustomed rest on the first day of the week, are sufficient evidence to us that the law of the Sabbath is of physical as well as moral obligation, and that its precepts cannot be violated with impunity."

McMicking never stooped to squabble. A man of principle, serious, a bit pedantic, he pressed forward, always reasonable, always forceful enough to command the majority of the expedition. He was, said one who knew him, "a true Christian gentleman, a genial companion, a ready writer and speaker, and withal a man of strong character."

On June 30, the party reached the South Saskatchewan River, three hundred yards wide. A single Hudson's Bay bateau was available to ferry all the carts, people and animals across. It lay on the far side of the river. A. C. Robertson, of Goderich, a jail-keeper's son, who was already emerging as one of McMicking's senior lieutenants, and who was the strongest swimmer of the party, swam the river and fetched the boat over with the help of one other man. It took ten hours to move the party across. Every beast had to be unharnessed, every cart unloaded, and the wheels pried off before it could be fitted onto the ferry. Back and forth the little boat laboured, carrying six carts at a time while the horses, oxen and cattle were forced to swim across. One man, Robert Kelso of Acton, almost drowned hazing laggard animals into the water. He was revived by artificial respiration, pummelled back to life, and the wagon train moved on.

At Fort Pitt, the Hudson's Bay factor warned McMicking of rough country, faint trails and unruly Indians ahead. A mass meeting tightened up the organization. McMicking was promoted to colonel; Robertson, the swimmer from Goderich, was named captain. The meeting decided that the party would split into four groups who would travel together in close order and that a guide would be hired to lead the way to Edmonton.

And then came the rain! It began in earnest a day out of Fort Pitt and did not let up for eleven days. No one who has not camped out night after night in an unending downpour can comprehend the misery this means: clothes soaked, tents saturated and leaking, blankets forever damp, provisions soggy, dry wood non-existent. On Saturday, July 12, the deluge grew so heavy that the party could not move. On Monday, it was forced to halt after two hours because the guide could not see the trail. Yet, in the midst of all this soggy discomfort, there was merriment. On July 16, after supper, in the centre of the corral, thirty-two Overlanders formed a musical society complete with vocalists, violinists, flautists and others. While the rain pelted down, the hastily organized orchestra and choir entertained the camp.

Now the rivers were transformed into torrents and even the smallest creeks were too dangerous to ford. Between July 18 and July 20, the party built eight bridges. The shortest was forty feet long; some exceeded one hundred feet. Once, when no trees were available, McMicking ordered the swollen creek filled with carts to form a passage.

July 19 was the worst day of all. Most of the party had been neck-deep in water and every one was soaked to the skin; every stitch of clothing, packed or worn, was dripping wet. In the tents the water was four inches deep. Men used wagon boards, piles of brush, buffalo robes – anything to raise themselves above the ooze. The following day was the Lord's but, for once, the Overlanders were forced to break their Sabbath rule. They threw a sixty-foot bridge across a roaring creek and fled to higher ground.

There was one further obstacle: a two-hundred-foot ravine with a foaming torrent at the bottom, its sides so steep that no man or animal could keep his feet while sliding downward. Trees had to be felled for a bridge, a trail opened up, and carts and cattle let down the flanks by ropes. On the far side, one of the men riding ahead spotted the palisades of Fort Edmonton in the distance and the party, revived by the spectacle, broke into cheers. Wrote McMicking:

"During the preceding eleven days our clothing had never been dry, we had just passed through what we considered a pretty tough time, and the toil-worn, jaded, forlorn and tattered appearance of the company was in striking and amusing contrast with our appearance a few months before; so marked, indeed, was the change that our most intimate friends at home would scarcely have recognized us. But our courage was still unbroken and, although we had been so much longer on the road than we anticipated, we had yet full confidence in our ability to reach the El Dorado of our hopes...."

The inhabitants of Fort Edmonton, cut off from the world as if on another planet, greeted them eagerly for news. Here the Overlanders learned that the carts must be abandoned; the land rose steeply toward the mountains and only packhorses could make the journey. The prices of animals and saddles rose almost immediately on this intelligence, and some members of the group were forced to sell provisions to raise money. The Schuberts, for instance, sold their cow. But, like many others, they kept their ox as a pack animal; there weren't enough horses to go round.

Archibald Thompson from Queenston panned for gold in the river and claimed he'd found some colours; these were almost certainly mica. But a man named Timoleon Love, who said he was a seasoned prospector but who was, in actuality, a charlatan, insisted there were riches to be found on the eastern slopes of the Rockies. Twenty-five men peeled off from the main party to follow this will-o'-the-wisp; none found so much as a grain of gold.

For the remainder, the trail would lead through the Yellowhead Pass, the traditional fur traders' route to the interior of British Columbia. On July 29, the Overlanders broke camp and headed west in high spirits, refreshed at riding horseback, sure that they would reach the goldfields in a matter of weeks. Actually, the worst part of the journey lay before them.

They had one hundred and forty pack animals with them, but none knew how to adjust a saddle, balance a load or secure it with a diamond hitch. They learned these things on the trail. At St. Anne's they faced a river with all the timber on the opposite side. Four men caught two oxen, tied their clothes to the horns, drove them into the freezing waters, hung onto their tails, breasted the torrent and felled a gigantic poplar tree on which the others crossed. Here the unfortunate Morrow, still scarred by his earlier accident, was battered again: his steer bolted, he clung to its horns and was thrown to the ground, where the animal promptly stamped all over the face that had been bruised weeks before by a cartwheel. Morrow, however, was determined to get to the Cariboo. He recovered after eleven days at the St. Anne Mission and joined a second party of Overlanders following behind.

The trail grew worse. The forests were so dense that an advance party had to chop a passage through the coniferous jungle. Somebody had waited behind in Edmonton for the mail from Fort Garry. He rejoined the party on August 2, with a copy of the *Globe* of May 16. It was full of reports about the American Civil War. Great Britain had just recognized the Confederate states as belligerents. This was the last news the party had of the outside world until they reached the Cariboo.

In the chill mornings, the dew, freezing as it fell, hung from the leaves like icicles. One river was too deep to ford and too broad to bridge: everybody was forced to swim across. In the spruce swamps, the horses could only flounder until their packs were removed. The men themselves became beasts of burden, leaving behind them a trail of discarded tools. At the McLeod River two men, trying to ford on foot, were swept away and almost drowned, but saved at the last instant by their comrades.

Then, on August 13, the Overlanders got their first magic glimpse of the Rockies, one hundred miles ahead of them, the snowy peaks floating like clouds in the brilliant blue sky. They were enraptured; none had ever seen a mountain before. Five days later, camped in the foothills, McMicking could exclaim over "a view at once sublimely grand and overpowering."

The most dangerous section of trail lay dead ahead along the south side of the Athabasca River, up a high shoulder of Mount Miette, "with its cold and craggy cliffs, crowned with eternal snows." Near the top, the narrow defile led between a perpendicular wall of rock and a dizzy precipice. At fourteen hundred feet a packhorse missed his footing and tumbled four hundred feet down the cliffside; he was hauled back up, miraculously unharmed. But later two more slid over the side and were lost.

The McMicking party was moving through history. Around

them lay various crumbling monuments to the fur trade. From Mount Miette they could see the deserted Hudson's Bay post of Jasper House on the north side of the Athabasca. They passed it at midday and the next day happened upon the rotting logs that marked the site of Henry House, built in 1810. In one two-hour period that day, they crossed the raging torrent of the Miette River seven times. The following day, August 22, they passed over the continental divide and entered the crown colony of British Columbia.

They had expected to reach the Cariboo in two months from Fort Garry. Already they had spent three months on the trail and were only at the midpoint of the mountains. Their stock of food was perilously low; indeed, their pemmican had run out. Some parties slaughtered their oxen; the Schuberts killed one of their horses; others shot squirrels, a porcupine, and several small birds. On August 24, a Sunday, unable to find grazing land for the stock, they again broke the Sabbath stricture and travelled all day. With heavy irony, McMicking reported on their supper that night: "We dined this day upon a dish so delicate and rare that it might have tempted the palate of Epicurus himself; so nice, indeed, was it, that I have some little hesitation in naming it lest we might be censured for living too luxuriously by the way. It was a roasted skunk, which our guide prepared and served us in true Indian style."

Pastures became more difficult to find. The animals were beginning to fail. A few miles east of Tête Jaune Cache, a horse slipped into the Fraser and drowned, taking all his pack of cooking utensils with him. At this point the provisions were very low; many of the Overlanders had run out of flour and were subsisting on dried beef; Shuswap Indians appeared with fresh fish and serviceberries; the travellers were glad to trade ammunition, clothing – anything – for food.

The Cariboo beckoned; but where was the Cariboo? The Shuswaps had never heard of it. Most of the easterners had thought of a pass as an easy way through the mountains. Instead they were faced with a forested slope, flanked on both sides by huge precipices and torrential cataracts. It was all very beautiful in midsummer; windflowers, mountain roses, bluebells and cornflowers sparkled in the sunlight; the fragrance of grass and hemlocks rose sweetly to the nostrils. But there was danger ahead where the Fraser River lurked – that barbarous waterway whose discoverer had named it, for the best of reasons, the Bad River.

Ten days' travel down the Fraser, the Indians said, lay the trading post of Fort George. But the route was dangerous in the extreme, a nightmare of canyons and white water. The Indians shook their heads sadly at the idea of the Overlanders taking to the river. "Poor white men," they said. "No more see white men."

An alternative route lay directly to the south. Fourteen days' travel to the headwaters of the North Thompson would bring the travellers to the white man's pack road, a foot deep in snow. Was this the trail from Oregon to the Cariboo? The party was in a quandary. If they went south, they might be frozen in for the winter before they reached the goldfields. If they followed the Fraser in its great loop west, north and south again, they might all drown. After much palaver the party split in two. The larger group, under McMicking, would take a few cattle and challenge the Fraser in rafts and canoes. A smaller group, including the Schubert family (Mrs. Schubert was now heavy with child) would take most of the stock and head south for the Thompson.

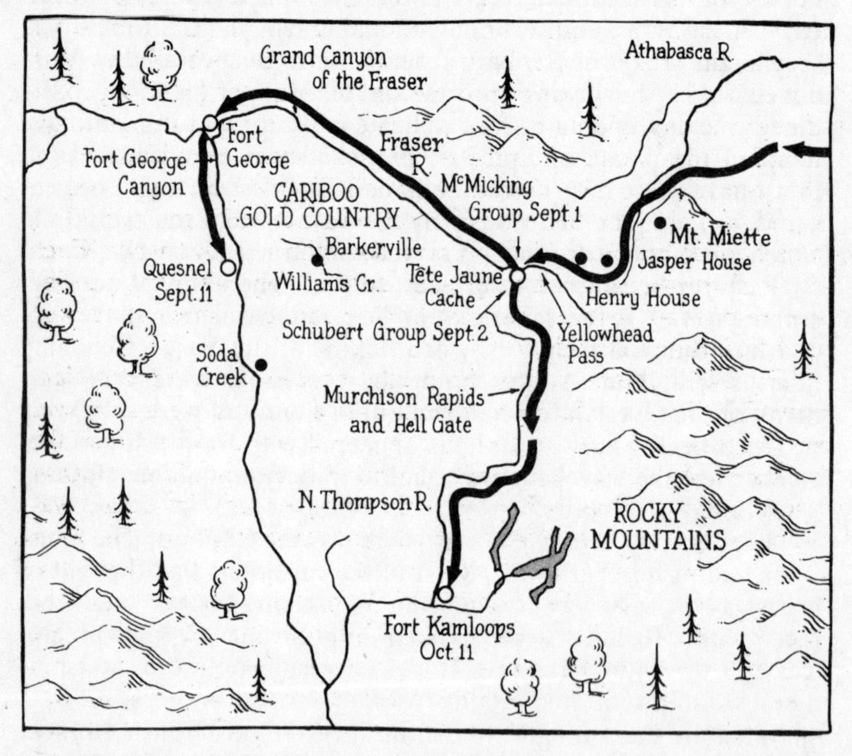

These were different men from the eager, optimistic goldseekers who had set out so jauntily the previous May. Exhausted but hardened by travel, their faces gaunt, burned by sun and wind, their clothes in shreds, their food heavily rationed, they seemed to have lived a lifetime in a single summer. Look at them now as they prepared to face, without a tremor, a river that had for half a century daunted the most experienced explorers. The early fur traders had plunged down these hazardous rapids in canoes manned by seasoned Indian guides, but now a group of greenhorn easterners have arrived intent on running the rapids without any help in hollow cottonwood logs or on huge rafts with fences on the sides and cattle tethered to the decks.

The rafts they built were forty feet long and twenty feet wide. The men from Huntington, Ontario, fastened two rafts together – eighty-five feet of timber, enough to hold nine head of cattle plus passengers and freight. Some stitched buffalo hides together and stretched them over wooden frames. Many took live animals with them; others butchered their oxen and took the meat. With the Indians standing on the bank and uttering doleful warnings, the McMicking party set off down the river on September 1, led by Eustace Pattison and two men from Toronto in a big cottonwood canoe. The smaller party left the following day for the Thompson.

Thomas McMicking was captain of a thirty-two-man raft named for his home town of Queenston. Most of his fellow passengers were members of that original group. It was the same on the other rafts: each group was bound together by a sense of its own community. The current was a swift five knots, the course serpentine, the channel narrow, the weather cold and wet. The men cooked meals on the raft and sometimes ran at night. Each party chose its own camping time, so that the rafts kept passing and re-passing one another while the lighter canoes shot well ahead of the main body.

Eustace Pattison's canoe reached the rapids of the Grand Canyon of the Fraser a full two days ahead of the leading raft. It was obvious that the hollowed-out cottonwood log could not run the rapids, so the three men attached a lariat to its snout and tried to line it along the bank. The tow rope snapped and the canoe was swept away, carrying with it everything they owned. For two days Pattison and his two comrades lay out in the clothes they wore without food or bedding, exposed to rain and cold. The exposure began to tell on the nineteen-year-old. By the time the next craft arrived, forty-eight hours later, he was in a bad way.

Two canoes, lashed together, appeared in the white water, manned by Robertson, of Goderich, and two fellow townsmen. The snarling river seized their craft, ripped it apart and capsized both boats. Robertson, being the best swimmer, told the other two to hang onto one of the upturned canoes while he swam to shore to get help. Off he struggled only to be swept away into the icy waters, never to be seen again, a loss that shocked the party when the news was known. The canoe drifted onto a shoal in midstream. Shortly after that the big double Huntington raft appeared; these men had had the foresight to equip their craft with a canoe which they now used to pick up the stranded men. McMicking's raft, not far behind, picked up the ailing Pattison and his shivering companions.

When McMicking first approached the rapids at dawn on September 6 – the only warning was the terrible roaring of the waters breaking the morning stillness – he barely had time to get his raft ashore before being drawn into the maelstrom. The party pondered the situation, examining the shoreline for possible portages. But there was no way around: "We saw no alternative; we had either to run the rapids or starve where we were." Finally it was decided that ten men would remain on board the raft to handle the sweeps. The others would work their way along the shoreline, inching along narrow granite ledges, above the torrent, or taking hesitant advantage of the shaky footholds of treetrunks that the Indians had built where the cliffs fell sheer to the water's edge. The raft was untied and pushed out into the racing current. McMicking described the scene:

"Onward they sped like an arrow. They seemed to be rushing into the very jaws of death. Before them on the right rose a rocky reef against which the furious flood was lashing itself into foam, threatening instant and unavoidable destruction and on the other side a seething and eddying whirlpool was ready to engulf in its greedy vortex any mortal who might venture within its reach. With fearful velocity they were hurried along directly towards the fatal rock. Their ruin seemed inevitable. It was a moment of painful suspense. Not a word was spoken except the necessary orders of the pilot, which were distinctly heard on shore above the din and tumult of the scene. Now was the critical moment. Everyone bent manfully to his oar. The raft shot closely past the rock, tearing away the stern rowlock, and glided safely into the eddy below. The agony was over. The gauntlet had been run and all survived. The issue of the ordeal was announced by an involuntary cheer from the brave hearts aboard the raft, which was heartily responded to by those on shore."

All the others rafts shot the rapids safely using similar techniques. Beyond the canyon, the river broadens and the current slows. To make up time, the McMicking raft floated all night, with only one man posted to watch. It was a terrible risk to take for, unknown to any, fifteen miles of continuous rapids lay ahead. Awakened hastily, the men struggled with the sweeps to keep a course through a channel studded with masses of rock. They did not succeed. The raft struck a rock and stuck fast. Three men immediately swam ashore with a line, secured it to a tree and managed to pull the raft free.

At 8:45 on the morning of September 8, the McMicking raft, having navigated the great curve of the Fraser, reached Fort George. Eustace Pattison was now seriously ill, apparently with diphtheria, his resistance badly weakened by exposure. That night he died, to be buried in a rough grave in a strange land, some six thousand miles from the home he had left, with such high hopes, the previous spring.

At the trading post McMicking was warned that the Fort George Canyon, fifteen miles downriver, was too dangerous to run. Emboldened by his earlier experience, he decided to chance it. All the rafts ran the rapids successfully, including the eighty-five-foot Huntington raft, which made the most difficult passage. A shelving of rock lay across the principal channel; the resulting cataract formed a whirlpool below. The big raft leaped over this fall and buried its nose in the waters below as the Indians, watching from the shoreline, threw up their arms and emitted a sad moan, believing all the white men to be drowned. Every man and animal on the raft was swimming but, having fastened themselves to the logs by ropes, retained their purchase as the raft, nosing out of the foaming water, raced down the remainder of the spillway like a toboggan on a slide.

There were more rapids and more adventures ahead, but all seemed tame compared with the ordeal of the Grand Canyon. Now the party began to get some hint that the goldfields were near: on the sandbars they came upon a party of curious pigtailed men in wide hats, mining with rockers. It was the first time that any of these easterners had set eyes on a Chinese.

The party reached Quesnel, the northern gateway to the gold country, on September 11. The remnants of the two other parties of Overlanders, who had left Fort Garry in May, followed some weeks behind along the same route. The last of the three parties lost two men in the Grand Canyon.

The thirty-two Overlanders and their hundred head of horses and cattle, who had separated from McMicking to head south for the North Thompson River, reached Fort Kamloops, far to the south, on October 11. All were in bad shape. One man had drowned and all their provisions and baggage had been lost in the nine-mile stretch of the Thompson known as the Murchison Rapids. At the lower end of this cataract the banks narrow to enclose the river between two high, perpendicular rock walls, fifty feet apart. Through this crevice the river rushes at top speed and then makes a right-angle turn. It was here, at Hell Gate, that most of the rafts were smashed and lost.

This party, who trekked overland to Kamloops, was in pitiable shape, but its members were far more concerned for the Schubert family than for themselves. The Schuberts and several others had decided to continue on downriver by raft, Mrs. Schubert being so heavily pregnant that walking was a near impossibility. They had no food, and when they stopped at an Indian camp hoping for provisions, the Indians, who had never seen a white woman before, became hostile. One woman, seeing the cowhide rope to which the raft was tethered, accused Mrs. Schubert of trying to steal her cow, and tried to set the raft adrift.

The next Indian village was deserted. When the Schuberts went ashore they came upon a grisly spectacle; half-rotted corpses lay every which way, victims of the terrible smallpox epidemic of the previous year. Potatoes were ripening in the fields, unpicked, and for the next four days the Schuberts lived on nothing else. They reached Fort Kamloops, on the west side of the North Thompson, on October 13 – and not a moment too soon. Early the following morning, Catherine Schubert gave birth to the first white girl born in the interior of British Columbia. She named her Rose because, it was said, the family existed for several days on rose hips, an edible that Catherine remembered from her native Ireland. Thomas McMicking could not contain his admiration for her. He wrote that she "has accomplished a task to which few women are equal; and, with the additional care of three small children, which but few *men* would have the courage to undertake."

By mid-October, all of the goldseekers were within reach of the goldfields. Why, then, did they not rush to the Cariboo, eyes aflame, hearts beating wildly, to stake claims and work ground? For the irony is that only a tiny fraction of them bothered to seek the bonanza that, in the first instance, had taken them westward. The majority of the Queenston party took their rafts downstream to Fort Alexandria, where they went to work building the wagon road from Clinton to Soda Creek. Most of the others went immediately to Victoria and thence by boat to San Francisco and home.

Why? Part of it, no doubt, was disillusion brought on by the realization that, while they were struggling across the prairies and over the mountains, men much closer to the scene were staking the richest ground. Perhaps some of those who reached Quesnel on that triumphant day in September found their elation dampened by the spectacle of disenchanted men retreating on foot from the gold country, heading for the coast, dead broke. Only then did they understand that they had been hoaxed, not by fast-talking confidence men, but by their own false optimism.

That is not the whole story. Though some of the Overlanders left for the coast with a sour taste in their mouths, others clearly felt that they had triumphed in unexpected and more enduring ways. Perhaps, in their hearts, they had always known that the gold was a false lure, and that they had really travelled thirty-five hundred miles for reasons that had nothing to do with material gain. They had tested themselves and had not been found wanting. The long trek across the continent had brought out the very best in them. Others had passed that way before, and others would again, but these men were not explorers or fur traders; these were sedentary amateurs seeking adventure under the acceptable guise of business.

In the face of the discouraging reports leaking out of the Cariboo fields, the wonder is that some of them actually worked on the placer claims with varying degrees of success. It isn't surprising that one of these was Augustus Schubert, who stuck it out for eleven summers before rejoining his family in Lillooet, where his resourceful wife ran a hotel. Another who persevered was a veteran of the Huntington raft, James Wattie, who staked a claim on Williams Creek and got enough from it after two years of toil to open a woollen mill at Valleyfield, Quebec.

Dozens of others remained in British Columbia to ply their trades as blacksmiths, millwrights, contractors and storekeepers; some of these went on to become community leaders, aldermen and pillars of local society. Thomas McMicking became sheriff and county clerk in the city of New Westminster. There, in 1864, his wife and family joined him; and there, in 1868, ironic tragedy struck him down. The man who had survived the worst white water in all of British Columbia was drowned in a vain, noble attempt to rescue his little son from the same Fraser River which, just six years before, he himself had conquered.

Others of his party survived well into the twentieth century. His brother, Robert Burns McMicking, the young telegrapher, rose to become general manager of the B.C. Telephone Company; he died in 1915. Augustus Schubert survived until 1908 and his wife, a legend in her later years, lived on until 1918. All these people left their mark. Long after the colony had become a province and more than one railroad had reached the coast – when Fort George was a real estate man's paradise, the canyons of the Fraser had become tourist attractions and the goldfields had been converted into ranching country – the pioneers of '62 were honoured as living links with the past. Of them it was said, and always with awe, "He was an Overlander." There was no greater accolade.

9
The Odyssey of Cariboo Cameron

The scene, as it has often been described by popular writers, seems to have been lifted verbatim from a Victorian melodrama. One can almost see the asbestos curtain rising on the small stage to reveal the setting: a humble prospector's cabin lit only by a flickering candle; a simple cot in which there languishes a lovely woman, her features drawn and pale; two bearded men in mackinaws on their knees beside her; *sounds off*: a howling gale; *effects*: confetti snow, blowing through the window.

The woman opens her eyes. "John! John!" she cries. "Promise me, you'll take me home. Promise me you will not lay me to rest in this unkind country!"

The bulkier of the two men tries to soothe her: "Now, Sophia, you're not going to leave me."

He rises to prepare some medicine, but as he does the woman, half hysterical, struggles up and gasps one final word: "Promise!"

"I promise," comes the choked answer, and, almost on the instant as his partner raises the sick woman's head to receive the potion, she expires.

One questions the dialogue; it is a little too contrived, more than a touch theatrical. But one cannot doubt the incident. It occurred in the early morning of October 23, 1862, in the shack community of Richfield, a mining camp in the Cariboo country of British Columbia. We have Robert Stevenson's word for it; he was one of the men in the cabin. The other was his closest friend, John Alexander Cameron of Glengarry County, Canada West, soon to be known as "Cariboo" Cameron, the richest miner in British Columbia and perhaps also in the Canadas. But Cameron's fame derives less from his wealth than from the Gothic sequence of events that flowed out of that bedside promise. If the scene in the cabin belongs in a Grade B melodrama, those that follow belong on the wider canvas of a nineteenth-century novel. There was, in fact, such a novel, *The House of Cariboo*, published in 1898, and based in part on the incidents of Cameron's life; even his surname was used. But in this instance, fact could not be transposed into fiction. The novel omitted the real melodrama because the truth was too bizarre: a deathbed promise following on a fabulous gold strike; a coffin and a sack of gold dragged for four hundred miles through impassable snows; a body pickled in alcohol to preserve it from the furnace of the tropics; and to cap it all, a public disinterment twelve years later – a corpse uncovered before a crowd of shocked and disbelieving villagers.

Nonetheless, the record is unequivocal. These things happened; eyewitnesses recorded them; three generations of popular writers have profited from them. The wonder is that so many have felt it necessary to embellish a tale that needs no embroidery.

John Cameron was born in 1820 in Lancaster, near Cornwall, in the County of Glengarry, Upper Canada. His father, Angus, was an immigrant farmer, a Highlander who could trace his ancestry back in a direct line to Donald Cameron, Chieftain of Lochiel. Young Cameron worked as a hired hand on the farm of his uncle John, near Summerstown on the St. Lawrence, but farming was not for him. There was in his make-up a streak of that mysticism which seems to be part of the psychic baggage of born prospectors. He was a dreamer; he believed in dreams; he dreamed of finding a fortune, and when the news of the great gold strike in California filtered East he determined to leave for the West. His neighbours laughed at him when he announced that he would prospect for gold. "Typical John Cameron dreams," they said.

California was not an easy frontier to reach; Cameron did not arrive until 1852 after trudging on foot across the Isthmus of Panama, an appalling forty-mile struggle through dripping jungles, malarial swamps, and cholera-infested shack towns along the route of the uncompleted Panama Railroad. Two brothers, Roderick and Allan, followed in 1854, and all three worked in the goldfields until 1859, when John Cameron returned briefly to Glengarry to marry his fiancée, Sophia, the willowy daughter of Nathan Grove, a veteran of the battle of Lundy's Lane, who owned a farm in the nearby township of Cornwall.

Cameron was in his fortieth year; Sophia was twenty-seven. The difference in age was not unusual at a time when a man needed "prospects" in order to take a wife. Cameron's prospects were just that: reasonably good placer ground in California. The happy couple set off for the Pacific, this time crossing the isthmus in comfort on the newly completed railroad. Sketchy accounts exist of Cameron's success and then failure in the California diggings. He did well for a time but then fell victim to that optimism, which also tends to be an ingrained trait in goldseekers; he overextended his resources constructing a flume to bring water to a mine that was already played out. To add to the problem, a serious depression was at that time sweeping the continent. But this did not really concern Cameron because reports were beginning to seep out about new gold finds in the Crown colony of British Columbia, first on the Fraser River and then farther north in that hazy section of the map known as the Cariboo. Men with colourful nicknames were striking it rich in narrow willow-choked valleys. On Antler Creek in 1860, Doc Keithley was reporting pans of seventy-five and one hundred dollars; by the spring of '61, the entire creek was solidly staked. By then Dutch Bill Dietz had given his name to Williams Creek, a fairy-tale stream so rich that one man took twelve thousand dollars from a fraction of ground between two claims, thus earning himself the title of Twelve-Foot Davis.

Creek after creek in the Cariboo yielded similar dividends, and the rush was on. On October 25, 1861, the little hamlet of Victoria was treated to a singular spectacle: a group of miners from Williams Creek arrived with eighty thousand dollars in gold dust, all from a single claim. An awestruck crowd at the Hudson's Bay wharf followed them as they headed for the Wells Fargo office, the heavy canvas bags of gold slung over their shoulders. The crowd squeezed into the office to watch the gold being placed in the Wells Fargo safe. The safe slammed shut, but the members of the crowd did not disperse; they stood as if mesmerized, gazing at the strongbox as though it were an icon, trying to pierce the door with X-ray vision, seeing the gold in their minds' eyes. Every man in the throng that day, it was said, announced his intention of going to the Cariboo the following spring.

Gold fever raged across the continent and leaped the ocean. In England, young men thirsting for adventure and sudden wealth in an unimaginable wilderness swallowed the fiction of the transport companies and laid out hard cash for what was billed as a joy-ride across the empty plains and through the mountain passes. A handful actually made it.

Crews deserted vessels; clerks left their posts. Hundreds poured off the ships into the tiny colonial backwater of Victoria, transforming it into a bustling city of tents. City men in top hats and boiled shirts, who didn't know a Long Tom from a sluice box, rubbed shoulders with kilted Scots and California miners in high, hobnailed boots, armed with bowie knives, derringers, and six-guns. Up from California by way of Portland on February 27, 1862, came the creaky side-wheeler *Brother Jonathan*, bursting with seven hundred and fifty passengers. The list included the names of John Cameron, his wife Sophia, and their fourteen-month-old daughter, Mary Isabella Alice. The family's circumstances were desperate. Cameron had forty dollars to his name. The child, wrapped in a blanket, was critically ill.

She died five days later in the Royal Hotel, a blow that all but prostrated her parents. But almost at the same moment fortune turned up in the guise of a young man named Robert Stevenson, a fellow Glengarrian. The two men – one twenty-four, the other forty-two – formed a remarkable if somewhat one-sided friendship that would last, off and on, until Cameron's death.

Of the two, Cameron had the more commanding presence – a massive Scot with a high forehead, clear eyes, straight nose, and vast beard. It was the eyes that everybody noticed: chill blue, they seemed to bore right through you. Stevenson was slighter then and neater, with a short clipped beard, a thin moustache, and the kind of pageboy hairstyle fashionable at the time and favoured by such romantic figures as the actor and future assassin, John Wilkes Booth. A number of portraits exist of both men at various ages. All are alike in one aspect: Cameron stares soberly at the camera; it is not too much to say that he glowers. Stevenson seems always good humoured: his eyes twinkle and in the later, less stiff-necked portraits, when the developments in photography encouraged subjects to be more casual, he smiles. This was his nature. Where Cameron was morose, stubborn, and often temperamental, Stevenson was obliging, constant, and cheerful. We do not know what it was that drew him almost instantly to the older man – a neighbour but a stranger; it is possible that he saw in him a substitute father because his own father, who had originally accompanied him to the West, had returned to Glengarry; but the attraction must have been powerful, for it never really faded. By Cameron's standards, his new friend was well-to-do. Cameron was nearly destitute. Stevenson set about making him rich.

Stevenson had left Glengarry at twenty-one, when news of the Fraser strike first reached Canada West. He was too late – or thought he was – and joined a new stampede to the Similkameen country in southern British Columbia, where he survived a series of adventures including, it is said, a volley of poison arrows from the bows of hostile Indians. He found little gold but secured a government job – customs officer at Osoyoos – which he quit when news of the bigger strikes in the Cariboo reached him in the spring of '61. Learning that pack horses were in great demand in the gold country, the shrewd young man bought one hundred head, drove them to Lillooet, and sold them at a profit of ten thousand dollars. On he went to Antler Creek, acquired a gold claim, and bought a building from which to launch a supply business.

Few miners were prepared to brave a Cariboo winter. In December, some two thousand, Stevenson among them, made the long trek out to the coast – four hundred miles of it on snowshoes – and then by boat across the strait to Victoria, where a tent city blossomed. Stevenson planned to return to Antler Creek the following year with a pack train of supplies. To do that, however, he would have to delay his departure until late spring when the trails were passable for horses. In Cameron he saw a solution to that problem. Cameron was sturdy; Cameron was dependable; Cameron could wait behind to supervise the pack train while Stevenson went on ahead with the first wave of returning miners.

He took the older man over to the Hudson's Bay store, introduced him to the chief trader, and, after an hour's parley, went security for two thousand dollars' worth of goods, which were placed in Cameron's name. Then, on April 2, he left for Antler Creek on a twenty-one-day journey through snows often seven feet deep. There he opened a store and in less than four months cleared eleven thousand dollars – more than most prospectors made from their gold claims.

Cameron and his wife arrived on July 25, but without the pack train. Something had happened. We do not know the details, but there had been a quarrel between Cameron and the freighter, Alan McDonald – a quarrel so bitter that the two were now deadly enemies. It was the first hint Stevenson had of Cameron's stubbornness and irascibility, a quality that would contribute to the bizarre events of a later decade. Again, Stevenson proved a friend in need. Cameron owed McDonald fourteen hundred dollars in freight money; Stevenson settled the account and had the goods delivered to the new boomtown of Richfield on Williams Creek where the latest strike had taken place. The supplies included a ton of candles of inferior quality, now badly broken after being carried on the backs of animals for some four hundred miles. Broken or not, they fetched five dollars a pound in a land of sky-high prices, where a pound of butter went for five dollars, a pound of salt for $1.50, and wax matches for $1.50 a box. By any standard the prices were incredible; in Toronto that year, a pound of candles sold for fifteen cents, a pound of butter for twelve cents, and and a box of matches for about fifteen cents. You could buy an entire barrel of salt for four dollars.

That summer, Billy Barker, a bow-legged English merchant seaman who had jumped ship at Victoria the previous year, decided to move into virgin territory below the Williams Creek canyon. Barker, a complete amateur, had decided to sink a shaft some distance from the rimrock above the creek in the belief that the prehistoric creek bed, where the gold lay, had been turned aside at that point. His story – the story of a naïve newcomer who strikes it rich as old-timers snicker – was to be re-enacted many times in this and future gold stampedes. While prospecting veterans made sport of him, Billy kept digging. On August 22, at fifty-five feet, he struck paydirt: five dollars to the pan. At eighty feet he took out one thousand dollars in gold in two days. The camp went wild.

Stevenson had already moved his business to Williams Creek. According to his own account he was tipped off by a Dr. Crane that there was good ground vacant about a half-mile below Barker's diggings. Crane wanted to stake immediately, but Stevenson was to recall that he held out for organizing a company of six friends, including Cameron and his wife. His solicitude for Cameron at this point is remarkable. He was forced to wait, he wrote, for more than a day before Cameron would come with the group to stake; the superstitious Scotsman had a prejudice against taking any action on a Friday.

There followed a disagreement between the two friends, which came close to being a quarrel. Again Stevenson backed down. He had wanted to stake on the right bank; Cameron insisted on the left. As it turned out, the right bank was richer; Henry Beatty of Toronto, who had an interest in that property, became a millionaire shipowner as a result of the booty he obtained from it; his son, Edward, rose to be president of the CPR.

Stevenson not only gave in to Cameron but he said he also insisted, over Dr. Crane's objections, that the claim be named the Cameron and not the Stevenson claim. As for Crane, he was swiftly eliminated as a partner by reason of some gunplay in a local saloon, an incident that got him thirty days in jail and a heavy fine. "We did not wish this kind of man in the same company with us," Stevenson later wrote. In his long account of the saga of Cariboo Cameron this is the only remark that might be described as uncharitable; if Crane had steered the others to riches, surely he deserved something.

Yet one must pause to consider the evidence. All tales of placer mining locations are notoriously tangled, especially in the minds of the participants. When a strike is made, the breathless scramble for land becomes confusing. Who can remember who told whom to stake what, and where? There is the further complication of mining law, which was in this instance especially rigid, holding that no man could own more than two properties; as a result, many claims were held by proxies. Stevenson's memory does not jibe with the record, which shows that six men, including Cameron – but neither Stevenson nor Crane – recorded claims on Williams Creek on August 25, three days after Billy Barker struck his first pay; and that on September 15, Stevenson recorded an adjoining claim to be worked with the Cameron claims. After that the chronology becomes more complicated: Stevenson, Cameron, and the others are frequently shown to be buying bits of their interest from each other or selling fractions to outsiders. One fact, however, is indisputable. One way or another, Stevenson was responsible for steering Cameron to one of the richest pieces of ground in the Cariboo.

The riches were yet to be proved. Until a shaft was sunk, the Cameron company's property was nothing more than a seven-hundred-foot strip of moss-covered clay and gravel. Cameron had other matters to concern him: a few days after the claims were registered, his wife, grief-stricken over the death of their child and weakened by the hardships of the trek into the interior, was struck down by typhoid fever. Cameron and Stevenson took turns nursing her, the latter tramping at midnight through the heavy brush and later through snow to the cabin at Richfield to make sure she took regular doses of the medicine that the pioneer doctor, Charles Wilkinson, had prescribed.

On September 26, with the shaft at twenty-two feet, bedrock was reached on the Cameron property. There was no gold. All work ceased. Two of the partners, discouraged, gave up and left for Victoria.

Sophia Cameron's condition grew worse until, at three o'clock in the morning of October 23, with the wind howling at sixty miles an hour and the thermometer at thirty degrees below, Fahrenheit, she exacted that memorable promise from her husband and expired – the first white woman to die in the Cariboo. A local miner was engaged to prepare a double coffin, the interior of tin or galvanized iron, the outer case of wood. Thus protected, the body was placed in an empty cabin on the outskirts of Richfield. There was no need to embalm it; the corpse was already frozen solid.

By this time, all but ninety of the several thousand miners working in the Cariboo region had fled to the outside world. Almost everyone who remained attended Sophia Cameron's funeral – the first of four that would be held. Two days later work began again on the Cameron claim and a new shaft was started; on December 22, again at twenty-two feet, Cameron and his partners struck it rich.

It was a chillingly cold afternoon. Cameron and Stevenson were working at the mouth of the shaft when they heard a cry from Richard Rivers, one of the original stakers, working at the bottom. "Come down here at once – the place is yellow with gold. Look here, boys!" and he held up a flat rock "the size of a dinner pail." Stevenson, lying flat on the platform and peering down, could see the gold sticking out of the rock. It was an electric moment; that one piece of rock, as it turned out, was worth sixteen dollars. Cameron scrambled down the shaft while Stevenson hacked away at some frozen muck that had been sent up that morning. From three twelve-gallon kegs of gravel he panned $155 in gold.

Cameron realized that he had one of the richest claims – if not *the* richest – in the Cariboo. But most of the gold was in the ground and could not be realized until it was washed after the spring thaw. Moreover, he was haunted by that deathbed promise. How could he scrabble for material treasure while his wife's corpse lay unburied? And of what use was gold anyway, when his happiness had been taken from him? Something was gnawing at Cameron, disturbing his sleep, bedevilling his waking hours, and that something was guilt. He blamed himself for his wife's death; greed for gold, he now felt, had caused him to push her beyond her resources, to drive her, in the midst of her grief, to a long wilderness struggle on an unkind frontier. Gold or no gold, he must get her body out of the Cariboo. But how? Between Williams Creek and Port Douglas, where the steamboats docked, was a four-hundred-mile wilderness of slippery mountain slopes, tangled trails, dense forest, and endlessly drifting snow. To transport her coffin through that complexity of natural barriers would require manpower as well as horsepower, and *that* would require money. The only answer was to sell part of his interest in the Cameron claim at a sacrifice.

He approached Charles Hankin, a shareholder in the Barker company, and revealed his secret. Hankin was allowed to climb down the Cameron shaft; what he saw caused him immediately to offer a fifty-pound sack of gold for a part interest. Thus enriched, Cameron made an offer to the ninety men left in the mining camp. He would pay twelve dollars a day and a bonus of two thousand dollars to any one of them who would agree to make the round trip with him to Victoria, where he intended to bury his wife's body temporarily. It was a fantastic offer at a time when a dollar a day was good pay for a workman, but after some consideration, every one backed away. Fifty miles to the south and all the way along the trails to the coast, smallpox was epidemic. It was the most virulent kind, the kind that killed or at least left pockmarks on its victims. Cameron was desolated. Even with the help of horses, he could not haul that sleigh alone, with all his supplies, the heavy double casket, and the fifty pounds of gold. What was he to do? At this point young Stevenson, ever the friend in need, volunteered. In vain Cameron protested that Stevenson had never had smallpox and so was not immune; Stevenson said he did not fear the disease, was willing to chance the journey. But, Cameron asked, who would run the mine in their absence? The enterprising Stevenson already had a substitute.

"Well," said Cameron at last, "if you'll go, I'd rather have you than any man in the Cariboo."

"I'll go and I'll pay my own expenses," his friend replied.

Stevenson's sparse diary still exists in the public archives of British Columbia, and it records that on Saturday, January 31, 1863, he "left Williams Creek in company with J. A. Cameron bound for Victoria with the remains of his wife." That blunt statement in no way conveys the immensity of the task the two men had set themselves.

In 1863, British Columbia was an unmapped wilderness, especially in winter – a realm without people. It had been a Crown colony for less than five years; before that it was the fiefdom of the Hudson's Bay Company, populated only by Indians and a handful of fur traders. Apart from a few hundred souls in the new stump-filled capital of New Westminster, the only real congregation of people was along the goldfields of the Fraser River and the Cariboo, and most of these vanished at the onset of winter. Even in summer there were as many people living in the sister colony of Vancouver Island as there were on the mainland.

To reach the Cariboo in summer was strain enough. The succession of routes that led into the interior from the head of Harrison Lake, where the steamer traffic from New Westminster ended, could scarcely be called trails, let alone roads, being nothing but "mud, stones [and] trees fallen in every direction" in the words of one traveller. The goldseekers were forced to flounder hip-deep through glacial streams or trudge for miles in muck to the knees, often in pouring rain, all the while vainly battling hordes of mosquitoes and flies.

In winter, the route was all but impassable, especially at the northern end, where a tentative trail some seventy miles long connected the main wagon road at 150 Mile House to Williams Creek. It was this first seventy miles that would be the most difficult, for in winter there was no semblance of a trail. When Cameron set out, the pathway was under seven feet of packed snow with another two feet of freshly fallen powder above. Behind

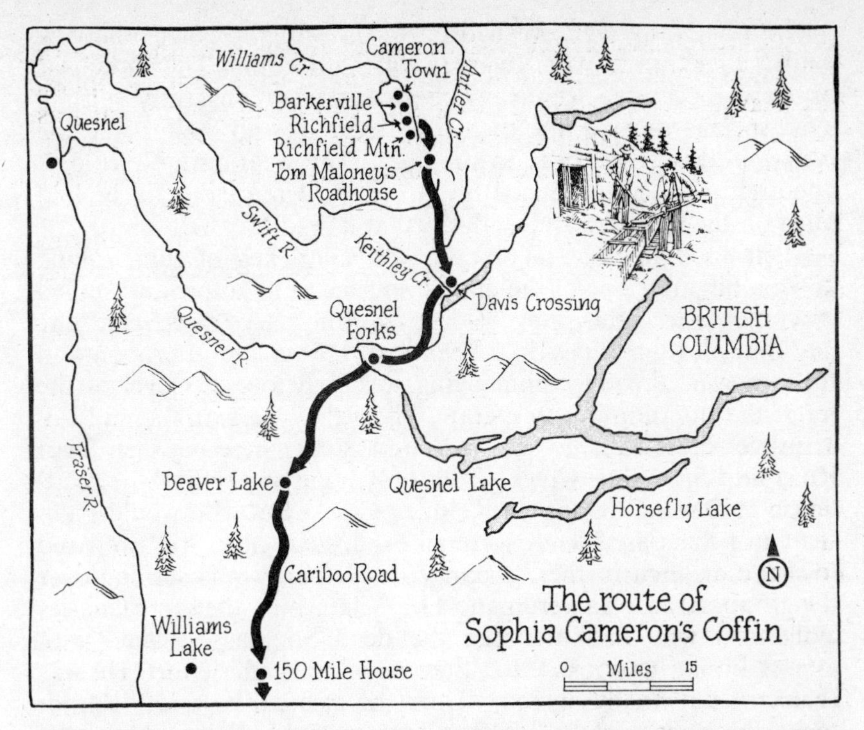

them, the two men dragged an awkward burden: the casket, fastened to a narrow toboggan scarcely more than a foot wide, on top of which were lashed blankets, food, and then fifty pounds of gold. With this preposterously top-heavy load the two friends faced the barrier of Richfield Mountain. Fortunately, twenty members of the mining community offered to accompany the cortège for the first few miles to help hoist the coffin and its burden over that rampart. These men, all of them on snowshoes, hitched themselves to a long rope, with Stevenson as guide, taking the head of the line. There was no trail to follow, "not even the mark of a dog's foot."

The climb was treacherous and slippery. The absurd load kept turning turtle. By noon, the party had managed to move the toboggan a scant three and a half miles. Many of the men lost their bearings and were worried that Stevenson, who suddenly turned off into a maze of green timber, was also lost. But he found what he was after: the faint furrow of Grouse Creek, whose frozen path would lead them to Tom Maloney's roadhouse. They reached it long after nightfall, with the thermometer at minus thirty-five, the wind blowing at gale force, and the snow piling into immense drifts on a treeless plain. The next morning, fourteen of the party returned to Richfield.

The remaining eight pushed on in the stinging cold, following Antler Creek and Swift River. It was hard going. The snow was dry and loose; the top-heavy toboggan was constantly turning over, spilling its load into the drifts; there was no shelter, and the men were forced to sleep in the open. The weather grew colder; one night Cameron glanced up at the spirit thermometer he had hung on the limb of a tree and saw that it read fifty below.

Their food ran out. Worse, a two-gallon keg of rum, rolling down a hill after one of the upsets, smashed into a tree and spilled its contents into the snow. Worse still, the party discovered one day that all its matches had been lost. It was late afternoon and the sun was already commencing to dip below the level of the trees; the situation was desperate. There they were, in the midst of a spruce forest with no sign of a trail, somewhere between Swift River and Snowshoe Creek. Their only hope was to find the roadhouse at Davis Crossing on Keithley Creek. But who would go in search of this oasis? They were all exhausted; none was prepared to move an inch further; a dangerous lethargy was settling over the group. At last Cameron and Dr. Wilkinson – the same Charles Wilkinson who had attended the dead Sophia – asked "with almost imploring looks" that Stevenson make the effort. He was reluctant but finally agreed. "Don't be afraid," he said, "I'll not make the least mistake." The doctor looked at him soberly. "If you do," he said, "we are all dead men."

He made no mistake. He seems to have had an uncanny sense of direction. He reached the roadhouse some hours after dark and immediately turned back, taking with him a quantity of bread, meat, and matches. Hours later he encountered the rest of the party who had been laboriously following his snowshoe tracks in the dark. Two of them – French Joe and Indian Jim – were carrying the blankets and the gold; the toboggan and the coffin had been abandoned in the forest. It took a day to retrieve it, after which four more men turned back to Williams Creek. Only French Joe and Indian Jim remained to push on with the two friends to the forks of the Quesnel, where they sought shelter in a hotel run by a mysterious Irishwoman known as Mrs. Lawless. She was, in actuality, Johanna McGuire, the "lost" daughter of Dan O'Connell, known as the Liberator, the first of the great nineteenth-century Irish leaders in the British House of Commons – or so Stevenson believed, and with some reason, for she had been identified by the brother of an Irish peer who had known her well in Dublin. Stevenson described her as "rather a wild creature [who] consumed a large amount of liquor" and steadfastly refused to reveal anything about her background. Gold rush camps attract such exotics. Mrs. Lawless tried to persuade the party to go back to Williams Creek because of the smallpox raging a few miles farther south, but all four men pushed on as far as Beaver Lake, at which point French Joe and Indian Jim departed. The date was February 10; it had taken eleven days to haul the coffin seventy-two miles.

A single Indian greeted them at Beaver Lake; the rest were dead of smallpox. It was not possible to inter the corpses in the frozen earth; they were concealed instead under hummocks of hardened snow. Stevenson counted ninety of these snow graves in the vicinity. More lay ahead, for the disease was raging all down the Lac La Hache valley. Cameron had bought a horse for three hundred dollars, which he hitched to the toboggan. Stevenson led the animal through the drifts while the older man, shoving and pushing and trying to keep the load upright, brought up the rear. There were snow graves everywhere: Stevenson recorded one hundred and twenty at Williams Lake.

The going grew easier on the newly improved Cariboo wagon road that led south to Clinton and on to Lillooet. Everywhere they encountered grisly reminders of the disease that had swept all of southern British Columbia that year. When the first horse died of exhaustion, Cameron purchased a second; it died also; he purchased a third for the last leg of the journey along the Lillooet-Port Douglas portage. Before the trip was finished, it, too, was worn out and useless. Jim Cummings, who joined the pair at Pemberton, described their slow progress along a slippery hillside:

"Cameron went ahead with the axe and cut out brush and stakes. Stevenson led the horse and I was trying to keep the toboggan on the road. My boots were nearly worn out and very slippery. We would all go down, the toboggan, coffin and gold dust, and get up before the horse. The horse got on to the job. He would turn his head to the mountain, then the whole thing would stop. It took a long time to get it back on the road – over four hundred pounds. I said to Cameron that I would take the gold dust off the coffin and pack it . . . . After that I could keep the toboggan from turning over . . . ."

At last the party reached the end of the trail at Port Douglas at the head of Harrison Lake. The little steamer *Henrietta* lay ahead – a welcome sight – but en route to embark the three men had to endure a grim gauntlet, passing down a road lined on each side with tents in which Indians lay stricken with smallpox. The flaps were raised sufficiently so that the dying, some of them turned black by the disease, could be clearly seen; and over the trail, like an unwholesome fog, hung the stench of death.

At New Westminster, the two men moved their burden onto a seagoing vessel, the *Enterprise*. On March 7, they reached Victoria after a journey of six hundred miles, four hundred of it through deep snow – a journey that Stevenson was to call "the most severe and trying I have ever experienced."

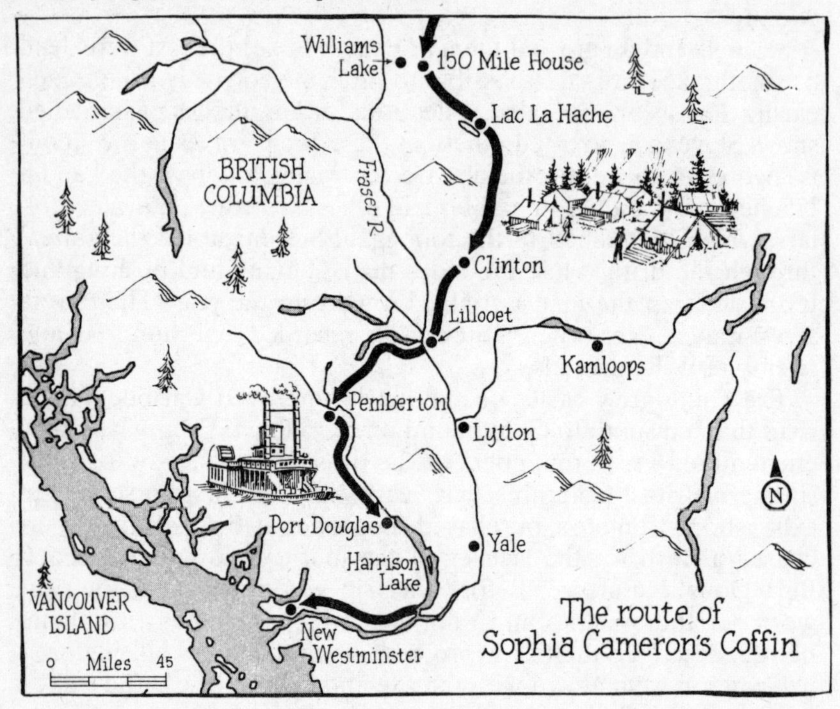

Cameron's intention was to leave the coffin interred in a local cemetery long enough for him to realize the fortune in his claim on Williams Creek: that achieved, he would set out on the long voyage home. Meanwhile, Sophia must be given a second funeral. The *British Colonist*, in its report on that melancholy rite, noted that the "arrangements here were conducted by Mr. Richard Lewis, undertaker, very creditably." That bland phrase scarcely did the matter justice, nor did it reveal any of the fascinating details. Cameron decreed that his wife's frozen body should be preserved in alcohol to prepare it for the future day when he would transport it across the cauldron of the isthmus of Panama. Lewis, who was also the mayor of Victoria, was equal to the task. He had a tinsmith drill a one-inch hole through the wooden and metal coverings. Into this small aperture he poured, over a period of three hours, twenty-five gallons of ninety-five proof alcohol. When the job was done, both Stevenson and Cameron stuck a finger into the hole to make sure the spirits had reached the top. The hole in the metal was soldered shut and the opening in the wood filled. The funeral cortège that wound its way to the Quadra Street cemetery that Sunday, March 8, was "the largest and most respectable . . . ever witnessed in the city." Eight hundred mourners, most of them Cariboo miners wintering in the capital, followed Sophia Cameron to the grave.

With Cameron's arrival in Victoria word of the big new strike, which had been seeping out of the Cariboo since late February, was confirmed. Whisper became rumour; rumour became fact; fact became published news. When gold was first found on the Cameron claim, the partners had agreed to keep it a secret, but there can be few secrets in a mining camp. Hankin's purchase of a single share for eight thousand dollars was already known and published, and now, as miners moved from tent to tent, wheeling and dealing in shares, half-interests, fractions and slivers of property, the law of supply and demand took over. The results made headlines. On March 15, Cameron himself bought an additional share in the Cameron company for six thousand dollars. In three days the price doubled. A man named Cunningham bought a share from Stevenson for twelve thousand dollars. Still the price rose. A fortnight later Stevenson decided he wanted back in; Cameron sold him a share for fifteen thousand dollars. As it turned out, these were all bargains. From this point on, the name of John Alexander Cameron would be linked permanently with the Cariboo goldfields. For the rest of his life and long after death he would be Cariboo Cameron.

The two men wasted no time in returning to British Columbia. They left Victoria on March 19 and arrived at Richfield on April 4, making most of the journey on horseback. Cameron, meanwhile, had written home that he had struck it rich. That summer, with the mine in full operation, his brothers Roderick and Allan joined him.

This was the Cariboo's bumper year, a year in which at least four million dollars in gold was sluiced out of the gravels of the creekbeds. (In 1978 that gold would be worth forty-four millions.) By summer, the wooded defile of Williams Creek had become a desert of stumps as four thousand newcomers built themselves log cabins. Two new communities sprang up downstream from Richfield – Barkerville, opposite Billy Barker's rich ground and Cameron's town – later contracted to Camerontown – opposite the company's diggings. Saws screeched, trees toppled, water wheels creaked, hammers clanged in smithies. At night the narrow valley flickered eerily in the glow of a hundred torches marking the heads of the shafts. In the makeshift saloons the newly arrived Hurdy Gurdy Girls smiled and capered. These were German dancers, *fraülein*s brought originally to California and now, following the trail of gold, to the dark heart of the new colony, accompanied by a French upright piano, the first in the district, lugged on the backs of four men for sixty miles from Quesnel to Barkerville.

The Cariboo was no longer a male preserve: sixty orphan girls from England had been imported to Victoria by the British Columbia Emigration Society; many of these, newly married to wintering miners, began to drift into town with their husbands. The nights were raucous with music and song, with the scraping of fiddles and the rattle of the piano, with the baying of dogs made manic by the moon, and the groans and cries of men intoxicated by Forty Rod – but rarely with the sound of gunplay, for firearms were taboo. British justice ruled in the gigantic and bearded person of Matthew Baillie Begbie, the legendary Cariboo judge. The old mulatto fur trader, James Douglas, now governor of the colony, had seen to that. Without the presence of Begbie, an intimidating imperial symbol with his fierce waxed mustachios and his piratical black slouch hat, the whole of the interior might have drifted by default to the Americans. Douglas had no intention of letting it slip away, as the Oregon Territory had once slipped away. His incredible wagon road, an extraordinary engineering feat designed as an umbilical cord to secure the goldfields to the seacoast, was already being blasted from the granite and quartz of the Fraser canyon. Here, in the heart of the empty colony, the seeds of a new civilization were being cultivated. Union in the Canadian confederation was less than eight years away.

Cameron was blind to all this hustle and clamour. It is doubtful if he even heard the music; his claim occupied all his energies. He worked it all that summer, a man urged on by inner furies: hired a dozen men to help him; built a double sluice box to wash the gold at a faster rate; drove himself with all the impatience of a man desperate to get the job done and be off. Guilt obsessed him. He could not rest until he had fulfilled his promise.

The richness of his claim is legendary. One anecdote gives a graphic idea of its value. When, in October, the Cameron brothers were preparing to leave, Roderick announced that he would take one last pan and make a ring for his wife out of whatever gold it contained. "No," said John Cameron, "I'll pan the final round." He did so and washed out close to a pound of gold, then valued at one hundred and twenty dollars.

Stevenson estimated that Cameron took $350,000 out of the

Cariboo, a sum whose value is difficult to comprehend in an inflationary era, especially when one remembers that interest was untaxed. It was easily the equivalent of three million dollars in 1978 terms. Nor is it likely that Stevenson's estimate included Cameron's take from an adjoining piece of ground purchased during his trip to Victoria. Since he could not legally hold more than two claims, he asked Jim Cummings, whom he had met on the trail, to stand proxy for him. Cummings worked the claim all summer and as Cameron prepared to leave, handed him the key to a strongbox containing one hundred thousand dollars in gold. Cameron had come into this additional fortune as the result of a dream in which he saw the pay streak of his own property running into the next. He was a believer in such portents. He sought out the owner of the adjoining claim and bought it for three hundred dollars. That happy windfall did nothing to weaken the mystical streak in his make-up.

Cameron tendered a thousand-dollar banquet to the men who worked for him and then, on October 6, 1863, he and his brothers and Stevenson left the Cariboo. It took some time to get underway; there was so much gold dust that eight horses had to be engaged to carry it. Cameron hired twenty men to guard this treasure, each armed with a Colt revolver. It was later said that if anyone had had the misfortune to emerge from the bush when the pack train went by, he would have been riddled with bullets, Begbie or no Begbie.

At New Westminster, the gold was melted into bars. Cameron went on to Victoria where he ordered his wife's coffin exhumed and a new outer covering constructed. On November 8, he and Stevenson embarked for San Francisco on the old steamer *Pacific*. At the California port the gold was converted into coin while the coffin, now weighing 450 pounds, was hoisted aboard the *Constitution* bound for Panama City. There it was transferred to the freight car of the world's most expensive railroad, where the fare for a jungle journey of forty-seven and a half miles was twenty-five dollars in gold. At Colon, on the Atlantic, they boarded another steamer, *Champion*, for New York. They would complete the journey to Glengarry by rail.

Cameron had encountered no trouble in San Francisco, but in New York he ran hard against a series of obstacles. The customs officials refused to believe that the coffin contained a body. Why did it weigh so much? What else was inside? If it actually contained a corpse preserved in alcohol why did it not gurgle, slosh, or splash? In vain Cameron tried to explain that besides filling it to the brim, he had surrounded the body carefully with old clothes so that it would not be battered during the trek to the coast. The dead woman's head lay pillowed on her favourite Paisley shawl, a wedding present from her mother.

The red tape in New York was serpentine. The two men were shuttled in a hired hack from office to office where each time Stevenson was required to swear that the casket contained a corpse and nothing more; that the corpse was that of Cameron's wife; that he had personally been present and seen the occupant expire; that the extra weight consisted of metal and alcohol. In each office – Stevenson insisted later that he must have been to a hundred – Cameron was required to pay a fee of two dollars. It is doubtful that the customs men were as sceptical or the Manhattan bureaucracy as muddled as this implied. Simple corruption is a more likely explanation. Tammany was at its height; the infamous "ring" of Boss William Marcy Tweed, which milked the city of at least thirty million dollars, was solidly entrenched. The town was riddled with graft. Cameron was an incidental victim.

At last the customs men declared themselves satisfied; one story has it that Cameron convinced them by offering to pay the way of one of them to watch the coffin buried at Cornwall. The two men had been bouncing around lower New York since eight that morning. Dusk was falling. But a further difficulty now presented itself; the overweight casket, lying deep in the hold of the *Champion*, had to be unloaded. It would require Herculean efforts to haul it free, for there was no winch aboard. The customs men secured a two-hundred-foot length of rope; they corralled seamen from the *Champion* and from neighbouring vessels and they even conscripted passersby into service – all at two dollars a head. This nondescript crew – some hundred men in all – leaned on the rope, heaved, tugged, wheezed, gasped, and finally yanked their burden out of the hold. Cameron set off at last for Glengarry County with his cargo, some hundreds of dollars poorer.

He arrived on December 22. The eight-thousand-mile journey around the continent from Victoria had taken forty-four days. As far as Cameron was concerned, the frontier was behind him; now he could forget the hardships, the struggle, and the tragedy and indulge himself with the wealth that the wilderness had provided.

It was not to be that simple. The frontier had changed Cameron, as it changed so many others. His experiences on the trail had contributed to his self-confidence but also increased his stubbornness. The seemingly magical fulfilment of his dreams had strengthened his mysticism. He had conquered the wild; he felt he was invincible; no one could tell him what to do.

After Christmas, he made arrangements for his wife's third funeral at her family's plot at Cornwall. It was assumed that he would have the casket opened so that her parents might gaze for the last time upon her face, but he had no such intention. Instead, he ordered the coffin further enclosed in a casing of sheet lead. This led to a painful scene at the cemetery. Stevenson reminded Cameron of a promise to open the coffin, which he claimed had been made in Victoria. Cameron refused. The younger man, now thoroughly angry, could be heard by every mourner in the graveyard.

"Cameron," he shouted, "the day will come when you will have to show her face. The people are not satisfied, and never will be, until you do show it. This is an awful mistake you are making. You made a distinct promise to me that you would do so, or I would never have left the Cariboo with her body and you!"

Again, Cameron refused. Instead, he asked Stevenson to sign an affidavit attesting to his wife's death. Stevenson, still highly irate, turned him down. He asserted that even Cameron's father-in-law had doubts that his daughter's body was in the coffin. The old farmer, pointing at the box, had remarked in a dubious tone: "Yes, they *tell* me she is there." This angered Cameron further; he refused to believe the story until a corroborating witness was produced. "That settles it," said Cariboo Cameron. "I will never show her face now to any person." And the coffin, unopened, was consigned to the earth.

His intransigence remains a mystery. Why was he so insistent on keeping the coffin closed? It was common practice for mourners to view the remains of the dead: corpses were often displayed in front parlours. It would have been a simple matter to satisfy the customs men in New York and the suspicions of his in-laws in Cornwall; yet even when his closest friend requested it, Cameron refused to comply. Was it because he shrank from looking again on the face of the woman whose death he believed he had caused by his own avarice? Or was it simply pride – a bitter pique against intimates who refused to accept his word? We do not know. But had he heeded Stevenson's advice, John Cameron would have saved himself a decade of grief.

The night of the funeral Stevenson stayed at the old Cameron homestead, and here the two old friends quarrelled again. Cameron's brothers and sisters tried to smooth matters, but, as Stevenson put it, "neither of us was satisfied." Early in February, the younger man left for the Cariboo. It would be a quarter of a century before they would meet again.

Now Cameron set about spending his money. He paid fifty-six thousand dollars for his uncle's farm at Summerstown – the same farm on which he had worked and dreamed as a youth. On it he built a cavernous mansion in the pompous but then popular style known as Italianate, complete with belvedere, projecting frontispieces, and stained-glass windows. Stone was imported from Scotland, marble from Italy, mahogany and other rare woods from the Philippines. He adopted a style to match his estate, driving about in a gold-trimmed carriage behind four dappled grey horses imported from Europe. He held flamboyant parties at the mansion, Fairfield, to which prominent citizens of the day were invited. He rode to hounds and nurtured political ambitions. A staunch Conservative, he sat on the platform when the member from Kingston, John A. Macdonald, visited the area.

He seemed obsessed by his wealth. He coveted a team of matched blacks owned by a neighbour, Donald McLennan. McLennan had no intention of selling, but when Cameron called, he invited him in for a drink. Cameron sat down, produced a leather pouch and, as he sipped his drink, began to fill the pouch with five-dollar gold pieces. He left with the team; he had made an offer McLennan could not refuse.

If he was indulgent with himself, Cameron was more than generous with others. When he dropped in for a drink at the local tavern, he would tip the man who held his horses five dollars, almost a week's pay. He bought all four of his brothers three-hundred-acre farms on the best available land on the banks of the St. Lawrence. On each farm he built a house, completely furnished with custom-built sideboards, matching chairs, expansion dining tables, and small pieces of mahogany, not to mention complete sets of silverware. Other gifts followed such as the eighteen carat gold belt, studded with diamonds, he gave his sister Mary.

Still brooding over Sophia's death, he married Emma Woods, the daughter of a well-to-do neighbour, described by a grand nephew as "a somewhat flighty wench whose giddiness must have contrasted sharply with the gentleness of his first spouse." The bride was twenty-two years his junior.

His temperament became unpredictable. He was often rude to the very relatives who were the objects of his generosity, perhaps because he felt they were more interested in his wealth than in his welfare. His fits of temper could be frightening: a physically powerful man, he was known to throw guests out of his mansion by picking them up and tossing them bodily through the ornate front door. He became a controversial figure in a community that distrusted lavish displays of wealth as much as it was suspicious of its sudden acquisition.

Rumours and gossip, mere whispers at first, then hoarser and more strident, echoed about the community. How was it possible for any man to have accumulated such a fortune in a single year? Nobody had ever done such a thing – at least, not honestly. How could anybody dig up that much gold in one summer? A working man would have to toil for . . . what ? One hundred years? No . . . far longer, at a dollar a day, to earn as much as John Cameron was said to have stored away. Why had he refused to open that coffin? What was the secret? What had he *really* buried in that churchyard: the body of his wife, as he claimed, or, more likely, a vast hoard of treasure? That would explain its weight; that would explain Cameron's adamant refusal to open it. Was his wife really dead? They had only Cameron's word for that, and his friend Stevenson had pointedly refused to sign a paper swearing to it. Did he in fact have a rich claim in the Cariboo? Again, they had only the word of a man who was behaving in a most eccentric fashion, flaunting his wealth, engaging in quarrels, flinging his gold about in a most un-Scotslike manner. *Could* it be that Sophia Cameron was still alive, perhaps held in thrall by some exotic native prince in that faraway wilderness, as distant and unknown as the moon, where white women were so rare that they might be worth their weight in gold? The whispers spread, grew louder, were half-believed, until they became a kind of Greek chorus, haunting the master of Fairfield.

Then, in the autumn of 1865, the rumours were given voice by a political opponent, a Lancaster physician, Dr. Alex Macpherson, who was heard to say that Cameron had not come by his money honestly and had, in fact, served a term in jail in the Cariboo. Macpherson had an axe to grind: Cameron had taken his brother to court, where he was fined for discharging a firearm on the Cameron estate. The doctor's accusation stung Cameron; enraged, he travelled all the way to Montreal to purchase a rawhide whip with which he intended to flay his accuser unless he recanted in writing.

The confrontation took place in a hotel sitting room. Several witnesses were present. Macpherson refused to sign anything; Cameron brandished his whip; cooler heads restrained him. Macpherson, however, charged his would-be attacker with assault. The results of the court case were inconclusive: Cameron was found guilty but was granted a new trial, which never took place.

The incident did nothing to halt the rumours; indeed, to many it seemed to confirm their truth. The Cornwall *Freeholder* attacked Cameron as a "shameless rowdy" and declared that "his conduct for the last year or two has been such as to incur the displeasure and contempt of his neighbours." Then it gave substance to the gossip by adding that "his conduct during his absence from the country probably does not reflect much credit upon him, and we must say that his mode of treating the author here of the rumour as to his imprisonment in British Columbia is not such as would be expected of a man who was conscious of its untruthfulness."

The newspaper went on to needle Cameron for his open display of his gold:

"It is all very well for Mr. Cameron to exhibit about his person a large quantity of the precious metal. No one needs complain about his 'cutting a swell,' as the popular phrase goes. He may drive his coach-and-four where ever he has the disposition to put on airs, and not excite the displeasure, although he may not avoid the ridicule of his neighbours . . . . But when Mr. C. assumes to introduce Lynch law into the community . . . he need not be surprised at the indignation which such dastardly conduct has in this instance created. To Mr. C. as a dandy we have nothing to say; but we can assure him that he will not be tolerated here as a ruffian . . . . Mr. Cameron has been away from home and like many other weak-minded persons has contracted some bad habits; let him relinquish them and the sooner the better."

The conviction grew that Cameron had something to hide. But he refused to clear the air. When one of his brothers suggested that some sort of explanation was in order, Cameron tossed him through a stained-glass window. When his wife urged him to make some sort of announcement to still the wagging tongues, he roared out: "I'm feeding most of the people who are doing the talking. I won't be pushed around by them." Nothing, it seemed, could move him. Again the question nags: *why?* Was it pride alone? Or was it something more arcane, the by-product of the mystic streak that persuaded him of the efficacy of dreams, convinced him that he was born under a lucky star, and now caused him to shrink from a deed that would disturb the ghost of the woman of whose death, he felt, he himself had been the instrument? A clue to this inner torment lies in the answer he flung back at a local judge who pleaded with him to still the outcry.

"My wife rests in peace," said Cariboo Cameron. "She will continue to rest in peace. If anyone disturbs her grave, I'll kill him."

Cameron lived with the calumny for more than nine years and kept his silence. Then, in the summer of 1873, an extraordinary story appeared in the *Sunday Times* of Syracuse, New York.

A Romance in Real Life. A Feast for a Novel Writer. Ten Years with an Indian Chief. Just Retribution.

Fifteen years ago there lived on the banks of the St. Lawrence, near the village of Cornwall, a man named Cameron of near Scotch descent. He dwelt until after maturity, with his parents in their rugged homestead in a poor log-house, and then he married from among his associates, a good girl, who afterwards did her best to help her husband on in the world. But somehow fortune always frowned, and the couple found life an uphill road.

At last, seemingly convinced that they could barely make a living on a farm, Mr. Cameron bestirred himself among his acquaintances and relatives and picked up money enough to purchase a passage for himself and his wife to Australia, which was then in a fever of excitement over the gold discovery. Nothing more was heard from the wanderers for five years, when all at once Mr. Cameron returned, and bearing with him

A STRANGE BURDEN!

It comprised, first, a coffin with the embalmed remains of his dear wife, and second, unbounded sums of money, all in glittering gold!

His report was that instead of going to Australia as they had contemplated, they had finally brought up in the Fraser River region, at a point called Cariboo. That he there got possession of a claim, which he had worked so successfully, and yielded so well, that he was the possessor of untold wealth, and he was in constant receipt of more. These facts were proven by the after events. Moreover, he said, with tears in his eyes, that his poor wife had died in that inhospitable country, and that his fortunate wealth and his love for her had prompted him to have her body embalmed that he might bring her home and bury her among friends. This was done; and then commenced a series of lavish expenditures on his part. First, he bought the old homestead and erected thereon, a grand and princely mansion, of Milwaukee brick, surrounded the ample grounds with a unique and costly wall, purchased his parents and other relations comfortable homes, and seemed bent on the most lavish hospitality and generous use of his wealth in every direction. And still his store never seemed to diminish, and the people all blessed him, and copied him and united in calling him

CARIBOO CAMERON.

Everybody in the northern part of our state knows Cariboo Cameron, and he had not an enemy. But look at the sequel. After ten years of uninterrupted prosperity, during which he had risen to the very top of the social scale,

THERE CAME A CRASH!

And it came in an unthought of manner. One dreary night, late in the evening, a rap was heard on the door of the Cameron mansion, and a poor weak woman was admitted, who begged for shelter for the night, and it was granted. Nothing special was thought of her, until next morning, as the family – the jovial husband, the happy wife whom he had married a year after his return, were seated at the breakfast table, the strange woman came from her room, walked straight in front of Cameron, and asked in an agonized tone,

"Do you know me?"

"My God, yes, I do!" was the reply, and Cariboo Cameron fell senseless to the floor.

The woman was thrust hastily aside, and Cameron was restored to consciousness, but the moment he escaped from the house he left the country, and has not been heard of since then. That was last week.

And now comes a most horrible tale from this first sad wife, for the poor woman was none other than Cameron's wife, whom he had taken away so many years before. For the past ten years she has been the unwilling prisoner and wife of an Indian chief near Cariboo, to whom Cameron had

TRADED HER

for the claim that yielded him all his wealth.

That claim contained unbounded stores of gold, and its wealth was known to none but the Indian. After the bargain was struck Cameron supplied himself with great quantities of it, put the rest in the hands of a partner, who has worked it since, and sent Cameron's share to him.

THE COFFIN WAS TAKEN UP

and found to contain a mass of clay!

Of course the poor woman who has been so foully dealt with, will step into the possession of the valuable property left on the St. Lawrence.

Who ever read a chapter more replete with incidents than this, and it has all the additional interest of being fact.

It is hoped that the guilty fleeing wretch will be caught, and dealt with as he deserves.

This astonishing tale says a good deal about the standards of journalism, the laws of libel, and the gullibility of the public in nineteenth-century North America. That it should be published at all is incredible; that it should be believed is staggering. Yet it must be understood that British Columbia a century ago was scarcely known to the outside world. Who really knew what weird rites were practised among the savage tribes who roamed that dark labyrinth of forest and canyon behind the bulwark of the Rockies? Just as the Elizabethans believed that strange creatures with flat heads and single eyes lurked beyond the unexplored rim of the world, so credulous Easterners were prepared to accept the fantasy of a native chieftain exchanging a golden hoard for the body of a white maiden.

With the rumours out in the open, Cameron realized that finally he must act. He published an advertisement in the Cornwall *Freeholder* announcing that on Tuesday, August 19, 1873, he would have the coffin raised from the family plot at Cornwall and cut open so that all present might look upon the face of his dead wife. The entire population was invited to the opening, to take place at another burial ground, the Salem Cemetery, nine miles east of Cornwall, only a few hundred yards from Fairfield.

Here before a crowd of hundreds of the curious and the morbid, the outer casing of the casket was removed. Then the tinsmith began his work.

Cameron stood at the new graveside, head bowed, his late wife's family beside him. His brother Duncan, standing directly behind him as the coffin was opened, noticed red and white streaks on the back of the bereaved man's neck and thought he was about to suffer a stroke. Later he learned what was in John Cameron's mind: what if some vandal, in search of rumoured treasure, had opened the coffin? What if the body had been disposed of and the box sealed again? If there was no corpse, Cameron was convinced he would not leave the cemetery alive.

His fears were unfounded. As the metal was worked open, the face of the dead woman appeared, almost perfectly preserved; only the eyes were sunken. A cry rent the air; it was the dead woman's mother. "*It's Sophie!*" she cried. She had recognized her daughter and the Paisley shawl beneath her head, its colours faded by the alcohol.

Hundreds now filed soberly past the opened casket. That done, Cameron asked if they were satisfied that the remains were those of his first wife. All agreed that they were.

"Dust to dust," said Cariboo Cameron. "Pour off the alcohol."

Twenty-five gallons splashed on to the ground, burning the turf; months later visitors to the cemetery would point out the spot where no grass grew and repeat the story.

Sophia Cameron was given that day her fourth and final funeral, her last resting place marked by a marble memorial four feet high, running the full length of the grave and surrounded by an ornamental fence fixed in a base of cut stone.

The episode, in his nephew's phrase, "did something" to Cameron. He stepped up the pace of his living and spending. On the first day of each month he held court in the front hall of Fairfield, seated behind an ornate carved desk, listening to the appeals of neighbours, relatives, and complete strangers, and dispensing largess.

His standards of judgment were uncomplicated. He would fix his ice-blue eyes upon each petitioner and ask: "Are you an honest man?"

If the answer was a flat yes, he was inclined to refuse. But if the answer was "I try to be," the request was usually granted. Cameron's loans were generally in the range of one hundred dollars, a considerable sum at the time.

If he was trying to buy respect, he did not succeed. The very people who grovelled in that pillared hall were later to jeer at the "crazy old prospector" who went through a fortune in less than a generation. What *was* Cameron's motivation? His nephew believed he was trying to buy his way out of a self-inflicted purgatory.

His investments began to turn sour. He plunged into gold properties in Madoc, Ontario, and Beauce County, Quebec. He built a lighthouse at Port Magdalen. He took a contract to dredge the Lachine Canal. None of these ventures paid off. But the real financial blow came when he bought a working sawmill with two million feet of dressed lumber and a timber limit on Lake Superior. Cameron, the man who had squandered hundred-dollar bills on strangers, quarrelled with an employee over the sum of $3.50. The disgruntled worker set fire to the mill. Cameron had no insurance. Shortly afterwards he lost the timber limit in a law suit. In 1884, he tried to recoup by investing in yet another gold mine, this one in Nova Scotia. But Nova Scotia was not the Cariboo, and Cameron lost the remnants of his fortune.

The Cariboo! It haunted his mind and obsessed his dreams. Some of his relatives had banded together to mortgage their properties and raise a few thousand dollars for the man who had been their benefactor; others with shorter memories refused to join. Cameron went through it all in a few months. What did it matter when he had already resolved to make a new fortune in British Columbia? All of the old optimism returned; he, John Alexander Cameron, would go back to the frontier and, he promised, within three years come back in triumph. Had he not done it before? Had he not followed his dreams and seen them come true? It would all come true again.

No need now to make that exhausting journey across Panama. The newly completed Pacific railroad would speed him and his wife to the coast in a few days. On May 11, 1886, the *Colonist* noted his arrival: "Old British Columbians experienced a genuine and agreeable surprise yesterday when the once familiar form of John A. Cameron appeared on the streets." The paper also noted that Cameron "looks as young as he did 23 years ago." That was journalistic licence. Cameron's hair and beard were white, his massive figure shrunken. He left his wife in the capital and set out for the Big Bend of the Fraser River, where he staked a claim on Carne Creek. He did his best to work the ground, but heavy rains in the summer of 1887 broke not only his dam but also his health. Reluctantly he abandoned the claim, returned to Victoria in November, and, enfeebled by a haemorrhage of a lung, spent the next ten months in convalescence.

But he would not give up, for the Cariboo still called. Surely there must yet be gold in those golden valleys! His old friend Robert Stevenson, now a prosperous farmer in the Fraser Valley, came to Victoria to renew a long-dormant friendship. In vain he tried to persuade Cameron to give up his dream of the Cariboo; it was not possible to make a second fortune in a worked-out mining camp. Cameron stubbornly refused to heed his advice. Off he went to the Cariboo, wearing his $150 Persian lamb coat, a relic of his former wealth, "an emaciated old man . . . a wreck of his former self," to quote the *Colonist*'s later obituary (journalistic licence works both ways), "but with the fires of his enterprising spirit unquenched."

The Camerons put up at Mason's Hotel in Barkerville, but this was not the Barkerville that Cameron had known. As for Camerontown, it was a ghost community, its shacks crumbling before the invading forest. There are few sights more depressing than a dying mining camp. The roofs of log cabins untended cannot withstand the weight of the winter snows and are soon crushed. Doors hang open, creaking and banging in the wind. The panes in the saloon windows are quickly shattered. Rust and rot take over. Willow and alder creep through the plank sidewalks, blurring the perimeter of the community. Trudging up the familiar length of Williams Creek, Cameron came face to face with decay: old lengths of cable tangled in the gravels; crumbling mineshafts; the skeletons of wheelbarrows; and the valley floors washed down to bed rock, scoured clean of gold.

The dream was shattered. He returned to the hotel and took to his bed. His wife tried with little success to rouse him. On Wednesday, November 7, 1888, he turned his face to the wall and died. The doctors diagnosed the cause as "paralysis of the brain," but the handful of old-timers in Barkerville had a different explanation: they said that Cariboo Cameron, at the age of sixty-eight, had died of a broken heart.

Nobody struggled this time to take the coffin back to Summerstown, although the task would have been immeasurably easier. He was buried, instead, in the frontier community that briefly bore his name, almost on that site where his dreams had come true and far, far away from that other grave whose occupant could now be truly said to rest in everlasting peace.

10
Ned Hanlan and the Golden Age of Sculling

Was there ever a world champion like Ned Hanlan? I doubt it. He was one of those athletic paragons who, like meteors, dazzling in their brilliance, flash across the sky only to flare out as suddenly as they burst forth. Hanlan of Toronto – the fastest sculler in the world, almost certainly the fastest sculler in history (all but one of his records still stand after a century) – is it possible that he achieved it all in just ten years? Consider his history: champion of Burlington Bay at nineteen; champion of Canada at twenty-two; champion of America at twenty-three; champion of England at twenty-four; champion of the world at twenty-five; beaten four years later at an age when most men are still clambering slowly toward the crest of their careers. Hanlan was finished as a world champion before he reached thirty; but what a champion he was!

He was to sculling what Roger Bannister was to the mile run. His triumphant decade, 1874–84, was one of those glorious accidents when the accomplishment of an athlete and the popularity of a sport coincide and enhance one another. Hanlan *made* sculling; it might also be said that he unmade it, for he was the de Gaulle of oarsmen. None who followed had his flair. Sculling is not the world's most exciting sport; it lacks the speed of skiing, the danger of sports-car racing, the drama of the greater spectator sports. But Hanlan had the showmanship, the theatre, the pure *pizazz* to turn it into a spectacle.

When Hanlan rowed, the world turned out to watch. In Canada, crowds of ten or twenty thousand came to see him row – more than turned up for Grey Cup matches in a later century when the country was five times as large. He outclassed his opponents; could and did run rings around them. But not for him the long lead, the dull finish. Better to counterfeit collapse, draw a gasp from the crowd, or make it laugh, circle back from the finish line, stage any number of bravado gestures to bring applause from the spectators and groans from his rivals – anything to juice up the audience. Better to row just hard enough to make it *look* like a race. Only once in his ten-year string of victories did Hanlan need to go all out for speed, and that was on the remarkable day when he rowed alone after his opponent's shell had been mysteriously sabotaged. To prove that he had had nothing to do with the crime, to show that he could beat any man alive on the water, Ned Hanlan rowed a five-mile course at a speed that had never before been attained and that has never since been surpassed.

Hanlan's style and showmanship brought him an adulation that has rarely been equalled. He was remarkably good-looking, with the regular features and curly hair so fashionable in the engraved advertisements of the day: "The handsomest gentleman I or anyone has ever seen," to quote the words of a contemporary. In all the accounts of the period of Hanlan and his victories, there was scarcely a snide word written about him; he was undeniably likeable, a man apparently without enemies, the perfect sports hero.

Of the private Hanlan we know very little, except that he was happily married (in 1877) and the father of eight children. The glimpses we have of him are the public ones, and they are all remarkably serene. In all his appearances he seems to be a man without neuroses or observable weaknesses (unless one counts his propensity to clown during a race). His private life must have been equally untroubled, since nobody apparently thought it worth writing about.

He was small for an oarsman, a shade under five foot nine and weighing a mere hundred and fifty pounds. Many of the scullers he vanquished were his physical superiors; but what Hanlan lacked in strength he made up in style. He rowed without apparent fatigue. Often his opponents, straining every muscle, found they were working twice as hard as Hanlan but not travelling as fast. His single-seat shell, someone remarked, seemed to have been drawn along the waters as if by an invisible string.

Hanlan's effortless style grew out of his mastery of sculling techniques. His long stroke was developed because he thoroughly understood some of the technical innovations of the day: the extended rowlocks, for example, and the sliding seat. Hanlan did not invent these new devices, which came into use about the time he began to row in earnest, but he mastered them to such an extent that he revolutionized rowing. In former days, scullers used to gain extra leverage by sliding back and forth on buffalo skins.

Hanlan, who became known as the Father of the Sliding Seat (he was the first to adapt it to the single-seat shell), perfected an odd kind of crouch which, together with his acute sense of pacing, made him unbeatable. He used the seat and the rowlocks to extend his arms so that his stroke was always longer than that of his opponents. In his ten-year heyday, he took part in some three hundred and fifty races. He lost no more than half a dozen.

The rise of rowing as a spectator sport in eastern Canada coincided with the decline of the pioneer era after Confederation. The adventure and the excitement had moved westward. Gold had been discovered in British Columbia; the North West Mounted Police were being formed; the Pacific Railway enterprise had just been launched. But in the settled areas, barn raisings and stump-blasting bees were giving way to roller skating, snowshoeing, tobogganing and, above all else, to boating. Basketball had not yet been invented. Baseball was in its infancy; the big leagues had scarcely been formed. Ice hockey was a minority game confined to amateurs. There was no Stanley Cup, no World Series. Rugby, football and soccer had scarcely reached the embryo stage. Lacrosse, of course, was highly popular; but rowing was *the* international sport and in no country in the world was it more popular than in Canada.

The increase in leisure time helped. On Sundays and holidays everybody seemed to be out on the water. Toronto and Hamilton harbours vibrated with craft of every shape and description. When a four-oar crew from Saint John, New Brunswick, went to Paris in 1867 and defeated crews from England, France, Germany and the United States, there was no holding the rowing enthusiasts back home. Hanlan was just twelve years old in 1867, living on Toronto Island (where his father ran a store), rowing three-quarters of a mile every day to school and working as a fisherman in his spare time. He was raised, as they say, with a pair of oars in his hands. The Hanlans were poor shanty Irish and young Ned could not even afford a proper shell. His first boat was a home-made contraption, fashioned out of a two-inch plank, sharpened at both ends, with a seat and an outrigger mounted upon it. Hanlan was probably the first Canadian sports hero to break through the barrier of class: the boating world, after all, had social connotations and the yacht clubs catered to the topmost crust of society. But the day would come when members of the Royal Canadian Yacht Club would be pleased to escort Ned Hanlan home in style and welcome him as one of their own.

He was sixteen when, as a member of a three-man crew of fishermen, he rowed his first race. Two years later he switched to single-seat sculling. By May of 1876, he had acquired such a local reputation that a group of backers made the daring decision to enter him in the International Centennial Regatta in Philadelphia. The wiseacres scoffed; imagine sending a callow youth, unknown outside his own community, to compete with some of the world's most seasoned professionals!

Hanlan almost missed the big time. Just before leaving Toronto he learned that the police were after him for bootlegging liquor on the island. He hid out in a friend's house overnight, but the police caught up with him at the Toronto Rowing Club. Hanlan slipped away to the boathouse float, jumped into a skiff, and skimmed away across the harbour. It makes an apt little tableau: the frustrated bluecoats fuming at the dock while the future world's champion makes the best possible use of his technique to evade them. Far out in the lake a pleasure steamer, crammed with roistering members of the German Club of Toronto out on their annual picnic, was chugging off for Lewiston, New York. Hanlan with his long, fluid strokes easily overtook the sidewheeler and was soon happily ensconced among the *lederhosen* and meerschaums, out of reach of the Canadian law.

He was joined in Philadelphia by the man he had recently bested for the Ontario championship, Billy McKen. They trained quietly each morning. In the evenings, while Hanlan caught up on his sleep, the convivial McKen made the rounds of local taverns, placing bets on Hanlan for his Toronto backers. Hanlan astonished and nettled the big New York gamblers by winning the first two heats against American favourites. That would never do; the decision was made to put him out of the race. Fortunately for Hanlan, but unhappily for McKen, they confused the two men. Somebody poisoned McKen's beer; the following morning his legs buckled under him and he was shipped back to Toronto on a stretcher. To the astonishment of all, the pink-cheeked, curly-haired 21-year-old nobody went on to win the final heat – and in the fastest time on record. He returned in triumph, the summons forgotten, the scoffers confounded. A vast crowd was on hand at the bayside to greet him on his return as, atop a hook and ladder wagon, he led a torchlight parade to a welcoming banquet at the Queen's Hotel. In a single race, Ned Hanlan had become one of the international demi-gods of sport.

In those days champion scullers were owned by syndicates in much the same way as boxers were owned in a later era. Hanlan was backed by the Hanlan Club – no social institution but a hard-headed business enterprise, organized for profit. (One of its members was the local American consul, Colonel Albert Shaw.)

Though regattas were drawing thousands, it was the matched races that held the most appeal because, like prizefights, they featured only two men – challenger and champion. In such races, the backers put up prize money and fenced off the course for paying customers. The real profit, however, lay in the side bets placed before the race. The same scullers would meet again and again, as racehorses do, on different courses. Skulduggery of various kinds was not uncommon: Billy McKen was not the only man to succumb to poison before a contest. Gamesmanship was also used to neutralize opponents. One famous sculler indulged in a series of false starts to exhaust his rival. Another purposely picked a fight with his adversary just as the race began; the angered sculler found he was still arguing at the starting line while his tormentor shot two lengths into the lead.

In 1877, Hanlan's career appeared briefly to falter. He had broken an outrigger in one regatta and lost a second race at Boston when he was disqualified for fouling an opponent. When Wallace Ross of Saint John, then the Canadian champion, challenged him to a five-mile race with a purse of one thousand dollars a side, his backers started to hedge their bets. Ross, having just set a new record for four miles, was the heavy favourite. Hanlan's backers began putting some of their money on the other man. In spite of this lack of support Hanlan remained calm, worked out regularly, ate heartily, slept peacefully. In fact he took a siesta on the day of the race and had to be wakened to go out onto the course. The odds were eight to one on Ross, but Hanlan, pulling at a steady sweep of thirty-two strokes a minute, was a length ahead at the half-mile mark and had doubled his lead, without effort, by the time the first mile was passed. Ross, pulling at thirty-seven strokes a minute, kept forcing himself to the utmost; one observer felt that he was wrenching himself apart. Suddenly, at the mile-and-a-quarter mark, he dug his sculls too deep and was seen to plummet headlong into the water. Hanlan was awarded the Canadian championship.

Hanlan's imperturbable sculling style, the ease with which he managed to skim across the water without perceptible effort, was psychologically devastating. Again and again one finds his opponents coming to physical grief as a result of tension, over-exertion and, perhaps, frustration. One of Hanlan's tactics was to set such a searing pace in the first few hundred yards that rival scullers tended to give up. Not long after he beat Ross, Hanlan won the American championship against Evan "Eph" Morris, a noted oarsman from Pittsburgh who, according to a contemporary account, "made such a terrible effort to retrieve his fortunes that it is very doubtful if he has ever been the same man since." Hanlan literally drove some of his opponents out of professional competition.

One of these was Charles Courtney, a carpenter from Union Springs, New York, who had won the amateur championship at Philadelphia in 1876 when Hanlan won the professional. Courtney was a big man, well over six feet, heavier than Hanlan and fifteen years older. Between 1878 and 1880, he and Hanlan took part in three match races, which were the most peculiar and most questionable of the Toronto sculler's career.

The first match took place at Lachine, Quebec, on October 3, 1878. The match was for twenty-five hundred dollars a side, but the citizens of Montreal were so enthusiastic that they added an additional six thousand dollars to the already substantial stake. Multitudes poured in from all parts of the United States and Canada to watch the contest. Courtney started out as the betting favourite but the odds suddenly changed at the last moment. When Sheriff Harding of Saint John shouted "Go!" the money was on Hanlan, one hundred dollars to sixty.

To the onlookers it appeared to be a seesaw race, but the experts soon knew that Courtney was hopelessly outclassed. At two miles Hanlan was in the lead. After the turn, at the four-mile point, Courtney almost caught him and began forcing Hanlan off the course. Hanlan warned him to straighten out and as he did so, the Toronto sculler pulled ahead and won. That night there was an ovation for the two men in Montreal's Windsor Hotel and a grand reception the following night at the Victoria skating rink, but those who had seen the race were not satisfied. Some claimed Hanlan had only won because Courtney had intruded on his lane. Others whispered darker suspicions: that Courtney had agreed in advance to lose the first race and that Hanlan's backers had obligated him to throw the second. These suspicions weren't dispelled by the curious events that took place during the later matches. But before that, Ned Hanlan had an appointment overseas.

His backers had matched him against John Hawdon, then considered to be the coming champion oarsman of England. The two men would compete on the three-and-a-half-mile championship course on the River Tyne. English boating experts laughed at the idea of a Canadian crossing the Atlantic to row against a man of Hawdon's proven skill. They backed their man heavily, not knowing that Hanlan's syndicate had matched him against Hawdon as a mere test, preparing for a more significant encounter with William Elliott, then the champion of England. When Hanlan began training on the Tyne, every effort was made to conceal his style from the bookies; but it was no use – by race time the odds were on Hanlan, two to one.

Here, for the first time, Hanlan indulged in some of the horse-play and gamesmanship that was to infuriate his English and Australian opponents. Hawdon started off at a vigorous thirty-eight to forty-two strokes a minute. Hanlan, with his longer and easier sweep, pulled at a little over thirty and took the lead. Soon he was three lengths ahead of Hawdon and the odds on the Canadian – for those who still wished to bet – rose to one hundred to one. As they passed the meadows, packed with spectators, Hanlan actually stopped to bail out his boat, nodding and laughing to the people who were running along the bank. "Poor Hawdon," wrote a reporter, "was painfully struggling along but in a piteous plight, thoroughly exhausted." As the crowd shouted and laughed, Hanlan allowed himself to fall back until he was only a couple of lengths ahead of his frustrated rival. Again he spurted forward, bowing and smiling to the cheering crowd. He finished four lengths in the lead, but had he wished he could have humiliated Hawdon by half a mile.

The match race with Elliott, the English champion, was set for June 16 on the same course. Scores of Canadians from Toronto, Montreal, Windsor and Belleville were on hand to cheer their man. The river was so black with boats that navigation was almost impossible. Hanlan appeared just before noon and took off his cap as the crowd cheered; he was wearing the familiar dark blue singlet and shorts, which had earned him the nickname of the Boy in Blue. Elliott was stripped to the waist. In the accounts of Hanlan's major races his opponents are always described as perspiring freely; but the Boy in Blue never doffed his singlet.

Hanlan was an easy favourite with the gamblers and quickly proved it. At first it seemed to Elliott's backers that the race would be tight; later they realized that the Canadian wasn't really trying. Elliott had not mastered the long slide and the swivelled rowlocks; his oars dug too deeply into the water, splashing and ploughing away in contrast to Hanlan's perfect style. "The style in which Hanlan moves his oars. . .must attract notice," one sportswriter noted. "The broad blades skim so close to the surface of the water that they are scarcely seen. . . .On the water Hanlan and his boat are as much in harmony as an animate and inanimate object can be. His sliding is as methodical and regular and as free from apparent effort as the motion of the driving shaft of a locomotive engine when running at a regular rate of speed." Hanlan beat the English champion by ten lengths and broke the course record by fifty-five seconds. To the sporting press of England he was "the most speedy and finished oarsman that was ever seen on the Thames or Tyne."

The new champion of England returned to a tumultuous welcome. He sailed to New York, took a train to Niagara and boarded the lake steamer *Chicora*. Ten miles out of Toronto, every conceivable craft that could be mustered was waiting to greet him: five large sidewheelers loaded to the gunwales with cheering people, all the yachts of the Royal Canadian Yacht Club and a scattering of small craft. As the *Chicora* steamed by, the entire flotilla lined up behind her, the whistles shrieking, the crowd yelling and the bands playing "Hail the Conquering Hero." Hanlan, standing on the roof of the pilot house, waved to the throngs cramming the Yonge Street wharf. That evening he appeared before an enormous gathering at the Horticultural Gardens to receive an address of welcome from the mayor.

All contemporary accounts describe Hanlan as a modest and totally moral man. An acquaintance recalled that, in all the years he knew him, he never heard him utter a vulgar word, nor had he been "party to a suggestive story.... Morally he was the cleanest man I had ever known." In 1933, a biographer wrote that "of all men, he combined the most likeable qualities. Unreserved, gracious, kindly, clean, humorous, honest and sporting, are just a few of the virtues attributed to the world's new demi-god. He is accredited with those two sterling qualities, friendliness and cleanliness of mind." Yet Hanlan's good name was certainly besmirched, if only temporarily, during the second of his notorious races with Charles Courtney.

The match was set for October 16, 1879, in the little upstate New York town of Mayville on Lake Chautauqua, which had given its name to the famous literary and scientific tent circuit. The promoter was A. T. Soule, of Rochester, the proprietor of a stomach tonic known as Hop Bitters and the owner of the Hop Bitters Baseball Team. Soule's plan was to bring Courtney and Hanlan to Mayville for a purse of six thousand dollars, if the businessmen of the town would pay him five per cent of the take they received from the tens of thousands who would surely arrive to watch the match. The locals needed no prompting. They built a grandstand two thousand feet long with seats for fifty thousand. A railroad, which built a special spur line, brought in an observation train half a mile long from which spectators could watch the race in comfort. Steamboats began to sell tickets and even old barges were patched up and made ready for the event at five dollars a seat.

On the eve of the race the little town of one thousand found itself swamped. Hotels raised their prices from a dollar a day to twelve dollars. It was said that five thousand people were forced to sleep on chairs, tables and floors. Others rented piano crates, bales of hay, corners of barns as sleeping accommodation.

The town sizzled with rumours. Courtney was said to have developed a new and secret method of training. Hanlan, it was whispered, had concealed a bellows in his shell for extra propulsion. The odds on both men shifted hourly. The referee, William Blaikie, complained that he had heard persistent rumours of a fix. He tried to close down the betting pools but pressure from the railway and from Soule, who was getting five per cent of everything, including the gamblers' take, forestalled him.

Courtney started as the favourite, but when the contestants' form was observed during the final day of training, the odds dropped to even money: both men seemed to be in the peak of condition. After that the betting went crazy. The odds swung back to Courtney in the teeth of new rumours: one hundred to ninety, one hundred to seventy-five, even one hundred to fifty. It was said that the Canadians, possessed of information that their man would throw the race, were desperately trying to hedge their bets. At one point odds could be obtained on Courtney at one betting box, on Hanlan at another. Finally, the sheriff agreed to close the boxes; when they were allowed to reopen, two hours later, some gamblers refused all further bets because they had no idea what odds to offer. The New York *Sportsman* reported that "the fancy could not find out who had fixed whom to do what."

Few were able to sleep during the stifling night that followed. The following morning, at nine, a stunning piece of news shook the community. Down Main Street on a velocipede came a tinhorn gambler crying: "Boys, it's all off! Charley Courtney's boat's been sawed."

A terrifying scene followed as hundreds of furious men choked Main Street for three blocks attempting to find out what had happened. They soon learned that the news was correct: both Courtney's skiff, *Hop Bitters*, and his practice shell, had been sawn in half at a time when the two watchmen, entrusted with guarding the boathouse, had unaccountably left their post and gone to the village to "play a little casino."

The rage of the crowd was understandable. Courtney was cornered and interrogated. He denied all knowledge of the incident. His trainer had discovered the damage the previous evening but said he hadn't wished to disturb Courtney's night's rest. Nor had he informed the press or anybody else of the disaster. Attempts were made to force Courtney to race in a borrowed shell. He bluntly refused. Blaikie, the referee, his face white with anger, announced that the match would be held anyway.

And so Hanlan sculled the five-mile course alone – and magnificently. He finished in 33 minutes, 56¼ seconds, breaking the record by 1 minute, 14¼ seconds. He was formally declared the winner, but his victory was Pyrrhic; Soule departed, after withdrawing all his money from the local bank, leaving Hanlan with a rubber cheque for six thousand dollars. The gambling pools also declared all bets off and returned the bettors' wagers, minus a one per cent handling charge. Nobody involved with the race, with the exception of Blaikie, emerged untainted.

Who had sawn Courtney's boat, and why? There is little doubt that the contest was fixed from the start. In order to get Courtney to race at all, Hanlan's backers had had to promise that he would win the second of the three matches. As David Ward, of the Hanlan Club, said, "How else would we have got Courtney to the scratch? A log chain wouldn't have dragged him there unless he knew he could win." The stumbling block was Hanlan himself, who had not been told of the arrangement. The Boy in Blue had no intention of throwing the race; one rumour said that he had already turned down a gambler's fifty thousand dollar bribe to lose. Undoubtedly the Toronto contingent knew this, because one of Ward's friends tried to place a quiet bet on Hanlan the day before the contest. But the secret leaked out. The Courtney camp discovered the double cross and told Courtney that the Canadians were welshing on their promises to ensure his win. The boats were undoubtedly sawn with Courtney's knowledge, and perhaps at his instigation, to prevent his further humiliation and, more important, to save all the money that had been staked on the outcome.

One thing is certain: Courtney was never a match for Hanlan. In spite of their discomfiting experience with Courtney and Soule, Hanlan's backers signed him up for a third race set for May 19, 1880, again under the sponsorship of the Hop Bitters salesman. This time, however, they had another oarsman on hand, just in case Courtney backed out. Sure enough, a few hours before the contest, Courtney developed a "blinding headache." His backers forced him into the contest and he actually started off in the lead. He wavered swiftly, stopped to bathe his brow in the water, fell back, and after two miles, quit altogether as the crowd howled in derision. That was the end of Courtney as a single-scull racer.

That November, Hanlan rowed the race of his career in England against the self-styled champion of the world, Edward A. Trickett, of Sydney, Australia. William Harding, the *Police Gazette's* sporting reporter, wrote that "perhaps in the history of boating there never was so much excitement over a race, or such a vast amount of money wagered."

Trickett was a six-foot, four-inch giant – jumpy, anxious and sullen. Hanlan was fifty pounds lighter and five years younger. Trickett, having defeated the English champion, Joseph Sadler, was claiming to be the world's greatest oarsman, even though he had never raced a North American sculler. He knew Hanlan was the man to beat, had even had a shell built and rigged like Hanlan's and had tried, not very successfully, to emulate the Hanlan style. His backers, the Thompson brothers, well-known Melbourne bookmakers, believed their man could beat any sculler in the world. Even after watching Hanlan's impressive training sprints on the Thames, they did not change their minds. "It is almost incomprehensible," Harding wrote, "that so many intelligent men could have been so strangely wrong."

The race was to be held over the famous Oxford and Cambridge boat race course from Putney to Mortlake on the Thames. Every bridge, on that unpromising November morning, was crowded from first light with spectators, peering through the fog and drizzle. Thousands more blackened the riverbanks for the entire four and a quarter miles of the course. Half a million dollars had been wagered on the outcome, with the English joining the Australians in backing Trickett. In Canada, the wise money was on Hanlan. Two days before the race the queue of people buying bank drafts for that purpose ran two blocks down Yonge Street from the Bank of Montreal in Toronto. In that city alone, forty-two thousand dollars was wagered on the Boy in Blue, enough to cause a last-minute shift in the odds.

But in truth, what had been billed as the Race of the Century turned out to be a farce, enlivened only by Hanlan's showmanship. The two men set off at 12:14 p.m. From the start Trickett appeared tense and anxious; clearly he was overtrained. Hanlan, by contrast, gambolled to the stake boat, apparently unconcerned about the outcome. At the moment he got underway he appeared to be criticizing his opponent; it was not until well after the starting signal that he turned his attention to the stern of his skiff and began to devote his energies to the race.

At the end of the first mile Hanlan was two lengths ahead of his rival. Trickett, labouring heavily, was observably outclassed. At Biffen's boathouse, Hanlan began to clown. He stopped rowing for a moment, leaned back in his boat, indulged in a leisurely survey of the scenery, and then took up the oars in a half-hearted way, "as though he would prefer to linger did not circumstances compel his progressing." He moved thirty yards, stopped again, moved on again, stopped again and thus continued by fits and starts down the course.

Trickett's face was pale, his expression wild. Hanlan, four lengths in the lead, now indulged in "a piece of harlequinade, the like of which has never before been witnessed in a race." He dropped his sculls clumsily into the water, fell forward onto his face and lay there for a moment or so – long enough to elicit groans from the spectators, who thought he had suffered some sort of seizure. Suddenly he sprang upright, resumed his oars and went back to work, laughing. There was an answering roar of relieved laughter from the crowd.

During this display, Hanlan's straining rival had almost overtaken him. Again Hanlan skimmed merrily away. Now he began to row with alternate oars, stopping repeatedly, looking cheerfully about, dawdling and clowning. He spotted his old rival, Elliott, in a boat beside the course, rowed over to him and chatted as they moved along side by side.

The Bull's Head Inn, Hanlan's headquarters, hove into view. His backers cheered. Hanlan produced a white handkerchief and waved cheerfully. As one of them later remarked: "I fully expected him to stand up in his boat and dance the Highland Fling." He won the race by seven seconds; he could probably have won it by a mile. In this contest, which saw more money wagered than had ever been bet on a sculling race, Trickett never had the ghost of a chance. There were some that day who seriously suggested that Hanlan's skiff was propelled by some kind of hidden machine. Nonetheless the audience was satisfied. "Hanlan's sculling was worth travelling a hundred miles to see," declared a writer for the London publication *Sporting Life*.

Hanlan now carried the official title of Champion Oarsman of the World. He was probably the first bona fide world's champion of anything. Except for boating there were as yet no international sports contests. The modern Olympic Games, which would introduce the idea of world championships, were still sixteen years in the future. But Hanlan was an international figure, handsome, clean-cut, still boyish but, with his fashionable new soupstrainer mustache, mature enough to be mobbed by women. His picture and his name were reproduced on Hanlan scarves, Hanlan shirts, Hanlan belts, Hanlan ties and, of course, Hanlan snuff boxes. It was said, truly, that no other Canadian was so well known in the English-speaking world. In Australia, a town was named Toronto, to honour Hanlan's prowess.

Hanlan successfully defended his world title six times. Elias Laycock of Sydney, Australia, who had won the International

Above: *Hanlan makes a laughing stock out of New York sculling ace Fred Plaisted at Toronto Bay, May 14, 1878. The judges didn't even bother to take the time.*

Below: *Hanlan's boathouse at Lachine, Quebec, on the eve of his race with Charles Courtney on October 3, 1878.*

Thames Regatta, was the first of the challengers. The race took place on May 22, 1881, on the Nepean river at Pendrith, Australia. En route, the champion staged profitable exhibitions: at Honolulu, for instance, hundreds of curious natives swam around his boat to watch him as he rowed. But Australia was an anticlimax. The odds on Hanlan were four to one; few would risk a wager. The promoters had invested heavily on the course, fencing in a space along each bank of the river with corrugated iron and erecting a big grandstand near the winning post. But the crowd was not as big as expected; Hanlan was too good. In the race that followed, his sweating opponent removed his jersey halfway down the course, but Hanlan stayed cool. A hundred yards from the winning post he allowed Laycock to catch up. When the two men were level he shot ahead with three or four powerful strokes and, amidst great excitement, won by a bare length. He had now won the Aquatic Championship Challenge Cup three times – from Elliott, from Trickett and from Laycock. Under the conditions of this race it was his forever. It can be seen today in Toronto's Marine Museum.

He raced Trickett again on the Thames on May 1, 1882. In Toronto, the *Globe's* headline told the story: THE INEVITABLE PROCESSION OF TWO REPEATED/VERY LITTLE BETTING AND LESS EXCITEMENT. Hanlan was a five to one favourite; Trickett again seemed anxious and nervous. In the race that followed, the Canadian played his usual cat and mouse game, rowing all the way to the finish line and then turning back to his rival, rowing even with him and spurting ahead to beat him by a length. "Never was there a victory so thorough and complete," the *Globe* reported. Trickett never appeared again in a major race.

Hanlan kept his title for four years, and then the inevitable decline began. If it is true that great champions experience ecstasies of triumph not given to the common herd, it is equally true that they must face a concomitant bitterness of defeat. Each loss becomes a little death, and as age advances, the losses can only accelerate. Hanlan was finally beaten at twenty-nine by an Australian ferryman named William Beach. His backers were astonished and chagrined. Hanlan blamed the climate and the treacherous and unfamiliar Paramatta River. Others blamed the round of banquets and receptions that had preceded the match. But the real culprit was time. Hanlan tried twice more to beat Beach; twice more he lost. Smaller races, more frequent defeats followed. Crowds still turned out to watch his demonstration of trick sculling. But the adulation slowly died. As late as 1897, Hanlan, who never admitted or believed he could be beaten, was still issuing challenges. By then there were no takers.

Yet he never lost his popularity. The citizens of Toronto presented him with a twenty thousand dollar house and a piece of freehold property on Toronto Island where he built a hotel. It is still known as Hanlan's Point. They hung a gigantic portrait of him ten feet high and six feet wide, in their city hall. In 1898, when he finally rested his oars, they elected him alderman for Ward Four. When he died on January 4, 1908, at the comparatively young age of fifty-two, ten thousand people filed past his bier. Almost two decades later, Hanlan was still remembered. In 1926, Toronto financed, at a cost of seventeen thousand dollars, a twenty-foot statue to him on the grounds of the Canadian National Exhibition – the only statue in the world ever erected to a sculler. On it is engraved this tribute: "Edward Hanlan, the most renowned oarsman of any age whose victorious career has no parallel in the annals of sport." It has been said of Canadian heroes that they are rarely honoured in their own country. Happily, that was never the fate of the Boy in Blue.

Ned Hanlan, October, 1878

11
Sailing Alone Around the World

May 6, 1896 – the South Pacific: The sun burnishes the sky and the sea is limitless. In all the vast circle of the ocean, there is only a single moving speck, a sloop barely thirty-six feet long, aptly named the *Spray*, sliding westward on the hot breath of a tropic breeze, like a fly scudding across a polished table. Her decks are empty. There is no one at the helm. Is she, then, a ghost ship conjured up, like a mirage, in the mind of a fever victim? Scarcely; for in all that infinity of water there is none to mark her passage. She is alone in the immensity of the southern sea and she will remain alone and unobserved for seventy-two days – seventy-two days without a stop, from Robinson Crusoe's fertile isle of Juan Fernandez to the coconut palms of Samoa, seven thousand miles as the gull flies. And this is only a small part (one-sixth, to be precise) of a long and remarkable odyssey.

Old Slocum sits hidden in his book-lined cabin aboard the *Spray*, totally alone, as he has been since he departed Yarmouth, Nova Scotia, the previous July. Old? Actually he is fifty-two. It is just that his face is leathered by the sea and the winds – the skin nut brown and crinkled, the chin and ears a little grizzled – that his hands are gnarled and knobby, that his body is all bone and muscle, and that he has already lived a lifetime and more. Supple as a bobcat, agile as a monkey, he is the most experienced salt-water man of his age, but also an anachronism – a committed sailor in a world that has done with sail. The days of the clippers have ended. The bustling ports of Saint John, Lunenberg and Halifax have wound down. The big rafts of squared timbers have all but vanished from the Ottawa River and life is beginning to speed up. In Boston, the first American subway has just been completed. In Detroit, the first commercial automobile has just made its appearance. And on the sand dunes of northern Indiana, a man named Octave Chanute is ushering in a new age of flight, with the development of a successful glider. Joshua Slocum, the out-of-work sea captain, cares nothing for this; too old a bird to learn new tricks, he has chosen this moment to do the impossible. He is sailing alone around the world.

He is acutely aware of being alone – alone with the vastness of the horizons, the play of the winds, the wells and currents of the sea, the moving sun and the wheeling stars. The very coral reefs, he will write, keep him company. His living companions are the flying fish that slap onto the glistening deck each night, the whales that cruise majestically past, the sharks, whom he calls "the tigers of the sea," and the birds: the men o'war soaring high above him, the red-billed tropic birds wheeling and arcing in the sky, the gulls and boobies screeching in his wake and settling on his mast.

With the sun rising astern and the Southern Cross abeam every night, he sprawls out in his cabin (for the *Spray*, which he has fashioned with his own hands, miraculously steers herself), reading his way through his library (Lamb, Addison, Gibbon, Coleridge, Cervantes, Darwin, Burns, Longfellow and his two greatest favourites, Robert Louis Stevenson and Mark Twain), poking about in his galley (trying his hand at fish stew and hot biscuits to lighten his regular diet of potatoes and salt cod) and occasionally (very occasionally) digging out his sextant to check his latitude.

Carried forward as if on a vast, mysterious stream, he is at one with his surroundings, feeling "the buoyancy of His hand who made all the worlds " – Old Slocum, veteran of a hundred sea adventures, survivor of a dozen murderous encounters, master of the ocean's finest sailing vessels (gone, now, every last one of them, sunk, beached, stove in, ravished, abandoned to the rot); Old Slocum on the greatest adventure of all, an adventure no one else has dared; Old Slocum, owner, master, mate and crew of a cockleshell, sailing all by himself around the world. Forty-six thousand miles. Three full years. Another lifetime.

For what else is there left for Slocum? He has been everywhere, seen everything, done everything – everything but this. He has been around the world five times on more ships than his hands have fingers, shuttling cargoes across the seven seas: he has stacked hay out of Montevideo, salt cod out of Kamchatka, coal from Nagasaki to Vladivostock, gunpowder from Shanghai to Taiwan, natural ice from Hakodati, sugar from the Philippines, timber out of Brazil. He has broken three mutinies (killed one man, maimed another) and survived outbreaks of fever, cholera and smallpox, not to mention storms, typhoons, hidden reefs and the thunderclap explosion of Krakatoa, which killed thirty-six thousand persons in August of 1883, but not Joshua Slocum, who managed to sail the *Northern Light* past the smoking island three days before the eruption that filled the sea around him with floating pumice and buried his decks in hot ash.

He has seen everything, met everybody, from Garfield Hayes, president of the United States, to Bully Hayes, South Seas pirate and blackbirder. He has made fortunes. His race to catch the crack mail schooner out of Honolulu brought him a five thousand dollar sack of gold. But he has also lost everything. The lovely barque *Aquidneck*, "as close to a yacht as a merchantman can be," with its parquetry floors, its grand piano and its blue and gold staterooms, was battered to pieces off the coast of Brazil with a full cargo of timber, leaving Slocum a pauper.

Since the age of sixteen, Slocum's whole existence has revolved around salt water. All seven of his children were born at sea or in foreign ports and the wife who bore them, the marvellous and beautiful Virginia – who could kill a shark with a single shot from her .32 and who had sailed with him on every voyage – sickened and died at sea, leaving him "like a ship without a rudder." He had married again but it was never the same; Hettie, the new bride, sailed with him and the four surviving children on the most extraordinary voyage of all: fifty-five hundred miles from Brazil to the Carolines in the thirty-five-foot *Liberdade*, a weird cross between a Cape Anne dory and a Japanese sampan. But that was all for Hettie; she never went to sea again. Slocum closed the shutters on what had been a warm and congenial personality and set a solitary course for himself.

So here he is, all alone as he prefers to be – Joshua Slocum, a Bay of Fundy boy from Annapolis County, Nova Scotia, born in 1844 into the age of the clipper ships: a seaman at sixteen, a first mate at eighteen, master of his own ship at twenty-five and at thirty-seven, captain of the *Northern Light*, the finest sailing vessel afloat. Joshua Slocum, master mariner, washed up at fifty, stubbornly refusing to come to any accommodation with steam power or iron hulls, preferring to work as a carpenter in a shipyard but forced out of that, too, for want of a fifty-dollar union fee. Joshua Slocum, picking up odd jobs on Boston harbour boats and hating it, dreaming of the great days of canvas, when he was king of the ocean, dreaming and hating his work until, on one black day, an entire load of coal mixed with dirt ("Cape Horn berries" they call it) half-buries him. In that moment, Slocum, casting his mind back to the *Northern Light* (two thousand tons, three decks, 233 feet long, full-rigged), can stand it no more. He quits his job and determines to return to the sea. He will make the longest possible voyage in the smallest possible craft and he will do it all alone.

Spring, 1893: In a pasture at Fairhaven, not far from New Bedford, Massachusetts, the hulk of an ancient oyster sloop lies rotting in the grass. Slocum can have her; her owner, a retired whaler, is a friend. Like a sculptor gazing on a lump of Carrera marble, Slocum sees a new ship hidden somewhere in the old. He will keep very little of her – only the model, the lines and the name: *Spray*. He cuts a new timber from the woods at Poverty Point and replaces a rotting one, then another and another – new timbers for old until the hull itself is new. He cuts an oak for her keel (she had been a centre-boarder but a drop keel is too likely to ship water at sea). He hauls a spruce trunk from New Hampshire for her mast. He cuts down another oak from the pasture for her stem piece, so tough that months later it will split a coral patch in two at the Keeling Islands without a scratch to itself. People come to watch in astonishment as the new ship takes form from the carcass of the derelict: thirty-six feet, nine inches overall; fourteen feet, two inches, beam; four feet, two inches deep in the hold; nine tons net; rigged as a sloop – a big craft for a lone man to handle. She has no engine, no power windlass, and no navigational aids except for a compass, some charts, a sextant and taffrail logs. But there's a secret to her, which even Slocum doesn't yet know. Later yacht designers, analysing her dimensions, will conclude that he has hit upon a perfectly balanced vessel. Ballasted with cement, she will be almost impossible to capsize. He has worked on her for thirteen months, supporting himself with odd jobs in the intervals, and she has cost him exactly $553.62.

Though the *Spray* claims Boston as her home port, Slocum's voyage will really begin at Yarmouth, Nova Scotia. He has come up to the Bay of Fundy to spend a month in the home town he ran away from, more than a generation before. (His father, a Methodist deacon, came from Loyalist stock; his mother was a Digby lighthouse keeper's daughter.) He must decide now which way to circle the earth: westward, round the Horn, or eastward, through the Mediterranean, the Suez Canal and the Red Sea? He hesitates, chooses, changes his mind; he will go east. He is without a chronometer – he cannot afford the fifteen dollars it wlll cost to have his old one cleaned and reset. So he buys a tin clock in Yarmouth for a dollar; its face is smashed – no matter.

But he has food. He has two barrels of ship's bread soldered up in tin cans (it must be soaked six hours before he can make bread pudding). He has flour, baking powder, salt, pepper, mus-

The famous Spray *is shown at the left rigged as a yawl– a mizzen sail behind the helm.*

Below: *Joshua Slocum as he looked a few years before he vanished with his ship.*

tard and curry. He has salt beef, salt pork, ham and dried codfish – real slabs of it, "thick as a board and broad as a side of sole leather." He has condensed milk in tins, butter in brine and muslin, eggs hermetically sealed, potatoes which he will roast in their jackets, sugar and tea, and coffee beans which he will grind himself. He will not need to buy fresh fruit, meat and vegetables: a man attempting such a voyage receives such perishables as gifts at every port he touches.

July 2, 1895: Slocum and the *Spray* clear Yarmouth harbour at a fast eight knots, scurrying to get clear of the track of the ocean liners which might run them down at night. He has designed a self-steering mechanism and discovers that it is successful beyond his wildest dreams. He had expected that the *Spray* would hold her course trimmed close to the wind, but now he finds that she can keep it up with her boom broad in a stiff breeze and a lumpy sea. It is a godsend. He can lash the helm and sleep while the sloop holds her course.

As the fog closes in (the familiar Atlantic fog of his childhood), it seems to Slocum that his past life is running before his eyes like a series of magic lantern slides. A babble of voices chatters in with the wind – all the voices he has heard in all the corners of the earth. The fog lifts, the weather clears, but he cannot shake off the realization that he is totally alone. He begins to shout commands, fearful that in the long days ahead he may lose his ability to speak; then, to keep himself company, he roars out sea chanties. The *Spray* races across the waters, leaving the biggest freighters in her wake, to the astonishment of their captains. Slocum's spirits begin to lift.

He reaches the Azores in just eighteen days. He has some newspaper dispatches to mail (he hopes to pay for the voyage by describing it in the press). He takes on a cargo of various fruits, the gift of the islanders, and sails off again, making a meal of fresh plums and old cheese – a combination that brings on a terrifying attach of stomach cramps. He barely has strength to haul down the mainsail and set the *Spray* on course when he falls to the cabin floor, delirious. For two days and two nights, his mind is wild with visions. The ghost of the pilot of Columbus's *Pinta* stands at the wheel talking to him. The ghost's advice is sound: don't mix plums with cheese. When he recovers, finally, he discovers the *Spray* is still on course, and going like a racehorse. He throws the plums overboard and dines on fish hash, stewed onions, pears and coffee. Later that day he harpoons and roasts a turtle, with fried potatoes on the side. When he reaches Gibralter on August 4, he finds that

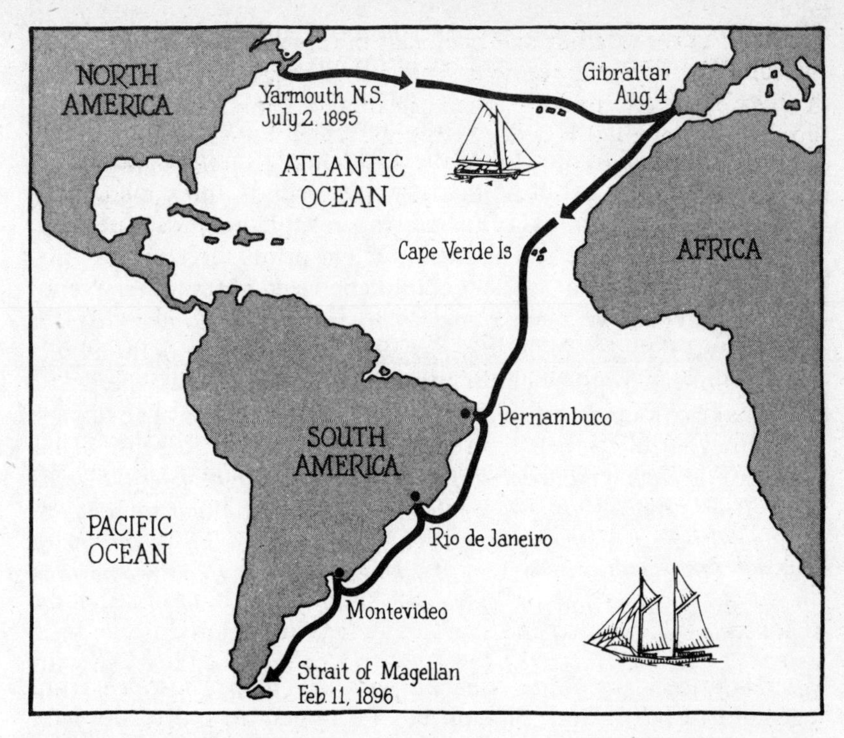

he has crossed the Atlantic in faster time than any vessel except for the big steamers.

And here he learns that he must turn back. The British officers who greet him, fête him, wine, dine and picnic him, urge him to avoid the Suez and the Red Sea. These narrow waterways are infested with pirates to whom a lone man in a small boat will be an easy victim. So Slocum must turn about and set the *Spray*'s course westward for Brazil.

Irony of ironies! He is scarcely back in the Atlantic before he encounters pirates. A Spanish felucca is in his wake, manned by a gang of ruffians intent on plunder. He changes course; the felucca follows. He veers; the felucca veers. He puts on sail but the felucca, a swift and slender sailboat, continues to close. Slocum prepares for an unequal fight; and then a monstrous wave strikes both ships, tearing loose the *Spray*'s boom. Slocum puts the helm hard down, pulls down the jib, hauls in the mainsail before it is shredded, and snatches up a rifle to ward off his attackers. He turns to fight and finds he has been saved by the elements: the same wave has torn away the felucca's mast.

He is totally used up, too tired even to cook a flying fish that has landed on his deck. Now he realizes, perhaps for the first time, that the voyage will call for "exertions ardent and lasting." In all his life he has never reached such a point of exhaustion. He sets the sloop on course, rolls into his bunk, and sleeps.

He sails with the tradewinds across the Atlantic, the helm lashed for most of the time, the little ship running without his hand. In his snug cabin he reads, writes, mends and cooks. He is still composing accounts of his adventures for the newspapers but there will be few takers. The Boston *Globe* prints three pieces only, then ceases; Slocum takes too long between dispatches. Newspaper readers have been tuned in to the modern journalism of Hearst and Pulitzer. Nelly Bly has already beaten the fictional record of Phineas Fogg by circling the globe in seventy-two days.

It takes Slocum forty days to recross the Atlantic. The voyage is so uneventful he feels himself again possessed by a sense of his isolation: *Leaving the Cape Verde Islands out of sight astern, I found myself once more sailing a lonely sea and in a solitude supreme all around. When I slept I dreamed that I was alone. This feeling never left me; but, sleeping or waking, I seemed always to know the position of the sloop, and I saw my vessel moving across the chart, which became a picture before me.*

Down the coast of South America past Uruguay: The *Spray* runs aground in hard sand. Slocum has fashioned a kind of dory for himself by sawing a proper dory in half and boarding up one end. In this stubby craft he sets out to free his ship. The leaky dory turns turtle. Slocum reaches for the gunwhale as she goes bottom up, for he suddenly realizes that he cannot swim, but remembering all the wiseacres who have predicted he will never return, he determines to survive. He hauls himself back onto the dory, rights her, paddles ashore, and with help frees the sloop.

Down the coast of Patagonia heading for the Horn: The seas are in a fury. A single, towering wave, masthead high, comes roaring down, swamping the *Spray*. She reels under the impact, rights herself and sails on.

Into the Strait of Magellan: Slocum is about to face his greatest ordeal. He has already seen mirages: an albatross sitting on the water looms up large as a ship; two sleeping seals appear as monstrous whales. Now, as he enters the Strait, steering between two great tide races (the wreck of a great steamship looming out of the foam), the mirages become audible. He has scarcely reefed his sails and retired to his cabin when he thinks he hears a warning cry: "*Spray*, ahoy!"

I sprang to the deck, wondering who could be there that knew the Spray so well as to call out her name passing in the dark; for it was now the blackest of nights all around except in the southwest, where the old, familiar white arch, the terror of Cape Horn, rapidly pushed up by a southwest gale. I had only a moment to douse sail and lash all solid when it struck like a shot from a cannon .... For thirty hours it kept on blowing hard.

He puts into Punta Arenas, the Strait port, and here an Austrian named Samblich makes him a present of a box of carpet tacks and advises him to strew his decks at night, for brigands haunt these waters, preying on vessels in trouble. The port captain urges him to wait until a gunboat can escort him, but Slocum is impatient to move on. Shoot straight if the savages surround you, the port captain tells him.

February 20, 1896: Slocum's fifty-second birthday. Back in the fury of the Strait again he has encountered the dreaded williwaws, terrible gales that suddenly strike vertically down the mountain slopes – "chunks" of wind, in fact, to use Slocum's word – that can uproot trees or anything else in their paths including any unfortunate vessels that happen to be in the way. He has reached Cape Froward, the southernmost point of the continent of South America; and here he has a dime-novel encounter with a group of native pirates led by one Black Pedro, a renegade Spaniard and notorious as the worst murderer on the bleak island of Tierra del Fuego. They attack the *Spray* in armed canoes, shrieking "Yammer-schooner!", a kind of beggar's plea. Slocum must prevent them knowing he is alone. He pops into his cabin, flings off his clothes, dons a new outfit, pops out again, holds up a bowsprit dressed as a sailor and then, as his pursuers try to close, fires a shot across the bow of the nearest canoe. Black Pedro fails to live up to his name; he and his gang turn tail.

The *Spray* clears Cape Pilar and enters the Pacific. But now a violent storm springs up and she is driven southeast down the coast of Tierra del Fuego towards Cape Horn. She runs for four days before the gale, her mainsail in rags. Slocum rigs up a square sail to replace it. The seas are mountainous and in the distance he can hear the deafening roar of tremendous breakers. As dawn lightens the sky he finds that he has entered the dreaded Milky Way of the Sea, a foaming labyrinth of hidden rocks and tiny channels churned into a perpetual fury. Years before, aboard the *Beagle*, Charles Darwin had written that any landsmen seeing the Milky Way would have nightmares for a week. Writes Slocum: *He might have added "or seaman" as well.* The ordeal that followed he later describes as the greatest sea adventure of his life. Others will compare it with the triumphs of Magellan and Drake and it will be called "in point of pure seamanship, the most remarkable of all."

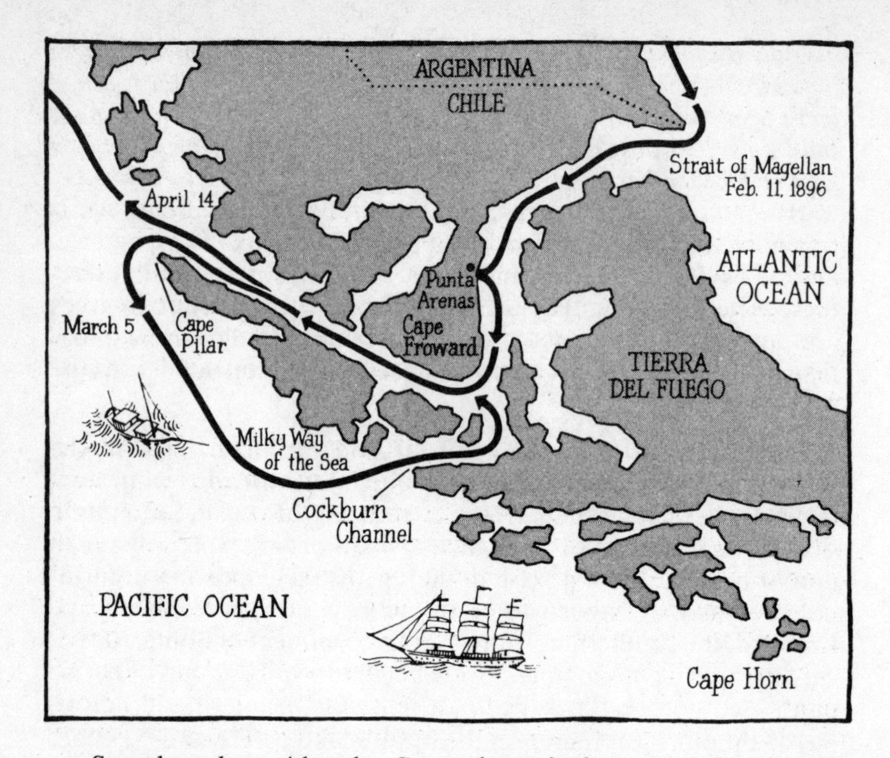

Somehow he guides the *Spray* through the maze of rock and foam to the comparative safety of some small islands. But his vessel is being blown east into the labyrinth of the Cockburn Channel which leads again to the Strait of Magellan. He has come almost full circle and there is nothing he can do. "Jaded and worn," he contents himself with a meal of venison stew; then, after sprinkling his deck with tacks, he turns in. At midnight he is awakened by a terrifying series of shrieks. A group of natives has boarded the *Spray*, bent on booty and murder; terrified by the tacks and howling like a pack of hounds, they are already leaping into their canoes and fleeing into the night. Slocum goes back to sleep.

Two days later, still trapped in the channels, he salvages a barrel of wine and an entire cargo of tallow from the wreckage of a doomed ship. The tallow comes in eight-hundred-pound casks, which Slocum must winch aboard by hand. But the old sea trader knows its value; later he will make a fancy profit from its sale.

Again he tries to head the *Spray* towards the Pacific. Again he fails. Again he is attacked by Fuegians, who launch a shower of arrows at him, one of which sticks fast in the mainmast. Slocum seizes his old Martini-Henry repeating rifle and drives them off. The land is as cruel as the inhabitants: black, broken cliffs that rise directly from the fury of the sea; sere slopes denuded of trees by the williwaws; dismal, foam-swept islands, half-hidden by the combers.

Day after day he struggles to sail west out of the prison of the Strait. Six times he is driven back by the gales. An Argentine cruiser offers to tow him east to safety; but that would mean giving up and that he will not do. It is almost two months since he cleared Cape Froward. He tries one more time and finally he succeeds. The *Spray* veers so close to the shore that her mast becomes entangled in the branches of the tree. Slocum calls out to his ship "as an impatient farmer might to his horse." *Didn't you know you couldn't climb a tree?* Clearly she has become, to him, a living companion.

April 13, 1896: The *Spray* sails out into the Pacific and a giant roller washes over her as if to cleanse her of the memories of those frustrating weeks. Slocum has been at the helm for thirty hours without rest. But soon the sloop is under full sail, jib full out, main unreefed and, for the first time, the jigger spread from the aft mast, converting her, temporarily, into a yawl. Next stop: Juan Fernandez, the island of Alexander Selkirk, the real-life castaway who was Defoe's model for Robinson Crusoe. They reach it in ten days.

Here, on this "blessed island" (Slocum's phrase) are lovely, wooded hills, fertile valleys and pure bubbling springs. There are no snakes and no wild animals and none of the frustrating trappings of civilization: a total absence of liquor, policemen and lawyers. All forty-five inhabitants glow with health and the children are beautiful. A boatload of natives arrives to greet the mariner who treats them to a breakfast of coffee and doughnuts cooked in the salvaged tallow. They are delighted. He shows them how to make doughnuts and then sells them the tallow; they reward him with a pile of gold coins salvaged from the wreck of a Spanish galleon. There are other rewards; he scampers about the hills with the children, picking wild fruit, including ripe quinces which he will preserve as he sails out again across the empty Pacific on that long seventy-two-day leg to Samoa.

What are his thoughts as the *Spray*, almost unaided, carries him westward? He writes that he is *en rapport* with his surroundings, that he feels the presence of the hand of God, that he has made companions of the birds, the fish, the mammals and the reefs (and, he might have added, the uncannily human *Spray*). Oddly enough, though sailing before the mast is a lonely life for most seamen, Slocum is not used to such loneliness. He has never cottoned to the kind of ersatz marriage which has been the fate of so many ship's captains: brief honeymoons snatched between long

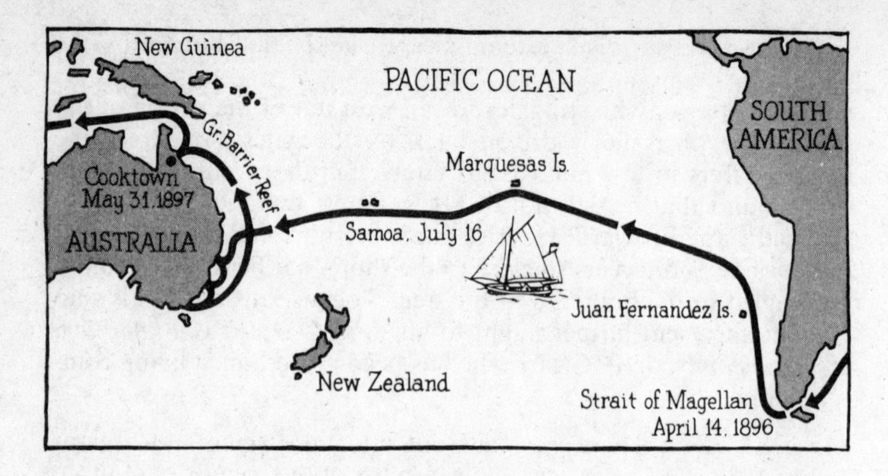

periods at sea. His beautiful, part-Indian wife, Virginia, had accompanied him on every voyage, from their first honeymoon trip out of Sydney, Australia, to Cook Inlet, Alaska (which ended in shipwreck) to that last, sad voyage aboard the *Aquidneck*. She had been the ideal shipboard wife, schooling her children, sewing and embroidering, playing the grand piano, all aboard ship. When a mutineer stabbed Slocum's first officer aboard the *Northern Light* in 1882, Virginia had covered her husband, a revolver in each hand, as he subdued the crew. Her death at thirty-four was a terrible blow. In his loneliness he had taken to visiting spiritualists but this could not bring her back. Nor could his twenty-four-year-old cousin, Hettie, whom he married two years later, hope to fill his first wife's shoes. After that one remarkable 5,500-mile voyage on the *Liberdade*, they drifted amicably apart. For the rest of his life, Joshua Slocum will be a loner.

July 16, 1896: The *Spray* casts anchor in Samoa. Three lissome women approach in a canoe. "*Talofa lee*," they carol: *love to you, chief.* They cannot believe he is all alone. *You had other mans, but you eat 'em.*

Slocum is far more interested in the widow of his great hero, Robert Louis Stevenson. She comes down to greet him personally and presents him with her husband's four beautiful volumes of sailing directories for the Mediterranean and another for the Indian ocean. He takes the books with "reverential awe." He is invited to use her husband's desk to write his letters but he cannot bring himself to sit in that hallowed spot.

He spends an idyllic month in Samoa and then sails off again, this time for Australia where more enthusiastic welcomes await him, not to mention a shower of presents, including a telescope and a new set of sails. Here, he recoups his finances, moving from Sydney to Melbourne to Tasmania, lecturing as he goes to paying audiences. Then he swings north again, past Sydney, Newcastle, Brisbane and Rockhampton, towards the entrance to the Indian Ocean.

May 24, 1897: The *Spray* moves gingerly through the Great Barrier Reef directly opposite New Guinea. Again Slocum has occasion to remark upon her self-steering capacities. From Thursday Island to the Keelings, a run of twenty-three days and 2,700 miles, he spends no more than three hours at the helm. He lashes the wheel and lets the ship scud along on her own; no matter where the wind is, abeam or dead aft, she sails faithfully on course. After leaving the Keeling Islands, Slocum is lost to the world; he has neglected to write home and in New Bedford the newspapers report that he is lost at sea. It is not until he arrives at the island of Mauritius, off the coast of Africa, that the New York *Evening Post* is able to correct the error. The date, by now, is September 21.

Meantime, he has been the chief actor in a comic opera scene on the remote island of Rodriguez, a flyspeck in the Indian Ocean, some thousand miles east of Madagascar. The local abbé has been filling the islanders' heads with terrifying tales of the approaching Antichrist, a piece of sermonizing calculated to keep them on the narrowest of pathways. Suddenly, into the harbour, scudding before a heavy gale, her sails all feather-white and her single gaunt occupant holding down the deck like a bearded prophet, comes the *Spray*. Down to the jetty flock the faithful crying that the Antichrist has truly arrived: "May the Lord help us, it is he and he has come in a boat!" One elderly creature makes for the safety of her home, locks herself in, barricades her doors as Slocum advances up the street, and refuses to emerge from her self-imposed prison for the full eight days he spends on the islet. The others soon re-

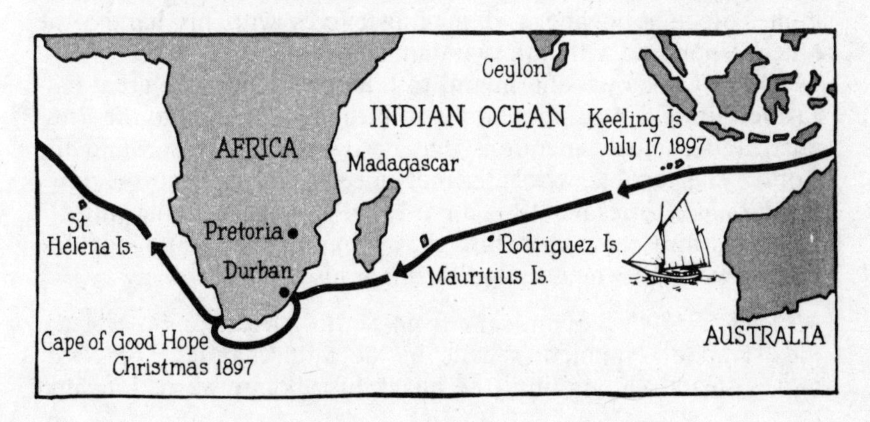

cover and entertain him royally. The abbé invites him to his convent in the hills for an overnight stay and when finally he prepares to depart, wishes him a safe journey – whatever his religion. Slocum, the freethinker, cannot resist a slight dig: *My dear abbé, had all religionists been so liberal there would have been less bloodshed in the world.*

Then through the Mozambique channel to Durban, fighting against a hard four-day gale. The *Spray* is famous by now: a signalman on a bluff station reports her progress from fifteen miles off. At eight miles he signals a piece of news that confounds the sceptics: the *Spray* is shortening sail and one man, working alone, has reefed the main in just ten minutes. Three minutes later, the news is rushed to a Durban morning paper and as Slocum reaches port a copy is handed to him.

In Durban, Henry Stanley, the greatest explorer of the age, is brought to meet him. *Mr. Slocum I presume*, or some such greeting. Livingstone's saviour is fascinated that the ship has travelled through treacherous waters without any built-in buoyancy compartments. What would happen, he asks, if the *Spray* should strike a rock? Slocum's answer is succinct: *She must be kept away from the rocks.*

A more bizarre trio of savants awaits his pleasure. Their master, "Oom Paul" Kruger, president of the Transvaal, is firmly convinced that the earth is flat. The Word of God has said so and the Word of God cannot be wrong. The three Boers are struggling with a thesis to prove this contention and Slocum is a prize catch. Alas, not such a prize, for he has just girdled the globe and is convinced that it is spherical. The flat-earthers are annoyed; they pore over a Mercator's projection of the world showing the *Spray*'s track and point out triumphantly that it looks remarkably flat. Slocum leaves them to their deliberations but the following day encounters one of the fanatics on the street. They engage in pantomime, Slocum bowing and making curves with his hands, the other responding with flat, swimming movements.

Off to Capetown and inland to Pretoria to meet the great flat-earther himself. A prominent jurist introduces Slocum to the President and clumsily mentions that he is on a voyage around the world. The terrible word "round" incenses Kruger: "you don't mean *round*!" cries he. "It is impossible! You mean *in* the world!" He turns away, crying "Impossible! Impossible!", and not one further word does he utter to Slocum or his companion.

March 26, 1898: Slocum sails from South Africa for St. Helena, the island of Napoleon's exile in the mid-Atlantic. The *Spray* moves steadily along until the quack of a booby warns him that land lies dead ahead. He takes a swig from a bottle of port as a toast to his invisible helmsman, the pilot of the *Pinta*, and prepares for the inevitable receptions. He is a celebrity by now. He lectures, dines with the Governor, accepts a fruitcake from the first lady of the island and, unhappily, the gift of a goat from an American friend. The goat is a disaster. Safely ensconced aboard the *Spray*, he begins to eat his way through the ship. No rope can hold him; he devours them all. Then he turns his attention to the charts of the Caribbean and gobbles them up. Finally he munches Slocum's straw hat. Slocum must suffer the presence of the ravenous goat for a thousand miles, until at Ascension Island, in mid-Atlantic, he kicks him ashore.

He crosses the Equator off the coast of Brazil. An American battleship, the *Oregon*, speeds up behind and hoists a puzzling signal; Slocum has difficulty reading it because he has no binoculars. Finally, he makes it out: *Are there any men-of-war about*? He is baffled. No one has been able to tell him that war has broken out between the United States and Spain. *Let us keep together for mutual protection*, he signals back. The *Oregon* ignores this badinage and steams away.

Chartless and cursing his late passenger, the goat, he racks his memory of wind and water as he approaches Tobago and Trinidad. He moves from island to island, packing lecture halls with spirited accounts of his adventures. He is becalmed for eight days in the horse latitudes, the sea so smooth that each evening he can read by candlelight. A three-day gale follows the calm and he begins to weary of the ocean – "tired, tired, tired of baffling squalls and fretful cobble-seas." For more than three years he has lived with the whistling of the wind in the rigging and the slop-slop of the sea against the sloop's sides, music to any seaman after a stint in the doldrums, "but there was so much of it now and it lasted so long!" In the Gulf Stream late that June he is savaged by a terrifying storm, hailstones pelting down on the *Spray* and lightning pouring from the clouds in an almost continual stream.

On June 25, the elements strike again. A tornado has cut a swath through New York City. Slocum sees it coming and receives it with bare poles; even so, the little *Spray* shivers as it hits, heeling over on her beam ends and then, miraculous as always, rights herself and faces out the storm. Slocum is powerless and knows it. *What is man in a storm like this?*

June 26, 1898: Slocum reaches Newport and journey's end. Because of the war, the harbour is mined and he must hug the rocks as he brings his sloop into port. At one the following morning he casts his anchor. He cannot suppress a sense of triumph: he has gained one pound and feels ten years younger; the *Spray* is as sound as a nut and hasn't leaked a drop – since leaving Australia he hasn't even bothered to rig his pump.

But no bands greet him. No children appear with kisses and garlands. No civic dignitaries clamber aboard with plaques and medals. No reporters seek him out. For America is at war; it is the *Maine* that people remember, not the *Spray*. There are some, in fact, who believe that Slocum is a charlatan until he produces his yacht licence, stamped in every port he has visited; that shuts up the sceptics.

Slowly, the extraordinary character of his feat begins to sink in. He gives a lecture in the New Bedford city hall to an audience of old salts. The *Century Illustrated Monthly* asks him to write an account of his voyage. He docks the *Spray* in South Brooklyn and there, in the cabin that has become his true home, he writes, in the spring of 1899, a book-length account of his adventures. The magazine publishes it in nine instalments, and Slocum is charmed to find himself in print next to his hero, Mark Twain. Published later between hard covers, *Sailing Alone Around the World* is translated into six languages and, for the next seventy-five years will be read continuously as one of the great classic stories of the sea.

But for Joshua Slocum, life begins to go slightly sour. There are no more worlds for him to conquer, no more seas to sail. He suffers from that let-down feeling that always comes at the end of a great adventure or a heroic ordeal. Restless and at loose ends, he contemplates a dozen schemes, but they come to nothing. He wants to pilot a ship in the Spanish American War; he wants to start a college for boys aboard a clipper; he wants to take the *Spray* to the Universal Exhibition in Paris; he wants to make a trip to Iceland by submarine; he even wants to learn to fly. There are no takers.

There is one brief interlude. In 1901, reunited with Hettie, he tows the *Spray* up the Hudson and Erie Canal to Buffalo for the six-month-long Pan-American Exposition. Here he and his sloop go on display in competition with hula dancers, Eskimos, Chiquita the Human Doll, the Scenic Railway, the Trip to the Moon, forty-two Indian tribes, the Temple of Music and the U.S. Cavalry's reconstruction of Custer's Last Stand. His visitors' book fills three volumes and includes the signature of President William McKinley, assassinated on these very grounds.

With his profits, he decides to become a landsman. He buys a house and farm at Martha's Vineyard, plants fruit trees, prepares descriptive lectures about his adventures. But this kind of lecture is no longer in vogue: newer and more fascinating entertainments have arrived with the new century. Barnum has just joined Bailey to promote the Greatest Show on Earth. Buffalo Bill's Wild West Show is attracting thousands. Chautauqua has captured the small towns. The birth of the nickelodeon signals a new age. When Slocum left Yarmouth, the bicycle craze was at its height; now the automobile era has begun. There is no place for a man and a sailboat. More than half a century will pass before people begin to think again about sailing alone around the world.

Joshua and Hettie drift apart, again quite amicably. The farm loses its charm. By 1905, Slocum is back again aboard the *Spray*, moored off the Maine coast in the summer and sailing to the West Indies in winter to harvest conch shells and rare orchid plants, which he hopes to present to the new president, Theodore Roosevelt.

Then, in the spring of 1906, the squall of scandal blows over him. At Riverton, New Jersey, a twelve-year-old girl goes aboard the sloop. A few hours later her father claims that she has been attacked. Slocum is charged with rape. There has been no rape – that much is clear; a doctor confirms it and the father agrees, but he calls Slocum "a fiend . . . posing in the limelight of cheap notoriety." Slocum is arrested, jailed, held without bail, the charge reduced to committing indecent assault. At the preliminary hearing he makes an odd statement: if the misdemeanour had occurred, then it must have been during one of the mental lapses to which he is subject. Mental lapses? It is the first and, indeed, the only indication that he suffers from them. He spends forty-two days in jail and then is haled before a judge who reproves him, orders him to pay costs and forbids his return to Riverton – a queer and indecisive ending to a baffling incident.

What actually went on that spring day in the cabin of the *Spray*? Was there a sexual advance? Was it simply the imagination of an impressionable child? Or was it something else – at once more tenuous and more explicable – a desolate old sailor attempting, in his loneliness, to reach out to another human being? No one will ever know. Slocum himself does not contest the charge and apparently it has little effect on his reputation; for he sails immediately to Oyster Bay where he delivers one lone orchid (the others have died during his incarceration) to the President who, in his turn, entertains him royally at his home on Sagamore Hill.

These are pinpoints of excitement in an otherwise dreary half-life. Slocum is running down, like a leaky schooner, his personality increasingly waspish, his appearance more and more slovenly and his sloop, once so trim and shipshape, filthier and filthier. He is withering away, a man born out of his time, an old salt clinging to the past, a caricature in a shapeless felt hat, a collarless shirt and vest, unbuttoned trousers, and old, unpolished felt boots. Old Slocum, closed up tight, impenetrable, a mystery even to his sons.

There must be one more adventure. He is sixty-five years old and more than a little slack, but he is determined to undertake a new voyage – he and the *Spray*. Together they will penetrate the mysteries of that most mysterious of rivers, the Amazon. He will sail his sloop to Venezuela, follow the Orinoco and the Rio Negro to the headwaters of the great river and then set his course downstream into the unknown sponge of the jungle. Slocum has dreams of grandeur; he is confident the natives will mistake him for a god and, if they do, he intends to be ready for them: he will take along one of Mr. Edison's new-fangled gramophones.

November 14, 1909: Once again Joshua Slocum boards the *Spray* on a voyage that no one has made before. He sets sail from Tisbury and drives the *Spray* into the very teeth of a gale blowing in from the east. The little sloop scuds along as always, white sails billowing in the wind until she vanishes beyond the horizon. And that is the last that anyone sees of her. She and her master vanish without a trace. No shred of sail, no splinter of wreckage, not so much as a floating spar or a waterlogged straw hat remain to give a clue to her fate. His ship – his home, his faithful and sole companion, his last, true love – is with him to the end.

Slocum's first wife, Virginia, at 33.
He never really recovered from her death.

12
The Adventures of Wilfred Grenfell

Wilfred Grenfell was the perfect schoolboy hero. "Perfect" is the proper adjective. For most people at the century's turn and in the three decades following, Grenfell – Sir Wilfred as he eventually became – *was* perfect: missionary to the dispossessed; surgeon to the abandoned; adventurer in a foreign clime; saint and healer, evangelist and teacher. The well-to-do of Boston, Philadelphia, Manchester, and Toronto, hypnotized by his every word, revelled in the certain knowledge that they were in the presence of a living legend. In an era when the word *charisma* was unknown, the Labrador Doctor glowed with a compelling aura. Seeing his restless, muscular figure pacing the stages of countless auditoriums and listening to his tales of hardship, despair, salvation, and adventure, thousands were moved to contribute small fortunes for the succour of Newfoundland fishermen and Labrador liveyeres, whose lives they could hardly comprehend and whose environment seemed as mysterious and as remote as that of Katmandu.

Grenfell knew everybody, and everybody knew that he knew everybody. He was equally comfortable in the presence of royal dukes, Eskimo hunters, and the swilers of St. Anthony. He hobnobbed with Mackenzie King, Winston Churchill, King George v, and Teddy Roosevelt. In the long list of young Ivy Leaguers who cheerfully paid for the privilege of serving under him (often performing the most menial chores) one finds such names as Nelson Rockefeller and Henry Cabot Lodge. To these the name Grenfell was magic: it bespoke Christian selflessness of the highest order, sacrifice rendered bearable – even glamorous – by the lure of high adventure beyond the rim of civilization.

To those who worshipped him – the newspaper readers who revelled in his Sunday supplement exploits, the doyens of society who gripped his hand at fêtes and levees, the thousands of members of the various Grenfell societies who gave him their unstinting support – the Labrador Doctor was a man who could do no wrong. He got results; he raised millions; he changed the lives of thousands of Newfoundlanders for the better. None could deny those accomplishments. Yet to those who knew him intimately, and who admired and even loved him, he was not entirely perfect; there were certain flaws of temperament and character that never crept into the public prints. He was not a good administrator, nor was he an especially good doctor; he was irritatingly casual about money; he could on occasion be perverse, bumbling, even juvenile; and he never seemed content to stay in one place for any length of time. There was a breathless schoolboy impetuosity about Grenfell that his colleagues found maddening yet at the same time attractive.

No incident illustrates this better than his miraculous brush with death on Easter Sunday, 1908. The Ice Pan Adventure, as it came to be called, cast Grenfell as larger than life. It was for the Labrador Doctor what Khartoum was for Kitchener, what the Livingstone encounter was for Stanley. But it was also a foolhardy and dangerous exploit that almost took the lives of several fishermen in addition to Grenfell's own.

He was forty-three, at the height of his abilities and approaching the peak of his celebrity. He was not handsome, but he was certainly attractive, with a pudgy, almost cherubic face that radiated geniality – a very English face with little crinkles around the eyes, a short, nondescript moustache (a little ragged, but not too bristly), and prominent teeth. His face was tanned, his muscles were taut, his body was elastic. He was, in his own phrase, "fit as a brickbat."

He had just returned from conducting Easter service in the little church at St. Anthony, a fishing village on the northeastern tip of Newfoundland, which he had made his headquarters. Two fishermen were waiting; they had come sixty miles from Brent Island to inform him that a boy on whom he had recently operated was critically ill with blood poisoning.

Grenfell dropped everything. Nothing would do but that he dash off, almost on the instant, without waiting for the two messengers who needed to rest their dogs before proceeding. There was no sense in it. Sooner or later he would have to wait for them to guide him to the island. But it was not in Grenfell's make-up to pause; movement for him was a tonic, idleness a soporific. Off he dashed in his *komatik*, his seven best dogs strung out in front of him, his little black spaniel, Jack, leading the way – off across the ice-covered boulders of the east coast and through the ragged forests. Grenfell to the rescue!

His dress was distinctly odd. Under his coat and overalls he was wearing, for reasons that have never been satisfactorily explained, a football uniform from his college days, which, after twenty years, he had unearthed from the mothballs in his trunk, consisting of Oxford University running shorts, red, yellow, and black Richmond football stockings, and a flannel shirt. This peculiar garb added a bizarre touch to the events that followed.

Brent Island lay on the far side of Hare Bay, sixty miles to the south. It was spring breakup – the most dangerous season for travel. It rained that night, and a bitter wind blew from the east, causing the ice to crack in the harbours. Grenfell's first stop was Lock's Cove, eighteen miles from St. Anthony on the north shore of Hare Bay. There he spent the night as the wind stiffened and veered to the west, as the temperature dropped and the snow hardened, as the ice in the bay broke into pans, growling and crashing eerily in the dark.

Grenfell was advised to wait until conditions became more settled; he refused. He was urged to follow the shoreline and not to venture on to the uncertain ice, and for a time he held to that plan. But he could not resist a short cut directly across the bay, and this nearly proved his undoing.

The wind dropped. Suddenly, the doctor became aware that the ice beneath him had turned to slush. So rapidly was it breaking up that there was no time to turn back. He tore off his outer clothes, flung himself on hands and knees in order to distribute his weight, and urged the dogs forward. The land lay a tantalizing quarter mile distant. But the harder the dogs pulled, the deeper the runners sank into the slob ice.

A long struggle followed in the slush-filled waters. Grenfell hacked the traces clear of the sinking sled and managed to get the dogs on to a tiny pan of ice. It was not large enough to hold them all. The doctor fashioned a rope from the traces, tied it to the lead dog, and tried to persuade the animal to swim to a larger pan, twenty yards away. The dog refused. Grenfell tossed a piece of ice to the other pan and commanded his spaniel, Jack, to fetch it. All seven huskies leaped into the water to follow, dragging Grenfell with them.

His situation was desperate. He had lost his cap, coat, gloves, overalls, thermos, matches, and fuel. Five miles to the north he could hear the immense pans grinding together and thundering against the cliffs. No vessel, he knew, could survive in that turmoil. And the wind was moving the ice out to the sea.

He was freezing to death, and he knew it. In one of his several accounts of the incident he tells how he considered stabbing himself to make a quick end of things. (It was clearly no more than a passing thought; it is impossible to imagine the Labrador Doctor attempting suicide.) Instead, he stabbed three of his dogs to death and was bitten in the process. He skinned them, wrapped the hides around his shoulders, and constructed a windbreak out of the carcasses. Behind this bloody bulwark he crouched, cuddling for warmth against his biggest dog, as the wind drove his precarious floating island out to sea. When the wind dropped he even managed to sleep until midnight. At dawn he rigged an extraordinary signal flag, using the frozen legs of the dead dogs as a staff and a shirt tied to it with bits of old harness rope as a pennant. By this time he was close to delirium.

He was saved by something very like a miracle. The only man on all that coast who owned a telescope happened to be standing late the previous afternoon on the south shore of Hare Bay. Into his field of vision, a tiny object moved: an ice pan "no bigger than a kitchen floor" on which were huddled a man and five dogs. He recognized Grenfell's wiry figure and set about organizing a search party. A boat had to be dug out of the packed snow and by the time that was done it was dark. There could be no attempt at rescue until morning, and by then the west wind would almost certainly have carried the marooned party far out to sea. Nonetheless the attempt had to be made: "Ef the doctor's gone, dat's the end o' the French shore and St. Anthony. 'Twill all go down . . . 'E's the one keeps us all going."

At dawn, the lookouts on the headland spotted the pan several miles to seaward but still within the bay. The intervening area was a chaos of broken, grinding ice. For no one but the doctor would five men have risked their lives in such seas, but "his life was worth many. We wouldn't let a man like that die without trying."

The sick boy's grandfather, George Reed, skippered the crew. He steered; the others rowed, often hauling the boat across ice pans or ploughing it through thick slush until they came within sight of their goal. Grenfell, when they reached him, looked years older, a scarecrow figure, bloody and ragged, his face grey and uncustomarily sober. They forced tea down his throat, but he could not speak. Later, on shore, he tried to argue that he be allowed to drive his dog team alone back to St. Anthony, but they would have none of that.

At the hospital he was given morphine to force him to sleep. Still suffering from exposure and shock, he insisted, when he woke, on dictating the story of his adventure to Jessie Luther, the occupational therapist at the hospital. That account, much embellished and often retold, became the basis for a best-selling book and numberless newspaper features and magazine articles. But was the trip really necessary? A day or so later, the boy whose life the doctor had set out to save was brought to the hospital by boat (the ice having temporarily cleared from the coast), where he quickly recovered.

There were some who would say that the whole adventure was a publicity stunt. It was scarcely that, though Grenfell was a master of publicity. It was simply the saga of a man who, having suffered a real peril through his own impatience, exploited it by his own zeal. There was nothing deliberate about Grenfell, nor was he troubled by self-doubt, second thoughts, or introspection. Like so many other nineteenth-century adventurers – Englishmen all – he was a man driven to risk with enough of a sense of drama to make capital from it. His was a special type of imperial derring-do – the same kind one finds in a Chinese Gordon. His was also, it goes without saying, a special kind of luck.

He was descended on his father's side from that Sir Richard Grenville of *Revenge* fame immortalized by Tennyson and Kingsley. His father, a classical scholar and sometime public-school headmaster, switched course in the midstream of life to become a slum chaplain in London. He suffered intermittently from mental illness and died in a nursing home in Wales when his son was twenty. There is some evidence that he committed suicide. However that may be, it was his mother who was the real influence on Wilfred Grenfell's life. She was always "Dear Old Mum" to him; he wrote to her regularly and at voluminous length until her death. When he was fifteen she had given him a book, *A Soul's Enquiries Answered.* He carried it with him all his life, scribbling homilies in it from time to time. In his fiftieth year he was still her little boy: there is a remarkable account by a Reverend Henry Gordon of Grenfell taking afternoon tea in her bedroom in 1914. "I can see him now," Gordon recalled, "stretched out on the hearth with his head in his mother's lap, and I have never doubted ever since that it was from her that he drew so much of his spiritual strength."

Yet one senses that his father's decline and death had its effect, for it was at that time that Wilfred Grenfell experienced an extraordinary religious conversion. He was studying medicine at the London Hospital Medical School, an indifferent scholar but an ardent athlete: swimmer, weight thrower, rower, and rugby player. Medicine became a passion only when he fell under the aura of Dr. Frederick Treves, a brilliant surgeon who would later be knighted for saving the life of Edward VII in one of history's earliest appendectomies. Treves, like Grenfell, was a man of action: swimmer, water-polo enthusiast, yachtsman and cyclist. Like Grenfell, he had a flair for the dramatic. The young student, hero-worshipping the older man, found his own natural propensity for self-dramatization heightened by the model of this second father.

Then, in 1883, Grenfell, nominally a low-church Anglican, wandered into the revival tent of Dwight L. Moody, the American evangelist, and was born again. For ten months, Moody and Ira Sankey, a gospel singer, had been offering Englishmen the theatre of tent evangelism. At first a thorn to the established church, they had at least received some measure of grudging acceptance. Grenfell arrived in the middle of a long prayer, found it boring and was about to leave when he heard Moody tell the congregation to sing a rousing song "while our brother finishes his prayer." Grenfell was inspired by the practicality of the act. He decided to give this down-to-earth form of Christianity his best try. He would attempt to "make religion a real effort as I thought Christ would do in my place as a doctor, or frankly abandon it."

Like many other young men of his class, he was yearning for a mission in life, and Moody's muscular Christianity offered it. It was, after all, the missionary age. A kind of lull had descended over the world; Britain had been the dominant nation for a century; the dark corners of the globe had been mapped and conquered; there was no war. Public-school boys, searching for an outlet for their energies, often found it in evangelism. Off they went to the jungles of Africa or the rice paddies of the Orient or the slums of Britain to save souls.

Grenfell did not immediately plunge into mission work. He had said that he would either take up religion or abandon it. His mother, in the end, convinced him to stay with it. In 1885 – the year of his father's death – his commitment was reinforced at another Moody meeting where the evangelist's showpieces were the famous "Cambridge seven," young men who were either crack athletes or army officers. To Grenfell, here was something worth paying attention to: these were not pious milksops, prattling endlessly about theology; these were *doers*, men of action. When the saved were summoned to their feet, Grenfell, not without a certain embarrassment, pulled himself up from his bench. He left the meeting feeling that he "had crossed the Rubicon, and must do something to prove it." He had scarcely been converted from a life of debauchery; in fact, he had nothing to give up. His interests in sport, religion, and medicine – none of them profound – had simply coalesced. The life that faced him could hardly be called a life of sacrifice because he so obviously loved every minute of it.

Dear Old Mum was consulted. She sent him to the local vicar, who put him in charge of a Sunday school class – dull stuff. Grenfell relieved the tedium by teaching his charges to box and was promptly dropped – violence was un-Christian, prizefighting was for the lower classes. Grenfell proceeded to doctor bodies in place of souls. He received his medical degree, though Dr. Treves in his reports marked him "very poor" and "indifferent." Yet the two became close friends. In 1888, Grenfell was appointed house surgeon under his mentor at the London Hospital and also helped out at Treves's boys' camp in Dorset. Eventually this led to an appointment to the National Mission to Deep Sea Fishermen, of whose medical section Treves was chairman. And that, in turn, led to Labrador.

Grenfell rose quickly from missionary doctor to superintendent, often maddening his superiors by refusing to follow the rules, taking matters into his own hands, vanishing occasionally on expeditions of his own, preaching, endlessly organizing everything from brass bands to sporting events, treating both fishermen and shore folk (thus annoying the local doctors), baffling everybody by swimming every morning in ice-cold water regardless of season, fighting the liquor sellers, and raising money by lecturing in drawing rooms – an attractive, vigorous young man in a romantic occupation who seemed to have boundless energy.

Three years after the young doctor descended on the mission, one of its council members, Francis Hopwood, returning scandalized from a week's visit to Newfoundland, wrote a scathing report on the conditions of the land-based fishermen – the five thousand permanent residents of coastal Labrador known as liveyeres and the thirty thousand "stationers" who worked from the stationary fleets off the northeast coast of the island. Hopwood roused all England with his descriptions of people living below subsistence level, in filthy conditions, on leaky vessels or in old sod huts, forever in debt to the merchants of St. John's, whose profit margin was often 200 per cent. On all that bleak coast, he reported, there was not one doctor. Once a year a government physician spent an hour or two among the people in the larger settlements when the mail steamer called; that was all.

The press response was instantaneous. Public opinion was further inflamed the following year when forty fishermen working out of Trinity Bay were lost in a blizzard. The mission determined to dispatch a hospital ship to investigate. Grenfell, of course, volunteered to sail with her.

She left Yarmouth in June, 1892, a 110-foot ketch called *Albert*. Grenfell was officially ship's surgeon but liked to call himself "master mariner," although his certificate qualified him only to command *Vagabond*, a small yawl he owned with Treves. He managed to irritate the *Albert*'s captain by practising navigation and comparing it with the experts' and by training his black retriever to fetch and carry on deck. But the crew liked him because he pitched in and helped with the painting and led them in rousing evangelical hymns.

St. John's was in ashes from its second disastrous fire when the *Albert* sailed into harbour. Even so the conditions of the eleven thousand homeless were not as bad as those of the people he was about to visit. A thousand schooners were sailing north to the fishing grounds. The *Albert* followed in their wake, along the bleak and mist-shrouded shores of northern Newfoundland and Labrador. Little had changed here since Cartier had damned it at first sight. Headland and shoreline were devoid of any colour – a drab monotone – no speck of green upon the dark ridges, no sliver of blue in the sullen skies, the grey cliffs sodden with spray, the grey rocks blurred by creeping fog, the grey beaches spattered by dirty foam, the stunted conifers rising darkly from a patchwork of soiled snow, the whole landscape like a faded photograph. And the people, too, were faded, old beyond their years, the children like aging dwarfs with peaked, grey faces, the women all bones and hide, the men, battered by the elements, shapeless in dun-coloured clothing. Yet all were marvellously hospitable and generous, for, having nothing, they gave everything.

Grenfell was horrified. He knew the slums of London, but here was poverty on a scale he had never known existed. It was not only the underdogs of society who were poor; *everyone* was poor. And half the population seemed to be sick. "The women seem to me all ill from one cause or another," he wrote to his mother in August. The concept of welfare aid for those unable or unwilling to work had no meaning in a society where men lived their lives in peril and exhaustion, hobbled by lifelong debt. Jolly sports, inspirational hymns, medical succour – none of these were enough. Life was unalleviated hell. Boats leaked, clothes were stitched together from flour sacks, huts were worse than hovels. The people suffered from rickets, tuberculosis, scurvy, infected amputations. Their remedies were lunatic: they tackled disease by swallowing lice or wearing charms of deer's teeth; they poulticed abscesses with a concoction of herbs mixed with paint; they warded off diphtheria with a cod's head tied around the neck. They resisted treatment because it meant time off from work, and those who did not work starved. To be sent to the nearest hospital (at St. John's) meant economic disaster. Some told Grenfell that the coast had no use for a doctor; only survival of the fittest made the economy possible. But Grenfell persisted: he recorded treatment that summer for nine hundred patients, many deformed, crippled, blinded, or incapacitated through continued neglect of such minor conditions as ingrowing toenails and tooth decay.

These people lived with death and with the harbingers of death: the fury of the intemperate seas; the grinding terror of the moving ice packs; the everlasting fog that shrouded the lurking rocks; the gales that tore houses and ships to pieces. In one storm in October 1867, forty vessels had been lost and forty fishermen had died while fifteen hundred people were driven, homeless, on to the shore. A North Labrador hurricane in October of 1885 had sent eighty vessels and seventy men to the bottom and flung two thousand men, women, and children on to that savage coast in a state of starvation. Grenfell became a walking repository of horror stories which he would use to advantage in his money-raising lectures in the years to come:

"One man nearly lost his life slipping under an [ice] pan. These pans rushed together with irresistible force. Another man told me that he had both his legs broken and eventually cut off by being nipped between two pieces in their sway."

"One man only was reported to me today as getting weak on the ice; that is, he gave in. When a man can go on no longer and resigns himself to sleep and ultimate death in the snow the saying is that he 'gets weak.'"

Under such conditions, Grenfell could not restrain himself. When the *Albert* returned to St. John's after its three-thousand-mile journey that summer, he went after the Newfoundland government. The government crumpled under his onslaught with surprising swiftness. It promised to build two hospitals on the northern coast. Grenfell organized a committee of merchants and politicians whose task was to get the mission in England to broaden its scope, which had hitherto been focused solely on the plight of North Sea fishermen, and to set up a permanent base in Newfoundland.

That done, he sailed for home in the *Albert*. There was only one extraordinary incident on the journey, but it was typical of Wilfred Grenfell. He had organized the crew into cricket teams. The ball went over the side. Without a moment's thought the doctor leaped overboard to retrieve it. The ship slowly tacked about. In its wake, Grenfell could be seen triumphantly holding his prize aloft. He was picked up, and the game continued. He was fond of games; life, after all, was a game – a contest with the self.

But the mission council in Britain was not happy with Wilfred Grenfell; nor would it ever be. It now had eleven ships under its wing, and Grenfell was supposed to be superintendent in charge, a middleman between the fleet and the London council; but the problem was that Grenfell would never remain in one place. The council moved him from his headquarters in Gorleston to London, where it was hoped he would stay put. He did not. He insisted on working throughout the winter aboard the North Sea ships. He went off on speaking tours to raise money for the new Labrador mission. He began to scrounge around for personnel. He spent so much time on Labrador business that there were no hours left for his official job. He wrote to the council explaining that he was too busy to be superintendent. The council, by now thoroughly concerned, forbade him to pledge mission money to Labrador without permission. That was as effective as asking a small boy to give up chewing gum for Lent. Grenfell, who had no money sense, ordered equipment on impulse and had the bills sent to the mission. For the mission council the doctor posed a constant dilemma: he was unavailable when wanted, sloppy, careless with funds, as perverse as a tabby cat, and not always responsible; but he *did* seem to have the knack of raising large sums, and he did have the public's ear. If only Wilfred Grenfell would conform! If only those marvellous talents could somehow be channelled as his superiors wanted them channelled! If only – but this was wishful thinking. The hierarchy threw up its collective hands and sent Dr. Grenfell back to Labrador in the summer of 1893.

Off he sailed in the *Albert*, taking two doctors and two nurses to staff the proposed hospitals at Battle Harbour and Indian Harbour. He had managed to scrape up funds enough to buy a forty-five-foot steam launch, which he christened *Princess May* after May of Teck, the future Queen Mary, and had talked the Allan Line into shipping the vessel to St. John's at a bargain rate. In this cockleshell he intended to steam up the Newfoundland and Labrador coasts, an undertaking that drew guffaws from seasoned seamen in St. John's.

Princess May had an eight-foot beam, and she rolled like an eel. Unlashed gear tumbled overboard every time she pitched, and she pitched constantly. The engine faltered; Grenfell had not bothered to check it over. The compass was two points out; he had not checked that, either. He was, at best, a Sunday sailor ignorant of the finer points of navigation. At the outset he almost ran into a cliff and was forced to hail a passing fishing boat to get his bearings. He had no charts worthy of the name, the only ones extant being those made by Captain James Cook in the previous century.

No matter: off he blundered through reefs and shoals, sheltering at night in coves thronged with the sick, pleading for treatment (for his arrival was always broadcast by some mysterious form of moccasin telegraph). Clearly he was having a wonderful time. He was also fostering a legend.

Late one evening he arrived at Battle Harbour, the site of one of the new hospitals. The *Albert* had preceded him. Grenfell dropped his medical staff but did not stay; he darted south again with only an engineer as crew, through the Strait of Belle Isle and along the southern coast of Labrador, picking up the occasional passenger, including a Roman Catholic bishop and a Methodist preacher whom he put to work as deckhands. Then north again, grounding in shallows and on rocks, struggling clear somehow, cruising deep into unknown inlets, shooting game birds, casting for salmon, sketching the foreshore, and rejoicing in the whole adventure. Up the Labrador coast he chugged to Indian Harbour, site of the second hospital, where he again encountered the *Albert*, and then on north to Hopedale, where he was firmly warned to go no farther. But, typically, he did go on for another 160 miles, watching for reefs from a ladder lashed to the mast, visiting with the people, preaching and doctoring and gathering material for a devastating report for the mission council. The living conditions of the liveyeres were almost unbelievable; the doctor discovered that a typical hut constructed of sod, mud, and old boards would house as many as fourteen persons and all their dogs. Equally infamous was the truck system, through which the merchants of St. John's kept the fishermen in thrall; their purchases always seemed to exceed the profit from their catch. In Grenfell's innovative mind, the idea of a system of co-operatives was beginning to take shape.

Back down the coast he went by fits and starts. The *Princess May* was the last boat to leave Labrador that winter. When she ran short of fuel, Grenfell tore the roof off the cabin and burned it. When he lost his compass overboard, he navigated by eye. When he reached Twillingate he learned that he had been given up for dead: a London newspaper had printed his obituary; only Dear Old Mum, with her abiding faith, refused to give up hope. When at last he reached St. John's he raced three steamers into the harbour, with one of his casual passengers – a Salvation Army captain this time – playing the violin on deck. His arrival was a small triumph. He had taken his improbable craft three thousand miles without lights or accurate charts. The *Albert*, on the other hand, had encountered a gale, run aground, and been hammered on the rocks. She was hauled off by a rescue boat and had lost her jib boom in Belle Isle strait. Her captain's comments, when the doc-

tor cheerfully moored the *Princess May* beside him, went unrecorded.

The *Albert* sailed back to England without Grenfell. He had decided to cross Canada at his own expense – and without permission – to raise money for a third Labrador hospital. When he returned to London the following February, the response from the mission council was decidedly chilly. The funds he had raised were not for the work of the mission as a whole but "for the work of Dr. Grenfell." The man seemed to be starting a fiefdom of his own!

Still . . . he *had* raised a great deal of money. He had crossed Canada on a CPR pass wangled from that old Labrador hand, Sir Donald Smith, the man who drove the railroad's final spike at Craigellachie. Now the mission learned that under Grenfell's gentle prodding, Smith had donated a steamer to the cause, to be named, of course, *Sir Donald*. It was valued at eighteen hundred dollars, a bit more than the fifteen hundred it had cost to repair the *Princess May* after Grenfell's summer journey. But the gift turned out to be a mixed blessing. It was a foregone conclusion that the doctor would captain the new vessel. Back to North America he went in late August of 1894, picked up the prize, and worked her through the Strait of Belle Isle. As he sailed her triumphantly into Battle Harbour, he struck a reef, damaging her so badly that she was out of commission for a year. With the *Princess May* also disabled and the *Albert* ordered back to England, he was forced to make do with a twenty-foot jollyboat. It served his purpose, which was to keep moving. "I never feel at ease," he wrote to a friend, "unless I am moving along day and night."

When he returned to England in December of 1894, the mission was forced to admit that he was an asset. He published his first book, *Vikings of Today*, and donated all the profits to the cause. He was now known as the Labrador Doctor and becoming a popular lecturer in spite of a nervous stammer and a rambling style. Subject matter triumphed over technique as the doctor spoke of a frontier few knew existed and a lifestyle that most could not imagine. The poverty and the isolation were beyond the ken of his listeners. It was hard to believe that St. Anthony, the major port of northern Newfoundland, with a bigger concentration of people than anywhere on the coast, had a permanent population of seventeen families. It was equally hard to believe that these cod fishermen and sealers were so badly off that their women often became reluctant prostitutes on schooners in exchange for food for their families. And was it really possible that white Christians with British ancestors treated rheumatism by wearing a haddock's finbone around the neck?

It was Grenfell's conviction that much of the poverty was the result of the system perpetuated by the Water Street merchants of St. John's, who paid the fishermen for their catch not in money but in sugar, vegetables, clothes, even liquor. So enslaved were the people that, in order to keep on the right side of the merchants, they preferred to maintain a slight debit balance. Grenfell's response was to launch a fishermen's co-operative at Red Bay, one of the poorest of the Newfoundland communities. He had scarcely accomplished this, in the summer of 1895, when the mission council pulled him back to England, apparently for good. Another doctor, Fred Willway, would take over the work in Labrador; Grenfell, whose profile was becoming alarmingly high, would go back to the North Sea trawlers.

The council thought it had divorced him from Labrador, but he was not easy to muzzle. Grenfell insisted on talking about it as if he were still involved. One of his most captivating stories concerned a crippled Eskimo boy named Pomuik, who had been on display at the Columbian Exposition in Chicago in 1893. Grenfell, with his flair for the dramatic, always referred to him as "Prince Pomuik" because he was the son of a minor chief. When the exposition ended, the boy was unceremoniously abandoned in Newfoundland and told to find his way home to Labrador. A Boston Congregationalist who had befriended the boy in Chicago called on Grenfell to help find him. Grenfell obliged. He traced Pomuik to the head of a Labrador fiord, near death, his crippled thigh badly infected. He sent him to hospital at Indian Harbour, where the leg was amputated. Pomuik died after Grenfell returned to England, and the Labrador Doctor wrung tears from his audiences as he recounted the story. The Boston link stood him in good stead, for it opened the door to connections with wealthy New Englanders.

The council was now determined to keep a tight lid on the irrepressible doctor. The very word "Labrador" was to be expunged from his vocabulary. At the General Meeting in 1898 he was specifically instructed not to mention it. But Grenfell would not be stifled. "I was told not to say a word about Labrador," he said as he began to speak, "but I am going to transgress . . . " and he was away in full spate. The following summer Dr. Willway asked to be relieved; Labrador was too much for his wife; the climate and the isolation had broken her health. The council was cornered; only one man could take Willway's place, and after an absence of almost three years that man returned to Battle Harbour, where crowds cheered, flags flew, and guns fired a salute. The legend was now secure.

The doctor's letters home to his mother – they are voluminous – are revealing. He delights in shocking her in the same way that he would deliberately shock an audience into a sense of guilt:

"Only two days ago I was in a starving man's hovel. I asked the mother, as usual, how many children? She replied: 'Only two now, the other two are better off.' Dead of chronic starvation."

Yet Grenfell's style is so brisk that the effect tends to be muted. His letters display a kind of bluff heartiness that plays down pain and despair:

"I was eight miles off visiting a poor fellow, out of whose leg I cut a large tumour . . . . The poor chap was half starved and fainted twice the first night when I began, so I had to give him food and begin in the morning again. I had only a local anaesthetic, cocaine, but it worked splendidly. I had to sew him up, six stitches with black thread from his wife's box as I had no sutures. These I sterilized and took them out last night. My driver and servant had to hold the man and get another man to hold the wound open. Luckily he did not faint, though, poor chap, the sweat ran off his brow like a sponge."

Grenfell was not an intensely sensitive man. Had he been, it is doubtful that he could have survived psychologically. His tales of hardship and heartache are rather like those of a college boy describing a game of rugger. In one letter home, written during his first trip to Labrador, he did strike a poignant note:

"One poor Eskimo called Jonas had both his hands shot off. I cut one arm at the elbow and would have taken off the other another day but mercifully he never recovered . . . . As I left the shore last night it was 10:30, dark and blowing. His poor wife heard my call for the *Albert*'s boat and came out to bid me good-by, she would not let go of my hand and I left her standing on the rocks after I had gone, crying as though she would break her heart. She could not speak English but just pointed up to signify that we should meet again in Heaven. It just made me cry outright."

This is a moving scene, but then Grenfell had to add: "Certainly these people are very affectionate and have the same feelings we have, though not, I believe, quite so acute." This is the gentleman missionary speaking, the country squire, the public-school boy, the Oxford blue. The lower classes, like domestic pets, must be looked after, but they cannot be expected to love or hate, to feel joy or sorrow to *quite* the same degree as their betters. "Missionary as I am," Grenfell had written to Dear Old Mum in 1896, "I fully believe in strict discipline as the best thing for the uneducated classes."

Yet it would be unfair to fault him for being what he was – the product of his time and of his background. His letters reveal him as the perennial schoolboy, rejoicing in the frontier life. He was at last able to spend a winter in St. Anthony and his gusto is infectious: "The first snow is on the deck – I'm just revelling in it," he wrote to his mother. As for the harsh Atlantic winters that drove so many fishermen to despair, it was "one long delight":

"My dog team is very smart. Red & blue tassels & every dog with a bell. My komatik with whale bone runners is a beauty. It is most exhilarating flying over mountain and valley, over sea flake behind the fast dog team."

Life was a lark to Grenfell and never more than when he was on the move: "It is a wonderful coast and I suppose I'm the only man on earth who can take a steamer down it at full speed."

Even his harshest descriptions of life in bad weather aboard his newest ship, the *Strathcona* (its donor now raised to the peerage) have a kind of *Boy's Own Paper* quality:

"Just fancy cleaning fish in the dark on deck in the blinding snow and rain of the past month with gales of wind blowing and constant waves coming over soaking all hands to the skin. The head piece that Granny made comes in after a night watch hanging with icicles and the men's beards and noses positively glisten with icicles. Just fancy, too, carrying water out of your stockings and putting them on again before going to bed and merely leaving your legs hanging out of your bunk to allow them to dry on . . . ."

At the end of his life, the doctor summed up his credo in a single sentence in a letter to a friend: "When two courses are open my plan in life has always been to take the most venturesome." To him life *was* a magnificent adventure. Did it ever cross that nimble but insouciant mind that the hardships of the Labrador and Newfoundland coasts, which he saw as a sporting challenge, were to the fishermen a source of unrelenting horror from which there was no escape? Only rarely in his letters home did Grenfell manage to capture the pathos of the situation. He was too busy flexing his muscles, dashing from one adventure to the next, pounding on the doors of the idle rich, to stop and reflect upon the reality around him. He was, after all, trained as an orthopaedic surgeon. All surgeons, one of his colleagues has said, are extroverts and orthopaedic surgeons more extroverted than most because theirs is a skill that deals entirely with bones and joints – solid things that either work or don't work; thus their occupation requires little self-examination.

Dr. Grenfell carried this lack of introspection into his evangelism. His faith was simple, all embracing, and untroubled by doubt; it never changed. He believed in deeds not words. His was a religion of action: "Christ's man should be a man first and foremost – a man among men." The muscular Christian saw faith as a contest, a wrestling match with the Devil. Early in his career, when suffering terribly from seasickness, he wrote his Dear Old Mum that "in Christ I can do all things and I just got up and had a run up and down. It's a nasty fight but can and must be won." He had little in common with the orthodox churches: "I've come to judge people's religion by their spirit and their works. Some of our honest talkers here are thieves and robbers in my estimation."

The worst thieves and robbers, in Grenfell's estimation, were the traders who exploited the peoples of the coast. He declared war upon them. As a justice of the peace, he prosecuted them for bootlegging. As an agent for Lloyds, he hit them for faking wrecks and scuppering old hulks for insurance money. His methods were unorthodox; he once threatened to take a man's wooden leg in lieu of a fine. He spread himself thin, yet he got results. By 1899, his first co-operative at Red Bay was able to declare a 10 per cent dividend. Within a few years, he had seven more in operation.

He saw the need to instil in the people a sense of community; without it the movement could not grow. And so that winter in St. Anthony he plunged into a flurry of activity: there were soccer games, shooting matches, duck hunts, obstacle races, concerts. St. Anthony was to be his headquarters, the hub of his empire; he would make it grow. Its people would build their own hospital; he led them into the forest to cut the lumber by hand. Other buildings would follow, and on each would be a Biblical quotation: "Whatsoever ye do, do it heartily for the Lord." That phrase, adorning the industrial workshop, summed up the Grenfellian credo.

In the summer he was off again up the coast. In London, the members of the mission council, who had deceived themselves into believing his sojourn was temporary, gave up their attempts to lure him home. The best they could hope for was to put a curb on his spending but this was more easily demanded than achieved. By 1900 his hospitals were treating four thousand patients a year, for everything from toothaches to brain tumours. Grenfell ignored all instructions to be frugal.

He plunged into new ventures. Apart from a little trapping, the people of the coast depended on two staple harvests – codfish and seals. The doctor set about to diversify their resources. He launched a co-operative lumber mill and an experimental farm. He founded an entire range of cottage industries, the manufacturing of hooked rugs, ivory and wood carvings, deerskin mitts and sealskin boots, the weaving of cloth and the preserving of foodstuff. He tried to get the coasts charted in order to bring in tourists, sent his own coastal sketches to the Royal Navy, urged the Canadian government to prospect for minerals. Some of the schemes worked, at least temporarily. Others aborted. At one point he ordered three hundred reindeer to be brought from Finland to launch a new industry; it was not a success.

He had, in the meantime, incurred the wrath of the traders along the coast and some of the merchants and ecclesiastics of St. John's. That opposition surfaced in 1905 with a vicious article in the St. John's *Trade Review*, which accused him of making a personal profit from his ventures. "We are not surprised," the *Review* declared, "to hear that he will soon retire from the Mission with what the sinful and the vulgar would call 'his whack of spondulicks.' " This opening shot touched off a volley of criticism led by the Roman Catholic archbishop, who had been irked by Grenfell's attacks on orthodox religion and his brand of evangelical Protestantism, not to mention his plans for non-denominational schools, which were opposed by Catholics and Anglicans alike. "Grenfell," the archbishop wrote, "is not needed on that shore and his work is not only useless but worse than useless. It is demoralizing, pauperizing, degrading."

The doctor fought back. He forced the *Trade Review* to apologize under the threat of a libel suit and, with the mission council publicly backing him, was able to prove false the archbishop's long list of charges against him. Meanwhile he had launched a new project, one of his most successful – an orphanage in St. Anthony for children found starving, deserted, naked, and homeless.

But the focus of his life was changing. He spent less time preaching and ministering to the sick and more time raising funds. He was an indifferent surgeon – some called him mediocre – who had succeeded largely through a remarkable bedside manner. A colleague, Dr. Theodore Badger, who worked with him on the *Strathcona*, has described Grenfell's medical approach as "almost like the laying on of hands. He didn't do much surgery. He had a few pills which he shook out of his pocket. But when you were talking to him it was as if nobody existed in the world but you." This personal magnetism made him uncommonly effective as a fund raiser. To Badger he was "one of the most unselfconscious men I have ever known. He would just walk onto the stage without a note in his hand and talk to the wealthy . . . tell them what he thought of them." The wealthy, in agonies of guilt, would dig into their pockets. In a single month in the United States, in 1906, Grenfell raised twenty thousand dollars for his work, an extraordinary feat when one realizes that this was an English doctor with an upper-class accent asking Americans to support welfare work in a British colony.

But, then, Grenfell broke all the rules of platform deportment. He was not a good speaker in the conventional sense. He rambled; he went beyond his time; he made appalling gaffes. He told one audience of Christian Scientists that they should have more sense than to spend millions on a monument to a "silly old woman" – the silly old woman being Mary Baker Eddy, the founder of the sect.

He was astonishingly blunt. "And what do you get out of all this work, Dr. Grenfell?" a plump businessman asked him. The doctor poked him in the paunch. "Not this, anyhow," he said.

He had no compunction in pointing to a string of pearls around a dowager's throat and exclaiming, "Those are worth twenty thousand dollars; that money would be better spent helping the people of Labrador."

He had a poor platform style, but he did have a sense of theatre. At a meeting in Boston, he introduced three orphans from Labrador, and on the impulse of the moment proceeded to auction them off to foster parents, taking the money for the mission. The children were, of course, returned to the orphanage at St. Anthony. Grenfell could size up an audience like a politician. His speeches, like his books, fitted the style of the period and his recital of life in Labrador never failed to grip his listeners.

He had a special appeal to Americans of the pre-war years. The British were already disturbed by intellectual doubts, but the Americans were still idealists, vastly impressed by the Labrador Doctor's image as a man of action, risk, and accomplishment and by his simple muscular Christianity. The sons of the well-to-do from Harvard and Yale flocked to Labrador each summer as WOPS – Workers Without Pay – to toil as stevedores, cooks, dish-washers, anaesthetists, and veterinarians and to follow their hero in a morning plunge from the cross-trees of the *Strathcona* into the freezing waters, followed by a ritual race to the closest ice pan.

By 1906, Grenfell was a world figure, awarded the CMG in the King's birthday list of that year and the hero of a variety of sentimental books and magazine articles. Edward VII had him to the palace; Andrew Carnegie made him a house guest and donated three thousand books to the mission; the Governor General of Canada put him up at Rideau Hall. Oxford bestowed upon him an honorary doctorate of medicine – the first it had ever given. In St. John's, the Bowrings were his hosts and companions. Did Grenfell, in the midst of dunning them for money, mention the unmentionable – the degrading conditions on the Bowring ships at the height of the seal hunt? We do not know.

He professed not to enjoy his honours. Fund raising, he insisted, was necessary but irksome; he hated asking for money. Possibly; but did he really hate the attention, the adulation, the recognition that he, Wilfred Grenfell, was receiving from heads of state? His very eccentricity was disarming. He would often turn up late on social occasions, improperly dressed. Was this entirely a pose? Probably not. He was in love with the sea and he enjoyed those exhilarating summers, testing himself against the rocky inlets of the Labrador coast. It was, after all, a continuation of his childhood, but with no parents in control. There was always something of the small boy in Wilfred Grenfell. "He did what he wanted to do and if somebody told him not to do something he would go ahead and do it anyway," Dr. Badger has recalled. He could be remarkably gentle; the word most often used to describe him is "lovable." But he could be ruthless when he did not get his own way; he could and did throw tantrums when others followed a course not his.

The Ice Pan Adventure of 1908, which increased his public stature, was typically Grenfellian. His impulsiveness, his incautiousness, his refusal to heed advice got him into trouble; his coolness and resourcefulness under pressure got him out. His sense of theatre and his courage turned the incident into an international act of heroism. The doctor had himself photographed in the costume he had worn that Easter Sunday – the Oxford shorts and the football stockings – waving aloft the shirt-flag on its staff of dog bones. The picture was taken in front of the hospital at St. Anthony, but the background was retouched to make it appear to have been made on the ice pan itself. Grenfell tended to play down the incident; he had the English flair for self-dramatization while appearing to deprecate his accomplishments. He knew the form – the form that makes a bloody siege "a bit of a rough go." The Ice Pan Adventure changed in the telling. When Grenfell rewrote it as a book for boys, he gave the impression that, immediately on being rescued, he had dashed back to St. Anthony behind a dog team. The truth was that he had been carried in, barely conscious.

By this date, the Mission to Deep Sea Fishermen wanted out. The doctor's disinclination to follow instructions, or even to report, was maddening. He was supposed to be a missionary, preaching the gospel; what was he doing organizing *handicrafts*? His charges were supposed to be deep sea fishermen; why was he working with shore folk, teaching them to weave and carve? And what on earth was happening to all the money – the money that was going into "special funds" (whatever *they* were!) that never reached England? Dr. Grenfell was ordering hospital extensions that nobody had authorized and ship repairs without a by-your-leave; he was inviting strange guests to the coast while forbidding others to come; he was behaving very like a dictator and – worst of all – he was changing the direction of the mission away from religion toward social reform. Too often his superiors read of his work in the newspapers before receiving his reports.

There were other changes. In 1907, he had helped set up a separate Grenfell Association of America in New York and another in New England. The mission council was upset at the use of the Grenfell name, but before it could move, the associations became legal entities. By 1908, the doctor was on bad terms with the council's agent in St. John's and a long, acrimonious, and complicated argument over funds erupted. No one questioned Grenfell's honesty, but his accounting methods were shockingly casual: checks were kited, funds were unaccounted for; records, when they existed at all, were incomplete. Grenfell belonged to that breed of enthusiasts – they have been called visionaries, and dreamers, and also bunglers and incompetents – whose ideas outrun their execution, who are impatient of detail, and who, in leaping from peak to peak, tend to strew behind them a litter of unfinished business and a perplexity of half-executed concepts, which lesser mortals must put in order.

The dispute over funds led to a not very satisfactory investigation, which, eventually brought about the formation in 1912 of the International Grenfell Association, almost entirely divorced from London, with Grenfell as Superintendent of Missions and a proper board of directors and a finance committee to look after the accounts.

Yet it must be emphasized that even those who were exasperated by the doctor's unorthodox approach found him an endearing man. His very offhandedness, his lack of pretension, his simple devotion to a cause that had seemed hopeless were attractive qualities. He had that rarest of abilities – it is found in certain politicians – of concentrating his full attention on whomever he encountered. The most casual stranger was made to feel important, convinced that Wilfred Grenfell was genuinely interested in him and in what he had to say.

In spite of his financial bumbling, none could deny that he got results. Without Grenfell there would have been no mission to Labrador. The secretary of the Mission to Deep Sea Fishermen who had originally been dispatched by London to investigate the financial tangle, had this advice for a later colleague:

"May I remind you and all associated with Dr. Grenfell that you have a man to deal with of peculiar temperament whose vices, paradox as it may seem, are his virtues. His extraordinary personality and his steam-power driving energy are his God-given virtues, which have led to his accomplishing an enormous amount of good . . . the gift of balance and judgment having been denied him, his strong personality and driving force result in his making errors and possessing methods and aims which an ordinary man would perceive and in littleness avoid. But whatever errors Dr. Grenfell makes and however wrong his methods may appear, judged by ordinary standards, you must never lose sight of the fact that his actions are prompted by the highest motives."

In the midst of this hullabaloo, Grenfell, at the age of forty-four, surprised everybody by taking a wife. He had seldom demonstrated any special interest in the opposite sex; his energies had been channelled in other directions. No doubt he found solace in the time-honoured and very Victorian therapy of the cold plunge, which, for him, was a ritual. He had said on one occasion in 1904 that he liked American girls – the Christian ones: they were so practical, so full of go and capacity. And it was to an American girl of impeccable social credentials that he became, at last, attracted.

She was Anne Elizabeth Caldwell MacClanahan, a twenty-three-year-old Chicago heiress and Bryn Mawr graduate, whose father, a successful lawyer, had been a Confederate officer in the Civil War and whose mother was the daughter of a Vermont judge. She had been "doing Europe" – the obligatory tour that was the birthright of every young American aristocrat (in Miss MacClanahan's case it was the last leg of a three-year trip around the world) – and was returning to America in May, 1909, when she encountered Grenfell on the deck of the *Mauretania*. More likely, he encountered her through her travelling companion, a prominent midwest banker and family friend named William R. Stirling. Grenfell was taking Dear Old Mum, then seventy-eight years old, on her first trip to the New World to see him receive an honorary degree at Harvard. It is likely that he saw in Stirling an important ally in his campaign for funds.

The doctor's own account of his first meeting with the autocratic and firm-minded Miss MacClanahan was highly romantic. He was, he said, attracted by her beauty and her background but proceeded to lecture her on the uselessness of her life as a social butterfly. "But you don't even know my name!" she retorted. To which he replied that he was interested only in her future name: Grenfell.

This charming anecdote seems a little pat. The future Lady Grenfell was no shrinking violet; the most cursory inspection of her character suggests that it was she and not the famous Labrador Doctor who was the dominant figure in a swift romance that led to a fashionable wedding in Grace Episcopal Church of Chicago in November of the same year.

Miss MacClanahan knew what she wanted. "All my life," she told a Chicago newspaper, "I have been interested in reading of those who have made sacrifices for the general welfare of mankind. I realized when I became a young woman that if ever my heart was won, the conqueror must be more than a mere figure in society or a successful business or professional man. The men I met – none of them – seemed to comply with my requirements. When I met Dr. Grenfell I realized at once that my ideal had been found." What Anne MacClanahan wanted, she generally managed to get.

The doctor brought his bride to St. Anthony by mail steamer in

January, 1910. It was not a propitious voyage for a honeymoon; the journey took nine days instead of the usual five because the ship encountered a blizzard and a gale, which drove the spray onto the vessel until it was "sugared like a vast Christmas cake." They arrived on a chilly night to a warm welcome. Skyrockets and flares lit up the sky; cannon and shotgun rent the air. A driver on a decorated *komatik* slid up to the dock, and the happy couple, perched upon the sled and followed by a long line of welcomers, were driven to the staff house where a bed-sheet banner flapped a "welcome to our noble doctor and his bonnie bride." The fisher families, silently lining the path, and the mission staff were treated to their first glimpse of the new chatelaine of St. Anthony: a tall, handsome, large-boned, and aristocratic girl, wearing a fashionable hat with a short veil on her piled-up hair. The American press had made much of her sacrifice in leaving high society for a life in the wilderness. One New York paper had gone so far as to depict her future home as a tiny log hovel. It was, in fact, to be a mansion, built on the hill above the mission – a two-storey edifice of local stone with a magnificent glassed-in verandah, central heating, and electricity, the grandest dwelling in the community. It was immediately dubbed "the Castle," a title that exists to this day.

Of this "Grenfellian mansion" (the doctor's own description) the new bride took imperious command. She had brought her own furniture from Chicago; the following morning she supervised its installation. She demanded a cook and got one. She ordered that a leaky roof be fixed; it was. Styles changed; informality vanished. People no longer dropped in, in the local fashion – not even Reuben Sims, Grenfell's guide, servant, and friend – they waited to be invited. Mrs. Grenfell was nothing if not regal. There was a quality about her that made the locals feel awkward. Clearly, she felt herself above them; and to this day in St. Anthony, stories are told to illustrate that point:

– About the time she held a dinner party and the cook, worried about the quantity of food, asked what would happen if anybody asked for second helpings. Replied Anne Grenfell, "They wouldn't *dare*!"

– About the workman who spent three days digging a trench for a drain and rang the Castle's bell, announcing that the job was done. Said Anne Grenfell, "Wait a minute, my good fellow," went back in the house, and returned with – an apple.

– About the woman who worked a sixteen-hour day in the summer preparing meals for the Workers Without Pay, a task so exhausting that she often slept in her clothes. When Anne Grenfell paid her for her week's work – a sum of a dollar and a half – she asked, "And what are you going to do with all that money now?"

In the first summer of their marriage, Grenfell took her with him on the *Strathcona* up the Labrador coast to show her the land he loved. He delighted in it all – in the people who brought him presents of rotting whale meat for his dogs; in the cool, northern nights when they bunked down amid piles of salt cod; in the smoky sod huts where they crouched down eating cod heads or "browse," which is soaked ship's biscuit mixed with cod and served with crisped pork fat. She loathed it – loathed every minute of it: the sea, the ship, St. Anthony; but, to her credit, she accepted it all without complaint, in her fashion.

She was a natural manager. She set out to organize her husband (a monumental task) and it is a tribute to her determination that she succeeded remarkably well. Without her, he would have been less effective. Dr. Badger remembers her, seated behind him on the stage at a fund-raising lecture, passing him a stream of little hand-written notes to overcome his notorious absent-mindedness: "Don't forget Mrs. Badger . . . Don't forget Dr. and Mrs. Little . . . etc., etc." She handled his mail and his appointments and took over from his brother, Algernon, the editing of his books and articles, some of which she virtually wrote herself. (Was that arch anecdote about the marriage proposal hers?) When Houghton, Mifflin, the publishers, congratulated the doctor on a story in the *Atlantic Monthly*, she replied: "I am much interested in it, as I did a great deal about it myself. I did all the polishing and worked for days over it." At St. Anthony she took over the marketing of goods produced by the cottage industries and raised a fund to send local children to schools in the United States and England. She also annoyed old friends by sending notes saying that her husband had no time for them. "She was boss; she ran him like a puppet," her son Wilfred, the eldest of the three children she bore the doctor, has said of her. He has also said that "she would have liked nothing better than to be the Duchess of St. Anthony" and that "she was one of those people who was never happy unless she was frantically engaged in activity for its own sake," a description which, he agrees, also applied to his father.

If these remarks sound less than filial, it is perhaps because the Grenfells were virtual strangers to their offspring. They wanted the best for them: a special cow to give them pure milk, a French governess – luxuries far beyond the reach of those who lived below and beyond the Castle – but they did not provide their children with the one gift that money cannot buy. Anne Grenfell rarely expressed motherly emotion. "The only time I ever remember her showing any sign of real love in the best sense of the word," Wilfred has said, "was when I was about four or five. As a sort of great privilege, handed down from above, I was brought to an upstairs room in the Castle and allowed to sleep in her room. I remember I regarded this as a sort of audience, as a tremendous privilege. It was manna from Heaven; but it's the only time I ever remember her showing anything. I don't remember her hugging or kissing me or any of us."

In later years the gap widened; Wilfred's memory is that he rarely saw his parents for more than two weeks out of a year. Anne Grenfell's time was reserved for her husband; *he* was her real child. She was determined that he would be even more famous than when she met him; to that end she would polish him as she polished his prose. She even managed to change the way he dressed; morning coats replaced the old tweed jackets; no longer did he wear mismatched socks and shoes. He had once been so indifferent to his appearance that he had been ticked off by court officials at the Palace and had appeared at Harvard wearing his Oxford gown over a yellow tweed suit and yellow shoes. There was something engaging about this; after all, it was part of the Grenfell legend. But he meekly accepted the change because "Anne told me I must dress properly because people expect it." The perverse boy, who in manhood had always had his own way, was once again under parental control.

She had decided from the outset that he would be most useful to the mission as a publicist and fund raiser. In this, no doubt, she was right; it also suited her own way of life, for she basked in the limelight. "Notables kept Wilfred talking for hours," she enthused in a letter to her mother when, in 1911, the pair crossed the Atlantic. "All London is crying out to meet us." Nellie Melba, the opera diva, occupied the adjacent deck chair on the *Mauretania*. King George sent for Grenfell and kept him talking for an hour about Labrador. Sir Ernest Shackleton, the Antarctic explorer, chaired a meeting at which Grenfell spoke. The Royal Geographical Society gave him a reception. Count Marconi offered to install wireless on the *Strathcona*. Dr. Treves, now knighted, invited the couple to stay at Windsor.

Anne Grenfell insisted that her husband leave the work on the coast to the team that he had trained, headed by Dr. John Little, a brilliant surgeon who had helped to eliminate beriberi in Labrador. By 1914 the little mission of the nineties had expanded into a vast and complicated organization: six permanent doctors and eighteen nurses, their ranks swollen each summer by fourteen additional doctors and one hundred and fifty WOP volunteers.

Four hospitals and six nursing stations treated more than six thousand patients every year. The annual budget, handled by a finance committee, had grown to sixty-six thousand dollars. All of this resulted from the inspiration of one man who had by now become a kind of walking flag for the enterprise that bore his name but who was spending less and less time on the coast. Instead, his wife commandeered the homes of the rich and powerful, where the couple stayed, accompanied by an increasing staff.

Grenfell was not immune from criticism. An entire generation of Labrador and Newfoundland traders had been forced out of business or compelled to cut prices because of the success of his co-operatives. In 1916, the merchants of St. John's petitioned the Newfoundland government to take away the mission's privileges because of bad publicity and unfair competition. Grenfell was presenting to the world a picture of a colony composed almost entirely of paupers; his institution was able to sell goods without paying duty or freight charges; the merchants wanted these perquisites curtailed or abolished. A commissioner was appointed to investigate the complaints. His report, laudatory of Grenfell and his mission, quenched the protests from Water Street, but there was little love lost between the doctor and the merchants of Newfoundland.

A few years before, when a customs officer had asked her if she had any spirits to declare, Anne Grenfell had let slip a revealing remark. "My husband," she said, "does not allow strong drink in the colonies." The Grenfell Mission was, in every sense, colonial. All of its doctors and nurses came from either the United States or England (except for one from Australia). Its young volunteer workers came from the good eastern universities. Most of its funds were raised outside of Newfoundland. No one in its hierarchy was a native Newfoundlander. And there were few if any Canadians among staff or volunteers. As one Torontonian remarked to Grenfell, the Canadians were quite used to ice and snow; to them there was nothing in the least exotic about the bald cliffs of Newfoundland or the bleak fiords of Labrador.

Grenfell's strength lay in his ability to romanticize one of the grimmest corners of the continent. But there was a potential weakness, too; the fact that the mission was an entirely foreign effort. One can understand, if not sympathize with, the feeling in St. John's that these were "outsiders" come to stir up the natives. There was something just a little patronizing about these strangers. The Prime Minister, Sir Richard Squires (to whom Grenfell privately referred, in a letter to a friend, as "a thief"), was infuriated by the doctor's impassioned descriptions of the sufferings of the liveyeres. Squires was trying to coax a good credit rating for the colony from the financial interests of New York and London, but everywhere he went he "came upon the bloody trail of a man named Grenfell." He openly accused the doctor of blackmailing the consciences of generous foreigners with lurid lies.

This view was not supported by the people of the coasts. At the height of one of the public attacks on Grenfell, one of them wrote to the St. John's *Evening Telegram*:

"He gets the salt brine in his eyes for he is out in all weathers . . . . Let those who speak ill of him follow after his heels . . . . Not only do the people of Labrador look for Grenfell, but forty thousand fishermen look for him sooner or later . . . they know the magnificent work he has done . . . . There is not a fisherman I know or a fishing skipper that sails a vessel to Labrador has anything but good to say of Grenfell or his work, and it would be to our shame if one of us could not give Grenfell our everlasting gratitude."

Yet, as the years moved on, the doctor saw progressively less of the coast. He wintered for the last time in St. Anthony in 1918-19, the year of the great influenza epidemic, a tragedy that was to make the mission workers heroes in the world's eyes, for they struggled day and night against impossible odds. The statistics are shocking: in Okkak, a community of 270, every man died; only thirty-nine women and children survived. At Cartwright, forty children were orphaned. Dogs, neglected and starving, attacked the dying. Entire families succumbed, and their huts were burned over their corpses to kill infection. The plague put an additional strain on the mission. Grenfell, impulsively ordering more buildings, boats and repairs, sank it deeper into debt. But what if the doctor were himself to die? Face to face that winter with the uncertainty of life, the mission came to realize that the leader was not immortal. If he went, where would the funds come from? There was only one answer: Grenfell himself must raise an endowment fund of at least one and a half million dollars to perpetuate his work. Instead of cruising north that summer, he reluctantly agreed to return to the lecture platform.

To the great satisfaction of his wife, he moved his family to Boston and set off on a tour of the United States, Canada, and Great Britain. By crowding as many as three lectures into a day he was able, by the end of the first year, to raise more than half the required amount. He returned each summer to Labrador, but his visits grew shorter. His mother died in 1921. The following year the *Strathcona* was lost at sea. In 1924, nearly sixty, exhausted by fund raising, he was persuaded by the directors of the International Grenfell Association to embark on a nine-month cruise. It was designed to help him recuperate, but he could not relax; the lectures, the receptions, the appeals for funds, the constant correspondence with the mission all continued.

The following year he returned to London, formed the Grenfell Association of Great Britain, and cut himself off from the Mission to Deep Sea Fishermen, whose contributions to his Labrador work had for some time been minimal. Whipping about Britain in a second-hand car that frequently broke down, he was, as always, an enormous hit. He commanded overflow audiences; hotels refused to bill him; porters and waitresses handed back their tips as donations; typists worked for nothing; youngsters volunteered as WOPS. The lure of the Labrador wilderness – the lure of the unknown – tempted the imagination of young Englishmen as it had once seduced the doctor himself.

He had published thirty-five books and hundreds of articles, and his wife was busily revising and enlarging his biography. By 1926, both were in bad health. She had been treated for a tumour she must have suspected was malignant; he had suffered his first major heart attack. Yet in spite of this, and in spite of a worse heart attack three years later, he continued his fund-raising efforts.

He would have much preferred to cruise that dark and brine-encrusted coastline, diving into the freezing waters of a morning, prescribing for the fishermen, preaching to the liveyeres, and living a carefree adventurous life; but this was not to be. One February he found himself at his "lowest ebb" in a hotel room in Birmingham, Alabama, and sat down to pour out his thoughts in a letter to his friend George Warburton, the General Secretary of the YMCA for North America:

"Talking for money – talking – talking – talking – sometimes to individuals, sometimes to crowds. But talking. I wasn't bred that way and I look forward to the day of my deliverance. Do you love the open and the silence of the woods and the next-to-nature life, and the challenge of the wild? Here I hear of it in Labrador. I see it and pass by – never still, always urged on and on, as if I must fall off the edge some day . . . ."

He was laden with honours: Lord Rector of St. Andrew's, a Livingstone Gold Medal, a Fellowship in the Royal Geographical Society, and a knighthood. He was now Sir Wilfred Grenfell. The title was shared, with considerable pride and not a little hauteur, by his wife. In St. Anthony a local acquaintance committed the unpardonable error of addressing her as "Mrs. Grenfell." "*Lady* Grenfell to you!" came the frosty reply.

He had reached the pinnacle but had passed his prime. He was like a sports hero who has lost his crown but refuses to admit defeat – a boxer vainly attempting one more comeback. At the hospital in St. Anthony he was tolerated and sometimes indulged; but he was not always welcomed, for he could be a disturbing and irritating influence. Dr. Charles Curtis, in charge of the hospital, lacked Grenfell's brilliance and bedside manner, but he was a better organizer and a better surgeon. For some years he had been the real head of the mission, and it irked him when his mentor would suddenly turn up, come roaring into the hospital, seize a white coat, and go into the wards or the operating room to tackle cases of which he knew very little. There is one tale in which Curtis, having prepared a patient for operation, arrived to discover Grenfell kneeling at the bedside in prayer. "I would prefer you to leave off praying," Curtis said acidly. "My patients are not dead yet."

Grenfell had always been a creature of impulse. Now the trait became more erratic. He would drop groups of children into the already crowded orphanage without knowing their names and forgetting where he had found them. He would walk into one of the co-operatives, pick up armfuls of clothing, and order the clerk fired when she told him he could not take the items without their being listed on a receipt. The WOPS continued to be his sole responsibility; sometimes they turned out to be drug addicts or alcoholics, shipped off by their parents for a cure and useless when they arrived. He invited important guests to visit St. Anthony and then went off cruising, leaving them to be entertained by others. He took on patients and left their after-care to the staff. He once brought in a dying man who had no identification and whose body had to be disinterred from the Protestant graveyard when his worried wife, a Roman Catholic, wrote to inquire about his whereabouts.

Nelson and Laurance Rockefeller, whose father was a financial supporter of the mission, were WOPS in Labrador in 1929; they found the experience a little disillusioning. When Laurance was stricken with appendicitis and brought into the hospital at St. Anthony after a difficult trip down the coast, Grenfell offered to perform the operation himself. In the words of a Rockefeller aide, the offer was "politely declined – the young Rockefellers were having their doubts about putting Laurance in the hands of an ailing man functioning under rather primitive conditions as to antisepsis."

Yet in spite of it all, he retained his ability to mesmerize. Curtis encountered it one day, after a shipload of tourists arrived at St. Anthony. "I'm going down to have a talk with them," Grenfell remarked. Curtis urged him not to; he was not invited – it would be an intrusion. "I don't care whether I'm invited or not," Sir Wilfred retorted. "I'm going." He approached one of the ship's officers and identified himself. He was told that the passengers were at lunch and would not want to be disturbed. "Well," said Sir Wilfred, "I'll just talk to them anyway for a couple of minutes." He walked into the dining saloon and began to talk as his listeners nibbled. He talked for five minutes; the nibbling ceased. People began to ask questions; Grenfell replied. The five minutes stretched to forty-five. At last Grenfell was finished. "Thank you very much for letting me talk to you," he said. "I would like to be able to go back to the hospital with three thousand dollars in my pocket." He got it.

He made one last voyage to Labrador in 1932. As always there were photographers and cameramen present as the sixty-eight-year-old doctor was shown gliding across the sea, propelling a kayak. But he suffered a stroke that year, and the directors suggested he resign as superintendent. Lady Grenfell was having none of that; but he did agree to give up his sole right to choose and send volunteers.

The couple retired to a handsome white-painted house in Vermont where he continued to write long, rambling articles and letters until his doctor forbade the activity. Anne Grenfell was in great pain from cancer and the resultant X-ray treatments, but she continued her work, raising funds herself, sorting out her husband's mail, protecting him from irritating letters and calls, and polishing up the best of his earlier writing for a new book to be entitled *A Labrador Logbook*.

By 1938 both were invalids. Grenfell's high blood pressure made him increasingly irrational and intolerant. Sometimes, it appeared, he was not quite sane. He had been forced to resign as superintendent of the mission in 1937, henceforth to be known as Founder. It irked him. In a letter to Harvey Cushing the following year he quoted Huxley: "The idea that one is becoming useless is the greatest shock a real human organism can experience."

Anne Grenfell was sent to Boston in October of 1938 for what was to be the last in a series of operations. She had been in great pain for years and had born it stoically; no whisper of discomfort, no murmur of complaint ever passed her lips. She worked until the end, as she had for almost all of her adult life, in the interests of her husband. When he checked into a small hotel near the hospital with his male nurse-cum-secretary, she made sure that he was not told she was dying. All of her considerable ambition had been channelled in one direction. In those final days, when she knew her disease was terminal, did she come to regret the narrowness of that devotion? There is evidence that she did. "For God's sake," she told a friend at one point – and she was in tears – "keep your children with you always. Don't farm them out." When she died, hers were not at her bedside; nor did they attend her funeral.

Her husband, with his abiding faith in the afterlife, accepted her death. She had left him a touching note, which she had managed to scrawl just before the end: "I'm going to leave today, I think – but I shall never be far away." Only after she was gone did he discover that she had squirreled away all his records, papers, drawings, and photographs for posterity.

Clearly he missed her, and yet there is more than a suspicion that he felt the kind of release a schoolboy does when the term is over. After the funeral, he came back to the home of his friend Dr. Badger, who was suffering from pneumonia and had been unable to attend the last rites. Grenfell went to his friend's bedside, then crossed to the window and, staring out, remarked, "You know, Ted, for the first time I can lead my own life." It is possible to believe that, at that moment, he was staring not at the Boston skyline but at those far shores where the cry of the gulls is lost in the clamour of the storm.

It was characteristic of Anne Grenfell that to please her husband she had asked that her ashes be scattered either at sea or at St. Anthony – the two places she most heartily detested. And so, in the summer of 1939, Sir Wilfred Grenfell set out on a final visit to his headquarters on the northeastern tip of Newfoundland. It was a far different community from the frontier settlement he had first seen almost half a century before. The hospital was thriving. The fishermen were raising crops and cattle. Old men were at work carving; the women were sewing clothes from deerskin and from the tightly woven cloth that Grenfell had suggested and that still bears his name. He cruised north on the mail steamer to welcoming crowds and then, on his return, was given the mission tender to skipper across the Strait of Belle Isle. When he left in August, the years seemed to have fallen away; his health, both physical and mental, had improved to an astonishing degree.

His recovery was close to miraculous. At one point he had been so totally disoriented that he had forgotten where Labrador was and could not recognize even such old friends as Ted Badger. Now he was alive once more. He returned to the lecture platform, and only those who had heard him in his prime knew that he was less than what he had been.

Death held no terrors for him. He had been living with death since his first heart attack, had brushed against it long before that among the ice floes of Hare Bay. He had always seen it, as he saw all of life, as a great adventure. "When I actually was looking at death, sitting on that ice pan with no material hope whatever of ever seeing land again," he wrote to his friend Warburton, "I was just as keen about what I was going to see on the other side of the horizon as I was to get back and see what I thought I had left forever behind me."

And did not death also bring freedom? For all his life, the schoolboy in him had chafed at restriction, rebelled against the constraints of convention, financial responsibility, executive red tape; his happiest moments had been spent on the frontier of the Labrador coast, alone in the wilderness of the ocean, captain and crew of his own craft, free to voyage wherever whim took him, father to his flock, protector of his people, master of his own fate and that of others.

Freedom. It is a word that crops up in his correspondence over the years. In one of the last letters he wrote (to a woman friend), on September 5, 1940, he mentioned it again:

"I'm supposed to be under sentence of death from heart trouble. You know how I look on death – as the greatest advance in life . . . soon we shall ourselves get free of this human temporary habitation and know what real freedom is . . . ."

The following month – the date was October 9 – at the age of seventy-five, he played a rousing game of croquet with his secretary and a visiting professor. He went upstairs for a rest before dinner and there, in his sleep, the Labrador Doctor embarked upon his last great adventure.

13
The Revenge of Mina Hubbard

On June 27, 1905, two oddly similar expeditions were launched from trading posts on opposite sides of the North West River to map and explore the interior of what was then called, with considerable validity, "darkest Labrador."

One expedition made its headquarters at the Hudson's Bay post on one side of the water; in charge was a stocky lawyer and outdoorsman from New York City named Dillon Wallace. The other expedition was located on the opposite shore at the French trading post run by one M. Duclos. It was headed by a small, neat, and determined widow of thirty-five, Mina Hubbard.

Both expeditions had identical objectives. Each was intent on completing the work of Mrs. Hubbard's late husband, Leonidas, who had starved to death on the Susan River two years before during an abortive attempt to travel across the unmapped heart of Labrador to Ungava Bay.

Dillon Wallace and Mina Hubbard had once been friends, drawn together by a mutual attraction to the dead man. Wallace, Hubbard's closest male crony, had almost died with him on the previous expedition. Now he and Mrs. Hubbard were no longer speaking, the estrangement made embarrassing by their proximity. It was not easy to avoid one another, for they had no option but to travel from Rigolet at the head of the Hamilton Inlet aboard the same boat. Wallace, who was nervous and uncomfortable in Mrs. Hubbard's presence, did his best to keep his distance. As for Mina Hubbard, she loathed Dillon Wallace – despised him, hated him, detested him. When she learned of his presence aboard the *Harlow*, the ship that would take her from Rigolet to North West River, she "trembled like a leaf for an hour." She was determined that if anyone completed her dead husband's work it would be she. For the two expeditions were engaged in more than simple exploration: they were bitter rivals in a race across the broken surface of an inhospitable plateau that no white man had yet conquered. They were racing not only against each other but also against the calendar. If they did not reach Ungava Bay by the end of August, they would miss the season's only steamer and be forced to spend the entire winter in each other's company in the cramped quarters of the George River trading post. It was a prospect that neither wished to contemplate.

To understand the reasons for the contest, it is necessary to meet the main characters and follow the singular chain of events that led to the tragedy of 1903 and its extraordinary aftermath.

Mina Hubbard was born Mina Benson in April, 1870, on a farm near Bewdley, Ontario, not far from Rice Lake. She studied nursing in New York and after graduation was assigned to Leonidas Hubbard, Jr., a young journalist convalescing after a bout of typhoid fever. Hubbard was the son of a Forty-Niner who had left the California goldfields for a more prosaic life as a farmer in Michigan. The younger Hubbard, "high strung and sensitive" in Mina's phrase, had developed a romantic love of the outdoors, an attachment nurtured by the stories of his grandfather, a frontiersman and an Indian fighter. The young man, possessed of "a driving energy to have a part in the larger work of the world," was graduated from university at Ann Arbor in 1897, wangled a job on a Detroit newspaper, moved to New York to the staff of the *Daily News*, wrote editorials for the *Saturday Evening Post*, lost his job as a result of his illness and, on recovery, decided to free-lance. His first article was accepted by *Outing*, and from that point on he did most of his work for that magazine.

In January, 1901, he married his nurse. Although she was two years older (thirty-one to his twenty-nine), he called her "my girl." She called him "Laddie," and as far as she was concerned he was perfection itself, "utterly fearless, resolute, persistent," possessed of "a beautiful simplicity, a gentleness and interest that rarely failed to disarm and win admission where he desired to enter." There was more: "Added to this equipment were a fine sense of humour, a subtle sympathy and a passionate tenderness for anyone or anything, lonely or neglected or in trouble. . . ." In short, a paragon without fault or blemish; in Mina Hubbard's eyes he would never be anything else.

Hubbard's closest friend, Wallace, was nine years his senior. The two had been drawn together by a mutual, if somewhat unrealistic attachment to the outdoors; they yearned for the frontier life, for the thrill of crossing unknown country, of walking where none had walked before. They saw only romance; the hardships they ignored or brushed aside.

Dillon Wallace was a self-made man with a remarkable background. At the age of thirteen, with his mother dead and his father's legal business a failure, he had taken over and single-handedly run the family farm in Orange County, New York. When the farm was lost, he worked first in a grist mill and later mastered the art of telegraphy as a Morse operator while saving all the time for a future education. He put himself through law school and, in 1897, entered private practice in New York. Clearly, Dillon Wallace was a man who felt he was capable of anything he attempted, but when Hubbard first met him, around 1900, he was at the end of his tether, lonely and disconsolate over the death of his young wife of three years, a victim of tuberculosis, the ravaging disease of the day. Legal work failed to stimulate him; he found his therapy was the outdoors. In November of 1901, while he and Hubbard were on a camping trip on Shawangunk Mountain in New York, the younger man suggested as a distraction an expedition into the heart of Labrador.

Wallace was puzzled. "Now where in the earth is Labrador?" he asked. He had a vague idea of it being "a sort of Arctic wilderness" – nothing more.

But Hubbard was bubbling with excitement: "Man, don't you realize it's about the only part of the continent that hasn't been explored? As a matter of fact, there isn't much more known of the interior of Labrador than when Cabot discovered the coast more than four hundred years ago. Think of it, Wallace! A great unknown land near home, as wild and primitive today as it always has been. I want to see it. I want to get into a really wild country and have some of the experiences of the old fellows who explored and opened up the country where we are now."

Wallace was caught up in Hubbard's enthusiasm; yes, he would go with him to that unknown domain! It was, however, more than a year before Hubbard dropped into his law office to announce that the trip was on. "It will be a big thing, Wallace. It ought to make my reputation." Hubbard now saw himself as another Stanley, probing a frontier as dark and as mysterious as Africa.

At this time – February, 1903 – Hubbard was assistant editor of *Outing* and not without camping experience. The previous February he had gone on a snowshoeing journey with the Montagnais Indians of northern Quebec, and that summer he and his wife had camped around the north shore of Lake Superior, mainly in the interests of journalism. His editor, Caspar Whitney, did not share his enthusiasm for the Labrador excursion. "It was a trip with which I was frankly not in sympathy and from which I sought to dissuade Hubbard," he was to write. He bluntly told his assistant that he did not think it worth the money; however, because of his regard for Hubbard, he agreed to help finance him.

Hubbard insisted on planning the entire expedition himself. Through his magazine he had access to a rich store of wilderness experience, but he disdained it. He "neither took *Outing* nor its editor into his confidence," Whitney wrote. He asked no help or advice from anyone in selecting his equipment or the members of his party; this was to be his expedition and his alone; the glory would be his also. He had determined to travel lightly: too many provisions would slow down the expedition. It would be a small party: himself, Wallace, and a woodsman.

He wrote to the Hudson's Bay agent at Rigolet asking if he knew anyone who could be hired for such a journey. The agent was discouraging: everyone feared to venture too far inland. Finally, Hubbard engaged a Cree named Jerry from Missanabie, Ontario, but at the last minute the Indian backed out, not because he feared the wilds of Labrador but because he was terrified of the jungle of Manhattan. As he put it to Hubbard, he didn't "want to die so soon." Hubbard was fortunate in his replacement. From Eastmain, Quebec, on the shores of James Bay, he engaged a remarkable half-breed, George Elson, a solid, rangy, God-fearing outdoorsman, difficult to ruffle, easy to live with. Though Elson was half Cree, he looked more like a white man, with his black moustache and his pipe. And *he* was not in the least inhibited by the menace of the metropolis.

He had never travelled on a train and had never been in a city; it did not faze him. Hubbard and Wallace were supposed to meet him when he arrived at Grand Central; they missed the appointment. That did not faze Elson either. He had never travelled by cab, but he found a stand, rented a hack, and was trotted off to the office of *Outing* where Hubbard finally caught up with him, seated in the waiting room quite unconcerned.

Elson, in Wallace's later description, was "something more than a woodsman – he was a hero. Under the most trying circumstances he was calm, cheerful, companionable, faithful. Not only did he turn out to be a man of intelligence, quick of perception and resourceful, but he turned out to be a man of character."

It tells us something of Hubbard's misplaced self-confidence that at no time did he ask Elson for advice about equipment or other arrangements for the expedition. Elson had expected to plan the provisions and set the travel schedule, but he found, to his surprise and chagrin, that Hubbard intended to use him only in a minor capacity. With all the optimism and arrogance of the amateur, Hubbard decided he alone would plan the details and make the decisions.

The three men, with Mrs. Hubbard, left New York on June 20, 1903. On July 5, they reached the Grenfell Mission at Battle Harbour. Here Mrs. Hubbard debarked to return by another steamer to her home at Congers, New York. The idea that a woman might take part in a journey of exploration was then inconceivable; it was adventurous enough merely to express a desire to be a telephone operator. Mina Hubbard parted from her husband at 6.00 a.m. in a cold, drizzling rain, stepping into a small boat in which she was rowed to that bleak and rocky shore, still mottled by a patchwork of old snow. She had been married for just thirty months, and she did not know when she would see her husband again. She cried. He tried not to. As yet there was no hint of a breach with Wallace, who wrote: "She was very brave. . . . Poor little woman! . . . I stood aside with a lump in my throat as they said their farewell." It was to be their last.

There exists a pencil sketch of Hubbard, made in New York about the time of his marriage. It shows a rather ascetic-looking man, finger to forehead, hair in a prim part, pince-nez centred on a thin, sensitive face, looking very much the man of letters. A stylish rendering. The photograph taken at Rigolet shows a different figure: a bantam cock of a man, dressed for the trail, legs astride, feet planted on the ground, jaw set. Wallace, in the companion photograph, looks a little more nondescript, a little less self-assured, with a large moon face, slashed in the middle by the downward curve of a dark moustache, the eyes also drooping as if in concert.

Hubbard's objective was to explore the eastern and northern areas of the Labrador peninsula, these being the least known. The interior plateau, a jigsaw puzzle of schist and granite, quartzite and basalt, rises steeply from the coast to a height of two thousand feet. This rolling wasteland of timeless rock and ragged scrub is pockmarked by innumerable lakes and marshes from which swift rivers pour off to every compass point, descending through a constant succession of cataracts and rapids. In Hubbard's day, the only means of travel was by canoe, and even that was considered dangerous. Because the condition of the rivers made it impossible to transport sufficient food for any considerable period, the plateau was shunned by white men. Game was not always plentiful, and there were scores of instances of Indians dying of starvation among those riven rocks and skeletal larches.

The plan was to follow the North West or the Naskaupi River

(there was some confusion as to whether these were the same) to Lake Michikamau and, from the northern end of that body of water, to strike across the height of land to the headwaters of the unmapped George River and perhaps, if time allowed, to follow that river to Ungava Bay. En route the party expected to witness the great caribou migration across the Labrador interior – something no white man had seen – and to spend some time observing the habits of the Naskapi Indians, then the most primitive on the continent. Hubbard's plans for returning were a little vague: these would depend on how far the season had advanced. They could go across country to the St. Lawrence; they could retrace their own route; or they could go down to Ungava Bay and pick up a boat for Newfoundland. Hubbard's view of the Labrador interior was blithely optimistic; his plans to cut across the peninsula, as he outlined them to Wallace, seemed to envisage nothing more fearsome than an excursion across Manhattan Island on roller skates.

It was not to be that easy. The only useful map of the peninsula was that of the Geological Survey of Canada, based on information gathered by that remarkable wilderness traveller, A.P. Low. Much of Low's material came from hearsay. His map showed only

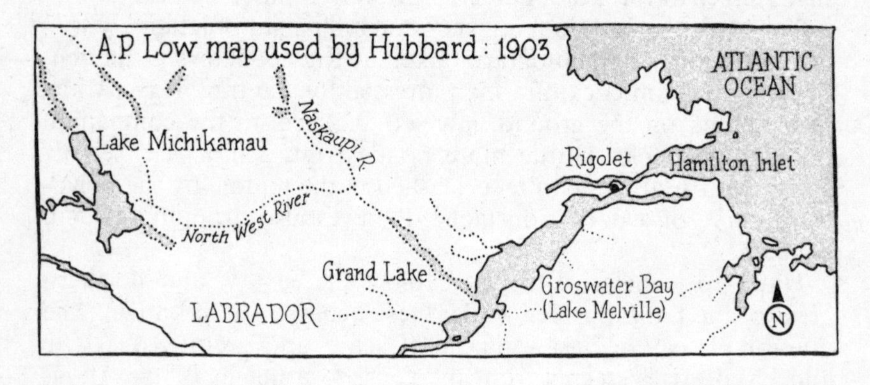

one major river, which he called the North West River, rising at Lake Michikamau and flowing into Grand Lake. There were five. At Rigolet on Hamilton Inlet, Hubbard and Wallace talked to several natives who convinced them that Low's North West River was actually the Naskaupi. Nobody bothered to tell either man that there were other rivers as well; it did not occur to the natives – who knew this part of the country as intimately as Hubbard knew his home village of Congers – that anybody could miss the obvious. But miss it they did.

At Rigolet almost everybody predicted that the expedition would never return. Hubbard brushed these prophecies aside;

indeed, he welcomed them, for he said it would make his work seem more important in the end. "He could do it and he *would*." At the North West River Post at the south end of Grand Lake, the Hudson's Bay agent was the only man to show any enthusiasm for the venture. When the party left, at nine on the morning of July 15, the others were "grave and sceptical and shook their heads at our persistency in going into a country we had been so frequently warned against."

They set off on one of those marvellous northern days that remain in the mind long after the hardships of the trail have been blurred and softened by the cumulus of memory. The air was crisp and heady with the incense of the evergreens; the sky was a clear robin's-egg blue; sunlight danced on the dark waters of the lake. The prospect was pleasing: all they needed to do was paddle to the head of the lake, find Low's river, and follow it to Lake Michikamau at the top of the Labrador plateau.

They found it – or thought they did – the next day, just after noon, a swift stream about 125 feet wide. It never entered their heads that they could be wrong. But they had made a tragic error. The mouth of the river they sought, the Naskaupi, was five miles behind, its mouth divided by a wooded island that concealed the opening. The river they entered was the Susan, "a river which was to introduce us promptly to heart breaking hardships," a forbidding tangle of rocks and cataracts that forced them to struggle knee-deep in the icy water as they tracked their loaded canoe around rocks and through eddies. The portages, which seemed endless, were worse; day after day they manhandled their craft and their supplies through gullies and swamps, hands, faces, and wrists swollen by the bites of blackflies, clouds of which often filled their nostrils and caused their eyelids to puff up so badly they could scarcely see. The cheesecloth and ointment purchased in New York against such an eventuality proved useless.

They were lost but did not know it, persisting in the belief that this was Low's North West River. Tom Blake, a half-breed at Rigolet who trapped at the upper end of Grand Lake, had told them they would encounter close to twenty miles of good paddling. Hubbard concluded that Blake was wrong; it did not occur to him that he might be himself. Nor did he listen to Elson. To lighten the load on the portages he began to discard supplies – clothing, a five-pound pail of lard, coffee, several pounds of flour, a box of milk powder. In vain Elson argued that these would be needed. Fifteen days and eighty miles out of the North West River Post, Hubbard still believed himself on the right route. The river forked and the three men followed the south branch, believing it

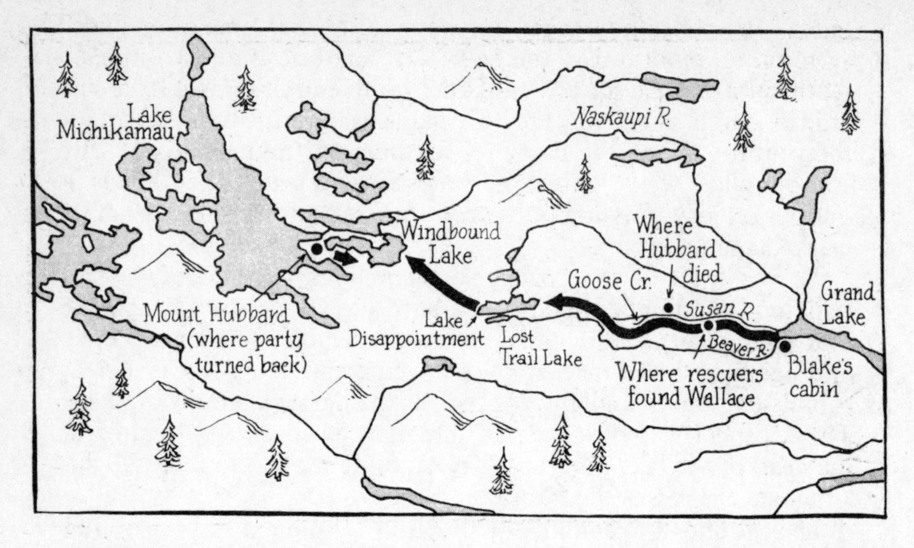

would lead to Lake Michikamau. Actually, they had turned up Goose Creek, a tributary of the Susan. Eventually, in the course of a portage, they lost it and crossed to a different river, the Beaver. They had no way of knowing that they were now following an old Indian trail to Michikamau. Then they wandered off that, too. As they moved westward they named some of the features along the route, and these tell their own story: Lost Trail Lake . . . Windbound Lake . . . Lake Disappointment.

Hubbard's diary, which has been preserved, reads very like all diaries of abortive wilderness excursions. It begins with enormous zest: "Pancakes, bread and melted sugar at 3 o'clock. Bully. Dried apple sauce and hot bread, bacon, coffee . . . for supper . . . Bully. Apples and abundant sugar great comfort. Keep us feeling good and sweet and well fed." Then, as the insects did their work, as the supplies diminished with alarming swiftness, as the portages grew wearier and limbs weaker, the diary becomes a record of slow disillusionment. Within three weeks the trio had run out of lard, sugar, bacon, salt, and flour. The trout they managed to catch and the geese and the single caribou they shot were not enough to maintain their strength, for they lacked fat, the one resource absolutely necessary for men struggling with heavy loads. When the caribou skin turned rotten and was crawling with maggots, Hubbard and Wallace were persuaded by George Elson not to throw it away. Keep it, Elson told the astonished pair, "we may want to eat it some day." That day was not far off.

Both Hubbard and Wallace quickly wore holes in their moccasins; they had not thought, as Elson had, to bring an extra pair. Hubbard lost two of his toenails and cracked the skin on his heel;

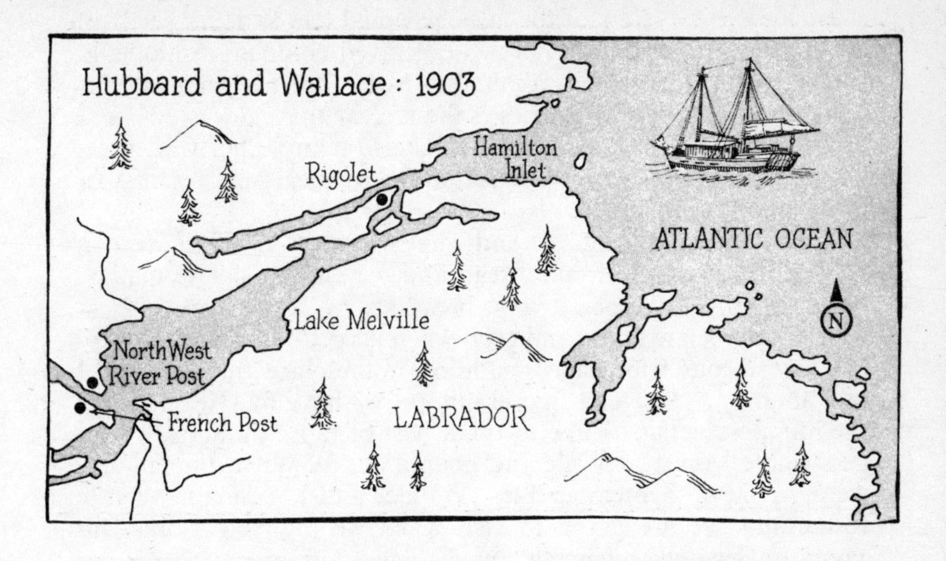

he had not thought to bring adhesive plaster, either. By early August, his clothes were in dreadful condition, his trousers ripped clear down the leg from the waist. "Don't know how to patch them" he confided to his diary, "no stuff." He had not foreseen that eventuality, either. Yet he was able to add: "Spirits high."

He refused to entertain any thought of turning back, and the other two dared not suggest it. "Failure makes me shudder," he wrote in his diary on September 6. By that date he was a grotesque sight. He refused to take a bath, not because of the cold – the first snow fell that day – but because he was "ashamed of my bones ... I'm a walking skeleton." Two days later he wrote: "Moccasins in tatters, socks and duffle hang out at every angle and catch on every bush. Pants in rags from knees down – could trade pants and footwear with the raggedest tramp I ever saw and be better off. It is depressing, so is grub lack. Hard to keep up courage when hungry – but we do it. ..."

The following day, September 9, Elson and Hubbard crossed a small lake, climbed a mountain (later to be called Mount Hubbard), and saw in the distance, at last, the lonely sheet of water for which they had been searching.

"It's there! It's there!" Hubbard shouted to Wallace on his return. "Michikamau is there, just behind the ridge. We saw the big water! We saw it!"

They saw it but could not reach it. A storm on the lake – which they named Windbound – held them in camp. Then lassitude gripped them. Wallace began to notice a change in Hubbard. To this point he had been full of the work at hand, of the mountains and rivers to be conquered, of the tales he would tell, and, above all, of the stories he would write. Now he "craved companionship" and began to talk intimately about his early life, his relatives, his home. Hubbard's diary entries make it clear that he was obsessed by two subjects – home and food. Like so many other wilderness journals, his contains long descriptions of meals he has had or meals he hopes to have:

"W & I talk of restaurants and what we would do if we were in New York. We would take bread and pie and chocolate mainly. Never dreamed one could want bread so. . . ." And again: "How we will appreciate home and grub when we get out. Coffee, chocolate, bread, pie, fried cakes, puddings – these are what W. and I talk about. . . . We tell of good dinners we have had, dwelling on the minutest details. I like to think best of those dinners at Congers where M. sat opposite and poured coffee. What dinners they were!" And on September 14: " Wallace and I . . . made a list of restaurants we are going to visit when we hit New York. Our tastes are decidedly plebeian. I would delight to enter a mission restaurant on the Bowery and eat flour and bread at 2 cents a plate. . . . I would like now best of all big slices of boiled pork, bread . . . and sorghum or New Orleans molasses. . . ." And so on and on for page after page, listing all the food he *should* have taken and would take on another trip or even on a picnic in the Hudson Highlands: oatmeal, rice, flour, bacon, fat pork, beans, baking powder, salt, sweet biscuit, sugar, marmalade, onions, potatoes, raisins, figs, dried fruit, tomatoes, chicken – the very words seemed to intoxicate him, as if the act of putting them down on paper nourished him – "then some good stews, soups, French toast, syrup, pancakes, omelettes, sweet biscuits and jam with a broiled steak and chicken roast . . . canned pork and canned plum pudding must also go in the menu. . . . Mina and I must study delightful camp dinners now and carry out the nice little woods dinners we started. . . ." The scribbles continued on, and then these glum words: "Hard to keep off depression . . . . All hungry."

The day after Hubbard composed that extended gastronomic fantasy, George Elson, sitting around the campfire with the other two, began to tell stories of Indians who had starved to death in the bush. That was scarcely tactful. Hubbard stood up, pushed some partially burned sticks into the flames, turned his back on the fire and, deep in thought, walked down to the lakeshore, staring out into the windswept waters – a gaunt, haggard figure in rags, dashed by the spray. Finally he wheeled about and walked briskly back.

"Boys," he said, "what do you say to turning back?" Wallace was stunned, Elson relieved. They ate their last bacon and rice and talked feverishly of home and food. But the storm held them on the lakeside for five more days.

During this period of waiting Hubbard held long conversations about his wife with Wallace. He felt guilty because he believed he had not given her or their life together the attention they deserved. "That's real happiness, Wallace – a good wife and a cheerful fireside. What does glory and all that amount to, after all? I've let my work and my ambition bother me too much. I've hardly taken time for my meals . . . ."

They had been more than two months on the trail. Winter was setting in. By September 24, six inches of snow covered the ground. How could they hope to get back to North West River in their weakened condition? "We were almost as thin and almost the colour of the mummies one sees in the museums," Wallace wrote. The talk turned less to food now – they were subsisting almost entirely on berries, the occasional grouse, and sporadic feasts of fish – and more to their childhood memories. Hubbard, suffering from the recurrent diarrhoea that had plagued him almost from the outset, was too weak to do his share of work. By October 4, he was staggering as he walked and suffering lapses of memory. "On this last day of our long portage he came near to going to pieces nervously," Wallace wrote. "When he started to tell me something about his wife's sister, he could not recall her name. . . . For a long time he sat very still, his face buried in his hands, doubtless striving to rally his forces. And the most pitiable part of it was his fear that George and I should notice his weakness and lose courage."

On October 11, with the weather bitterly cold, the three men tried to lift the canoe and carry it the thirty yards to the water's edge. They could not raise it onto their heads and it crashed to the ground. For the first time each was forced to admit to the others that they were weaker than they had dared acknowledge and that "if we ever got out of the wilderness it would be only by the grace of God."

Still they staggered on, dragging the canoe over the portages and finally abandoning it, leaving everything behind that was not strictly needed, so that their passing was marked by a trail of discarded paraphernalia; sextant, axe, waterproof camp bag, film, blankets – everything that could be shucked off save a Bible, comforting passages from which they read aloud to each other every night.

They reached a river. It was, as Wallace later discovered, the Beaver. Elson wanted to follow it, but Hubbard insisted that they keep to their original trail. Elson did not argue; Hubbard was leader. Their only hope would be to find the lard, flour, and milk powder they had discarded early in the journey. They were ready to eat anything, and when they came upon an old flour bag, they scraped the residue into a pot of water with some leftover bones and devoured the result. Then they found a box of baking powder and ate that, and another box, half full, of mustard, which they also ate. When Hubbard came upon this last item, he could not control himself. Tears trickled down his cheeks as he said, "That box came from . . . my home in Congers. Mina has had this very box in her hand. It came from the little grocery store where I've been so often. Mina handed it to me before I left home. She said the mustard might be useful for plasters. We've eaten it instead. I wonder where my girl is now? I wonder when I'll see her again? Yes, she had that very box in her hands – in *her* hands. She's been such a good wife to me."

He could go no further. Instead, he insisted that Wallace and Elson try to reach the abandoned flour and lard. Elson would then continue on to seek help while Wallace would return with the provisions.

The following day all three made their wills, and Hubbard urged that if he died Wallace should write the story of the expedition and give his diary to Mina.

In his own diary, George Elson described the moment of parting:

"Just before starting, Mr. Wallace says that he is going to read the 13th chapter, First Corinthians, and so he did.

"It was time to start.

"Mr. Wallace went to Mr. Hubbard and said, 'Goodbye, I'll try and come back soon.'

"Then I went to him and tried to be as brave as Wallace.

"When I took his hand he said, 'God bless you, George,' and held my hand for some time.

"I said, 'The Lord help us Hubbard. With His help I save you if I can get out.' Then I cried like a child.

"Hubbard said, 'If it was your father, George, you couldn't try harder to save.'

"Wallace came back to Hubbard again, and cried like a child and kissed him; and again I went to him and kissed him and he kissed me, and said again, 'The Lord help you George.'

"He was then so weak he could hardly speak.

"We came away."

That scene haunted George Elson for the rest of his life. Almost thirty years later, in the winter of 1932-33, when he was living in Moosonee, Ontario he would come to the station of the Temiskaming and Northern Ontario Railway to reminisce with the agent, W.G. Brittain, about his days in Labrador. Elson's visits were regular; Brittain could predict to the minute the time at which he would walk down the pathway. The routine was always the same: Elson would walk in, say hello, and then tell the story of his trip with Leonidas Hubbard. He told it in great detail – it took two hours – and always in exactly the same way. On each occasion, when he reached the point in his narrative where he left Hubbard behind to look for help, George Elson would begin to cry; tears would stream down his face and he would take from his pocket a clean red handkerchief to wipe them away. Then he would continue with the tale.

Elson and Wallace came upon the discarded flour the following evening – several pounds of it, black with mould. They divided it. Elson headed down the valley toward Grand Lake, twenty-five miles away, while Wallace was to retrace his steps to the point fifteen miles back where he had left Hubbard.

A blizzard sprang up; it would last ten days. Elson warned Wallace to stick to the river – never to leave it for any reason – and then he plunged off into the snow, walking only in his socks, making slow time in the drifts. He had no mitts and was forced to make some from the sleeves of his undershirt to keep his hands from freezing. He found the abandoned coffee, milk, and lard, and these, with a partridge and a porcupine, gave him enough strength to continue. In the evening, to keep up his spirits, he read a chapter from his Bible and sang a hymn, "Lead, Kindly Light." He reached Grand Lake on October 26, followed the shore, came to another river (it was the Beaver, which, had they taken it as Elson urged, would have led all three to safety), decided to swim across in the floating ice, suffered terrible cramps, and turned back just in time. The following day he built a crude raft, which took him to a small island before it collapsed beneath him.He made a larger raft and, talking to himself all the while ("telling myself what a fine raft it was"), managed to reach the far shore and make camp. That night he went to explore a nearby point and, as he rounded it, saw a sight he would never forget. Just a hundred yards away lay a small boat, the first sign of civilization he had seen since he left Wallace. A moment later, a human sound broke the silence – harsh and grating, yet immensely comforting – the scream of a small child.

"I cannot tell how I felt. I just run the direction I heard the sound. The next, the roof of a house I saw. Then I came on a trail. I saw a girl with a child outside of the door. As soon as she saw me she run in and a woman came out. I sung out to her before I came to her. Meeting me she looked so scared. Then I shook hands with her and told her where I come from. She took me in the house and told me to sit down. But I was – well I could not say how I was and how glad I was."

The woman was the wife of Tom Blake, the Grand Lake trapper. Her presence was fortuitous: the cabin had just been built; the family had moved in only the week before. Blake and his brother plunged off at once to fetch two more men; the four then set out to rescue Wallace and Hubbard. Elson gamely offered to accompany them, but they convinced him that he could not stand the pace.

Wallace, meanwhile, struggling in knee-deep snow, had become hopelessly lost. In his delirium, he thought he heard his dead wife calling to him through the storm, a phantom whisper, sighing in the wind. He lost count of the days; actually he was travelling in a circle. One night, building fires more by instinct than by conscious effort, he boiled his moccasins and ate them. He was prostrate in the snow, half dozing, when four swarthy men on snowshoes loomed out of the blizzard. He gazed at them stupidly as in a trance; it was some time before he realized that they were not apparitions. He must have presented a bizarre appearance – a tattered, bony wraith "standing in drawers and stocking feet with the remnants of a pair of trousers about his hips, there in the midst of the snow covered forest."

Two of the rescue team stayed with Wallace; the others set off in search of Hubbard. His tent was only a short distance away, his corpse inside, wrapped in blankets. He had died soon after the others had left him after writing a long passage in his diary, which ended with these words: "I am not suffering. The acute pangs of hunger have given away to indifference. I am sleepy. I think death from starvation is not so bad. But let no one suppose that I expect it. I am prepared, that is all. I think the boys will be able with the Lord's help to save me."

Wallace's rescuers turned over to him all of Hubbard's effects. They were prepared to bury him where he perished, but Wallace insisted that the body be taken to New York. Because of the weather, that took some time. It was not removed from the tent until mid-March and did not arrive at Battle Harbour until mid-May where, still frozen, it was sealed in a lead-lined coffin to be buried later that month at the cemetery in Haverstraw on the Hudson.

Wallace accompanied the body back to New York. His own recovery had been slow; he had, in fact, almost lost a leg from gangrene. Ironically, the young medical student who saved it,

George Albert Hardy, a tubercular convalescent, caught a chill and died on the trip out from North West River.

Mina Hubbard learned of her husband's death in a brief telegram sent in January, 1904: "Mr. Hubbard died October 18 in the interior of Labrador." In March, she received the letter he had written to her before his death and also his diary but not his maps and field notes, which Wallace considered his property. To say that she was prostrated by the news of the tragedy scarcely describes the depth of Mrs. Hubbard's despair; her husband had been the very centre of her existence, the orb around which she, a minor planet, had revolved. She could not conceive of life without him. All that remained for her was to erect a monument – not some stark and useless pillar but a living document, a testimony to his wisdom, his courage, his selflessness, his . . . *perfection*.

She turned to Wallace: Wallace would create the monument. Wallace would tell the world about her Laddie's remarkable struggle with the wilderness – his explorations, his sacrifices, his heroic death. She was prepared to pay handsomely: one thousand dollars, a substantial sum in the fall of 1904. Wallace agreed, signed a contract, and in his turn engaged a ghost-writer, Frank Barkley Copley, to help with the task. The result, constructed from Wallace's and Hubbard's diaries – with many purple patches by Copley – became an enormous best-seller entitled *The Lure of the Labrador Wild*. It pleased the public; it pleased Hubbard's parents and his sister; but it did not please Mrs. Hubbard.

The book, written in the breathless, exclamatory style popular at the time, scarcely made Hubbard out to be a saint. Wallace yielded to no one in his admiration and love for his friend but he did not try to omit from the narrative those moments on the trail when the younger man was discouraged and depressed; when he had worried aloud that he had led his comrades into a tight spot; when, with tears in his eyes, he had talked of home and Mina. Such evidences of human frailty Mrs. Hubbard could not abide; she wanted them excised from the manuscript. It was far too sensational, far too, well, *popular*; she had asked, or thought she had asked, for a eulogy; she had received instead a parcel of Sunday supplement prose. She demanded changes; Wallace refused. The book, which eventually went into twenty-three editions, was published exactly as he wanted it.

It contained passages that must have cut her to the quick: "Undoubtedly the boy was beginning to suffer from homesickness – he was only a young fellow, you know. . . ."

The *boy*! How dare Wallace use that word to describe someone who was to her a man in every sense, and more than that, a man above all other men – a saint! And here was Wallace, in his subtle way, attempting to put the blame for the failure of the expedition on him. On August 30, so Wallace wrote, he had seriously considered whether or not he should "strongly insist" that the party turn back, but had decided against it, knowing so well Hubbard's determination to do what he set out to do. Wallace had treated Hubbard's stubbornness with some delicacy, but not delicately enough for Hubbard's widow. On October 14, he portrayed Hubbard as adamantly insisting on retracing their steps along the old trail rather than taking the Beaver River, as Elson suggested. "The question was settled," Wallace wrote. "Hubbard was the leader." Really, it was too much! In Mina Hubbard's view, the mean-spirited Wallace was absolving himself of all blame for her Laddie's sacrifice and death – her Laddie, who was "oh, so brave and glad hearted and beautiful," so noble that she felt "wretched and mean and unbeautiful . . . when I compare myself to him." Those excerpts from her later diary suggest that Mrs. Hubbard became a little unhinged by the growing realization that her Laddie was lost to her forever. Her worship of him took on a mystical, almost religious quality. In her diary she expresses herself as awestruck that a man of his calibre could "honour with his love" a mere mortal such as she – and a wretched, mean, unbeautiful mortal at that; "and yet *he loved me*!" she wrote, underlining her amazement at that miracle. And this was the man whom Wallace saw merely as a homesick boy!

There was, perhaps, more to it than that. For Wallace had cheated her out of the last six months of her husband's life. Wallace had experienced that intimacy, which she could never know, that draws men together in moments of crisis. It may well be that, subconsciously, she had from the beginning been jealous of the man-to-man palship that had seen the two of them go off together into the mountains of New York State without her – cutting her off from her husband in the first year of their marriage.

In Mrs. Hubbard's eyes, her Laddie could do no wrong. Then what *had* gone wrong? Slowly she came to believe – and her diary reveals it – that the villain in the piece must have been Wallace. Why had he not got back to her husband with the flour? She refused to believe that he had been weak, lost, and close to death. No: he was more concerned about himself; he had, in fact, by his cowardice and weakness let her husband die alone of starvation, when he might easily have been saved. Now here he was, publicly announcing that he, Wallace, would finish her husband's work; he would not even return to her the maps and field notes. "The work must be done," Wallace quoted Hubbard as saying, "and if one of us falls before it is complete, the other must finish it. . . ." "His words," Wallace wrote, at the conclusion of the manuscript, "ring in my ear as a call to duty . . . perhaps it is God's will that I finish the work of exploration that Hubbard began."

Mrs. Hubbard first read those words in January, 1905, when Wallace submitted the manuscript to her. She was repelled. Wallace was about to snatch all the glory, all the honour, that rightfully belonged to her Laddie. *No!* It could not be permitted. One can almost see Mrs. Hubbard's eyes glisten, her jaw set. If anyone completed the work it would be a Hubbard. Without delay she announced that in order to vindicate her husband's name, she would undertake to complete "his work." She would write her own book, and in it, as she was to confide to her diary, she would "let all the world know that he was loved and honoured, almost worshipped, by the one whom he honoured with his love."

All of which explains how it came about that Mrs. Hubbard and Dillon Wallace arrived at the twin trading posts at North West River on the same boat but did not speak. The two books that were published as a result of their subsequent adventures are notable as much for what they leave out as for what they recount. In Dillon Wallace's *The Long Labrador Trail*, there is no mention of Mrs. Hubbard. In Mrs. Hubbard's *A Woman's Way Through Unknown Labrador*, there is no mention of Dillon Wallace, only an oblique reference in the preface expressing the hope that the inclusions, as appendices, of her husband's diary and that of George Elson "may go some way towards correcting misleading accounts of Mr. Hubbard's expedition, which have appeared elsewhere." But the diary of Leonidas Hubbard, Jr., as she published it, was not complete. Most of those obsessive, mouthwatering visions of food, which suggest a certain derangement, a growing weakness of mind and spirit, were stricken out; so were most of the references to tattered clothing, worn-out moccasins, Hubbard's attacks of diarrhoea and vomiting, and his more desperate references to homesickness. So also were many of the references to Wallace.

In her version of the tragedy, Mrs. Hubbard did her best to remove all blame for faulty planning from her husband's shoulders. In spite of contradictory evidence from the editor, she insisted that the Labrador journey was an assignment for *Outing* magazine. Again, in spite of evidence to the contrary, she insisted that her husband did not plan his own inadequate outfit; the impression she left was that the planning was Wallace's. Finally, she placed the responsibility for the expedition's tragic ending on the weather. It was, she pointed out, correctly, "a season of unprecedented severity." Had the winter been normal, she wrote, "he would still have returned safe and triumphant."

No doubt she believed it. Her own remarkable journey through the lonely heart of Labrador reads like a pleasant Sunday jaunt in comparison with the horrors suffered by her husband's party. She was sensible enough to hire George Elson as her guide and to follow his instructions carefully. In addition to Elson, she had three other sturdy and experienced woodsmen to shepherd her across the Labrador plateau: Joseph Iserhoff, a Russian half-breed; Job Chapies, a James Bay Cree who spoke little English; and a fifteen-year-old Montagnais boy, Gilbert Blake, who Mrs. Hubbard persisted in believing (to his annoyance) was an Eskimo. The party planned to travel in two canoes – and in comfort: besides the stove, the balloon-silk tents, the waterproof bags, and a vast amount of food, there were also, for Mrs. Hubbard, an air mattress, a feather pillow, and a hot-water bottle.

She did not look like an explorer. A small slender woman with delicate features, she is best described as comely rather than beautiful – her hair piled high in the Gibson Girl fashion of the day, her nose small and pert, her chin receding but determined. In the artist's rendering of her profile that accompanies her book, she appears remarkably bland and passive; there is no hint of the passions revealed by her diary, of the elation she felt in following in her husband's footsteps, of the anguish that gnawed at her when she contemplated a future without him. Ten days out of North West River, she confided to her journal:

"Very tired, very sad, very glad to be here and getting on with our work. Two years ago last night, Laddie asked me: 'Will you miss me, sweetheart?' Two years ago this morning we said: 'Goodbye.' Sometimes it seems too much to bear. This work keeps me from being utterly desperate. Wonder what I shall do when this is done?"

For Mina Hubbard, the long trek across the peninsula had a justification apart from the one to which she publicly admitted: for her it was an escape, a postponement of reality, a therapy. By planning and organizing, by moving ceaselessly, by keeping busy, she shored herself up against the contemplation of what seemed an empty future.

She dressed for the adventure with a practicality that did not detract from her femininity: a short skirt over knickerbockers, high boots, a sweater with a belt (adorned with a knife and a revolver), and a felt hat with a mosquito veil. She did not make her husband's mistake of taking one pair of footgear; she had knee-length leather moccasins, high sealskin boots, a pair of low seal sneakers, three pairs of socks, five pairs of stockings, to say nothing of three suits of underwear, two pairs of gloves (one of wool, one of leather), a rubber automobile shirt, a long Swedish dogskin coat and – a feminine touch – a blouse for Sundays. In the contemporary photographs she always looks as if she were the guest of honour at a fashionable picnic. The factor at the Hudson's Bay post, who originally believed that Mrs. Hubbard had set herself a fool's errand, took one look at her and quickly changed his mind. "You can do it," he said, as she stepped nimbly into one of the canoes, "and without any trouble, too."

She was relieved to be on her way, guided by George Elson, "the trusty hero, whose courage and honour and fidelity made my venture possible." Elson was determined to see her through to a successful conclusion. He felt that somehow he had failed her husband, that his abilities as a woodsman were in question, that his honour, too, must be vindicated. The task would not be easy: he must guide her across five hundred and fifty miles of wilderness, much of it unknown, and he must do it within two months; the Hudson's Bay supply steamer, *Pelican*, was due to arrive at the George River post on Ungava Bay during the last week in August; there would be no other until the following summer. Also there was the race with Wallace; Mrs. Hubbard wanted to be the first to reach Ungava Bay and to be able to write that she was first. She watched anxiously for signs of Wallace's passing and, to her satisfaction saw none. She slept that first night out "as if in a most luxurious apartment."

The Hubbard Labrador Expedition was more properly the Elson Labrador Expedition. George Elson watched over Mrs. Hubbard as a mother cat watches over its kitten. On June 30, she left her knife behind; Elson would not let her go back for it; he went himself. She lost the tube for her mattress pump and realized that she could not sleep properly on the ground without growing very tired, "when I lose my nerve and am afraid to do anything." George solved the problem by blowing up the mattress himself each night. Once he found her standing on a rock gazing hypnotized, at the rapids below: "They grew more and more fascinating . . . so strong, so irresistible. . . ." He was quite firm with her: she might grow dizzy and fall; she must not stare into the rapids again, otherwise "we will just turn around and go back to North West River."

She grew fond of her guardians. "How easy I feel in the midst of them all," she told her diary. "Could not feel more so if they were my brothers. And no one except Laddie was ever as thoughtful and kind to me than they have been." At night she and George Elson had long talks beside the campfire. He told her of his childhood, of how he had learned to keep a diary, even though he had never seen anyone do it, and did not even know the word, but had wanted to learn to write and so made little books out of pieces of paper and then learned from other books his father bought him. She was charmed by this account. She suggested that he try to write about his experiences, perhaps a book for boys. A bond was growing between them.

One Friday late in July, while the men were making a portage, she asked permission to climb a hill. After some thought, Elson agreed to let her go. He urged her to take her rubber coat in case of rain, but, loaded down with two cameras, revolver, knife, barometer, and compass, she objected, and he did not insist. She was excited as a schoolgirl at being allowed to go off on her own. When a storm did come up she decided to push on farther than agreed upon because she was already wet to the skin. She set off through the rain for a ridge on the far side of a lake "with something of the feeling of a child who has run away from home, for it had been constantly impressed upon me that I must never go away alone. . . ." At the top of the ridge she looked down and saw the men on the edge of the bay, canoes drawn up on shore, brewing tea. She fired two shots to let them know where she was and noticed that they seemed to panic. They scurried up the ridge to meet her; but she had moved on, and it was some time before they caught up. Somewhat to her surprise she discovered that they were extremely upset: "Their faces were covered with perspiration and rare expressions, which were a funny mixture of anger, distress and relief and much more. They had been thoroughly frightened. I smiled at them but there was no answering smile from George."

"You have just had us about crazy." Elson told her, declaring that she should never have climbed the ridge in the storm. They would never again trust her to go off on her own; whenever she wanted to wander, one of them would go with her.

She tended to laugh off the experience, but Elson explained why they had been in such a state: "What would we do if you got lost and fell in the rapid? Just what *could* we do? Why, I could never go back again. How could any of us go back without you? We can't ever let you go any place alone after this."

She was truly sorry. She had not meant to frighten them, but their faces were still pale and their hands trembling so much she decided she must pass around her bottle of medicinal brandy. To her dismay, they drank it all.

The contrast between Leonidas Hubbard's struggle toward Lake Michikamau and that of his widow is so stark that the two accounts seem to be describing a different realm; and so, in some ways they were, for that earlier trip up the Susan to its headwaters

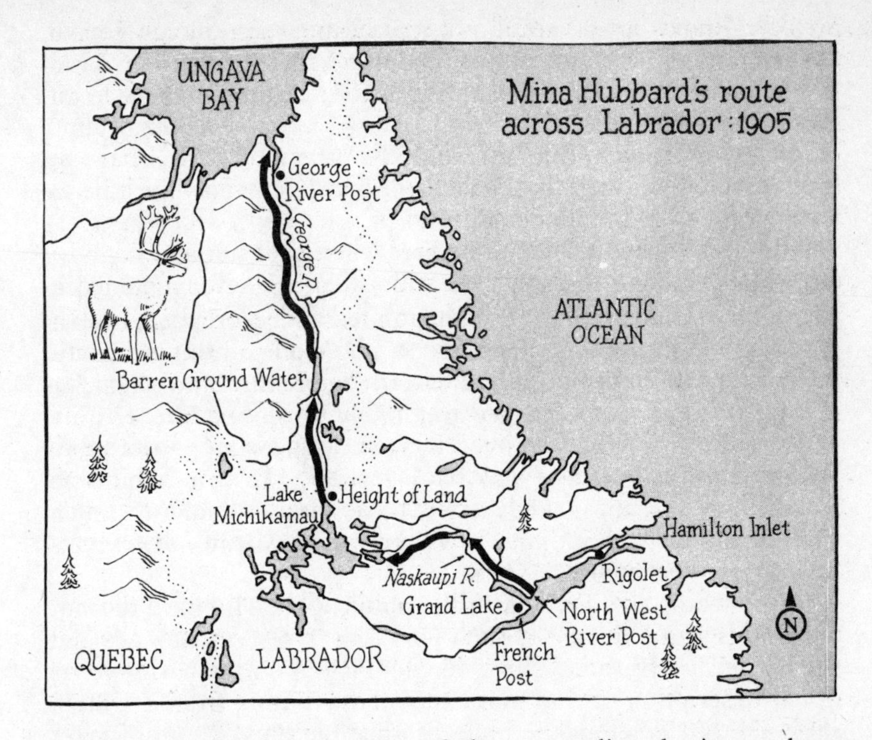

and then overland – a journey of almost unrelieved misery – bore no relation to the much easier voyage up the broad Naskaupi. Hubbard had neither time nor energy to wonder at the scenery; it represented only a barrier to his ambitions. His widow revelled in it: the torrents and cataracts of the upper river, "where water [was] pouring over ledges, flowing in a foaming, roaring torrent round little rocky islands or rushed madly down a chute," and the colours! – rocks a rich chocolate brown and in places almost purple, garlanded with mosses, grey-green and vermilion.

Ahead lay the first of their objectives, the great lake, the sight of which Mrs. Hubbard half dreaded because she knew it would bring back memories. Her husband's presence haunted her, and in her diary she gave vent to her emotions:

July 7: "Had a fine fire and I thought of Laddie's proverb 'On a wet day build a big fire.' It often seemed as if he must be standing just near and that if I turn I must see him. *Strange part* of all this experience *it seems* perfectly natural. . . ."

July 10: "How my heart aches with hunger and longing for him. It would be so perfect if he were here. How he would revel in it all. . . . It is all so wild and grand and mysterious and how his heart would beat with pride and joy in it all if he could be here. . . . So very, very beautiful and yet lacking that which completes and perfects. I have not his spirit, not that of the true explorer. I have to keep reminding myself all the time that I am the first of my kind to see it and I don't get any thrill out of it except only as I can make it honour him. . . ."

July 16: "Oh, what this trip would be if he were here. I have to keep reminding myself that the hills he is climbing now must be so much grander and more beautiful to escape an ever-recurring feeling that it is wicked for me to be here when he is not and Oh how desperately hungry and desolate and sad. . . . I never dreamed it could be so splendid. And the grander and more beautiful it grows, the more I hunger for the one who made all things beautiful, so much more beautiful by the spirit he breathed into them."

July 26: "Very, very hungry and lonely for my Laddie. His life and the spirit in which he lived in seem to grow more and more beautiful all the time as I look back to them. My own inability to measure up to them makes me feel so desolate. Wonder so much what I shall do without him. It will be the best I can but it seems such a poor best compared to his. . . ."

In the words she directed to the public, Mrs. Hubbard did not allow herself the luxury of such emotions. Only occasionally did she permit her private feelings to encroach upon the narrative, as in her description of that moment when, scouting from a hilltop, she was able to see in the blue distance the daisy chain of lakes through which that earlier party had made its way en route to Michikamau. "So much of life and pain can crowd into a few minutes," she wrote guardedly. "The whole desperate picture stood out with dread vividness. . . ."

By this time, as his diary entries reveal, George Elson had become greatly attached to her. At first his attitude was reserved, but as the journey progressed his remarks grew warmer:

July 1: "Mrs. Hubbard enjoying the trip very much. . . ."

July 8: "Mrs. Hubbard doing very well indeed in her travelling through such rough country. . . ."

July 17: "Mrs. Hubbard is enjoying her trip. She is so nice to me and a bright little woman she is. We are getting on fine."

July 23: "When I shot the caribou Mrs. Hubbard was after shading [*sic*] tears. I suppose it must remind her of the one Mr. Hubbard killed on our trip we had out here in Labrador. I feel very sorry for her."

By the end of July, the two had become close companions. She was genuinely interested in George Elson in a way her husband and Wallace had not been. He was more than her guide: he was her protector, her guardian, her big brother. Leonidas Hubbard had tended to think of him as an employee, a "woodsman"; Wallace had invariably referred to him as an Indian. But in those long talks around the glowing fire she showed an interest not only in his past but also in his future. He *must* write a book; she would help him. "Mrs. Hubbard, she is really so good and a really kind hearted woman she is," Elson wrote in his diary. "She is more than good to me. My sister could not be kinder to me as she is. How glad and proud my sisters would be if they knew how kind and what a good friend I have. Still I don't want to say she is only a friend to me, but that she is my sister. God will help her and bring her again to her good friends home to where she came from. She is so brite and smart and I am glad she does trust me. . . ."

This was one of Elson's longest entries and one of the most personal, but it was not quite enough. The following day he felt the need to repeat those sentiments: "I like her so much. She is really nice to us. I cannot speak enough good things about her. Oh I do wish I will be able to bring her out safe again. . . . I trust in the Lord. . . ."

On August 2, they reached Lake Michikamau. A wild demonstration followed, the men "jumping and waving their hats and yelling like demons." On a flat stone Mina Hubbard carved the words "HUBBARD EXPEDITION ARRIVED HERE AUGUST 2ND, 1905," adding the names of the members of the party. That afternoon they crossed the lake, with the call of the loons echoing down the empty waters. "It was weird and beautiful beyond words; the big, shining lake with its distant blue islands; the sky with its wonderful blue clouds and colour; two little canoes so deep in the wilderness and those wild, reverberant voices coming from invisible beings away in the long light which lay across the water." It was a scene no white human had encountered before and one that none will ever see again, for Lake Michikamau has vanished, lost in the vaster waters of the man-made Smallwood Reservoir that feeds the power project at Churchill Falls.

Other unique experiences followed. The great Labrador caribou herd, which no white man had ever encountered, was flowing east like a brown river toward the highlands between the George River and the Atlantic. On August 8, after leaving Michikamau, the party came upon it, "a solid mass" draped across a hillside. Shortly afterward, Mrs. Hubbard watched the herd plunge into a lake, forming an unbroken bridge of animals three-quarters of a mile long between the shoreline and a barren island far out in the water. For the next fifty miles they encountered thousands of caribou ("the country was literally alive with the beautiful creatures") and Mrs. Hubbard was able to report that "so far as I can learn, I alone, save the Indians, have witnessed the great migration. . . ."

On August 10, she added another record to her accomplishments. The party had portaged to a small lake. To the north lay a bog. Beyond that was a second lake, from which the water flowed in the opposite direction – north. At five that afternoon after travelling three hundred miles through the wilderness, she stepped out of her canoe "to stand at last on the summit of the Divide – the first of the white race to trace the Nascaupee river to its source." The canoes were portaged across the height and in less than an hour of paddling they came upon the outlet from the second lake – a tiny stream, which they identified as the George. By the time they reached its mouth, at Ungava Bay, it would be three miles wide.

In her diary, she allowed herself some moments of reflection:

"I wish I need never go back. I suppose I will never be taken care of in the gentle *careful* way I have been since we left N.W.R. I came away expecting to have all sorts of hardships to endure and have had none. . . . Labrador skies have so far been kind to us. Oh if they had only been so kind two years ago. . . . It has been a wonderfully interesting day for me. It has interested me in a way I did not suppose I should ever be interested again and in my heart tonight a touch of gladness that our work has prospered so far. It has not been perfectly done. I have felt my lack of training . . . deeply and keenly. . . . Yet even so we have opened the way. . . . And I can bring a tribute to the memory of my husband which he at least would think worthwhile. . . ."

There were worries. Could they cover the three hundred miles to Ungava Bay in time to meet the boat, due in little more than a fortnight? And where was Wallace? His name, if we believe Mrs. Hubbard's diary, evoked amusement and disdain from the other members of the party:

"Always there is much talk of the other party and their probable doings, esp. the probability of their getting lost. All are familiar with the story of W.'s prowess in wilderness travel. Geo. and Gil both know Stanton [a member of the Wallace party]. Gil says: If Stanton falls off of his seat in the canoe, he'll get lost. Geo: 'Well, W. won't make much progress on Mich. today.' Gil: 'I think it's blowing pretty hard on Seal Lake too, don't you?' Then his boy's merry laughter in which everybody joins."

The other worry was the mood of the Indians – the Montagnais and the little known Naskapi – who lived along the banks of the George River. Mrs. Hubbard detected some uneasiness among the men as they sat around the campfire. One evening she was made to realize what was bothering them. The Indians would not kill *her*. "No," said Gil Blake, "they wouldn't hurt a woman, I don't think. They want the women for themselves." It had not occurred to Mrs. Hubbard that she might be the prize in a bloody struggle. That night she lay awake in her tent "turning over in my mind plans of battle in case we should meet with treachery."

But the Indians were not treacherous, merely curious. On August 17, a cold and misty morning, the party espied on a hillside a dark, shapeless mass, which they took to be caribou until the glint of metal and the crack of a rifle dispelled the illusion. The men approached the Montagnais camp with some uneasiness until they discovered it was populated almost exclusively by women and children; the men were away trading at Davis Inlet. The women told the party that they would meet the Barren Ground People – the Naskapi – farther down the river and that they would receive a friendly reception. They also said that it would take two months to reach Ungava Bay.

Mrs. Hubbard was sick with disappointment. Should she turn back? For some days this worry had disturbed her sleep. She held a long palaver with her guides. The argument continued for some time, but finally the decision was made to continue down the George River and try to discover from the Naskapi Indians what their chances were of reaching its mouth in time to catch the *Pelican*.

Three days later they came upon the Naskapi camp. These Indians, dressed mainly in skins and hides, had little contact with civilization. No white man or woman had yet encountered them on their home ground. Mrs. Hubbard's photographs and observations would be unique. Over the objections of George Elson she insisted on visiting the camp and would have stayed longer had he not been impatient to move on. But from the Naskapi they received heartening news: Ungava Bay, they were told, was only five days down river.

Now Mrs. Hubbard became intensely aware that sweet victory lay in her grasp. They had seen no evidence that Wallace and his party had passed this way; *she* would be the one to complete her husband's work. Yet the slightest mistake could mean disaster; and potential disaster loomed ahead. As they hoisted sail on the canoes and slid across the surface of the slender lake known then as Barren Ground Water, they could hear in the distance the roar of the rapids. An almost unbroken stretch of angry white water, one hundred and thirty miles long, lay before them.

They were all worried. Job Chapies dreamed that night of danger; each man had a spare paddle ready beside him in case his should snap at a crucial moment. The river exceeded Mrs.

Hubbard's wildest nightmares; it was like a gigantic toboggan slide, a chute down which the canoes raced pell mell, past sharp rocks, around perilous curves, over slippery ledges, through boulder-strewn shallows, and under spray-soaked cliffs. The strain was intense on passenger and paddlers. Mrs. Hubbard, trembling with excitement after a night rendered sleepless by those insects whose continual patter on the tent "sounded like gentle rain," was never permitted an instant's relaxation in the canoe. She could not even allow herself to slap at mosquitoes "each bite of which was like the touch of a live coal. . . . It was most difficult to resist the impulse to grasp the sides of the canoe and to compel myself instead to sit with hands clasped about my knees and muscles relaxed so that my body might lend itself to the motion of the canoe."

The ordeal continued for the best part of a week. On August 23, George Elson and Job Chapies were nearly wrecked when their craft whirled about in the torrent and slammed against a cliff. The bottom caught on a rock but fortunately the canoe did not tip. The men leaped out, clambered to a perilous perch, and with ropes on either end succeeded in freeing it. Elson worried less about himself than about his charge. That night he wrote: " . . . what makes me so scared of the rapids is on account of having a woman in my canoe . . . because I don't want to get Mrs. Hubbard in any trouble. . . . Such a dear little lady and a sister to me."

On her part it was "almost unbelievable" that they had nearly reached their goal. "I begin to realize that I have never actually counted on being able to get there." Now, with Ungava Bay almost in sight, the strain became more intense. What if the *Pelican* had been and gone? The suspense was too much, the pace too slow.

"I did wish that the men would not chat and laugh in the unconcerned way they were doing, and they paddled as leisurely as if I were not in a hurry at all. If only I could reach the post and ask about the ship! If only I might fly over the water and not wait for these leisurely paddles! And now, from being in an agony of fear for their lives, my strong desire was to take them by their collars and knock their heads together hard. . . ."

In her diary entry of August 25, there appears a curiously obscure remark:

"Full of thought we are reaching the Geo. R. Post. It grows more and more wonderful and oh if Laddie were only here. . . . It has been another day of running down rapids, some of them have been particularly trying and hard to run. I have walked over several and once I thought we were certainly going to destruction.

Now that the work [is] so nearly done I don't want to though I dread going back. . . ."

If that passage means anything, it means that, at the back of Mina Hubbard's mind as she planned her trip to Labrador and later, as she struggled across the plateau, was the thought – almost the conviction – that she was going to perish. It is not too much to conjecture that she welcomed the prospect, for she believed devoutly in an afterlife. Her husband – that unbelievably noble man – had not been able to survive; what chance, then, did she, an inferior mortal, have? And what better death than one that would unite her with him under the same circumstances that had originally claimed his life?

But it was not to be, and now she must face that which she had not yet composed herself to face: the reality of a life without him. It is clear from her words that she had never for an instant been able to look beyond the day when she would reach the little fort on Ungava Bay. "What am I going to do?" she asked her diary and then answered, "I don't know."

Yet in retrospect she came to realize that she had found some measure of peace in this savage yet hauntingly beautiful land:

"Was thinking today how strange it is. I have not wanted to see anyone, I have been lonely for no one. We have come these months through this deserted wilderness and I have never felt as if I were far from home. I have felt more at home here than I have ever done any place since our home in Congers. But I mean to try to face the other life as bravely as I can and in a way that will honour the one I loved more than all the world and who loved me with such a beautiful, generous love. . . ."

On the final night of her journey she could not sleep, for she knew the race was not yet over. If she could make the ship in time, she could get her story and pictures out to the public before Wallace was heard from. "That would be the thing for me. If I am to be successful that would make it complete. Oh if it might only come out that way. How grateful I should be and how complete my victory and how completely it would make of no account W.'s reflection." She was convinced that, in this bitter contest, God was on her side, for she believed, with all the fervency of a Gordon or a Kitchener, that her cause was just. How could the Deity do anything to further the fortunes of the despised Wallace? "I believe His hand is with me," she wrote.

On August 27, exactly two months from the date in June when they had left North West River, they spotted deep in a cove a small huddle of buildings, nestling at the foot of a mountain of solid rock. They paddled up a little stream and poled their way over a mudbank. The agent, John Ford, came down to meet them, followed by a retinue of Inuit. There is extant a photograph of Mrs. Hubbard alighting from the canoe, a man at each arm to steady her. She looks perfectly composed in her hat and long skirt as if she were stepping off some royal barge. She inquired about the *Pelican*; had it left? No; it had not yet arrived nor would it arrive until the middle of September at the earliest. She was surprised at her reaction to this unexpected news: "There are times when that which constitutes one's inner self seems to cease. So it was with me when Mr. Ford uttered those words. My heart should have swelled with emotion but it did not. I cannot remember any time in my life when I had less feeling."

Rummaging about in one of the bags, George Elson found Mrs. Hubbard's sealskin boots, into which she changed for her walk across the mud flats. The agent's wife greeted her with the words: "You are welcome, Mrs. Hubbard. Yours is the first white woman's face I have seen for two years." Looking back, she was puzzled to discover that the men were still sitting in the canoes. Only then did she realize that the positions were reversed: "They were my charges now." A certain ceremony was obviously required. Back she went down the hill to meet them and thank them, "and Heaven knows how inadequate were the words." Later that day, from the window of her room in the post, she watched them setting up camp and, with a little pang, became aware of the gap already widening between them. "It was with a feeling of genuine loneliness that I realized that I should not again be one of the little party."

George Elson was more than a little in love with her. She had given him ambitions – to go to school, to set himself up as a trader on James Bay, perhaps even to become a writer.

"I am very sure [I] could write a nice little story. I am sure someone would be good enough to help me in doing so. Another thing is in my mind. I would like now to get married this fall, if I was lucky enough – if I could strak [*sic*] luck and could get a white girl that would marry me and especially if she was well learnt we then could write some nice stories because she would know lots more than I would but not likely I will be so lucky. I think some way my chances are small in that way, but I know that I would be very happy, I am very sure it is a happy life anyway. So many nice girls in the world and yet – none for me. . . ."

And again, a week later, on September 7: "In the afternoon Mrs. Hubbard and I working and talking about some things [of] great importance. Great afternoon. . . . I could not sleep last night awake all night, thinking lots of new things. Was up at 3 a.m.

What a happy life it would be if it would really happen. New plans so good of her to think so kind thoughts of me. She is more than good and kind to me."

Yet, as the days went by and the *Pelican* did not arrive, Mina Hubbard, using the time to prepare her story for publication, was not quite so enamoured of George Elson. He had persuaded Gilbert Blake to make a map of Grand Lake, and this aroused her suspicions. Was George planning to write his own account of the journey? "Am wondering whether I had better ask him to sign a written agreement not to write anything about the trip without my written consent and approach [*sic*]. I almost think I had. There would be no question about the thing then."

Was there something more? "Am beginning to see through quite a few things I did not understand before. He [George] has been contradicting himself lately in a way which makes me sick at heart. Makes me feel depressed and then I try to persuade myself I am wrong in my thoughts but I always suffer for that kind of thing."

The entry is tantalizing in its ambiguity. What exactly was it that disturbed Mrs. Hubbard? Why did she find it necessary to ask her four male companions to sign a joint statement in her diary that "we at all times treated Mrs. Hubbard with respect and each also declares his belief that Mrs. Hubbard was also treated with respect by other men of this party" and that "each also here records his promise that he will never, by look or word or sign lead any human being to believe that during the trip there was anything in the conduct of Mrs. Hubbard and her party towards each other that was unbecoming honourable Christian men and women . . . "? At Mrs. Hubbard's suggestion, and also their request, she prepared and signed a similar statement, which appears in Elson's diary. Were such protestations really necessary? Perhaps. One must remember the atmosphere of the time: a pretty widow alone for two months with four woodsmen could really give rise to gossip.

Whatever Mrs. Hubbard's reservations were about George Elson – and it may only have been that she felt he was not resolute enough in the ambitions she had for him – they were soon dissipated. She read portions of her manuscript to him and, on October 15, recorded that she had had "a pretty good talk" with him that night and felt "encouraged about him more than I have ever done before. How I hope he may work up to his possibilities. They are great."

At this point, the *Pelican* was more than six weeks overdue, and there was still no sign of the Dillon Wallace party of five. Then, the following evening, he turned up with a single companion, Clifford Easton, a forestry student from North Carolina. "They both look strong and well," Mrs. Hubbard wrote. "Wallace a little more coarse and common than ordinary. Looks positively repulsive to me. Felt a little nervous about their coming and now it is an end to peace of mind for me. Awfully hard to know what to do."

In his book, *The Long Labrador Trail*, Wallace was to write that he had decided at the outset to sacrifice speed for thoroughness and that he took scientists with him to help in research. These remarks do not ring true. The only scientific figure in the party was George Richards, an American geologist, whom he sent back when his expedition reached Lake Michikamau along with two others: Leigh Stanton, a Boer War veteran, and Peter Stevens, an Ojibway from Minnesota. Nor was Wallace's work as thorough as that of his rival. For reasons that are again obscure he decided not to take Hubbard's planned route up the valley of the Naskaupi but to try to follow an old Indian trail overland to the big lake. The party went astray more than once and found the journey hard going. They did not reach Michikamau until September 3, long after Mrs. Hubbard had arrived at Ungava Bay. The Hubbard party had come down the George River in twenty-five days; it took Wallace and his companion forty-three, in part because of the lateness of the season. There is no evidence that he observed the caribou herd or visited the Naskapi Indians. In short, he did not do what he set out to do, which was to follow in his dead friend's footsteps and complete his work.

That Mrs. Hubbard had done. Certainly Wallace was able to supply new information for maps of the country to the north of the Naskaupi, but Mrs. Hubbard's accomplishments were greater and were so recognized by geographical authorities. She had produced the first usable maps of the Naskaupi and George River system, had shown for the first time that Seal Lake and Lake Michikamau were in the same drainage basin, had proved that what geographers had supposed to be two different rivers – the North West and the Naskaupi – were actually one, and had produced notes on the flora and fauna of the region together with written and photographic observations on the lifestyle of the Naskapi Indians. On the other hand, the public found Wallace's book more entertaining than Mrs. Hubbard's partly, perhaps, because he had more adventures and mishaps and employed a more colourful and racy style. His chapter headings certainly suggest adventure; they also suggest a certain amount of fumbling and bumbling: "We Go Astray" . . . "Scouting for the Trail" . . . "We Lose the Trail" . . . "Disaster in the Rapids" . . . "Caught in the Rapids" . . . "Caught in the Artic Ice." Wallace no longer had need of a ghost-writer; he quit his law practice and became a popular story-teller, producing twenty-four more books, most of them for boys, before his death in 1939.

He did not long embarrass Mrs. Hubbard by his presence at George River. To her intense relief, he and Easton decided not to embark on the *Pelican*, which turned up two days after their arrival, but instead headed off for Fort Chimo and further adventures. On October 22, the entire Hubbard party boarded the Hudson's Bay steamer in heavy snow. Ten days later they reached Rigolet, where Mrs. Hubbard picked up a second steamer bound for Quebec. En route, she knitted a pair of mittens for George Elson. "How sorry I will be when we part," he wrote, " . . . I do wish her in every good thing. May God bless her. Dear little woman my best friend in the world and will always be I know."

They had talked of going to England together, but this was only talk. Mrs. Hubbard returned to New York, saw her book serialized in *Harper's*, then published on both sides of the Atlantic. She went to England in 1908 on a lecture tour to promote it. There she met Harold Ellis, the son of a British Member of Parliament. The vision of Laddie was fading more swiftly, perhaps, than she would once have expected. Before the year was out, she and Ellis were married.

But the memory of that wilderness interlude never left her. Like many before her who had experienced the frontier – Jogues, Cameron, Grenfell – she felt its pull, even at a distance of three thousand miles. She longed to return, to experience again those oddly satisfying days when the Unknown unrolled before her in a succession of lonely ridges, blurred by the haze of summer; when the great caribou herd thundered out of the west, so close she could see the velvet of the horns; when the leaping canoes breasted the wild water and she felt the cold spray lashing her face; mornings when the lichens were grizzled with frost; afternoons when the valleys turned misty with the new green of the larches; evenings when the lakes became drops of quicksilver shining through the conifers.

There was, as well, the memory of a special comradeship. She did not lose touch with George Elson. They continued to correspond and to plan a return to the wilderness. It was a long time coming. First there were children – three of them to be raised and schooled in England. Then, in the 1920s, Mina and Harold Ellis were divorced. Another decade went by before she was able to set her plan in motion. By then she was sixty-six. Elson had also been married – not to the white girl of his dreams but to a James Bay

Cree. In 1936 Mina sought him out at Moosonee, and the two old friends set out on a canoe trip up the Moose River. We do not know the details; if she kept a diary it has been lost.

Accounts of her later life are sketchy. During the Second World War, as in the first, she welcomed into her English home a number of Canadian soldiers. One was her grandnephew Edgar Benson, of Kingston, who was to become finance minister in the first Trudeau cabinet. He remembers her as a pleasant old lady, serving tea and crumpets. They did not talk of Labrador.

In old age, her mind began to wander. Her relatives placed her in a nursing home, and there one day, at the age of eighty-six, she went for a stroll. It was half a century since she had walked the long portages of Labrador. Did she recall those days, so far behind her, when she had crossed that desolate, lovely land of rock and rapid, with the shade of her lost Laddie constantly at her side? Probably not; for her thoughts had grown furry, the past was a muddle, the present a confusion. She strayed onto a railway track as she had once strayed up a distant mountainside, but this time there were no strong woodsmen to guide her to safety. A locomotive thundered out of nowhere. She stood, confused, directly in its path, and in the next instant was carried to her rest.

14
The Search for Gun-an-noot

There are no sad songs for Gun-an-noot, the invisible Indian. No banjos or electric guitars twang out the tale of his long exile in the mountains of British Columbia. Ira Hayes had his Johnny Cash but Gun-an-noot, who vanished for thirteen years, eluding all efforts to capture him, has yet to find his balladeer. Perhaps it is as well; he was a man of dignity and his saga would only be cheapened by the simplicities of the country and western circuit.

Yet this is the stuff from which folk songs are fashioned: the story of a man who shadowed his own pursuers, who regularly managed to visit his wife and family, who sired five children when he was on the run from the police. No one ever captured Gun-an-noot; when the time came he gave himself up, voluntarily.

The song of Gun-an-noot would have to be in a minor key. Beat the drum slowly for the Indian who wanted to live like a white man but was forced to revert to the ways of his forbears. Play the pipes lowly for Simon Gun-an-noot, who triumphed over his pursuers, but whose life, in its fullest flower, was wasted. Thirteen years is a long time to spend in caverns and in canyons, hiding out in the freezing cold of winter and the blast furnace of summer. Gun-an-noot might have become the most prosperous Indian in all British Columbia – rancher, merchant, solid citizen. Instead, his life was wrenched into a different channel. He was never to be the most prosperous; he certainly became the most famous. But for Gun-an-noot that kind of fame was ashes in the mouth.

He was a Kispiox of the Carrier Nation (so called because their widows carried the cremated ashes of their husbands' bones in a small pouch over their loins for two or three years after the death). His name, originally Zhumpmin-hoot, heavily Anglicized to make it pronounceable, meant "the little bear that climbs trees." He was born in 1874 in the village of Kispiox not far from the junction of the Skeena and the Kispiox rivers – totem pole country, some five hundred miles north of Vancouver.

For centuries his people had followed the customs of the Carrier Nation, a culture preserved as if in amber until the white presence began seeping through the forests, like ink on blotting paper. Now the loggers were coming in to hack away at the great cedars. White farmers were blasting out the stumps and churning up the soil. Roman Catholic missionaries arrived to give children Christian names – like Simon Peter. The members of the tribe began to wear the suits and sweaters of the white man, to abandon the old communal lodges in favour of single family shacks, to renounce the deliciously pagan ceremony of the potlatch. Simon Peter Gun-an-noot always wore his church medallion; more significantly, he began to believe that the best course for an Indian was to live as a white man.

In his childhood he had hunted and trapped on his family's traditional preserve, a hundred miles to the east at Bear Lake. But as he grew older he ranged farther afield until he came to know a vast area, ten thousand square miles in size, as well as most men know their own neighbourhoods. At twenty-one, he was a remarkable human specimen: six feet tall in his moccasins, two hundred pounds, light as a cougar on his feet and just as swift. With his Winchester .30-.30 he was a dead shot. It was said that he had once killed a bear with a knife and that he could straighten out a horseshoe with his bare hands. Gun-an-noot, growing a mustache like a white man, inspired that kind of tale.

But there was more to Gun-an-noot. Unlike so many of his fellow Indians he was an astute businessman. When he brought his pelts into the Hudson's Bay store, he did not accept the first offer. He bargained for cash and if the price wasn't right, he went elsewhere; sometimes he went as far as Vancouver.

He saved his money. In 1901, when he had enough to marry he took his bride, Sarah, and their first baby to Vancouver to buy supplies. Gun-an-noot had decided to embark on a venture that, for an Indian, was unheard of. He planned to open a store in his village.

He prospered. In the winter, the family closed the store and went trapping together. In the spring, they sold their pelts, bought more stock, increased their cash reserves. Gun-an-noot kept building up his equity; he bought a part interest in a sawmill, started a ranch on the Skeena, raised horses and cattle – a pillar of the community, until the world fell in on him.

In the winter of 1905, Sarah, newly delivered of her second child, elected to run the store while Gun-an-noot and his brother-in-law, Peter Hi-ma-dan, went trapping for the winter. They returned the following June, loaded with pelts, sold them for cash, and stopped for a brief celebration at the Two Mile House, halfway between the Indian village and Hazelton.

The community was then on the very edge of a boom. Real estate fever was sweeping the west, sparked by the construction of two new transcontinental railways. The Grand Trunk Pacific was due to pass directly through Hazelton on the way to its western terminus of Prince Rupert. The little village of two hundred souls was swelling and changing under the impact of the newcomers, one of whom, Jim "The Geezer" Cameron, had founded the Two Mile House to cater to the hard-drinking trappers, hunters, guides and Indians. It did not matter to Cameron that the law forbade him to serve natives. He had two charges pending against him already for that offence and another for operating an illegal gambling house. He felt no compunction about serving Simon Gun-an-noot and Peter Hi-ma-dan.

The incident that touched off the saga of Simon Gun-an-noot occurred that night and it involved Alex McIntosh, a member of the Charleston and Barrett mule train, camped nearby at Two Mile Creek. McIntosh was a pugnacious miner and half-breed, known for his willingness to brawl. Late that evening he got into a fierce struggle with Gun-an-noot and Hi-ma-dan over some remarks he made about Simon's wife. Gun-an-noot mangled McIntosh's finger but took a bad beating in return. He left the tavern vowing to "fix" McIntosh.

Years later, an Indian boy, Peter Barney, was to testify under oath that he had seen the unarmed Gun-an-noot ride off north toward Kispiox village. Later, he watched McIntosh ride off in a different direction – west – toward the hospital at Hazelton to have his finger dressed.

McIntosh reached the hospital, had his injuries attended to and headed back toward the pack train camp. He never reached it. Next morning his body was found on the trail, some distance west of Two Mile House. He had been shot in the back, apparently from an ambush. A short time later another body was found on the opposite side of Two Mile House, about a mile and a half to the north on another road leading out of Hazelton toward Kisgegas. It, too, was face up and it, too, had a bullet in the back. The corpse was later identified as that of a Frenchman, Max LeClair, one-time seaman, now a rancher and guide, who had only recently moved to Hazelton and was not well known in the area. A post-mortem revealed that both men had been shot between six and seven in the morning and that the shots, to the lower spine, were almost identical.

Constable James Kirby of the B.C. Provincial Police immediately jumped to the conclusion that Gun-an-noot was the murderer. He did not bother to search for cartridges or bullets or possible tracks left by the killer or killers. He arranged for an immediate inquest and some twenty men with hangovers turned up that morning, their recollection of the previous night's events understandably confused. Gun-an-noot and his brother-in-law did not appear. This together with Gun-an-noot's threat caused the jury to name him as McIntosh's murderer. The jury believed that the two men were also probably responsible for the murder of Max LeClair.

Gun-an-noot, apparently, was convinced that he would not get a fair trial from an all-white jury in Hazelton. Yet it is doubtful that either Indian could have been convicted on the evidence, which was both circumstantial and flimsy. Certainly, both men had a motive for killing McIntosh. But McIntosh, who had a criminal record and was a known molester of Indian women, had many other enemies. Moreover, Gun-an-noot had been seen riding in a different direction, unarmed, from his supposed enemy. Even more baffling was the murder of LeClair, a mild-mannered man whom the two Indians scarcely knew and who was almost a stranger in Hazelton. LeClair had not even been present at the tavern brawl the previous evening. Equally confusing was the position of the two bodies. McIntosh's corpse had been found west of the tavern on the Bulkley River road out of Hazelton. LeClair's had been discovered a mile and a half to the north on a different road. How was it possible for the same murderer to dash from one spot to the other and set up an ambush without being seen? Yet the nature of the bullet wounds suggested that both men had been felled by the same killer – an experienced and deadly marksman.

There was another curious occurrence which in retrospect seemed odd, though nobody thought to investigate it at the time. Jim the Geezer, summonsed once again for selling liquor to the Indians, vanished from town, never to return.

When Kirby and his deputies rushed to Gun-an-noot's store to arrest him they found that he and Peter Hi-ma-dan had fled. Unaccountably, Gun-an-noot had killed four of his horses. Why? Was it, as some believed, to prevent his pursuers from using them? But they had horses of their own.

On the way back to town Kirby encountered Nah-gun, the wanted man's father. Kirby clapped him into jail, hoping perhaps that this would draw the fugitive back into town. Then he set off on a two-week search, riding at the head of a posse in true frontier style, while a scene of pure farce was enacted back at the stockade. Kirby had deputized one Jake Ashman, a one-time coal miner from Nanaimo, to guard Nah-gun. The Indian sized up his prison and discovered that the outer wall of the latrine extended beyond the stockade. He told Ashman that he needed to use the outdoor facility. Ashman accompanied him. Nah-gun handed the guard his coat and vest, stepped inside the outhouse, closed the door, pried off two loose boards and slipped away into the mountains, leaving Ashman still holding the clothes and wondering what was taking Nah-gun so long.

With a fellow constable at his side, and six deputies close behind, Kirby was riding in hot pursuit of Gun-an-noot. Crossing the Kispiox River the posse was greeted by a chorus of howls; there, tied to trees, were Gun-an-noot's fourteen pack dogs. Kirby shot them all on the spot.

Constable Kirby mounted a series of searches in the summer and fall of 1906. All proved fruitless. The Indian Agency organized another party. It returned to Hazelton exhausted. For the next thirteen years, in spite of valiant attempts by much better men to smoke him out, Gun-an-noot remained at large, an invisible Indian, creating a growing legend. His hiding place was a vast rectangle, ten thousand miles square, a jungle of mountains and muskegs, lakes and trenches, rivers and canyons, plateaus and forests, stretching from the Nass River in the west to the Omineca Mountains in the east, from the Stikine in the north to the Nechako in the south. Gun-an-noot knew it as well as a taxi driver knows his own city.

The two Indians lived off the land, snared rabbits, shot grouse, deer and moose, angled for fish. Those who hunted them were not as mobile. The police carried their food in boxes; in wintertime when they could not use horses, they were forced to pack all their equipment on their backs.

Gun-an-noot did not lack for friends. In all those thirteen years no man, white or Indian, sought to claim the reward for his capture, even though it was raised from five hundred to twenty-three hundred dollars. The police, from time to time, tried bribery to discover the fugitives' whereabouts; the tribesmen remained totally loyal. One hundred skilled trappers roamed the Upper Skeena country; almost any one of them could easily have brought Gun-an-noot in. Instead, their grapevine worked for him, warning him when his pursuers were getting too close.

On many occasions Gun-an-noot was able to slip back to his home to visit his family. They in turn spent more and more time

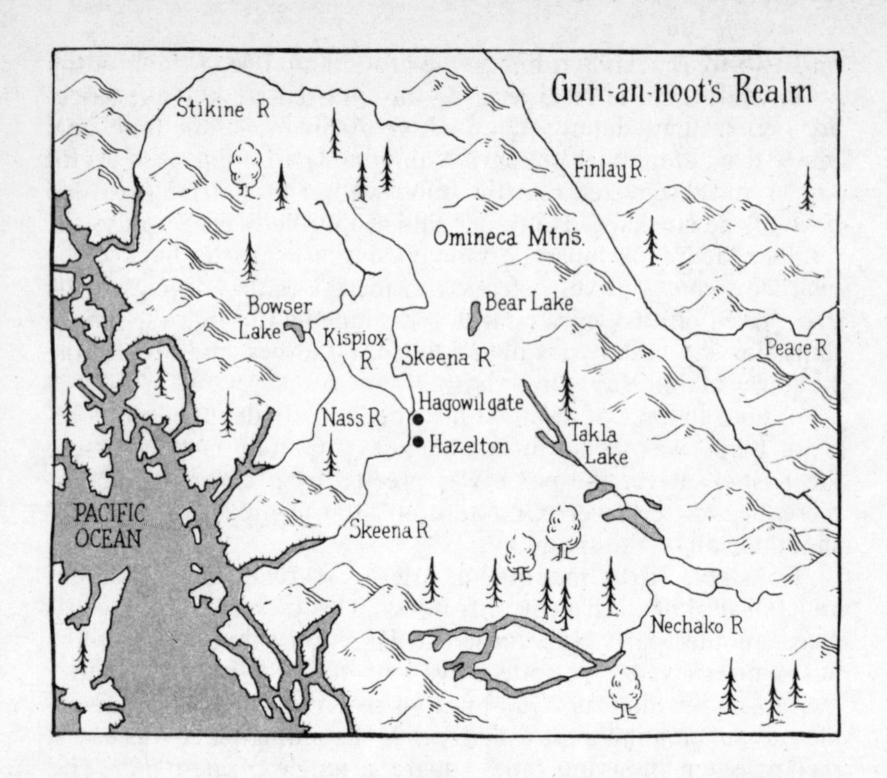

with him in the bush as the years went by. Unlike most men on the run he was able from the beginning to continue to support his wife and children. He trapped furs and sold them through intermediaries, who passed the money on to Sarah. Gun-an-noot was even able to afford a tutor for his offspring.

Intensive efforts were made to bring Gun-an-noot to justice by a government that feared his example would have a two-pronged effect, first on other Indians who might be inspired by it, and secondly on prospective settlers who might be frightened off by the thought of a dangerous fugitive at large in the wilderness.

The most experienced woodsman in the service of the B.C. police, Otway Wilkie, was selected to bring back the wanted men. Wilkie, who had a reputation for successfully tracking outlaws, launched his first expedition in the winter of 1906-7. Although he plunged deep into the heart of Gun-an-noot country, as far as Bear Lake, and although he came upon several of Gun-an-noot's caches and talked to men who claimed to have seen the two men, he emerged from the bush convinced that further searching was fruitless.

However he tried again the following winter, mounting a double-barrelled attack with two posses, one of which moved south from the Upper Skeena country and the other pushing northeast again to Bear Lake, the traditional trapping grounds of the Gun-an-noot family. His men combed the shoreline by raft and found nothing. Wilkie, with three others, then headed down the Bear and Stuart rivers and, although he did not learn about it for another dozen years, almost captured his quarry.

The two fugitives were setting rabbit snares in a box canyon near the headwaters of the Skeena. Just as they turned to leave, they saw Wilkie and another man approaching the canyon's mouth. A few more steps and their pursuers would see their snowshoe tracks, leading into the defile. Hi-ma-dan sighted Wilkie in his rifle and cocked the hammer. On an impulse, Gun-an-noot stuck his thumb under the hammer to prevent his partner from shooting. It was a fortunate move. At that instant Wilkie stopped, spoke a few words to his comrade and then, unaccountably, turned away and vanished into the twilight.

Gun-an-noot had learned his lesson. Never again would he be caught unaware. He could not afford to have men stalking him. From that point on, he determined that *he* would be the stalker. As Wilkie and his partner struggled back through the blizzard to Bear Lake, two shadows followed silently in their path.

The winter that followed was ghastly. Game was scarce, the cold almost unbearable. Many times the two fugitives were tempted to surrender themselves to the warmer, better-fed searchers in the valley below. But the hunters were often in as bad straits as the hunted. "Constable Jack Graham returned to us . . . exhausted and half-frozen," Wilkie wrote in his journal two days before Christmas. "His snowshoes had gone to pieces, his feet are in bad condition, and it took him twelve days to make the return trip from the fourth cabin of the Telegraph Line."

By January, Wilkie and his men were almost out of food. Two prospectors gave them frozen goat meat. They searched Kitkeah Pass, the Kettle and Otseka rivers and returned again to Bear Lake, empty-handed. Frostbite was taking its toll. On January 31, Wilkie was forced to call off the search, which he called the most difficult he had undertaken in thirty years of police work.

The searches continued; but no one came forward to betray Simon Gun-an-noot. His friends knew where he was and could always find him. One of these was George Beirnes, a Hazelton rancher who packed supplies on the old telegraph trail. When Gun-an-noot learned that the agent who was selling his furs was not passing on a price increase, he persuaded Beirnes to act for him. He left his pelts in a cache along the trail and his friend picked them up at regular intervals.

$1,000 REWARD $1,000

The Government of the Province of British Columbia hereby offers a reward of ONE THOUSAND DOLLARS for the arrest of

SIMON GUN-AN-NOOT and PETER HI-MA-DAN
(both Indians of the Kispiox Tribe),
or for information leading to the arrest of said Indians.

The sum of FIVE HUNDRED DOLLARS will be paid on the above-mentioned terms for the arrest of either of the said men.

The charge against them is that the said Simon Gun-an-noot and the said Peter Hi-ma-dan, on the 19th day of June, A.D. 1906, murdered Alec McIntosh and Max LeClair, near Hazelton, British Columbia.

By Order.

F. S. HUSSEY,
Superintendent, Provincial Police.

Victoria, B. C.,
August 9th, 1907.

The Great War came and the search for Gun-an-noot was temporarily suspended. When the Grand Trunk Pacific was completed through Hazelton to the coast the boom died. The British Columbia Provincial Police moved their headquarters out of the Hazelton district to Smithers. Kirby had long gone. A new and different kind of policeman, Sergeant Sperry "Dutch" Cline, was in sole charge of the Hazelton post.

Cline had lived in Hazelton for years before joining the police in 1914. One of his first moves was to take down the faded *WANTED* poster that had hung in the office for so long. He was trying to change the official attitude to make it easier for Gun-an-noot to come in. He stopped the badgering of Gun-an-noot's fellow tribesmen and he began to let slip a few complimentary remarks about the fugitive.

George Beirnes was also working on Gun-an-noot. In 1917, with the Indian's permission, he began to explore the possibilities of a surrender, taking Cline into his confidence. Cline gave him some advice: tell Gun-an-noot to get a good lawyer.

An ingenious plan now began to take shape with Cline, Beirnes and Stuart Henderson of Victoria as co-conspirators. Henderson was the leading criminal lawyer in the province, the son of a Scottish stonecutter, who specialized in defending Indians. With Gun-an-noot's permission, Cline and Beirnes had approached him to conduct the Indian's defence, when and if he should decide to surrender. Their idea, brilliant in its simplicity, was that Beirnes would "capture" Gun-an-noot, claim the twenty-three hundred dollar reward and turn it over to Henderson for his legal fees.

But Gun-an-noot refused to go through the charade of a faked capture. If he came in, he said, it would be of his own free will. That meant that he would have to trap for furs to pay for his own defence.

Two more years passed before Gun-an-noot was prepared to give in. Finally, on June 24, 1919, Beirnes and Henderson rode out to an abandoned cabin at Poison Mountain where Gun-an-noot was waiting. When the party reached Hazelton, Gun-an-noot insisted on riding alone to the police post. Cline that week had been called to a trial at Prince Rupert, and Constable John Kelly was sent from Smithers to replace him. The constable could not resist a nervous glance at the gun rack. Gun-an-noot reassured him: "You have nothing to fear," he said. "If I wanted to kill you, I could have shot you many times on the trail."

He was lodged in the Hazelton jail. Cline returned from Prince Rupert to find that his prisoner, after thirteen years in the open wilds, was suffering from claustrophobia. When Kelly put him into the cell he had broken out in a cold sweat, soaking himself so thoroughly that he needed a change of clothing. In return for Gun-an-noot's word of honour not to attempt an escape Cline stopped locking the jail. One night he discovered that it had been locked by accident. He rushed through the building, unbolted the door as quietly as possible and then walked into the cell where Gun-an-noot was sitting. Cline always remembered the spectacle that confronted him.

"He was crouched like a caged beast ready to spring, eyes aflame, every muscle tensed. I realized that I had to do something and do it quickly. So I turned my back to him and said, 'We're keeping the back door open, now. Come, I'll show you the way out . . . I guess Mr. Kelly forgot to tell you.' " Gun-an-noot followed him out into the yard and Cline left him there to relax.

Henderson had the trial moved to Vancouver, away from the passions that the murders had inspired in Hazelton. The charge was the murder of McIntosh, but the verdict was a foregone conclusion. Out of the past came a host of witnesses. Peter Barney helped to bury the case when he testified that the accused and his alleged victim had ridden off in opposite directions after leaving Two Mile House. Henderson did not put Gun-an-noot on the stand.

In his summation to the jury, Henderson said: "The prisoner has already been punished for a crime he did not commit by thirteen years of exile in a harsh northern wilderness. Throughout that time he has provided for his family. He endured an exile because he was afraid he would not receive justice in a white man's courtroom. It remains for you, the jury, to prove to him his fears were groundless."

The jury took fifteen minutes to acquit. Peter Hi-ma-dan, who surrendered a few months later, was freed following a preliminary hearing in Hazelton.

That is the gist of the story that I told in the original edition of *My Country*. But in a sense the story was unsatisfactory because several questions nagged. Who really killed the two men? Was there one murderer or two? What, if any, was the connection between McIntosh and LeClair? And if no connection, how was it that both were murdered in identical fashion within an hour? And why did Gun-an-noot kill all his horses?

Then, in the spring of 1977, I learned that Gun-an-noot's son David felt the time had come to tell the real story. But what *was* the real story? To find out I had to travel to the little mining town of Stewart, which nestles below the mountains at the head of the long Pacific fiord known as the Portland Canal. And there in the

King Edward Hotel I found myself sitting on the edge of my chair listening to the eloquence of David Gun-an-noot who is also, by virtue of his mother's lineage, Chief Legap of the Gitksan band of the Carrier Nation.

I found him to be a remarkable man – a man who had never had a single day of schooling because he was brought up in the wilderness. "My teacher," he told me "was an old gramophone." He learned English by playing old records over and over again and he taught himself to read by buying the appropriate sheet music and fitting the syllables of the lyrics to the recorded sounds. All his active life was spent out of doors. Until his mid-sixties he trapped and hunted for a living. Less than a decade before he had been alert enough and bold enough to accomplish the almost impossible feat of stopping an attacking grizzly bear while armed only with a .22 rifle.

At 71, he was suffering from heart trouble and was partially deaf and half blind. But when he told his story he did it without faltering and with none of those rambling excursions from the narrative that so often characterize the reminiscences of the aged. The oral tradition is engrained in his people. His voice, which tended to waver in ordinary conversation, grew stronger as he talked so that the tale, complete with dialogue, emerged with force and drama.

In the winter of his life, David Gun-an-noot wanted to tell at last the account his mother gave to him more than half a century ago, when she swore him to secrecy.

And what is the secret? The secret is that his father did it – did it and was proud of it; killed both McIntosh and LeClair and got away with it; changed the mode of his life only in degree; walked boldly down the streets of Hazelton and of Kispiox, the Indian village; shopped for rum at the Hudson's Bay post; lived on his ranch at Kisgegas; fathered a clutch of children, only one of whom (contrary to legend) failed to survive in the wild; trapped, hunted, and sold his furs to buyers who knew exactly who the vendor was.

David Gun-an-noot's account begins on that May night, seventy-one years ago, with his father walking into the Two Mile House hoping to buy some spring salmon. The place is crowded. Gun-an-noot does not really want a drink, but his pockets are full of money from the sale of his winter's catch and the women are imploring him to stand round after round of drinks. The evening grows boisterous. McIntosh, the packer, begins to pick on Peter Hi-ma-dan, who has preceded his brother-in-law to the tavern.

There is a struggle. Peter is knocked to the ground. Gun-an-noot intercedes, whereupon McIntosh pulls a knife and taunts him.

"I can sleep with your wife any time," David Gun-an-noot quotes him as saying, and the words hiss from his lips as he recreates the incident. "You'll never do anything about it. You'll never scratch my skin!"

A struggle follows; McIntosh goes down, but not before his knife has bloodied the Indian's face. More taunts by McIntosh about Sarah Gun-an-noot follow. Hi-ma-dan tries to break up the fight but by now his brother-in-law is in a fury.

"Before the light comes you'll be frozen blood!" he shouts at McIntosh.

"Run!" says Hi-ma-dan to the packer. "You better run! Hide! When he makes a promise you can bet he's going to keep it. He don't miss his promise!"

"Fuck him!" says McIntosh. "Fuck him! You'll never see an Indian scratch a white man's skin."

"He'll scratch your skin alright," Hi-ma-dan warns as he and Gun-an-noot leave the tavern. "You better go."

But McIntosh stays while Gun-an-noot rides to Kispiox village a couple of miles to the north.

Simon Gun-an-noot is in a black rage. He enters his house, seizes a rifle and mounts his favourite horse, Frank. There is no doubt that he wants to have it out with McIntosh. His sister-in-law Christine, Peter Hi-ma-dan's wife, fears the worst. She has managed to twist and loosen the cinch on Frank's saddle so that when Simon mounts the saddle turns turtle and he tumbles to the ground. This only increases his fury. The horses, startled, scatter. Simon seizes his rifle and shoots four of them. He mounts the fifth and dashes off toward Two Mile House.

Now, David explains, the tavern lies on the arm of a dog leg in the road between Hazelton and Kispiox. But a trail through the bush, wide enough for a single rider, acts as a short cut. Gun-an-noot takes the short cut and emerges on the main road west of Two Mile House.

Fate now takes a hand. If Alex McIntosh had not come riding past at that exact moment on his way back from the hospital, if he had stopped to argue when Gun-an-noot shouted at him, he might have lived, or so David Gun-an-noot believes. But when Gun-an-noot cries: "Alex! Stop! Remember what I told you!" McIntosh spurs his horse and the Indian, his fury increasing, drops him with a single shot.

Gun-an-noot turns back along the short cut, emerging again on the Kisgegas Road well to the north of Two Mile House. Again chance decides the course of events. At that exact moment Max LeClair comes driving past on a buckboard. He sees the blood from McIntosh's knife drying on Gun-an-noot's cheeks and, without thinking, taunts him: "Hey, you Indian! Fighting again, eh? Look at the blood on your face."

It is too much. Gun-an-noot raises his rifle and shoots LeClair dead. Thus begins the long exile of Simon Gun-an-noot and his family.

Yet, in David Gun-an-noot's telling, it is not quite the ordeal that most writers, including this one, have described. One must tread warily here. For his first thirteen years David knew no other kind of life. He did not know his father was a fugitive. For a long time he thought everybody in the world lived in tents warmed by B.C. heaters. The family thought nothing of moving a hundred miles in a single day, sometimes directly across mountain ranges. What would be a harrowing ordeal for a city-bred boy was, for him, a normal existence.

After the murder, they lost no time in leaving the Hazelton area, fleeing to the ranch at Kisgegas, more than fifty miles to the north. More than once Gun-an-noot doubled back on the trail to smoke out pursuers.

"What are you going to do – shoot them?" Sarah asked.

"Only if they put a gun on me," he told her. His son remembers that he always carried a 9 mm. pistol stuffed into his belt.

Gun-an-noot's father, Nah-Gun, so David Gun-an-noot believed, had been purposely allowed to escape in the hope that he would lead the police to the wanted men. But Nah-Gun, realizing he was being followed, hid in a hollow cottonwood log, evaded his pursuers and made his way to the ranch at Kisgegas. Here Gun-an-noot built a raft, took his entire family across the swollen Skeena, hacked a trail through the mountains and vanished.

The remarkable thing, in David Gun-an-noot's telling of the tale, is not so much that this tight group of men, women and children survived for thirteen years in the wilderness; it is that they spent so much of their time in civilization. David remembers wondering why his father always cast a careful eye about him when emerging from the woods onto a river bank; but he also remembers the later years when the entire family moved freely about in Kispiox and Hazelton.

Once, walking down the main street of Hazelton, Gun-an-noot almost ran into two of the Pinkerton detectives hired to flush him out of hiding. They did not recognize him but the Indian, taking no chances, vaulted a fence and vanished.

In Kispiox, David remembers, his father actually held an auction in order to get the best prices for his furs. The Hudson's Bay Company sent two buyers who bid against an independent. The Bay won. And Gun-an-noot also bought rum by the keg from the Hudson's Bay store, slipping in by the back door after dark. Meanwhile members of his family became familiar figures in Hazelton and Kispiox picking up groceries and other supplies.

Nobody ever turned them in. Early in the chase, two of Kirby's Indian deputies actually caught up with the fugitives. David's grandmother's remark at the time was told with great relish in later years to the younger children.

"Better pack your blankets and go home," she warned the two. "Or your shit will be cold by morning." They took her advice.

Gun-an-noot's most brazen public appearance took place when the first silent movie came to Hazelton in the days before the Great War. Everybody was talking about the new device that flashed moving pictures onto a white screen. Gun-an-noot could not contain his curiosity. He had his hair cut and his mustache trimmed. Then he bought himself a new suit, a good white shirt and a smart tie. Thus attired, he marched boldly into the movie house and saw the picture. All around him people were asking in whispers who the distinguished-looking stranger might be.

The family's headquarters was the ranch at Kisgegas on the Skeena. But their life was nomadic. They moved to Bowser Lake in the west, to Bear Lake in the east, crossing torrents, canyons, swamps and mountain peaks in the way city people cross roadways. When babies were born in the wilderness, Sarah slung them in a blanket and the family moved on.

David has never forgotten the day his father gave himself up. Though there had been negotiations with George Beirnes and the lawyer, Stuart Henderson, David Gun-an-noot believes that his father's ultimate decision to surrender was again triggered by pride, as the murders were. He had been, so David remembers, taunted by a fellow Indian, Moses Slamgeest. By 1919 his legend had assumed superhuman proportions and it may well be that the tale of the phantom Indian was used to frighten small children. At any rate, Moses was heard to sneer at Gun-an-noot, behind his back, in Kispiox.

"What's the use of him running around scaring people?" he asked. When those words came back to Gun-an-noot, the fugitive picked up a gun, rode into the village and confronted Moses, who promptly shut up. But the taunt rankled and one day Simon told his family: "I'm going to give myself up. I'm tired of people making up stories behind my back. If they're going to hang me, well, let them hang me. I've got to die some time."

David Gun-an-noot, aged 13, clung to his father.

"No, no," he cried. "I'm not going to let these white men hang you up."

"You're too young to understand," his father replied. "Look how many years it's been. You'll never fit into my tracks. You'll never be like that."

"For all my life," David Gun-an-noot told me, "I have remembered those words."

Most of the rest of the story is on the record. David remembers his mother telling him: "You're not going to live in this tent no more. You're going to sleep in a house and you're not going to use that candle no more. You're going to use a lamp on the wall."

In David Gun-an-noot's account the years that followed differed only in degree from the earlier ones. His father trapped at Bear Lake, and the family spent much of their time at Kisgegas. Gun-an-noot died in 1933, not of tuberculosis, as some have said, but of pneumonia, caught on the winter trail after his dogs broke away to chase a bear, leaving him alone without blankets or matches.

"I don't want to be buried in a town," said Simon Gun-an-noot. Appropriately, they were his last words. At his own request his tribesmen carried his body to the lake and laid it to rest beside that of his father, Nah-gun. Even then, Gun-an-noot's domain remained isolated from the world; it took four months for the news of his death to percolate out to civilization.

It remains wild, untravelled country to this day, far off the beaten tourist pathways, unmarred by asphalt, unscarred by campfires. Here the invisible Indian's name lives on in Mount Gun-an-noot and in Lake Gun-an-noot and in the legends of the Kispiox, who do not need a pinpoint on a map to honour his memory. It probably would not matter to Gun-an-noot that a mountain and a lake were chosen to mark his passage, though it might have amused him; during his lifetime all of the lakes and the mountains were his. Still, one can be certain that he would have preferred these natural monuments to the ephemeral accolade of a folk song in the Top Fifty.

15
Billy Bishop: The Lone Hawk

If you wanted to, you could make out a pretty good case for Billy Bishop as the Canadian Least Likely to Succeed as a World War One flyer. Consider the evidence:

Billy Bishop was a mother's boy. He spoke with a lisp, preferred dancing to the jock sports and was called a sissy by his classmates.

Billy Bishop was a rotten student. He cut classes to play pool. His report cards were terrible. His principal didn't think he'd amount to much.

Billy Bishop was a bust as a military cadet – the worst the Royal Military College had ever known. They would have thrown him out in 1914 for cheating at exams, but the war intervened.

Billy Bishop was a military misfit. His crime sheet carried entries for breaches of discipline and conduct unbecoming an officer. He drank so much champagne, going on leave, that he fell off a gangplank, bashed in his knee and was hospitalized for months. As a pilot he never could manage a decent take-off or landing. On his solo, he pancaked his training plane. The first time he took a Nieuport 17 into the air, he cracked it up.

But . . . when the war to end all wars had ended, Billy Bishop had become the world's greatest living air ace. He had shot down seventy-two enemy planes confirmed and many more which weren't officially counted – more, probably, than the Red Baron himself. He had won the Victoria Cross, two Distinguished Service Orders, the Military Cross, the Distinguished Flying Cross, the Legion of Honour and the Croix de Guerre with palm. There were no more honours left for him to win. Billy Bishop was a living legend and he was only twenty-four years old.

The schoolmaster who suggested Billy wouldn't amount to much had added a qualification: the one thing he *was* good at was fighting. Anybody who called Billy a sissy got beaten up. The odds against him were sometimes seven to one but that hadn't fazed Billy. Later on, in the air, the odds were often greater. Eddie Rickenbacker once said that Billy Bishop was the only man he ever met who was totally without fear.

On June 2, 1917, the greatest single day of his life, the odds were heavily against Billy. The field was still in darkness when he rose. The rest of the squadron was asleep. Billy was going out on his own, far behind the German lines, without support. He didn't bother to take off his pyjamas, just pulled his flying clothes on over them, trudged off to the mess hall, gulped some hot tea, then headed for the hangar, peering upward into the gloom. The weather wasn't good: heavy clouds at five hundred; light drizzle.

Walter Bourne, his mechanic, had the blue-nosed Nieuport on the field, its engine running. Billy pulled on his oil-stained leather helmet, made one last cockpit check and then was off into the darkness, experiencing "a loneliness such as he had never known before." His stomach felt hollow. It wasn't fear – he knew exactly what he was about to do, had planned it for weeks, prepared for it all the previous day – it was plain hunger; Billy wished he'd had some breakfast.

He was fifteen minutes behind the enemy lines before the Germans realized that a British fighter was over one of their airfields. Billy had no idea where he was, didn't even know the name of the aerodrome below him. (It was Estourmel, near Cambrai.) Coming out of the clouds he could see little black figures running out of the hangars toward their waiting planes.

He raked the field with machine-gun fire. An Albatros began to roll forward for take-off. Billy, two hundred feet above, poured fifteen slugs into it, just at lift off. It tilted; a wing dug in. Billy watched it ground-loop into a mass of wreckage.

A second plane was starting down the field. Billy pulled hard on his stick, gaining altitude for the kill. He fired a burst of thirty bullets but missed. No matter. The German was so unnerved he crashed into a tree.

Two other planes struggled into the air. Billy emptied the rest of his drum into one and watched it crash. The fourth plane attacked, its twin Spandaus flashing. Unarmed for the moment, Billy twisted and dodged, while changing ammunition drums. That done, he emptied the entire new drum – ninety-nine rounds – into the enemy aircraft. The German had no stomach to pursue as Billy streaked for home. As soon as his smoking gun cooled off he tore it from its mount and threw it overboard. He didn't need the dead weight; he needed speed.

The clouds parted. Four enemy scouts appeared above him. Billy kept his plane in the blind spot directly below, matching them manoeuvre for manoeuvre. They never saw him as he broke away, diving to one thousand feet over the German lines. Rifle and machine gun bullets poured up from the trenches. Billy's ears cracked with the sound of shrapnel ripping into fabric. He felt drained, all his early elation gone. He flew in a daze, a queer, sinking feeling in his gut. He felt he was losing his senses. The only thing that mattered was to get home.

When he landed, his comrades were still snoring in their beds; it was scarcely 5:30 a.m. Billy fired off his Very pistol to wake them and they crowded round: "How many kills?" *Only three; one got away.* Billy was being over-modest. He had damaged several other planes on the ground and wounded the pilot of the fourth Albatros. The raid was, according to the RFC's commander, "the greatest single show of the war." It won the Victoria Cross for Billy. He was the first Canadian airman to wear it – but there would be more.

The Canadians were among the greatest flyers of World War One. Of the twenty-seven super-aces – those who downed more than thirty planes – eleven were Canadians. Of the ten leading aces on the Allied side, five were Canadians. The Canadian flyers among them won 475 decorations, including three VC's.

They came from small, isolated towns, mostly in the west (Billy Bishop, from Owen Sound, Ontario, was an exception) – towns with names like Gladstone, Carberry, Keg River Prairie and Nanaimo. They were all free spirits, rugged individualists impatient with military tradition, reckless of rules and discipline, contemptuous of spit and polish. They took to aerial warfare because there were no military textbooks telling how it should be fought. The Canadians made up their tactics, invented their traditions, as they went along.

They handled their planes like spirited steeds. It was no accident that most of them were superb horsemen. Billy Bishop may have ignored hockey, football and lacrosse, but he learned to ride early and well. Above all they were crack shots. Billy had known how to shoot since his father gave him a .22 as a Christmas present and offered him a quarter for every squirrel he shot. He quickly learned to knock squirrels over with one bullet. In the air he treated Germans as squirrels; often enough he dispatched an enemy plane with a single burst.

The newspapers called him the Lone Hawk. Billy hated the name, but there was truth in it. The Germans hunted in packs but Billy liked to go off by himself between patrols, a solitary killer bursting unexpectedly from the clouds. "I doubt if mankind has ever known a lonelier job than that of the single-seat fighters of World War One," he wrote. The Canadians were used to lonely jobs, empty spaces, vast solitudes. Billy's closest rival among the Canadians, the naval flyer, Raymond Collishaw (sixty kills) had been a seaman on the West Coast and in the Arctic. Don McLaren, the number three Canadian ace (fifty-four kills), was raised in an isolated Indian trading post. Loneliness was in their nature.

It is doubtful if any of them intended to be flyers. Certainly the idea didn't occur to Billy. At the start of World War One, the entire Canadian Aviation Corps consisted of two men and a single airplane that never got off the ground. Billy, the horseman, joined the Mississauga Horse.

When his unit embarked for overseas on October 1, 1914, Billy was left behind, hospitalized by pneumonia and a mysterious allergy. One doctor said the allergy was caused by army food; another said it was caused by horses. Billy thought it was the result of parade-ground dust. The future didn't look too rosy but an old flame consoled him by sending a daily bouquet of flowers to the hospital. Billy, in a panic, turned them over to his sister before his fiancée could find them. There were several old flames in Billy Bishop's life, but all that was in the past. He was engaged to Margaret Burden, Timothy Eaton's granddaughter.

Out of the hospital, Billy transferred to the 7th Canadian Mounted Rifles. At twenty-one, he was the youngest officer in the regiment, and because he was a good shot, they put him in charge of the machine-gun section. The crossing to England was harrowing. The ship was overcrowded; the weather was vile; men and horses were seasick. As they neared the Irish coast, the U-boats moved in for the kill and ships to the port and starboard began to blow up and sink. Billy was petrified – or claimed to be. "I wonder if I shall ever come home to you," he wrote his fiancée.

Billy hated Shorncliffe military camp, one of the muddiest in all of muddy England, "an incredible mass of mud, muck and mire with the special added unpleasantness that only horses in large quantity can contribute." He had not expected the war to be like this. One day, up to his knees in the gumbo of the parade ground, he gazed up into the sky and saw a cleansing sight: a trim little fighter plane zooming out of the clouds. Then and there, Billy Bishop made up his mind to fight the war in the air. Without asking anybody's permission, he applied for a transfer to the Royal Flying Corps. At the War Office he was asked a lot of silly questions: *Do you skate well? Can you ride a motorcycle?* Sure, said Billy; you bet. He wanted to be a fighter pilot but that would mean a six-month wait – in the mud. But they needed observers: "the chap who goes along for the ride," as the War Office interviewer put it. Billy asked for a transfer and was taken on at once.

His first training plane was an Avro two-seater. The aircraft had no guns. It could barely get off the ground. In the air, it gasped and wheezed like an old Ford truck. But Billy was ecstatic: "This flying is the most wonderful invention," he wrote home. "A man ceases to be a human up there. He feels that nothing is impossible."

When Billy began his training, aerial warfare was only one year old and still in a primitive state. There had been some advances: pilots no longer threw bricks at each other or fought with rifles and pistols. The new aircraft were armed with light machine guns, synchronized to fire directly through the propeller. But the planes were often as dangerous as the enemy guns; and, none was so dangerous as the R.E.7, the experimental reconnaissance craft that was Billy's first combat machine when, as a trained observer, he reached France in January 1916.

The R.E.7 rarely reached a top speed of sixty miles an hour. It stalled at about forty-five. In the wind and sleet of northern France, take-offs and landings were nightmarish. In the air, as Billy put it, the R.E.7 was "as manoeuvrable as a ten-ton truck, but by no means as safe." It was supposed to carry four machine guns and a 500-pound bomb, but with that weight it couldn't get off the ground. On their first flight, Billy and his pilot jettisoned two guns and the bomb and just managed to stagger into the air.

Even with two machine guns, the plane was a sitting duck. Billy didn't see how you could fire either one of the guns through the maze of struts and wires that held the wings together. The plane, he said, looked more like a bird cage. Fortunately for Billy Bishop, there were no dogfights that first winter in France.

On the ground it was a different story. Billy, it developed, was accident prone. A series of mishaps kept sending him to hospital. Back in England, following a leave, he was out of action for the best part of a year with a cracked knee and a severely strained heart (the latter ailment blamed variously on brandy, champagne, the tensions of long patrols or a combination of all three.) These misfortunes merely convinced Billy that he wasn't meant to die.

Billy Bishop still wanted to be a pilot. In the summer of 1916 his own squadron had been nearly wiped out in the battles of the Somme. To complicate matters, his records had been lost. Worse, the medicos had declared him unfit for military service. But Billy had charm and Billy had made some powerful friends in England. He pulled strings and got himself accepted at a pilot's training course on Salisbury Plain.

Learning to fly was not the breeze that Billy Bishop, veteran observer, thought it would be. His instructor cursed him for being ham-handed at the controls. In desperation he allowed Billy to solo after only three hours flying time. In the air, without a companion, Billy felt lonelier than he had ever been. Somehow he managed to get the plane onto the ground again "with a spine-jarring 'plonk'" – the first of what were to become known as "Bishop landings."

Billy Bishop went back to France in March of 1917 to the 60th squadron of the RFC at a place called Filescamp Farm. The 60th was the most famous fighter squadron in France, thanks to one of its former members, Albert Ball. Ball, the leading British ace, was Billy's hero; he had attacked as many as forty German planes single-handed, and had shot down twenty-nine. His secret weapon was surprise. He would sneak up on superior formations and launch himself into reckless attack before the enemy could recover from the shock. Billy resolved that that would be his technique too. He had an added advantage: he couldn't miss with a machine gun. He was so deadly accurate he could shoot down enemy pilots before they knew he was behind them. And his eyesight was superb. Like Ball, he did not wear goggles in the air; he felt this interfered with his shooting; and he searched the sky with such intensity, turning and twisting in the cockpit to spot enemy planes, that the back of his neck was often rubbed raw.

The Nieuport 17 was a single-seat fighter with a rotary engine and a Lewis gun fixed on a mount on the top wing. The gun was easily manoeuvrable. It could be fired directly ahead over the arc of the propeller or it could be pulled back into the cockpit to fire straight up at an enemy passing overhead. Billy never allowed anybody but himself to handle his gun; he personally loaded every round into the magazine. He took a great deal more pains with his gun than with his plane; (the plane, to him, was merely a flying gun-mount.) On his first time out, returning from a patrol, he had crash-landed almost at the feet of the brigade commander, who immediately ordered him back to flying school.

Before the order could be put into effect, Billy Bishop experienced, on March 25, 1917, his first aerial dogfight. It was almost his last. Billy was rear man on a four-plane patrol at nine thousand feet when they ran into a squadron of Albatroses over the German lines. As the enemy planes closed in, the patrol banked to the left in a tight climb. Billy was a little slow. An Albatros, pulling up under the leader's tail, suddenly filled his gunsight. Billy, the one-shot squirrel killer, pressed the firing button and the German went into a dive. Billy figured he might be faking and gave chase. Sure enough, the Albatros pulled out of the dive. As it levelled off, Billy gave it another burst. Once more the plane went into a dive with Billy screaming down behind it at two hundred miles an hour. The Nieuport had one serious fault; pushed beyond normal speeds, the wings tended to break off. Billy Bishop was lucky; the wings stayed on but the motor coughed out. Billy didn't see the Albatros crash to the ground in flames – he was too busy trying to get his nose up and glide over to his own lines. He barely made it; the field into which he landed had just been captured by the Allies. It took several days to get his battered plane back to the squadron, but Billy Bishop had scored his first kill. They told him he didn't have to go back to flying school; he could stay in France and fight.

Billy met the Red Baron – or at least his famous Flying Circus – five days later on March 30, 1917. He was in charge of a patrol when the Baron's pack attacked and shot down two of his men. The following day, far behind the enemy lines, Billy got a partial revenge when he knocked one of the Baron's Albatroses out of the air.

The Red Baron was Manfred von Richthofen, leader of Jagdstaffel II, the deadly "hunting pack," based at Douai. The Baron was a bit like Billy – rugged, sturdy, wiry and short. But the Baron was dark and saturnine while Billy was fair with the features of a Paul Newman and the body of a James Cagney. The Baron had started in the cavalry, too, and got out of the mud and into the air, surviving a dangerous and inglorious apprenticeship as an air observer before becoming a killer pilot. The crimson spinner flying from his wing was his trademark. Billy soon had a trademark as well: a blue spinner on the wing, and a blue nose on his Nieuport.

April 1917 went down in history as Bloody April. Squadron 60 and Jagdstaffel II bore the brunt of the fighting, and the Germans were the clear victors. Richthofen alone shot down twenty-two planes to Bishop's twelve. The German Albatros was a faster machine with superior firepower – two machine guns to the Nieuport's single Lewis. And the German pilots were veterans. Number 60 Squadron suffered so many casualties that it had only five experienced men left at the month's end. One of them was Billy Bishop.

Billy learned fast. He got his third Albatros along with an enemy sausage balloon on April 5, five miles behind the enemy lines. Again his engine failed in a dive but Billy now knew what to do: keep pumping the throttle, his mechanic had told him. Billy pumped away as the Nieuport screamed toward the ground: two hundred feet . . . one hundred feet . . . fifty feet . . . thirty feet. At twenty feet the engine caught. Lucky Billy returned to fight another day and to write a letter home in his best Boys' Own Paper prose: "Three more pilots lost today. All good men. Oh, how I hate the Huns. They have done in so many of my best friends. I'll make them pay, I swear."

In 1916, flyers on both sides still operated with a certain amount of medieval chivalry, dropping wreaths over the aerodromes of dead enemies and even toasting captured fighter pilots in the mess. But Billy fought with hate. "I detest the Huns . . . I hate them with all my heart," he wrote to Margaret Burden. He experienced a thrill that was almost sadistic in watching a vanquished enemy crash. Like Richthofen, he had the true killer instinct, and not without reason. In 60 Squadron, Billy's friends went to their deaths almost as regularly as they answered mess call.

In the air, Billy Bishop kept his cool. On April 9, 1917 (Easter Monday – the day the Canadians attacked Vimy Ridge), he shot down three planes and came as close to death as any man can. His mechanic couldn't figure out how he'd lived, because his windshield was shattered by a bullet directly in the line of his head. All lucky Billy had was a graze. He kept the shattered windshield for the rest of his life – one of his few wartime souvenirs.

That night in the mess, with the others who had faced death with him, Billy Bishop let off steam. He drank champagne by the bucketfull, sang songs, recited, tap-danced on top of the piano, then poured more champagne on the sounding board to improve the tone. The squadron staggered to bed at three, rose again at dawn and flew off, low over the lines, to give ground support to the attacking troops.

By mid-April, thirteen of 60 Squadron's pilots were dead – men with whom Billy had caroused in the mess and fought beside in the air, men who had become, in a few days, closer to him than the friends of a lifetime. In less than a month Billy Bishop had become a combat veteran, the squadron's leading ace and commander of C–Flight. On April 20, after shooting down an enemy observation plane, he returned to find he'd won the Military Cross. There were drinks all round in the mess that night. But then there were drinks all round most nights. No one knew which round might be his last. Wakes and celebrations were indistinguishable.

The squadron lived daily with death but Billy Bishop didn't really believe that he would die. He was far more fearful of being taken prisoner. He found the British discipline oppressive enough; how could he ever stand a German prison camp?

Against that possibility, he kept a fine edge on his shooting with daily target practice. In the air he adopted Ball's tactics of surprise. On April 22, using a comrade as a decoy, he sucked five enemy single-seaters into a trap, swooped out of the clouds, dispatched two of them before the rest of his flight reached the scene, and chased the other three out of sight.

On the way home, Billy came to a decision. There would be no more twisting, turning and manoeuvring in the air; from this point on he would develop the quick, darting attack as the key element of his personal style.

Like a hockey player, Billy was on a winning streak. He made the most of it, for he was a man who liked to win, liked to be the best at whatever he attempted. On the last day of that bloodiest of Aprils, he took part in nine dogfights in two hours. He destroyed one enemy plane and forced down two more that morning. In the afternoon, he ran headlong into the Red Baron himself.

In eight months of combat, the Baron had shot down fifty-two planes. In five weeks, Billy Bishop's score was twelve. The previous day the Baron had scored four kills – an almost unheard-of feat. Now, on the eve of a furlough, he had vowed to equal that record.

Earlier that day, Billy had cheated the Baron out of a sure victory by breaking up his wolf-pack formation with his dive-and-zoom tactics. This time, with the odds five to two in his favour, the Baron was out for blood. As the seven planes (two British, five German), swirled and criss-crossed in the air, the Baron poured a stream of bullets into Billy's Nieuport. One entered the fold of his flying coat, another pierced his instrument panel. It was, Billy would say later (after he had cooled down), "the best shooting I have ever seen." But now, with oil drenching his face, he lost his temper and charged. Black smoke poured from the Baron's Albatros. For one ecstatic moment, Billy thought he had him. But the Baron had merely used an old trick to escape. He dove four thousand feet, flattened out, waggled his wings and was gone. When Billy counted the holes in his plane he found that the Baron had missed him by only six inches. "A miss is as good as a mile," he wrote Margaret. He and the Baron never met again.

April ended; the Baron went on his leave; the air war slackened off; Billy felt let down. He had some leave coming, too, and he needed it. He looked far older than his twenty-three years. He had fought forty battles in forty days, seen close friends plunge to flaming deaths, breathed far too many castor oil fumes from the Nieuport's rotary engine and drunk far too much champagne and brandy in those desperately jovial evenings in the mess.

Billy wanted to bring his score to twenty before he took his leave. On May 2, he fought from dawn to sunset and turned in three combat reports. He engaged twenty-three German aircraft, destroyed two and emerged without a scratch. His only problem came when he landed his plane at the day's end. It wasn't the Germans who smashed up his undercarriage; it was Billy.

On the day before his leave, Billy's hero, Albert Ball, came over from his squadron at Vert Galand to talk to him. Over brandies, Ball outlined a daring scheme. Why not sneak over the German lines at dawn, just the two of them, and destroy the enemy planes on the ground as they pulled out of the hangars? You bet, said Billy. Soon as I get back from leave. The following day he was whooping it up in London and Albert Ball was dead from enemy gunfire.

Billy Bishop now had the highest score of any surviving British airman; he also had the Distinguished Service Order – next to the VC the highest decoration his monarch could bestow. He was a celebrity and his leave, like all the leaves of that weary war, was a frantic attempt to cram as much living as possible into a fragment of time. He mingled in London society, dined with Princess Marie Louise, hob-nobbed with one famous Canadian, Lord Beaverbrook, and turned down a dinner invitation from another (Lloyd George's house leader, Bonar Law) in order to spend the time with a beautiful young actress. All these various connections, with the possible exception of the actress, would serve Billy well in later years.

Billy went back to France on May 22 and knocked down three more aircraft. But Albert Ball's plan kept nagging at him. Why shouldn't he do it alone? If he could reach the German airfields, unseen, at first light, he might just pull it off. Finally he decided on the day: come rain or shine, he would carry out his scheme on June 2. He spent the first of the month practising his shooting, poring over maps, checking out his plane. The following morning, before dawn, he flew off to win his Victoria Cross.

For the next fortnight, Billy Bishop scarcely took a day off. The odds were against him, but surprise was on his side. On June 8 he dove right through a squadron of six enemy scouts, knocking one out of the air, and continued his dive to safety before the other five pilots could gather their wits. His own plane eventually had to be overhauled and fitted with a new skin; there were so many patches on it, the extra weight was slowing him down.

For all his days with the squadron, Billy Bishop was subjected to the conflicting tugs of successive emotions. Elation was followed by frustration, frustration by defiance, defiance by despair.

despair by hatred. Frustrated by an inability to find the enemy, Billy led fifteen of the squadron directly over a German aerodrome where they indulged in a full-dress performance of aerial stunting above the astonished audience. "We should have charged the damned Huns admission," said his friend, "Black" Lloyd. The next day Lloyd was killed in a fight with two Albatros scouts and Billy was despondent. "I am thoroughly downcast tonight," he wrote. "Sometimes this awful fighting ... makes you wonder if you have a right to call yourself human .... I am so tired of it all, the killing, the war ...."

Billy went on a three-day leave to Amiens, had a fling with a beautiful French girl named Ninette and confessed it all in another letter to Margaret. The affair, he insisted, was more therapeutic than romantic. No doubt it was. When he returned to Filescamp Farm, he shot down five enemy planes in as many days. Billy couldn't seem to miss. He destroyed one with a single burst of ten rounds. He killed another at a distance of a hundred yards.

When the wet weather came at the end of June and flying was rendered impossible, the surviving pilots engaged in manic japery. Domestic animals were seized and painted in assorted hues. The smashing of gramophone records over various heads became endemic. Uniform-tearing contests were a nightly ritual. And the bar never closed.

A French pilot, making a forced landing through the overcast, was given a riotous champagne welcome. Billy inveigled him into a flying contest. Each tried to best the other in a series of wild manoeuvres under a low cloud cover. The Frenchman reached some kind of peak by scraping his wingtip through the grass of the field. Billy outdid him by rolling his wheels on the roof of the mess as he came in for a landing.

New planes – S.E.5s – arrived early in July: they had two guns instead of one and were forty miles an hour faster. Billy was ecstatic; but his euphoria vanished on his first flight: one gun wouldn't work; the other shot holes through the propeller. The squadron went back to the old machines while the new ones were being overhauled.

In his old, patched-up, blue-nosed Nieuport, Billy Bishop fought the highest battle of his career above Vitry at nineteen thousand feet. The single-seater wallowed in the thin air, barely responding to the controls. Billy's hands were numb with cold, his senses dizzy from lack of oxygen, his timing off. Twice he had the enemy in his sights at ten yards but each time his shots went wild. The second time his plane stalled and went into a spin. Billy swore he'd never fight again at that height.

He could hardly wait for the S.E.5s to be overhauled; the Germans in their faster planes were leaving him standing still. When the new planes finally arrived he was so excited that he decided to fight on his day off. That was the day Billy Bishop forgot to be cautious. He chased a pair of two-seaters down to five thousand feet – the ideal anti-aircraft range. The German gunners knocked him out of the air. His flaming S.E.5 crashed into a copse of poplar trees. Lucky Billy, hanging from the cockpit, was pulled out unscratched by some passing soldiers. His nerves shaken, he took two days' rest at Amiens, but on his return to Filescamp he took to the air immediately. Billy had heard too many stories about flyers who had lost their nerve after they crashed. He needn't have worried; his luck still held. On his first patrol he bagged two more of the enemy.

Billy Bishop, now one of the senior living British aces, had become too valuable to be wasted in the daily rough and tumble of aerial combat. With forty-seven official kills to his credit, they sent him to England as an instructor, made him a major, gave him a bar to his DSO, and put his picture in all the papers – the most decorated airman of the war. At Buckingham Palace, King George V pinned medals all over him. Billy was terribly embarrassed; his new boots squeaked audibly.

The hero went off to Canada to help with recruiting. At Montreal, a great, jostling crowd of dignitaries, reporters, photographers and plain citizens roared a greeting. Billy helped launch a Red Cross campaign and then visited his old alma mater, the Royal Military College, which only three years before had been on the verge of kicking him out.

Billy Bishop married his sweetheart, Margaret Burden, in the Memorial Church named for her grandfather. The four blocks between the Burden home on Avenue Road, Toronto, and the church, was dense with people. Billy and his bride went off to the Catskills on a honeymoon and then to the British War Mission in Washington. Billy's job was to help America build an airforce. Back in Canada, Billy made a speech about that: he said the Germans had nothing to fear from the United States' fighting forces; aircraft production was lagging seriously. Consternation! When he got back to London, early in 1918, he found himself under arrest. The incarceration lasted just ten minutes while Billy wilted under a stiff lecture about his verbal indiscretions.

Billy Bishop was given a new job. He was to form a fighting squadron of his own, the 85th, better known as the Flying Foxes. Training took up most of the late winter and spring. Before leaving for France at the end of May the Flying Foxes in one mammoth binge, managed to consume two hundred bottles of champagne. Their departure was accompanied by a certain relief. "Thank God," a leading actress was heard to mutter, as the curtain rose in a London theatre, "Bishop and his crowd have finally gone to France."

The front was even more hectic than wartime London. The Foxes arrived at the height of the great German spring offensive and were plunged immediately into a "carnival of destruction, which has no parallel in the annals of aviation." By the end of the month the squadron had ten kills to its credit: eight of those were Billy's.

In the mess, the Foxes enjoyed eggs Benedict, chicken livers *en brochette*, ice cream, champagne and Napoleon brandy. They caroused most of the night, flew off each morning on dawn patrol. Billy kept up with them in spite of a mountain of paper work. His favourite time for going out alone after the Huns was the evening, when his administrative duties were done and before the binges began.

The Foxes were soon moved to a permanent aerodrome near St. Omer. Billy was in high spirits: he now had sixty enemy kills confirmed. He took off from the new aerodrome one evening and in eight minutes got two more. Then he received some disheartening news; he was ordered back to London to help form a Canadian flying corps. Billy Bishop was so mad that the following morning he shot down three German planes in half an hour.

His total time with the Flying Foxes in France was just four weeks. In that brief period, with only twelve flying days, he destroyed twenty-five enemy planes, more than Eddie Rickenbacker, the leading American ace, was able to bring down in five months at the front.

On his last day, June 19, 1918, Billy Bishop was invincible. He climbed into a heavy drizzle and headed east toward Ypres, alone. In the clouds he lost his way and came down over Ploegsteert Wood. Just below him were three Pfalz scouts. As Billy swept down on them he spotted two more on his tail. He ignored them and opened up on the three in front from 120 yards. He killed the pilot of the rearmost plane and watched as it went into a vertical dive. The other two, scrambling for cloud cover, locked wings and crashed. Billy pulled up in a steep turn as his two rear attackers slipped past below. He came in at fifty yards and sent the fourth Pfalz crashing. Alone now, his compass broken, his bearings lost, he flew on in the mist, ran into another German two-seater, dispatched it with ten rounds. In fifteen minutes – his last aerial skirmish – Billy Bishop had destroyed five German planes.

The cautious British credited Billy Bishop with seventy-two official kills. The real total undoubtedly exceeded a hundred. As early as 1917, the War Office admitted an additional twenty-three "probable but unconfirmed kills." The RFC was sticky about confirmations. Billy, flying alone, knocked down many of his victims far behind the German lines where no Allied witness could spot the wreckage. Von Richthofen's score, on the other hand, was almost certainly inflated. The Red Baron had eighty kills to his credit when he was shot down in the spring of 1918. At least a dozen of these "victories" were planes that had made forced landings with their pilots alive. Nor did the Red Baron fight alone, as Billy did. Often enough he held himself aloof from battle, let his fellow pilots set up a victim, then swooped at the last moment. His fighting methods, wrote Billy, were "typically German."

When Billy left France, he was the greatest living ace on the Allied side. That record stood until war's end. He had forty productive years left to him but his greatest moments were over. In the dying months of the war there were more medals, more plaudits, more speeches. The inevitable postwar lecture tour followed. It was hugely successful until Billy collapsed onstage from appendicitis. When he returned to the platform, a month later, only ten persons showed up. War heroes were passé. The tour was cancelled.

Billy went into partnership with another Canadian ace, Bill Barker, who had won the VC by taking on single-handedly no fewer than sixty enemy planes and knocking down five of them. The two heroes formed a commercial aviation firm. The Canadian National Exhibition hired them to do stunts over Lake Ontario; the contract was cancelled abruptly when Billy dove directly towards the grandstand and looped at the very last minute, causing panic, fainting and (it was claimed) at least one miscarriage. Then Billy, testing a new two-seater, turned it over on landing, squashed his nose, damaged his eyesight and washed himself out of flying. That was it for the Bishop-Barker partnership.

But Billy's luck held. He invented a successful formula for a quick-drying paint and with the proceeds paid off his debts. He became front man for a Canadian firm in Britain. His contacts and celebrity easily opened doors; his native shrewdness at negotiation gave him a formidable reputation. He had, it was said "the face of an angel and the mind of a murderer." He could not stay still, kept taking on new sports and hobbies, always excelling, always trying to be the best. He played polo, learned golf, took up boxing. He became part of the high society of the Twenties. He chummed around with Ernest Hemingway, Scott Fitzgerald and

LEE KEEDICK *presents*

COL. W. A. BISHOP, V.C., D.S.O., M.C., D.F.C.

THE WORLD'S GREATEST ACE

Decorations:

Victoria Cross
Distinguished Service Order, with Bar
Military Cross
Distinguished Flying Cross
Special Medal British Air Fleet Committee
Legion of Honor
Croix de Guerre with Palm
The Medal of Gold Aero Club of France
Special War Medal Aero Club of America

OFFICIAL RECORD
72
Hun Machines

Unofficial Record
Over 100

Col. BISHOP is Hon. Aide de Camp to Governor General of Canada.

"AIR FIGHTING IN FLANDERS FIELDS"

AVIATION WAS A PRIME FACTOR IN WINNING THE WAR.

COLONEL BISHOP IS THE PREMIER AVIATOR OF THE WAR.

Exclusive Management LEE KEEDICK, 437 FIFTH AVENUE, NEW YORK CITY

One of the posters advertising Bishop's international lecture series.

Josephine Baker, mingled with royalty, drank champagne with Hermann Goering and, like so many others, was wiped out financially in the crash of 1929.

Once again, Billy's social connections came to his aid. He was soon on his feet again, vice-president of an oil company. A pillar of Montreal society, Air Vice-Marshal in the peacetime RCAF, Billy Bishop, impeccable in London-tailored clothes, driven to work by his personal chauffeur, was no longer the callow, hell-raising youth from Owen Sound.

Like his friend Winston Churchill, Billy was sure another war was coming. He began to spend more and more of his time trying to persuade the government to train pilots for the future Armageddon. To encourage the trend he himself joined the Montreal Light Aeroplane Club and took to the air again. On his first outing, he landed the plane on its nose. "Haven't lost my touch," said Billy.

In the summer of 1939, Billy Bishop, now Honorary Air Marshal of the RCAF and head of the Air Advisory Committee, figured out a neat way to sneak American planes into Canada without causing an international incident. The planes were landed at border strips, left purposely "unattended" on the American side, lassoed by Canadian airmen and dragged across, without violating the international boundary or American neutrality. That charade seemed to suit everybody.

After war was declared, Billy Bishop was put in charge of recruiting. The job was full time. For the first time since that earlier war, Billy was completely happy, every minute taken up. But he still made time to learn to play the piano and to practise three to four hours a day. Then he learned to play table tennis; not indifferently, but expertly. Billy always had to have a hobby, always had to be the best.

Billy's pace never faltered. He toured airforce bases, stimulating recruiting, travelling, lecturing, inspecting, even playing a role in a Hollywood movie about the airforce, driving himself once again as he had in those months at Filescamp Farm. In November 1942, in the middle of a speech to air cadets, he collapsed. The doctors said he wouldn't survive, but lucky Billy proved them wrong. He rested, recovered, and went back to work. But a lot of the old steam was gone; when he finally hung up his uniform in 1944, Billy Bishop was close to exhaustion.

In semi-retirement after the war, Billy Bishop, still restless, still curious, took up hobby after hobby. He subscribed to a correspondence course in typing; he learned ice carving; he spent hours reading. And then, one by one, the enthusiasms which had kept him alive were abandoned. Illnesses increased. He spent his winters in Florida but on his last winter he was too tired and too ill to come home. In the early morning of September 10, 1956, Billy Bishop died.

Billy Bishop's obituary appeared in the major dailies in most of the countries in the world. In Canada, his funeral was one of the greatest in living memory. Thousands lined the streets to see Billy go to his grave.

That was in 1956. In January 1975, the American men's magazine, *Argosy*, published a long article about the leading aces of two World Wars. "While World War I produced numbers of aerial 'aces'," the article said, "two names stand out from all the rest: Baron Manfred von Richthofen and Captain Eddie Rickenbacker." The article had a great deal to say about these two. It devoted three-quarters of a column of eulogy to the Red Baron and even more to Captain Eddie. It described certain other notables of World War One, including Roland Garros of France and the Dutch genius, Anthony Fokker. It even published a list of those it claimed were the greatest aces of World War One, with statistics on their respective victories. But in that list and in that text one name was conspicuous by its absence. Nowhere was there any mention of Billy Bishop. In 1975, the Lone Hawk was forgotten.

Bishop with King George V at Windsor Park, 1918

16
The Great Cross-Canada Hike

In the first six months of 1921 there occurred an extraordinary event, which made newspaper headlines from Halifax to Vancouver but which is now forgotten. Four men and one woman walked a distance of 3,650 miles from the Atlantic to the Pacific in a race that has never been copied or equalled. They did it for no particular gain or reward and for no particular reason except for personal satisfaction and, perhaps, for the fleeting fame that it gave them.

There was nothing remarkable about these five. If they had anything in common, apart from a determination to walk across the continent, it was that ordinary quality which is conjured up by such phrases as "average Canadian" or "man on the street." They were neither fanatics nor screwballs, as were the marathon dancers and flagpole sitters of the coming era. They were simply five unexceptional people who emerged from anonymous working-class backgrounds, strode swiftly across a large stage, and then returned almost instantly to anonymity, none of them materially richer for the experience. One is reminded of Andy Warhol's remark that in the future everybody will be famous – for fifteen minutes.

The story begins with a 20-year-old Halifax labourer named Charles Burkman, laid off in January 1921 after a year in the shipyards. Burkman had no intention of racing across Canada. He and an out-of-work acquaintance, Sid Carr, simply decided they would walk west at their own pace, perhaps as far as Vancouver, to look for a job.

Canada that year was in the throes of a depression – the result of the winding down of the wartime boom and the swelling of the labour market by thousands of returned soldiers. Vancouver, then as later, was a kind of mecca for the jobless. In bad times people tend to head for the west coast which is, after all, the one part of

Canada where you can sleep out under the stars for most of the year. As for walking – well, people walked a good deal more in those days. Children, especially in the rural areas, were used to walking several miles to school each day. Many men walked to work. Young men thought nothing of walking young ladies home of an evening. The country was on the edge of the automobile era but the motor car had not yet taken over. Radio was in its infancy; motion pictures had yet to become the universal entertainment. Walking was a pastime as well as a necessity. The Sunday afternoon drive had not yet replaced the Sunday afternoon walk.

Burkman and Carr planned to pay for their trip by selling specially made photographic postcards of themselves along the route at ten cents apiece, a respectable price at a time when newspapers could be purchased for two cents and some magazines for five. They also decided to offer regular dispatches to the Halifax *Herald,* an enterprising paper in those days, which specialized in stunts and contests. The newspaper responded with enthusiasm and offered to buy their dispatches.

The obvious route to take was that of the railways. There was, of course, no Trans-Canada Highway, and although the automobile was becoming popular (there were 1,150 *stolen* in Toronto the previous year), roads tended to be muddy, rutted and winding. In those days all the major Canadian communities (and many minor ones) were on the railroads, not the highways. Burkman and Carr planned to walk the CNR tracks to Maine, take a short cut across that state via the Maine Central right of way to Quebec and then follow the Canadian Pacific roadbed for the rest of the journey.

Neither man was in a hurry. They planned to take at least seven months to reach the west coast and they did not expect to travel more than fifteen miles a day in the winter, although they hoped they might increase the pace when they reached the prairies in the spring. What they envisaged was a kind of leisurely stroll, with time out to view the scenery or to linger in the towns and villages of rural Canada. It didn't work out that way.

The hike might easily have gone unnoticed if the *Herald* had not turned it into news by *saying* it was news – an early example of what the American sociologist Daniel Boorstin has called "the pseudo event." Carr and Burkman were featured on the front pages for two days before they actually set off in the wind and the rain on January 17, to the cheers of a large crowd and the good wishes of the mayor who gave them a personal letter for the mayor of Vancouver. Pathé News was on hand to film the start and in the months that followed Canadian movie audiences would get regular reports on the cross-Canada hike, along with Charlie Chaplin in *The Kid,* Pola Negri in *Passion* and Mary Pickford in *The Love Light.*

All this publicity had its effect. After the first day, Carr, employing a phrase now long in disuse, reported back to the *Herald* that "continental hikers are some pumpkins." As the two men plodded into Windsor Junction at the end of their first fourteen miles they could hear cries of: "Here they come!" That night meals were free and so was lodging; they slept together in the spare bed of a family who requested and got anonymity.

Two days and fifty miles later they were in Truro, feeling a little stiff from the unaccustomed exercise. Again, everything was free: meals and a room at the Stanley Hotel, an evening at the Strand Theatre, and the ultimate accolade – two free suits of Stanfield's unshrinkable long johns.

The temperature was down to ten degrees Fahrenheit the next morning as they set off briskly in the heavy snows, pausing at station houses along the way for free meals and, on one occasion, to listen to the station master entertain them on the piano. It was pleasant, easy going. But then, after five days and ninety-eight miles, they received a piece of news that was to change a leisurely walk into a fierce and often bitter race. In Dartmouth, the rival community across the harbour from Halifax, two other men announced that they would duplicate the feat and that they meant to better the time of the original hikers.

All the publicity had been too much for Jack Behan and his son Clifford. On January 21, the two men appeared at the *Herald's* office, armed with a letter from Dartmouth's mayor, and demanded similar press attention. The *Herald* was delighted to give it to them. The elder Behan made no bones about the competitive aspects of the race: "We are out to overtake Burkman and Carr," he declared, "and I am convinced that we will do so before they reach Montreal."

Both the Behans were "returned men," having served in the front lines with the Halifax Rifles, the father rising to sergeant, the son wounded three times in action. Jack Behan, aged forty-four, was used to walking long distances for he was a letter carrier; he was also an amateur sculler, past president of a local rowing club. Neither man had any money but they planned, also, to sell postcards of themselves en route. The Dartmouth Commercial Club outfitted them with breeches, boots and knapsacks.

Burkman and Carr took up the challenge at once, walking forty-three miles in two days: "You can tell the Dartmouth people that nobody will overtake us at any place between here and Vancouver unless we break our legs."

So now the race was on. Burkman and his partner turned down the luncheon proffered by the Amherst Commercial Club and plunged off into the driving snow before reaching Dorchester, "the hardest day we have had yet." The following day, under even worse conditions, they pushed twenty-seven miles to Moncton. "If we had the Behans along with us we would have shown them what hiking is," Carr wired back. Clearly, however, the fun was gone. The day, Carr wrote, had taken "some of the sap out of us." The Behans were already on the road, eight days behind, but announcing that they would make fewer stops; on their first day out they picked up a few miles on the leaders.

Now an odd thing happened. In spite of their bold reports to the *Herald,* Burkman and Carr slackened off. They loafed around Moncton until 3 p.m. and made only a few miles that day. Clearly, something was wrong. Later events suggest that a rift was developing between the two men – a rift that sprang from the changed complexion of the hike.

Arriving in Truro, the Behans waxed enthusiastic. "This hiking is great fun," Jack Behan reported. "I had no idea the kind of stuff that boy of mine is made of."

And on that same day, a *third* team of hikers, Frank and Jennie Dill, called on the *Herald* and announced that they, too, were prepared to walk at top speed across Canada. One can imagine the glee at the city desk when it was revealed that this was a man and wife team. Up to this point the story had had a whiff of the sports pages about it. Now it would attract a wider audience, espe-

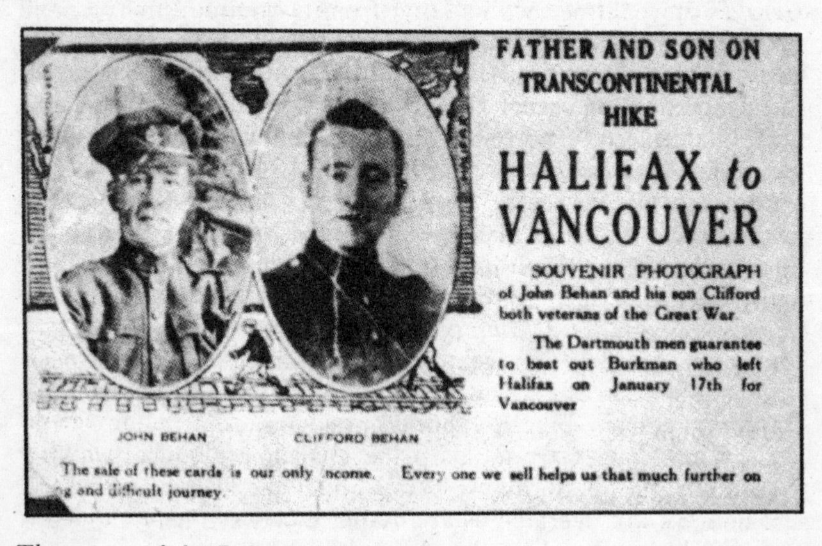

The postcard the Behans sold for ten cents to pay for the hike.

cially at a time when women's aspirations were making news. By 1921, Canada's suffragette movement had managed to push votes for women through in every province except Quebec and Prince Edward Island. Before the year was out, Agnes Macphail, an unknown school teacher from rural Ontario, would become the first woman Member of Parliament.

The Dills had been married for a little less than two years. Frank was a foundry worker in Dartmouth and had been a runner of some distinction in his home town of Windsor, Nova Scotia. But the dominant member of the family was clearly his wife, Jennie, and it is her personality that overshadows that of the others who took part in the cross-Canada hike. She emerges, in fact, from the sere pages of the 1921 newspapers, as a diminutive tigress, the strongest of the lot, fiercely competitive, pushing her husband forward, cajoling, nagging and threatening whenever he seems to falter.

She was a dark little creature weighing 128 pounds at the start – all of it muscle: a fisherman's daughter from Petpeswick Harbour, fond of the outdoors and a good hunter. She was one of the fastest women skaters in the Maritimes. The *Herald* was careful to point out, however, that there was "not a single suggestion of the mannish in her personality."

There was never any doubt, then or later, about who had prompted the pair to enter the race. "It was I who first suggested the trip," said Jennie. "We have both worked hard since we were married and now we are going to see the world." She made it sound like a holiday excursion but it soon ceased to be that. "We have no home ties," said Jennie, "not a chick nor a child." But Frank had a mother to whom he *was* tied. He did his best to phone her regularly, especially during the early stages of the walk.

The Dills announced they would leave on February 1, a week behind the Behans and fifteen days behind Burkman and Carr. They, too, would peddle postcards of themselves at a dime apiece (the nickel had yet to be invented) to finance the journey.

But even before the Dills left, the team of Burkman and Carr had a falling out. The split occurred on the banks of the Petitcodiac River on January 28, and it was Carr who made the announcement. Events were pushing him into a position which he could not control. He had not planned on a mad scramble from sea to sea and he said so. "I won't be forced into racing across Canada," he declared and took the train back to Halifax. One can sympathize with him now; nobody did then. Burkman became the hero of the hour, "the lone hiker," as the press was to dub him for the next five months.

The loss of his partner was a considerable blow to Burkman. Events were to prove that two hikers could force the pace – something mile runners have always known. And then there was the loneliness; it is not much fun to walk thirty or forty miles a day through empty country with no one to talk to or to urge you on. Burkman felt Carr's loss immediately but he plunged ahead nevertheless, covering a record thirty-three miles that day. At Sussex he announced his intention of continuing: "I have made up my mind to walk to Vancouver and if I have my health I will do it . . . . I have no hindrance now."

This attitude was much applauded and the public enthusiasm elated Burkman. Crowds gathered all along the way to wish him well en route to Saint John, which he reached the following evening. Scarcely pausing to rest his feet, he went to a dance and then the following morning hiked another twenty-four miles to Welsford, New Brunswick, totally confident of maintaining his lead. In Halifax, a group of businessmen announced they'd give him five hundred dollars if he reached Vancouver in six months.

The date was January 31, and Charles Burkman at that point had covered 298 miles. The Behans had walked 158, but they had narrowed the final gap between themselves and the leader by 23 miles.

The following morning, two thousand Haligonians gathered before the *Herald* building to bid Godspeed to Frank and Jennie Dill. The pair did not make very good time at first, held back by heavy snow and continually delayed by curious onlookers, many of them women – far more than had turned out for the others. At Truro, twelve hundred people cheered them and they sold 220 postcards. There was, of course, more free underwear from Stanfield's.

On that same day, Charles Burkman crossed into Maine. He made twenty miles in heavy snow and slept that first night in a logging camp. The Behans gained another six miles on him. They were pushing very hard; the following day they managed to cover a record forty-four miles, increasing their pace in the last two hours of the day to four and a half miles an hour – a very fast clip indeed. (The U.S. Army recommends an average speed of three miles an hour for long marches.) By Saint John, the Behans had gained a full two days on Burkman.

The Dills were still being held up by admirers. All along the route people were pressing gifts of food upon them, but there was no time to accept them all. At East Mines, the station agent, a Mr. McManaman, was lying in wait for them with tea, cakes, chocolates and cigars and nothing would do but that they stop. They

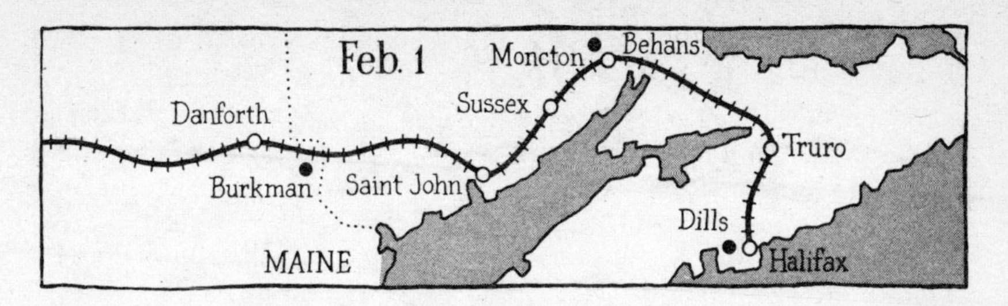

were, after all, celebrities, albeit instant ones, and everybody wanted to reach out and touch them in some way. So flustered was Mr. McManaman at the presence of real, live celebrities, munching cookies in his station house, that he quite forgot that he had prepared other refreshments for them. After the Dills left he could be seen trotting down the tracks, his arms laden with more gifts, urging them to slacken their pace.

The Behans had developed a system for walking along the rails in the snow. Jack walked on one rail, Clifford on the other; between them they carried a long spanner to maintain their balance. In Maine, Burkman got behind a snowplough, which made walking easier.

The Dills tried to adopt the Behan method but because Frank was tall and Jennie a little bit of a thing, they were forced to abandon it and walk on the ties. They were still losing ground. In Sackville there was an unscheduled delay; when the couple passed Mount Allison University, a covey of young women burst from that institution and fairly swamped Frank. Jennie, who wrote most of the dispatches to the *Herald,* commented with just a touch of acerbity that "I hope we do not pass any more girl college towns on this hike."

Back home, the wiseacres had been predicting that no woman could hike farther than Truro. Jennie was out to prove them wrong and that resolve gave her a competitive edge. "Tomorrow," she wired on February 3, "we will at least go as far as Moncton, twenty miles away, and perhaps *if Frank can stand it,* I'll take him further." That one sentence tells us a great deal about Jennie Dill.

On February 9, as the Behans entered Maine, Charles Burkman crossed the Quebec border and his pursuers gave up any hope of catching him before he reached Montreal. They were still setting the fastest pace: 23 miles a day, compared to 21.5 for Burkman and only 17.5 for the Dills. Burkman, because he was carrying on alone, was very popular. In Danforth, Maine, one pastor shooed his congregation out of the church and urged them to buy Burkman's postcards to help him on his way. "The fact that he has plugged along alone has won him a legion of friends," the *Herald*

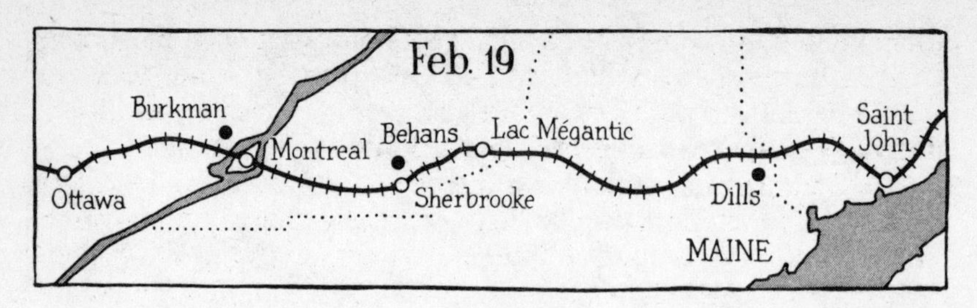

reported. There were fears for his safety in the lonely country west of Sherbrooke, Quebec, and one Springhill miner wrote in advising that he arm himself with a rifle to ward off wolves. But he reached Sherbrooke safely on February 15, having walked twenty-one miles that day. Said he: "I laugh when I think of the boast Jack Behan made about catching me before I reached Montreal. Already I can smell dear old Craig Street and hear the feet of the French girls skipping along St. Lawrence Main."

That day the Dills reached Saint John and were almost jailed as vagrants by a policeman who did not recognize Jennie in her breeches and knapsack until she was a few paces from him. He had heard all about her, of course – everybody had. A thousand people were waiting to welcome her farther down the line and one CNR trainman had even composed a poem to her:

And if your Frank gets weary
And talks of turning back,
Give him a dose of Nerveline
Or a bottle of Taniac.
Paint his spine with iodine
Put hemlock oil on, too,
But keep on going, Jennie,
Whatever else you do.

As the doggerel suggests, there was no doubt in the public's mind who was the stronger member of the Dill team. Women crowded about Jennie, asking questions, surprised by her diminutive size and astonished at her male attire (breeches and high boots), unusual in those circumspect days when dresses still trailed to the ankle. She was not in the least concerned about the slowness of the pace, confident that they could pick up the lost distance as the weeks went by. "By the time I get to Montreal I will be as hard as spikes," said she.

By this time, railwaymen along the route were placing wagers on the outcome of the race. Passengers on passing trains waved at the hikers, cheered and tossed out newspapers, candy, inspirational notes and sometimes letters from home (although most mail arrived quite legitimately at post offices along the route). All the walkers were offered rides on sleighs, cars and trains and all refused. Were they being tested? They couldn't be sure.

On February 19, one month and two days from the time he left Halifax, Charles Burkman reached Montreal, then a city of some six hundred thousand. It was, perhaps, the finest hour of his hike. The streets were black with people out to greet him on a crisp Saturday afternoon. The *Herald* had a man in Montreal to describe the triumph and he rose splendidly to the occasion:

"Bronzed like an Indian and aglow with radiant health, Charles Burkman, slim and boyish looking, strode into Montreal Saturday afternoon. As with head thrown back and chest out he marched through the streets he was a notable figure, youth and energy vibrated from him."

Burkman stayed at the Windsor, then Montreal's smartest hostelry and, in spite of his thirty-mile hike that day, spent the evening dancing. "He tripped the light fantastic for many hours and had no lack of admiration from his partners," was the way the press described it. Those, after all, were the dancing years. The one-step, the two-step and the waltz were giving way to new and faster steps and glides (such as the Gaby Glide) springing out of the music of ragtime and often imitating the struts of birds and walks of animals: the Alligator Crawl, the Turkey Trot, the Kangaroo Hop, the Bunny Hug and the longer-lasting Fox Trot. Newspapers were already referring to Burkman as "the smiling, happy-go-lucky daredevil" who was "dancing his way across the continent," and gushy letters were beginning to arrive from Halifax girls. "I have an appetite like a horse," Burkman declared, "and I sleep like a log." All that dancing held him up for a day. He slept well into Sunday and did not resume his hike until Monday morning.

At that juncture, the Behans, walking twenty-two miles in below-freezing weather, had already reached Sherbrooke, while the Dills had entered Maine. Burkman was holding to his average pace of 21.7 miles a day but the others had increased theirs slightly. The Behans were now making 24 miles a day while the Dills were averaging slightly more than 19 miles a day.

It was hard going in Maine. Jennie and her husband found themselves struggling through snow that often reached to their waists before the plough came through. It was so cold that one night frost formed on the comforter in the room in which they were sleeping. On a sharp downhill turn they were almost run over

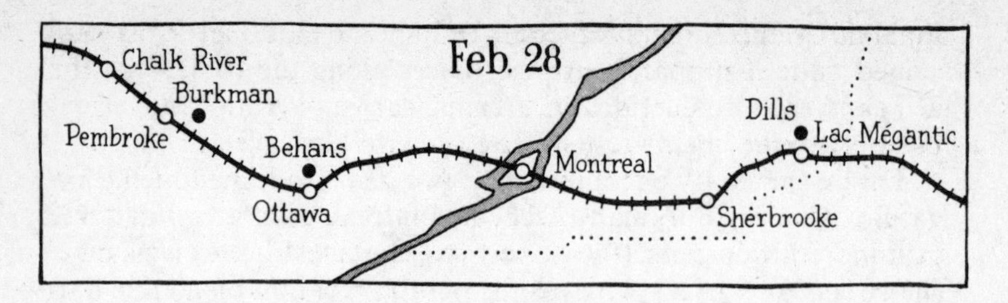

by a train that came coasting silently behind them. One day they made only eleven miles, but their spirits remained high. It was obvious that Jennie admired the lonely Burkman. "Good luck to him," she wired, when she learned that he was already en route to Ottawa.

But Burkman lost his way trying to take a short cut to the capital and the Behans gained another day. Now they were only four days behind. In Montreal they were fêted, as Burkman had been, and given gifts of tobacco and cigars from Benson and Hedges and new boots from the Knights of Columbus. Burkman, meanwhile, spent a full day in Ottawa being lionized by Nova Scotia members and senators. The new Conservative prime minister, Arthur Meighen signed his logbook; and the Honourable F. B. McCurdy, a Halifax business leader who was Minister of Public Works, played him a game of 100-up on his own billiard table.

The Behans were still pressing him hard. On February 28, they walked thirty-five miles to Burkman's seventeen. "We know we are closing the gap on Burkman and can almost hear him pant as he leads us in the race," Jack Behan reported. Burkman began to make extravagant prophecies that he could not hope to fulfill. He vowed to walk fifty-three miles to Pembroke "or bust," but rain and darkness frustrated that attempt. By this time the Behans were in Ottawa. The Dills, at Lac Mégantic, Quebec, were still losing ground.

Hampered by blisters, Burkman kept plugging along. At Chalk River, he reached the thousand-mile point in the walk after a hard thirty-two mile hike. He scoffed at reports that the Behans were on his heels. Said he: "if they are, my heels are much longer than I think." But the Behans, who thought nothing of walking until midnight, announced they'd catch him before he reached Winnipeg. In the empty, wolf-infested forests of northern Ontario, Burkman finally acquired a gun and lost a day at North Bay having it repaired. No one knew exactly where his pursuers were; for the first time since leaving Halifax they had failed to report.

The Dills, meanwhile, having celebrated their second wedding anniversary by plunging through heavy snow in the eastern townships of Quebec, had finally reached Montreal. Jennie was interviewed by a Miss M. J. Dewar, a society writer, to whom she confided that she considered the hike a honeymoon trip. "Rouge or powder would have been wasted on Mrs. Dill's healthy, tanned complexion," Miss Dewar wrote. "The financial cares of the trip weighed not at all on her as they did on her serious husband who perhaps realized more than she the gravity of the undertaking." Jenny had only one goal in mind: to prove that a woman could do whatever a man could do.

The Dills did not rest in Montreal, as the others had. Ahead of them the Behans had again stepped up the pace. At North Bay on March 10, they were only a day behind Burkman. A Halifax man bet a thousand dollars they'd catch him by March 12.

On March 11, the Behans were only nine miles behind their quarry. Burkman had devised an ingenious contraption that enabled him to walk on one rail while balancing himself with a stick that ran on a roller skate on the other. In this way he held off the Behans on the 12th and the Halifax plunger lost his money. But the gap remained narrow. At Sudbury, Burkman voluntarily gave up half a day visiting old cronies and didn't leave until half past one in the afternoon. The Behans moved into town later that same day and didn't stop.

Now the contest became heated. When he reached Chelmsford, Burkman asked a friendly telegraph operator to wire back to Azilda, a station between Sudbury and Chelmsford, to see if the Behans were planning to spend the night there. If so, Burkman would sleep at Chelmsford, secure in the knowledge that he held the lead. The Behans, however, fooled him. When they arrived in Azilda they told the operator they were stopping for the night. Instead they plunged on to Chelmsford. Burkman, meanwhile, went to bed in the Algoma Hotel. At two that morning the proprietor woke him to reveal that the Behans had arrived and were snoring away in the next room. Burkman dressed quietly and slipped off into the dark; but the Behans, who seemed alert to every possibility, soon learned of his escape and followed. In the faint light of dawn, five miles out of Larchwood, they finally caught up with him.

It was a memorable meeting. The rivals, strangers to each other, exchanged greetings and congratulations like old friends and then, in Jack Behan's words, "started off like three schoolgirls," the Behans walking on one rail (a remarkable balancing act) and Burkman on the other, keeping fairly even all the way. They stayed even for the rest of the day, arriving together at Cartier. Behan reported that "we hit a clip of 4 miles an hour for 5

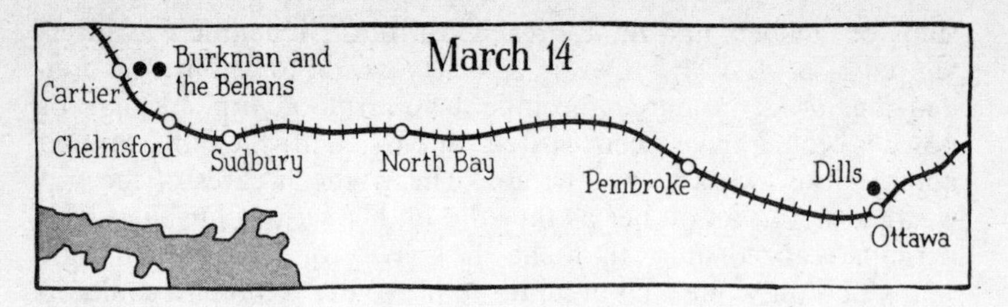

hours but Burkman, with his patent, stuck like glue and beat us 2 yards at the finish."

The Dills had reached Ottawa. Here they met Prime Minister Meighen and also the Liberal leader, William Lyon Mackenzie King, who was already campaigning against the Conservative party on whom he would inflict a crushing defeat the following December. The hike to Ottawa had given the Dills "the best day yet." Though they had taken one day longer than Burkman and five days longer than the Behans to reach the capital, they were beginning to gain back some of the time lost in the East.

Now the Behans found themselves locked in a duel with Charles Burkman as the three men made their way across the lonely Pre-Cambrian desert of northern Ontario. Here, in a land of stunted trees, cracked grey rocks and muskeg, the rivals stayed even. Then, on March 18, Burkman opened up a slight lead and reached Woman River ahead of the Behans. They expected that he would sleep there, since it was late in the day; but he fooled them and trudged on to the camp of an Italian section gang. The following day the Behans were led astray by an Indian guide who promised, but did not deliver, a short cut. They lost two days, blamed Burkman for the deception and confessed to feeling glum because their funds were low and their postcards weren't selling. In northern Ontario in 1921 there were few customers.

Somewhere in the dark forests to the east, the Dills had an adventure. A timber wolf sprang out of the bushes directly at Frank. Jennie downed it with a single shot. "I was by no means excited," she told her readers. She could not conceal her continuing admiration for Burkman who, though she had never met him, she now treated as an intimate friend: "We are hoping that Charlie wins and we only wish we had as many friends along the route as this boy has. Everywhere we go people speak in glowing terms of Burkman and state that they hope he beats the Behans." But the Dills were also stepping up the pace and increasing their average daily.

The Behans caught up with Burkman again at White River, traditionally the coldest spot in Canada. He had been keeping his whereabouts a secret, refusing even to wire the paper, to prevent his rivals finding him. That night all three men gave lectures describing their journey at the local YMCA. Two days later, at a little place called King, Burkman made another attempt to elude the Behans, slipping away before dawn in the bitter cold – minus 11 degrees Fahrenheit. He had not gone ten miles before he heard a familiar voice hailing him from the rear; it was Jack Behan. That day they walked an additional thirty-three miles to Heron Bay. The following morning the Behans managed to get off ahead of Burkman. Along the route people were saying that they slept like dogs – with one eye open.

Thus it came about that Jack Behan and his son Clifford were the first of the cross-Canada hikers to see the frozen expanse of Lake Superior. And here, at a watering station, they encountered the special train of the Governor General, Victor Christian William Cavendish, the 9th Duke of Devonshire, making the last of his cross-Canada tours before his term ended in July. Jack Behan made so bold as to approach a policeman to ask if the Duke would sign his logbook. The constable refused but Behan insisted on seeing the Duke's secretary who, having a more highly developed sense of public relations, immediately invited the hikers on board. The Governor General, a hefty, mustached figure, signed the book while the Duchess offered them a silver basket of fruit, urging them to take it all. This ritual complete, the vice-regal train puffed off, with the Duke and Duchess waving cheerily from the observation platform and the Behans, their mouths full of fruit, waving back until the train was out of sight.

Burkman had vanished again. "I found that sometimes telegraph wires leak," he explained later. "Jack Behan is pretty chummy with some of the folk up this way. I know that every day he arrived at a telegraph office he would try and locate me." On March 31, a dreadful blizzard hit the Middleton area. The Behans were warned not to attempt to move in the white-out but, having heard rumours that Burkman had passed them in the night, they set out anyway and managed to cover sixteen miles in spite of the raging storm. No living creature, least of all Burkman, crossed their path, which was hazardous in the extreme. At one stage they were forced to crawl nervously across a long trestle suspended sixty feet above a canyon. But where was Burkman? Had he been lost in the driving snows?

The following day was April Fool's Day: still no sign of Burkman. That day the Dills walked a record thirty-five miles with Jennie (by her own account) egging on her faltering husband for the last ten. The next afternoon, at Cavers, Ontario, Jack Behan and

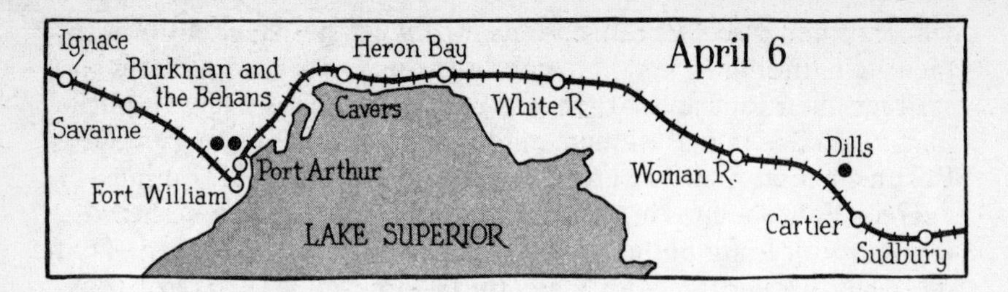

his son were picking up their mail at the post office when Burkman walked in and clapped them each on the back. He had hiked thirty-nine miles to catch them.

The rival hikers were glad enough of each other's company in the bleak nights that followed. They walked in the dark, always aware of the wolves lurking just beyond the dim circles cast by their flashlights. Stopping one night in an empty cabin, they shivered in the gloom as the wolves just outside the door howled at the moon.

The trio reached Port Arthur on April 6. This was Burkman's home town – his parents still lived here – and hundreds were at the station to welcome him. He had decided that nothing would prevent him from spending two full days with his friends and relatives: "I promised them that at home and I shall keep my promise. I had hoped, though, when I made that promise to have at least 7 or 8 days lead on the Behans, but since I have not there is no use to cry over spilt milk." He fully expected to make up the lost ground en route to Winnipeg because he knew all the short cuts from his boyhood days.

The Behans did not linger but moved right on to Fort William. "It may seem unfair of us to leave Burkman at Port Arthur," Jack Behan wrote, "but this is a race."

One does not have to read too deeply between the lines of the chatty newspaper dispatches to realize that Jennie Dill's admiration for Charles Burkman was causing domestic difficulties. In one of her earlier dispatches, Mrs. Dill had hinted at dissension when she wrote that Frank believed that Burkman was purposely lagging behind in order that he might walk the rest of the way with Jennie. Frank's suspicions had been aroused by the fact that Burkman was sending letters back to Mrs. Dill. "It's not often that I sigh," Jennie reported. "The other day I got a letter from Charlie Burkman and then today I got another one .... I told [Frank] that he was silly but he said it looked fishy to him ...."

This titillating hint at a romance with a woman he had never met was dispelled by Burkman when he left his home town. "He [Frank] need have no fear of me," he wrote. "I did write twice to encourage her along, as I think she is the pluckiest woman in Canada . . . . However, I am not waiting for any woman." After two days' rest, he admitted, "it took quite a bit of courage to start again." That day the Behans reached Savanne, 1,851 miles from Halifax, the half-way point on the great hike.

The Behans enjoyed being in the lead. They were, reported Jack, "feeling like two jack rabbits." Once again, Burkman's reports ceased abruptly and it was assumed he was again attempting a short cut. Actually, he had injured his hip falling off a slippery rail. It took him eight days to struggle on to Ignace, Ontario, which he reached on April 16, the day Babe Ruth hit his first home run of the 1921 season; the Behans had covered the same distance in four. The Dills, meanwhile, had arrived in Port Arthur and were closing fast.

Now the prairies beckoned – Winnipeg, then the third-largest city in Canada and after that Regina and Calgary. They were small towns then; Winnipeg, by far the largest, had fewer than 180,000 people. There were no skyscrapers. (The tallest building in the whole country was the new Royal Bank headquarters at King and Yonge in Toronto, whose nineteen storeys had recently overshadowed the fifteen-storey Dominion Bank across the way. Bankers, then as later, indulged in a literal form of one-upmanship.) Prairie horizons were dominated by church towers and grain elevators. Suburbs, drive-ins, shopping centres, supermarkets, motels, stop lights and parking lots all belonged to the future. The Canada which the 1921 hikers saw was still a country of villages and farms. More people lived in the rural areas than in the cities and one-third of the work force was employed in agriculture. The railway, not the highway, was the lifeline of the nation and the names of the villages that turn up in the hikers' logbooks – Nemegos, Cavers, Molson, Lydiat, Elkhorn, Wapella, Herbert, Enfold, Gleichen – have a musty, nostalgic ring to them; most of them are long gone, by-passed and left to shrivel away by later ribbons of asphalt.

The Behans reached Winnipeg on April 20 and promptly bathed their feet in the cold waters of the Red River. Burkman, recovered from his injury, had walked forty-five miles to Kenora that day and filed a report that had some of the flavour of a subtitle from one of William S. Hart's immensely popular western films: "I passed through several towns so early in the morning that the inhabitants were sleeping soundly, and the lone hiker departed without stopping to be greeted."

But Burkman's reports were growing terser as his daily mileage rates became more uneven. It became obvious that his morale was

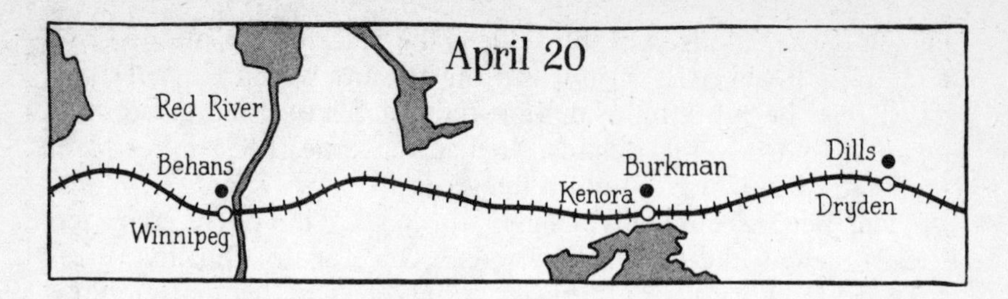

weakening and that he was reluctant to reveal how quickly he was falling behind. Even though the Behans took two days off to visit old army buddies in Winnipeg, Burkman was still a week behind them when he reached the prairie capital. The Dills, however, were picking up speed. The worst rainstorm of the trip did not stop them, as it had stopped Charles Burkman; they walked for twenty-seven miles and, according to the irrepressible Jennie, "had the grandest time."

It took Burkman 101 days to reach Winnipeg. The Behans made it in 86. The Dills managed to do it in 89 and were beginning to realize that they might win the race. "It is the Behans we are trying to catch," Jennie wrote. "I feel rather sorry for Burkman, who has been travelling in hard luck of late."

The days of blizzards and drifts were over. In the prairie spring, the snow patches vanished to reveal the glistening black of the world's richest soil. Soon there would be new obstacles: biting sandstorms, oppressive heat waves, maddening clouds of mosquitoes. But in spite of that, all five hikers made the fastest time of the trip crossing the plains. Burkman's feet were a real problem; his continuing blisters caused him to lose ground to the others. On May 9, while the Dills were passing through Whitewood, Saskatchewan, they were hailed by a telephone operator who connected them with Burkman only twenty miles ahead at Broadview. Unable to struggle on farther, the bottoms of both heels almost raw, he waited for them to catch up. For the past two weeks, he confided, he had barely been able to walk. They left him behind the following day and hiked fifty-one miles to Indian Head.

So now the contest was between the Dills and the Behans, who realized they were being pressed hard by the wiry little Jennie. "We will surely have to step out," was the way Jack Behan put it. Because of the heat, they travelled at night, reaching Medicine Hat on May 17 after a thirty-two mile hike. But the Dills were still gaining, having walked forty-four miles that day. They continued to gain in the days that followed; by May 22 they had cut the Behans' lead to sixty-one miles. It was Jennie who was forcing the pace and she was clearly proud of that role, as her dispatch from

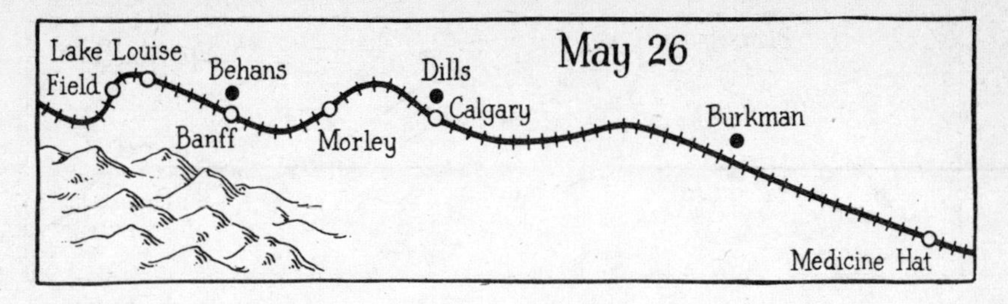

Bassano, on May 23, indicates:

"Race well in hand. Few will ever know what the struggle meant to me, although I feel fine .... Frank will never forgive me for the manner in which I have made him walk. When he wanted to rest I wanted to keep going, and while I do not think that Frank is a quitter, I pride myself with the thought that I have kept him going .... When we passed Burkman I felt sorry for him. Then I got to saying to myself, "Well; he is a man and he should be able to look after himself." I have often thought that if Burkman had a wife he would make better progress .... This wonderful hike has taught me a great lesson which I shall endeavour to teach my sex when the contest is over. The subject is not what men can do women can do, but what men have done women CAN MORE THAN DO."

There was a problem looming up, however. Frank Dill had a host of friends in Calgary, which the Behans reached on May 24, Victoria Day – a more important holiday then than July 1. The Dills were only two days behind them and Jennie was beside herself with fear that Frank might want to dally with his cronies: "I do hope that he will not stay longer than to get a bite to eat. I tell him that we will have lots of time to stay off and see our friends on the way back and that we should devote every minute of the time now to the hike."

Her worst fears were about to be realized. The Behans slipped out of the sleeping town, still bedecked with flags and bunting, at 7 a.m. on the 25th. They walked forty-one miles into the foothills and slept that night at Morley. At that point the Dills were still hiking along. They reached Calgary at two in the morning, having covered fifty-two miles. Jennie was still alert enough to dispatch a wire to Halifax: "This has been the longest hike we have made .... Frank would have been quite willing to stop at the 40 mile mark but I said, 'No, Frank, I am hungry to win the race, and there are Beans ahead.' 'All right, girlie, I am after the Beans if it takes all the pork out of me.'" Jennie admitted that she was tired but added, proudly, that she would soon be back in Halifax "where you

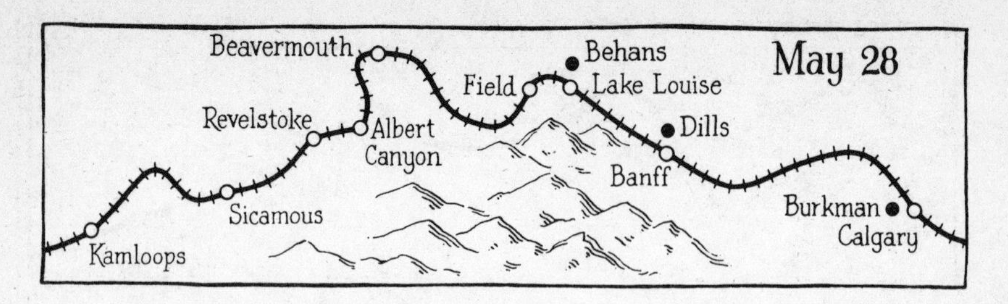

can all see what hiking has done for 'poor, frail Mrs. Dill.'"

To Jennie's grinding frustration, Frank's friends, all former Haligonians seeking their fortune in the cattle town, bore him off to the Kiwanis Club and kept him there until late afternoon. The couple was hard put to make ten miles in an unseasonable hailstorm before seeking refuge in a section house. There is more than a little bitterness still lingering in the report that Jennie filed almost a week later: "I do not think that I will ever forgive Frank for the long stay he made in Calgary, when he 'went out with the boys.' I told him not to stay more than 10 minutes and he stayed almost that many hours, and we lost practically a day and allowed the Behans to get out of our clutches for the time being." One suspects that the male readers of the Halifax *Herald* might at this point have been viewing the plight of Frank Dill with the same kind of sympathy which they had hitherto reserved for Charles Burkman, still plugging along gamely in the rear.

The Behans, meanwhile, having reached Banff at midnight, "so tired that we could hardly step over a match," were suffering nosebleeds brought on by the unaccustomed altitude. They were so exhausted that they could not move on the next day. Jack Behan had lost fourteen of his original 152 pounds. On May 28, with the Dills in Banff, the Behans were sleeping on the station platform at Lake Louise. The next day they crossed the Great Divide. Burkman at this point had passed through Calgary and was more cheerful – "in the pink of condition and in great spirits."

The race grew tighter. The Behans left Field on the morning of May 30; the Dills arrived on the same afternoon. Charles Burkman wrote: "Some, I suppose, will criticize me for letting a woman pass me, but few know what I have done since I left Halifax. It has been a hard, long, lonesome grind and many times I would have felt different if I had company, but I decided to stick and stick I will until I reach Vancouver." Anybody reading those words could not help but admire Charles Burkman.

At Beavermouth, the Dills lost a full day to the Behans; the next sleeping place was several hours distant and they did not have the strength to go further. That same day, June 1, was Clifford Behan's finest. He and his father were nearing Albert Can-

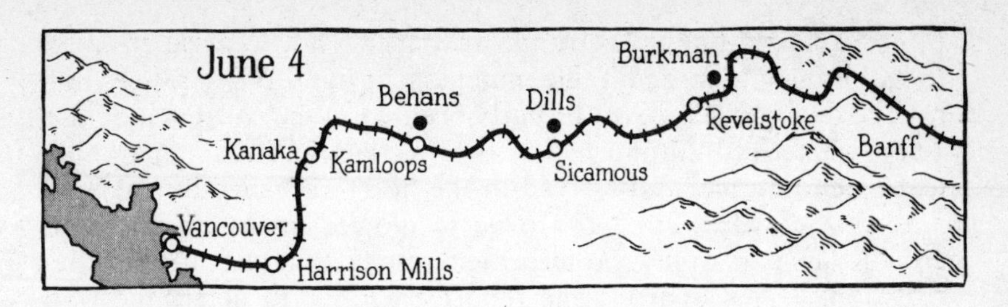

yon, within twenty miles of Revelstoke, when he fell to the ground, a spasm of pain searing his back. He urged his father to continue alone while he took the train to Revelstoke. Jack Behan went on "almost at a trot" and found Clifford in bed at the Revelstoke YMCA. A doctor had diagnosed his ailment as a cold in the muscle, probably caused by sleeping on the open platform at Lake Louise, and had prescribed rest.

Clifford stayed in bed for a few hours and then, so he wouldn't be accused of cheating, took the midnight train back to Albert Canyon. In the early hours of June 2 he repeated the walk alone to Revelstoke, only then realizing how difficult it must have been for Charles Burkman, trudging on, day after day, without human companionship. He arrived at 7 a.m. and after a few hours' sleep headed west with his father.

With the end in sight, the pace again began to accelerate. On June 3, each team walked twenty-six miles. On June 4, the Dills walked twenty-nine miles to Sicamous, British Columbia, but it was not enough. The Behans, afraid to sit down for more than a few minutes for fear of falling asleep, pushed on for fifty miles to Kamloops. At this point the Behans were 250 miles from Vancouver, the Dills, 334.

By June 8, the Dills had again pulled within a day of the leaders, but the pace was taking its toll. "It was a terrible ordeal we went through today," Jennie wired. The Behans were also exhausted. "The trip is wearing us both down," Jack reported. The Dills had set out, in their own words, "to see the world," but that objective had long since been discarded. The scenery was magnificent – the green expanse of Shuswap Lake, the frothing Fraser biting through its canyon – but there was no time now to look at the scenery; as Vancouver grew nearer the rest periods grew shorter. At Kanaka, 149 miles from their goal, Jennie reported gamely that she was in fine trim, "but poor Frank. He has had enough." Frank's feet were bothering him, "but he never complains." Burkman, meanwhile, racing across British Columbia, managed to walk forty-nine miles in one day to reach Kamloops and then pressed on again after only a few hours' rest.

On the morning of June 10, the Behans arrived at Harrison

Mills, just sixty-one miles from Vancouver. They were determined to reach the city in one single, magnificent jump. They rested during the day and set off in the early evening in the soft Pacific rain. They walked continuously for twenty-two hours, a remarkable feat of endurance, and arrived in the heart of Vancouver at 2:30 p.m. on Saturday, June 11, to be swallowed up by an immense crowd. The pair were weatherbeaten, tanned and haggard with exhaustion. "It was hard," one reporter wrote, "to determine who was the father and who was the son."

But who had won the race? Jack Behan was confused about the kind of victory they had achieved. They had certainly come in first, but the Dills appeared to be making better time. They had covered eighty-eight miles in two days and were now at Harrison Mills, where they got the news of the Behans' arrival. Jennie was chagrined and again blamed that fatal stopover in Calgary. However, she added, "unless something entirely unexpected happens we will win the race anyway from a time standpoint." She did not congratulate the Behans.

At North Bend, on June 12, Burkman wired his own thoughts: "I know I'm beaten in the great trans-Canada hike, but I'm going to finish it out and believe me I'll make better time in the home stretch than any of the other hikers." And so he did, walking from Field to Vancouver in just twelve days. The Behans had taken fourteen; the Dills took sixteen.

Jennie and her husband reached Vancouver on Tuesday, June 14, at 5:30 p.m. Mrs. Dill, it was reported, "looked more as if she had been on a picnic." She was fifteen pounds lighter than when she had left Halifax, a lean, hard-muscled 113 pounds. The Halifax *Herald* immediately declared that she and Frank were the winners; they had taken 134 days to cross the continent, four days fewer than their rivals, whom Jennie accused of cheating by sneaking aboard a train on the last few miles of their trip in order not to be defeated by a woman. It is a charge for which there is no substantiation.

Burkman was only a few days behind the Dills and he, too, received a warm welcome. He had taken 150 days to cross the country, two months shorter than the hike he had originally planned. During that period, other events of greater significance had occupied the headlines. In Boston, two anarchists, Nicola Sacco, a fish pedlar, and Bartolomeo Vanzetti, a shoemaker, were arrested for murder; their trial would become a political *cause célèbre*. Elsewhere, Marie Stopes was organizing the Birth Control League of America. And in May, in a barn near Guelph, Ontario, the Communist Party of Canada held its charter meeting.

A reception for all five followed and a group portrait was taken to commemorate the event. In the coarse-screened photograph the four men looked remarkably alike in their straw hats and cloth caps: clean-shaven, square-jawed Canadians, a little on the rustic side, totally unremarkable. Only Jennie stands out, standing a little forward of the others; and on those dark, mannish features there is something very akin to a smirk of triumph.

Once they had stopped walking, the hikers ceased to be newsworthy and all references to them vanished from the papers. None made money from the feat; and there is no evidence that the promises made at the height of the publicity ($500 from Halifax businessmen if Burkman made it in six months; "thousands" from a calendar company if Jack Behan made it in five) were ever fulfilled. In fact, the hike probably cost all the contestants some money. The Dills, for instance, spent five hundred dollars – a substantial sum in those days – and this was only partially defrayed by postcard sales.

Once the hike was over all five vanished into obscurity. Burkman, apparently, remained in Montreal; his name, as far as can be discovered, never again appeared in the newspapers. Frank Dill lived for only a few years after the event; he died in 1928. Jennie remarried and died in Halifax in 1941. The Behans, who outlived the others, moved to Massachusetts, where Jack Behan, aged eighty, was interviewed in 1956. It was he who had the last word on the great cross-Canada hike:

"We came home broke, our families in debt and we couldn't get work," he said. "We had to move to the States to pay our debts."

WOMAN SMASHES HIKING RECORD

Mr. and Mrs. John Dill Arrive in Vancouver from Halifax—Walked

Covered 3700 Miles on Foot in 134 Days [illegible]ring Letters to Re[illegible]ts Here

17 The Mysterious Safari of Charles Bedaux

It is not possible to contemplate the long list of luxuries that Charles Bedaux insisted on taking into the bush of British Columbia in the summer of 1934 without a small tingle of admiration. There was folly in it, of course; idiocy might be a better word. But the sheer *panache* of it! Here was a man reputedly setting out to explore country that was only partially mapped – country so rugged that it had defeated the Klondike stampeders with their iron rations of bacon and beans: country that had driven a party of Mounted Police to despair and exhaustion when they tried to hack a trail through it: a land of tangled forests, raging cataracts, gloomy swamps and chill mountain peaks. Yet Charles Bedaux had no more intention of roughing it than an Indian rajah setting out on a tiger hunt. The famous Nile picnic that the Duke of Sutherland once gave for the future Edward VII springs to mind: the provisions on that occasion included three thousand bottles of champagne, four thousand bottles of wine and liquors and twenty thousand bottles of soda water. The Nile is not the Rocky Mountain Trench, but Bedaux's own list of life's necessities, which he proposed to take into the Peace River and across the top of British Columbia to tidewater on the Alaska Panhandle, comes close to rivalling the Edwardian shopping list.

There was champagne, of course, cases of it; and French wines, both red and white, of good vintages. And case after case of those particular comestibles without which life would be scarcely bearable: pâté de foie gras and caviar, truffles and chicken livers, Devonshire cream and candied fruits. And the equipment! Fireproof tents woven from asbestos fibre; folding tables of aluminum; chairs, beds, bathtubs and patented washbowls; bush toilets of the latest design; nests of French cooking pots; rugs and cushions, tropical suits, cashmere sweaters, fur parkas and quilted pants, all of which Bedaux felt that he and his companions would require while roughing it in the bush. Twenty tons of gear and provisions! Entire armies have travelled on less. The Bedaux army consisted of forty-three persons, including a Spanish maid. The equipment was loaded onto five Citroën half-tracks, and later, when these failed, onto no fewer than one hundred and thirty packhorses. One horse carried nothing but ladies' shoes. Another was loaded down with a small library of French novels. If nothing else, Bedaux had style.

That, alas, is the only commendable thing about him. Had Bedaux been an engaging eccentric one might warm to him. Unfortunately he was a hateful man, apparently without humour, a martinet and a fascist, with all the bad qualities of a self-made millionaire and few of the good.

He was a creature of his period, a genuine Mystery Man of International Intrigue, the kind of shadowy figure that kept popping up in the novels of E. Phillips Oppenheim. When he died, by his own hand, the *New York Times* remarked that "there was an element of fantasy about his involved existence, a maze of loose ends, as there was about the lives of Sir Basil Zaharoff, Ivar Krueger, Serge Stavisky and Alfred Loewenstein." The *Times* went on to point out that Bedaux was the fourth of that group to meet with an unnatural end. Only the enigmatic Sir Basil died in bed of natural causes.

Bedaux moved in the same circles as these fallen titans – a world of international finance and government, of kingmakers and kingbreakers, of backstage manipulations and political wheeler-dealing, both democratic and totalitarian. His highly placed cronies included Herr von Ribbentrop, the Duke of Windsor and Pierre Laval. As John A. Macdonald once said of the Canadian steamship king, Hugh Allan, his only politics was money. In the end that would be Bedaux's undoing.

But when he arrived in Canada in 1934, few people knew much about Charles Eugene Bedaux, and what they were told, thanks to his own carefully orchestrated publicity, was all flattering. His lunatic escapade into the forests and muskegs of British Columbia was hailed by the Canadian Geographical Journal as "a scientific expedition made possible through [Bedaux's] ... enlightened generosity."

Exactly who was this enlightened citizen? Where had he sprung from? How had he amassed a fortune so grand that he could afford a Fifth Avenue apartment in New York, sprayed daily with quarts of lilac water, an entire grouse moor in Scotland and a castle in France staffed by thirty liveried servants?

He was the son of an impoverished French railroad worker. At sixteen, he had emigrated to New York, with only a few dollars in his pocket. That year, 1906, he kept himself alive scrubbing bottles and glasses in a waterfront saloon. He moved up to a nine-dollar-a-week waiter; later he worked as a sandhog on the East River tunnel. He saved his money, became an American citizen, and focused what was obviously a first-class brain onto a peculiarly American problem: how to get people to work more efficiently.

Shortly before the Great War, Bedaux set himself up in Cleveland as a business efficiency expert and there he started to spread the gospel of what he called the B-Unit – a means of relating time to movement in factory operations. The B-Unit has been described as an efficiency squeeze system designed to exact the last ounce of sweat from the workingman; it was to make the name of Bedaux a stench in the nostrils of organized labour. It was also to make Charles Bedaux fabulously wealthy.

By 1920, the emperor of efficiency had moved his headquarters to New York, where he presently installed himself on the fifty-third floor of the Chrysler Building in an oak-panelled office got up as a medieval monastery. This was the centre of an international spider's web which soon reached into eighteen countries, where Bedaux's time-study experts offered advice and counsel to wealthy industrialists. Soon Bedaux acquired the additional adornment of a socially impeccable spouse in the person of Fern Lombard, the daughter of a Michigan tycoon. A lean and lanky woman, with a darkly handsome face, she towered over her chunky, bullet-headed husband. Bedaux was only five foot six inches tall, but he was determined to be a big man in other ways. His expensively tailored figure became a familiar sight on Bond Street, Park Avenue and the Rue de Rivoli. In his several homes on both sides of the Atlantic he entertained the moneyed elite. But these minor indulgences were not enough. Bedaux wanted to show the world he could do things that no one else could.

He had made two earlier expeditions through British Columbia in 1926 and 1932. In 1930 he drove ten thousand miles across North Africa from Mombasa on the Indian Ocean through the Sudan, Egypt, Libya, Algeria and Morocco to Casablanca on the Atlantic. But these forays went generally unnoticed. Bedaux determined that the next one would make headlines and to that end hired a New York public relations man, Austin Carson, to build up press interest.

Why did he do it? Bedaux's most plausible explanation was that "I am just a nut who likes to do things first." A decade later, when his wartime connections with the Axis powers were revealed, some were to suggest, in hindsight, a more sinister motive. But Bedaux always insisted that his only interest was to challenge the impossible.

"It's fun to do things others call impossible," he said, at one of his press conferences. "Everyone says that to take a fleet of automobiles through the unmapped Rockies where there are no roads can't be done. I say it can. If I succeed, it will open up a vast region which has never been explored. The government hasn't much faith in me but I have done the impossible before."

Bedaux also talked of finding a northern outlet to the Pacific; about the possibility of prospecting for gold; about mounting big game heads for a Paris museum; and about testing tractors for Citroën, as he had done in Africa. Much of this was pure fantasy. There is no evidence that he did any prospecting or big game hunting. As for the Citroëns, he was soon to discover that northern British Columbia is not the Libyan desert. It was as if Rommel had attempted to fight a tank battle in the Alps.

Bedaux's route would lead from Edmonton to Fort St. John in the Peace River country of British Columbia, then northwest by way of the Prophet and the Muskwa rivers to the summit of the Rockies and thence on to Telegraph Creek and the Pacific. A good deal of this country was still a blank space on the map.

In February, Bedaux sailed to Paris to order the five tracked vehicles, especially built by the Citroën company for the venture. He had already engaged as his second-in-command an Edmonton geologist named John Bocock, who got clearance for the expedition from the British Columbia Department of Lands. The department also donated the services of two geographers, Ernest Lamarque and Frank Swannell, together with the princely sum of six hundred dollars. Since Bedaux was spending a quarter of a million on the expedition, this was hardly enough to pay for the chewing gum and cigarettes which Madame Bedaux handed out daily to the wranglers. For the hard-pressed department, it was a bargain – a heaven-sent opportunity to map some seventy miles of uncharted country lying between the Muskwa River and Dease Lake, mainly at Bedaux's expense.

In Vancouver, Bocock hired a surveyor, A. H. Phipps, and a radio operator, Bruce McCallum. In April, Lamarque took an advance party out of Fort St. John to mark the route, using small French tricolor flags as guideposts. Lamarque's party was followed by a second group of six men and fifty-six horses whose task was to hack a roadway of sorts for the tractors through the densely packed trees, brush and deadfalls. This party was led by a hefty Englishman, one Reginald Geake, a mysterious figure who seemed impervious to the elements; even on the coldest days he insisted on wearing khaki shorts and going hatless, his only adornment being a silk handkerchief tied around his head. A former British naval commander, Geake had ostensibly retired to Pouce Coupé in British Columbia; but his neighbours were firmly convinced that he was a member of the British secret service. The suspicion, never proved, was eventually given credence when Geake was mysteriously murdered in Mexico. No reader of Oppenheim could fail to be intrigued by the seedy implausibility of his demise: he was reportedly searching for gold in the company of a blind man.

In Edmonton, the remainder of Bedaux's polygot entourage was assembling. This included his Scottish gamekeeper, Robert Chisholm; J. A. Weiss, a professional Alpine guide from Jasper; Floyd D. Crosby, a movie cameraman from New York and his assistant; Charles Balourdet, the Citroën company's top mechanic; an Italian-Swiss countess, Signora Bilonha Chiesa, described as a big game hunter; Bedaux's wife, Fern, and her Spanish maid, Josefina Daly.

In June, Bedaux announced that this cosmopolitan assemblage would move to Jasper Park for "training."

"I suppose it sounds funny training for such a journey, but there's nothing like being fit when tackling something hard. We'll go up there and climb mountains and chase mountain sheep for a few days and that'll take the fat off us."

Much of the fat that came off must certainly have gone back on in the series of champagne parties and banquets that followed. In Edmonton, that June, the citizens became used to the spectacle of the newly arrived tractors, with their gleaming white paint and their nickel-plated accessories, rumbling around town on practice spins.

Finally, on July 6, the Bedaux Sub-Arctic (Citroën) Expedition was ready to depart. First, however, there was the inevitable champagne breakfast for Edmonton's upper crust; then, a full-dress parade down Jasper Avenue; and, after that, a farewell speech by the Lieutenant-Governor. When these civilities drew to their graceful close, the expedition rumbled off on the first leg of its journey – a five hundred and fifty mile run over a muddy, unpaved road to Fort St. John.

The tractors, spewing mud and pulling loaded trailers, crawled along at an average speed of four miles an hour. At the French-Canadian settlements of St. Albert and Morinville over the grinding of the gears came the sound of cheers. "Vive Bedaux!" the local citizens cried, waving tricolor flags. At Grande Prairie, the populace thrust up a ceremonial arch beneath which the mayor delivered a welcoming speech. And why not? It was the worst year of the Depression but Bedaux was spending good money for lodgings in small hotels and private homes.

The going was not easy, for that summer was one of the wettest on record. The fruitful Peace River soil, which has produced a succession of international wheat-growing champions, had already turned to gumbo, slippery as ice, thicker than glue. Clogged by mud, feed pipes and transmissions, differentials and brake-drums refused to function. Under these circumstances Bedaux was no longer the charming bon vivant. There was a nasty little scene at Tupper Creek involving a young dental student named Bill Murray who had been hired at the last minute. Bedaux was underneath one of the stranded half-tracks, trying to scrape off some of the mud. Murray was talking to a group of local girls. When Bedaux emerged, mud-stained, one or two of the girls made the mistake of giggling. Bedaux fired Murray on the spot.

Frank Swannell, the B.C. government surveyor, soon discovered that Bedaux was not really serious about mapping unknown country. When one of the tractors bogged down in a mudhole, Bedaux threw out a hundred pounds of Swannell's equipment rather than dispense with any of his own luxuries. As if that was not enough, the leader appropriated Swannell's surveying assistant, Al Phipps, and turned him into a personal servant.

On July 17, the expedition lumbered into the farming village of Fort St. John. Bedaux pitched his asbestos fibre tents in a local baseball field and, in a gesture which was literally flamboyant, attempted to set them on fire to prove their resistance. The locals gasped appreciatively; the well-heeled stranger was bringing prosperity to a town sunk in the depths of depression despair. He was offering four dollars a day (twice the going rate) to anyone who knew how to handle a horse, and seventy-five dollars (three times the going rate) for the horses. He purchased seventy-five animals and took on a dozen wranglers to handle them. That was merely the beginning: he had fifty steel tanks especially made in which the horses would carry gasoline for the Citroëns. Then he masterminded a farewell scene by his cameraman, Floyd Crosby, who had worked with the famous documentary film-maker, Robert Flaherty. Every one of the several score of men, women and children taking part in the scene was presented with a ten-dollar bill. It was estimated that Bedaux left something on the order of forty-five thousand dollars in Fort St. John; no wonder the Board of Trade threw a banquet for him.

The expedition was held up repairing the Citroëns until July

22. The departure, however, was delayed until three that afternoon in order to accommodate both speech-making and movie-making. The entire company spent an hour and a half standing in the mud of the main street while the newly broken ponies bucked off packs, riders and gas tanks. Indians arrived and were included in Bedaux's filmed epic. Finally, the expedition lurched forward for eight miles and at 9:30 p.m. set up camp.

The following day there was an altercation over the Citroëns between Bedaux and the French mechanic, Balourdet. The expedition had come to a stop before a small creek. The bridge was washed out and Bedaux, over Balourdet's objections, insisted that the half-tracks ford the four-foot-deep stream. The first car tilted over at a forty-five-degree angle and stuck fast. An attempt was made to bring the second one across on a floating bridge; it, too, tilted and was almost washed away. Finally, the crew set to felling trees to rebuild the bridge, while the two marooned vehicles were winched out of the creek bed and hauled across by cable.

The following day all five vehicles floundered in three hundred yards of swamp and had to be dragged out by cable. It took four hours to move one quarter of a mile. The front wheels of one of the trailers, overloaded with fourteen hundred pounds of winch and cable, splayed apart at the top of a slope; a day later it was ditched. The tree-cutting party up ahead had failed to cut low enough so that the tractors were constantly jamming their axles against raw stumps. On July 25, each car had to have a separate road cut for it through a swamp near Cache Creek. The day's run was no more than two miles and the tractors were in such bad condition that the company was not able to move again until the end of the month. In all that time they had moved a mere fifty miles beyond Fort St. John.

Meanwhile, to everybody's bafflement, Bedaux fired Bruce McCallum, his radio operator, his explanation being that the radio didn't work well enough to justify its extra weight, not to mention the food that its operator was consuming. As a result, the expedition was now out of touch with civilization. Bedaux attempted to solve the problem by sending back couriers from time to time with dispatches which were telegraphed from Fort St. John to New York and Paris. Without the radio, of course, Swannell could no longer get a Greenwich time signal and had to depend on the stars to chart the expedition's course.

All this time Floyd Crosby was grinding away with his camera under Bedaux's direction. One would have thought that the problem of rafting the Citroëns across the streams, hauling them out of muskegs, dragging them through the tangle of alder and willow,

Above: *Bedaux, at left, in the act of supervising one of his puzzling motion picture sequences.*

At left: *Bedaux dressed up one of the horse wranglers in this fake cowboy outfit to add a touch of what he considered to be authenticity.*

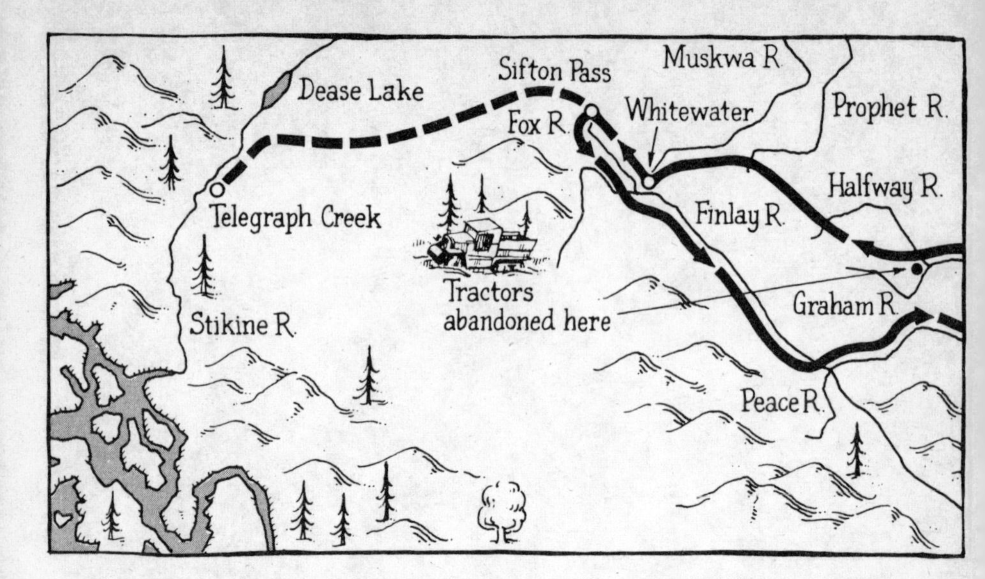

and winching them over precipices would have provided lively and dramatic fare. But the reality was not good enough for Bedaux. Over and over again he staged fictional scenes for the camera.

In camp, during that final week in July, for instance, one of the half-tracks was shown lumbering through the young poplars. Balourdet was at the controls while Swannell and Ev Withrow, the camera assistant, clung to the sidesteps, axes in hand, looks of grim determination on their faces. Al Phipps, Swannell's assistant, was then shown shouting a warning. As the half-track screeched to a stop, all the men leaped from it, dashed forward and began hacking a trail through the trees, watched by a band of baffled Indians.

The expedition struggled off again on July 31, leaving another ruined trailer in its wake. By this time the whole country was a quagmire. The rain never seemed to let up; in the first thirty-seven days, there were only five which might be described as dry. On some days the tractors could not move more than a mile.

Clearly, this was not Citroën country and it was tacitly decided that the vehicles would have to be abandoned. Two men were sent forward on a two-hundred-mile dash to tell Geake and his men to stop hacking out a road for the tractors; a packtrail would be sufficient. Meanwhile Bedaux busied himself with more scenes for his movie, as Swannell's diary entry for August 4 reports:

"Afternoon spent by our chiefs in rifle practice. In the evening a movie by flares simulating a fire in camp. I dash across in frantic

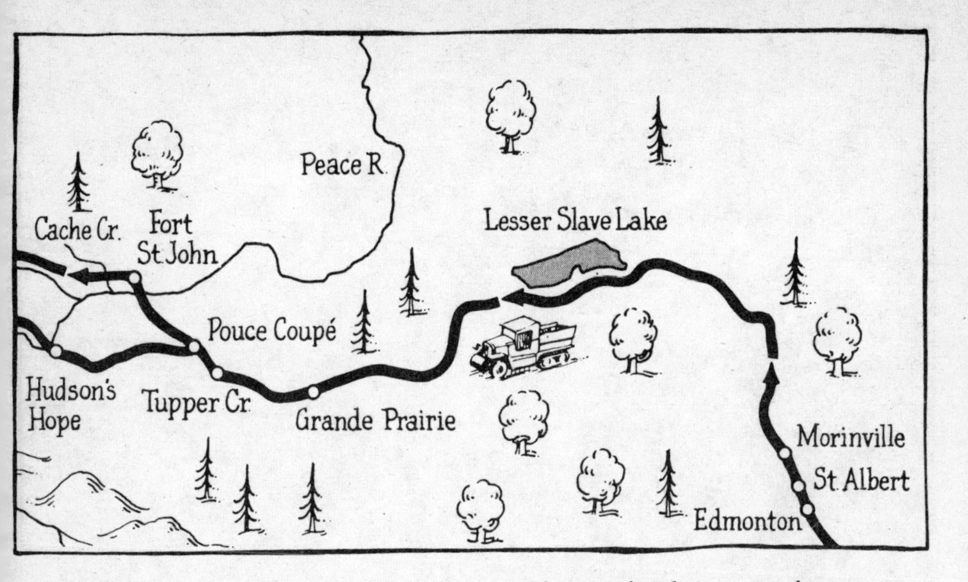

haste to save my tent – this is the cue for our buckaroo cowboys to drive the pack train in front of the camera. The others dash out of the tents with dunnage and Josefina finally emerges screaming. All went well except the pack horses stampeded and wouldn't face the flames."

Bedaux had conveniently glossed over the fireproof qualities of his asbestos tents.

On August 7, when the expedition reached the junction of the Graham and Halfway rivers, about ninety miles from Fort St. John, it became clear that the tractors could go no further. The previous evening, Swannell had recorded "cooks quarreling and everybody grumbling." But Bedaux intended to make the most of adversity. He spent the next four days making preparations for a spectacular movie sequence detailing the destruction of the tractors. He ordered that a rock bluff, rising a hundred and twenty feet above the Halfway River, be undermined. On August 11, two of the tractors were driven to the lip of the precipice and, as the cameras ground, the hill caved in and the cars made a spectacular plunge into the river as the drivers jumped free at the last moment and loads of empty boxes burst forth and spilled into the gorge below.

At four that same afternoon, Bedaux ordered his exhausted men to move the entire camp across the river. A frantic struggle followed to get the tents pitched before darkness fell. Everything had to be loaded aboard a raft and winched across by one of the tractors. It was 10:30 before the tents were raised but breakfast

Above: *An Edmonton crowd watches demonstration of a Citroën half-track.*
Below: *The reality. Horses struggling to pull tractor out of the mud.*

Above: *Madame Bedaux and her mysterious companion, Signora Chiesa.*
Below: *The raft that was used to destroy one of the Citroën tractors.*

was scheduled for 6:45 the following morning because Bedaux was planning another movie sequence.

This time he set his men to work drilling dynamite holes in the cliffs above a series of rapids. Bedaux's idea was to place one of the tractors on the raft, slash the cable and then, as the raft smashed into the bank, detonate the dynamite which would cause the entire cliff to collapse, submerging the raft and tractor. The plan went awry: the cameras whirred away behind screens of brush but the raft missed the cliff, swung clear and charged down the river for some twenty miles before it came to ground on a sandbar. (Some months later the machine was salvaged by a local rancher.) The blasting was also a fizzle; in Swannell's words, "the drill holes merely erupting upward like squibs." For Floyd Crosby, however, it was a useful practice session; he later went to Hollywood where he worked on everything from documentaries to horror pictures.

These minor setbacks did not appear to faze Bedaux. If the tractor hadn't actually been swamped by a falling cliff, it *ought* to have been. He reported all these spurious incidents as genuine accidents. The drowning of a packhorse became the drowning of a man. When one of his wranglers, Jim Blackman, took a rest at a nearby ranch, Bedaux, through his New York publicity agent, blew it up into a tale of a cowboy gone missing in the wilderness.

With the tractors gone, Bedaux bought thirty more packhorses. He now insisted on military discipline. Members of the expedition mounted their steeds at Bedaux's cry of "Aux chevaux!" and dismounted on his order, "Aux pieds!". The Prussian symmetry of these spectacles was marred, however, by the refusal of Madame Bedaux and Signora Chiesa to be hurried. The ladies did not mingle with the common herd; the so-called "big game hunter," in fact, vanished into her tent as soon as it was pitched and there is no evidence that she so much as shot a rabbit. The women's interminable toilets each morning, at the hands of Josefina the maid, caused maddening delays. At first the horses were saddled and ready at six, but when it was found that they had to stand around loaded for hours, the start time was advanced to ten. This did no good; the women merely drew out their preparations and were rarely ready to set off before noon. Bedaux made no attempt to hurry them.

As the long train of packhorses struggled toward the Rocky Mountains, the route grew rougher and marshier. The animals began to suffer from hoof rot, brought on by the constant immersion in mud; few days went by without at least one being shot. When that happened, some of the kit had to be abandoned, but Bedaux

Horse wranglers rigged up this curious contraption in order to teach Josefina, Madame Bedaux's personal maid, how to ride a horse.

refused to part with personal comforts. Several horses continued to stumble along loaded down with French wines, books and women's shoes. One afternoon, Bocock insisted that several hundred rounds of ammunition be discarded. Bedaux couldn't bear to leave it lying around in the wilderness; he had his cowboys fire it off into the air– "the craziest scene you ever saw," to quote Swannell.

On September 1, the party reached the Muskwa River and entered unmapped country. The mornings were chill and there were small flurries of snow. Bedaux decided that the time had come for his Swiss-born guide, Weiss, to make a quick reconnaisance on skis. Poor Weiss was forced to mount a horse every morning and ride in great discomfort with a pair of skis strapped to his back. The opportunity to use them never arose.

Balourdet, the elite Citroën mechanic, was now a man without a job. Bedaux put him in charge of the lanterns, a crushing blow to his dignity. The plight of the horses, scrabbling for meagre feed, worried him. Swannell recorded his concern, as the animals strayed farther and farther from camp in search of pasture:

"Waire 'ee going, ze 'orses, for eating?" Sometimes it took four hours to round the horses up again in the chilly mornings.

The expedition had caught up with the trail-blazing party when it reached the Muskwa and now numbered forty-three men and women and about one hundred and thirty horses. The cowboys began secretly dumping whole cases of canned food, blankets, cook stoves and unused reels of movie film. On September 13, when Bedaux reached Whitewater (now Ware) at the junction of the Fox and Findlay rivers, he was clearly preparing himself for failure. Lamarque and an Indian guide had been sent ahead seeking a route through the mountains to the expedition's objective of Telegraph Creek. If they found one, they were to telegraph Victoria which would relay the message by a broadcast to Whitewater. But the deadline for the message passed without any word. Bedaux dispatched two of his men to rent some power boats and then led the party up the Fox River to Sifton Pass on his own, believing Lamarque to be lost.

The expedition reached the pass on September 19, trekked on through heavy snow to the Drift Pile River and stopped. Food supplies were low. Horses were being shot daily. Some of the men were reduced to ploughing along on foot because there weren't enough fit animals for everybody. Bedaux decided that all must turn back.

He did not, however, neglect his motion picture epic. Floyd Crosby and his helper continued to grind out scenes devised by their master. At the Fox Pass, the missing geographer, Lamarque, arrived back at camp to witness a mind-boggling spectacle: all of Bedaux's cowboys were crawling around the campsite on their stomachs as if in the final throes of fatigue. Lamarque was anxious to inform Bedaux that he could now lead the party to Telegraph Creek but Bedaux began shouting at him and his Indian guide: "Go back into the bush and come into the scene on your hands and knees." Lamarque stolidly refused to be part of the charade. As for Bedaux, he did not share Lamarque's enthusiasm for the rest of the trip. (The telegram had been sent to Whitewater but it had never arrived.) Six power boats were waiting on the Findlay to bear him swiftly homeward. It was a nine days' trek back through the snow and that was enough for him. On October 10, the entire entourage boarded the power boats at Whitewater and made the cold, dangerous journey down the Findlay and into the Peace River to Hudson's Hope (covering in thirteen days by water a journey that had taken fifty-nine by land). There the wranglers were paid off while Bedaux and his guests left by truck for Pouce Coupé and the railhead.

Bedaux's retreat through the wilds of British Columbia had some resemblance to Napoleon's from Moscow. Dead horses, wrecked vehicles, tents, clothing, saddles, pack gear and cases of food littered the route. Some of the cowboys backtracked to salvage the more serviceable equipment. Bedaux himself, when paying them off, divided up the extra rifles, binoculars, stoves, saddles and cameras. Bert Bowes, the Fort St. John garage-owner, recovered four of the tractors. One served his garage as a wrecker until the early 1950s; another was employed all through World War Two as a tractor on a ranch. Parts from the others were used to reconstruct another which later found its way to a museum in Saskatoon.

Bedaux, however, still retained enough personal equipment to fill three trucks and two taxis. Bert Bowes' bill to move it all to the railroad station at Pouce Coupé came to two hundred dollars. Bedaux tipped him an extra fifty.

On October 22, at Pouce Coupé, the erstwhile explorer held a press conference in which he jauntily blamed the failure of his expedition on bad weather. He insisted that the original idea was sound, though he admitted that the Citroën half-tracks had not lived up to expectations. But some day, he prophesied, a highway would be built in the wake of the trail that he had blazed. In that he was partially correct; eight years later the Alaska Highway paralleled some of the same route taken by his expedition.

To Bedaux, this was a mere incident in a life crowded with adventure and intrigue. He followed up his British Columbia safari with later expeditions to India, Tibet and Persia. In 1937, he made headlines again when the Duke and Duchess of Windsor were married in his château in the south of France. That same year he tried to organize a tour of America for their highnesses; a bitter outcry from organized labour, which attacked his speed-up system and accused him of fascist sympathies, caused his speedy withdrawal from the venture. The charge of fascism was not hollow; later that year, Bedaux rented a summer home near Hitler's eyrie in Berchtesgaden and began to develop close associations with several leading Nazis including von Ribbentrop, the foreign minister, and Hjalmar Schacht, Hitler's financial wizard. In the war that followed, Bedaux acted as an intermediary between Pierre Laval's Vichy government and Berlin.

In 1941 he devised a plan for the German protection of the Persian Gulf oil refineries from Allied bombing. (The Germans had expected that Rommel's drive into Egypt would be successful.) After the United States entered the war, Bedaux gave the Germans valuable information from the files of his international company at Amsterdam. In the summer of 1943, he undertook, on Laval's authority, to construct a pipeline across the Sahara, which he had once explored in Citroën tractors. Its purpose was to relieve the scarcity of edible oils in the Reich. He had begun to assemble men and equipment for this task when the American army, in December 1943, overran the area and Bedaux was captured.

He was arrested and flown back to the United States just before Christmas, charged with trading with the enemy. He was kept in a cell in the immigration bureau where he regularly asked for sleeping pills to counteract his chronic insomnia. On Valentine's Day, Charles E. Bedaux was dead by his own hand, the victim of an overdose of the hoarded barbiturates.

When the news reached Fort St. John, people shook their heads sagely and declared that they had known all along that Bedaux was engaged in espionage. "Looking back on it," said Bert Bowes, the garage-owner, "the man was obviously a spy." In hindsight the entire expedition took on a sinister aspect: the firing of the radio operator, the fake movie-making (no one ever saw the film), the strategic importance of the route itself, the presence of the mysterious Geake – all these bits and pieces of evidence were dredged up to bolster the view that Bedaux was in the pay of the Axis powers, trying to find out if Alaska could be defended successfully from the interior.

If true, the Bedaux expedition must have been the most expensive and cumbersome cover operation ever mounted and Bedaux himself must go down as one of the most inept spies in history. But the real explanation, surely, is simpler. Charles Bedaux, *circa* 1934, was exactly what he claimed to be: a rich nut who liked to do the impossible; a self-made success squandering his funds on a fantasy; a middle-aged man trying to capture a childhood he had never known, playing with grown-up toys like movie cameras and nickel-plated tractors; a five-foot-six egotist trying desperately, and not very effectively, to be noticed.

18
The Man Who Invented Dan McGrew

His log cabin stood directly across the dusty road from our own home in Dawson City. It was the town's chief tourist attraction. Each summer, when the visitors poured off the sternwheelers, they boarded a yellow bus, which drove them directly to the poet's shrine. We children lay hidden in the long grass, peering at the strangers who squeezed through the door. We did not think to enter the cabin ourselves; I was fifty years old and a tourist myself before I saw its interior. It was, after all, no different from thousands of similar cabins that were strewn over every hillside for fifty miles out of Dawson, empty monuments, all of them, to the days of the great stampede.

We knew all about Robert W. Service, of course. A special edition of *Songs of a Sourdough*, his first and most famous work, lay in the parlour, specially bound in fringed caribou hide with real gold nuggets pressed into the picture of a gold pan that was burned onto the cover. He had left Dawson forever almost twenty years before but there were scores who remembered him – the diffident young teller, weighing gold in the Bank of Commerce, the man on the bicycle peddling alone along the old Klondike road, the recluse, retired to his cabin, scribbling verses with a carpenter's pencil on rolls of wallpaper. He had escorted my mother to a dance in the days when she was a young kindergarten teacher; he had even read the newest of his ballads to her – the one about Blasphemous Bill. She had told him it was awfully reminiscent of the one about Dan McGrew. He had agreed; that, he said, was what the public wanted.

In school we recited Service's verses. They were as real to us as the grey river, rolling past the town on its long journey to the Bering Sea.

The summer – no sweeter was ever;
The sunshiny woods all athrill;
The grayling aleap on the river,
The bighorn asleep on the hill.

Tintern Abbey and Dover Beach were light years away, but every one of us had seen the grayling leaping in the cold Klondike waters and knew exactly what a bighorn sheep looked like.

The winter! the brightness that blinds you,
The white land locked tight as a drum,
The cold fear that follows and finds you,
The silence that bludgeons you dumb.

Which one of us had not stood, hip-deep in the crusted snows, high on those wooded hills beyond the town and *heard* the silence of winter? None of us had ever seen Wordsworth's host of waving daffodils (they wouldn't grow in the Yukon) but each of us had "gazed on naked grandeur when there's nothing else to gaze on." Service's verse grew out of an experience we all shared. I remember, for instance, reading the first lines of "The Telegraph Operator":

I will not wash my face;
I will not brush my hair,
I "pig" about the place –
There's nobody to care.
Nothing but rock and tree;
Nothing but wood and stone;
Oh, God, it's hell to be
Alone, alone, alone!

And I remember, at the age of six, drifting down the river with my family and encountering just such a man. I can see him now, wildly dishevelled, running down from his telegrapher's shack on the bank, pleading with us to stop, stay, have dinner, stay overnight, eat breakfast. Stay for days . . . for weeks . . . as long as we wanted. And when, after our brief meeting we had to move on, running along the bank, crying out: Don't go yet . . . please . . . You've only just come. Please, don't go!

Service, in his lifetime, wrote some two thousand poems. Four, at least, are imperishable – and that is not a bad record. These are "The Law of the Yukon," "The Spell of the Yukon," "The Cremation of Sam McGee" and "The Shooting of Dan McGrew." The titles are part of the language and the stanzas are shouted, declaimed, whispered, carolled, parodied and mumbled by men and women, drunk and sober, boys and girls, comedians and actors, from school stages, in church halls, around campfires, in front of microphones, at father and son banquets, stag parties, smokers, reunions, in moments of high carnival and nights of revel wherever the English language is spoken.

Of the four, "The Shooting of Dan McGrew," is the most familiar. It has twice been made into a motion picture, was the subject of the first original Canadian ballet, was parodied by everybody from Bobby Clarke, the Broadway comic, to Guy Lombardo, has been recorded close to a dozen times and lives on in several obscene versions.

Tens of thousands of people are convinced that the story is true and these have included a suspicious number of Klondikers. In February 1934, the Canadian Press interviewed, in Regina, one Philip Gershel, aged seventy-one, who claimed he was the Ragtime Kid of the ballad. "I knew Dan McGrew and all the others," Gershel declared and went on to describe the Lady That's Known as Lou as a big blonde, "tough but big-hearted – a grand lady." Gershel said that the incident had taken place in the Monte Carlo Saloon in Dawson City and that Lou was married and living in Sioux Falls, North Dakota. Two years later, Mike Mahoney, whose story was to be chronicled in a bestseller, *Klondike Mike*, announced that he, too, had been an eyewitness to the fatal shooting. "I was right there when it happened in the Dominion Saloon," said Mahoney, who claimed that Lou was still alive in Dawson City. In 1940, the *Toronto Star* published what it claimed was an authentic account of the shooting which, it said, took place in Dawson in 1897. In 1942, in a motion picture version of *The Spoilers*, Rex Beach's famous novel about Nome, Alaska, the poet is shown sitting in a smoke-filled saloon, actually writing about Dan McGrew. The version was given added credence by the fact that Service played the role himself.

The facts are somewhat different. There was no Malemute Saloon in Dawson, no lady called Lou, no Dan McGrew and no shoot-outs. Service made up the story before he actually saw the Klondike. Of all his verses it is the least characteristic of the Canadian north. It is pure romance, based on Service's boyhood reading about the American Wild West and his own experiences in the camps of the coastal United States. It irked Service that of all the poems he published, it was this first one that made his name. He himself had long since tried to forget it. "I loathe it," he said. "I was sick of it the moment I finished writing it." Yet wherever he went and was known, he was asked to recite it.

A good many people, including several Klondike historians,

find it difficult to believe that Service wasn't within five thousand miles of Dawson City during the gold rush era. When the news of the great strike reached the outside world in July of 1897, he was a hobo in California. While others rushed north, Service headed for Mexico. For the next decade he was a drifter. In his remarkably vague memoirs (there is scarcely a single date) he tells us that he was variously a gardener in a rural bordello, a miner, a sandhog, a fruit picker, and a bum, eating food picked from gutters or begged at back doors or handed out at gospel saloons. Much of this must be taken with a shaker of salt. Service also suggested in his memoirs that he was raised in poverty in Scotland in a flat infested with rats, mice and cockroaches. This account so antagonized his several brothers and sisters that some of them were estranged from him. Service was not raised in anything approaching luxury, but the Glasgow district in which he was brought up was no slum. His grandfather was a postmaster, his father a bank teller. His mother inherited a small legacy and Service himself was weaned on the classics of English literature. After a spell as a bank clerk, he emigrated to North America hoping to be a cowboy in Canada, practising, over and over again, the quick draw from the hip with an air pistol. Instead, he found himself digging potatoes on Vancouver Island for fifteen dollars a month.

After the turn of the century, Service drifted back from the South to Canada. In 1903, he walked into the Vancouver branch of the Canadian Bank of Commerce, hauled out a dog-eared testimonial from his former bank manager in Glasgow, and was given a job. He worked successively in Vancouver, Victoria and Kamloops and then, in the fall of 1904, was sent to the bank's branch in Whitehorse, then a tiny village at the head of navigation on the Yukon River, some four hundred miles, as the salmon swims, from Dawson City.

For a man who was to become famous for his rough-and-tumble verse, Service presented a remarkably mild face to the world. In the hard-drinking Yukon, he remained a teetotaller, saving his pennies in the hopes of becoming financially independent. A lifelong agnostic, he agreed to act as a deacon in the church. A shy loner, he preferred solitary walks among the birches and aspens that fringed Miles Canyon, to the lively parties that whiled away the long winter. After his ballads were published Service had to face the astonishment of strangers who could not match his unassuming personality with the virility of his writing. ("His face is mild to the point of disbelief," one Canadian reporter wrote." And in Hollywood, the casting department at Universal balked at the idea of him playing himself; they said he wasn't the Robert Service type.)

At the church concerts in Whitehorse, the young bank clerk played the banjo, took part in amateur theatricals, produced a play and recited "Casey at the Bat" and "Gunga Din." Since childhood he had been attracted by the stage and all his life he revelled in role playing. When he first arrived in Canada he immediately donned a Buffalo Bill costume his father had bought for him. On a brief stint as a lumberman "I wore the rough overalls of the toiler, the denim shirt and heavy boots, but was prouder of them than I would have been of a suit from Savile Row." Each job, to Service, was a drama; and he tended to take jobs that allowed him time to dream. "The world has been a stage for me," he wrote, "and I have played the parts my imagination conceived. Rarely have I confronted reality .... "

In Whitehorse, with another church concert coming up, E.J. "Stroller" White, the colourful editor of the *Whitehorse Star*, suggested that, instead of reciting Kipling, Service might like to do something of his own. The idea appealed to Service; after all, in his younger days, he had written scores of poems, many of which had been published in Scotland; and in California, sitting around the hobo fires, he had sung many of his own songs. It was years since he had tried his hand at verse but he needed no prompting. Walking past the saloons on a Saturday evening and hearing the sounds of revelry a line popped into his head: "A bunch of the boys were whooping it up ... "

The rest came easily. When he reached the bank (the clerks lived in rooms on the second floor) Service decided to seek the quiet of the teller's cage to finish his ballad. There, he tells us, a bank guard, believing him to be an intruder, fired a shot from his pistol, which happily missed. "With the sensation of a bullet whizzing past my head, and a detonation ringing in my ears, the ballad was achieved."

Service, who never let the truth get in the way of a good story, admitted in the last year of his life that this particular incident was pure hokum. What followed, however, was as dramatic as fiction.

Service was told that "The Shooting of Dan McGrew" was too raw to recite in church and so, believing it worthless, he stuffed it away in a bottom drawer under some shirts. He continued, however, to write verse for his own amusement. A month later he met a mining man from Dawson who, removing a stogie from his face, suddenly turned to him and said: "I'll tell you a story Jack London never got," and thereupon spun a yarn about a prospector who had cremated his partner. Everybody laughed except Service who saw it as the core of a new ballad. In a six-hour walk in the moonlight he composed "The Cremation of Sam McGee," borrowing the name of the hero from the bank's ledger of customers. For the rest of his life, until he died in 1940 in Beiseker, Alberta, scarcely a day passed without the wretched McGee encountering somebody who asked: "Is it warm enough for you?" As a result of the poem, McGee's obituary made the *New York Times* and his cabin, like Service's, became a shrine in Whitehorse.

Service tucked the new ballad away in the same drawer, then went on to write more poems until the inspiration ceased. Some months later he showed his work to the bank manager's wife; she suggested he might make up a little souvenir booklet of some of his poems for friends at Christmas. Service decided to squander his hundred-dollar Yuletide bonus on the venture and suggested to a Scottish friend that he take a half interest. With a single crude phrase, the canny acquaintance did himself out of a fortune: "Ye can jist stick yer poetry up yer bonny wee behind," said he.

Service sent his cheque and his poems to his father, who had emigrated to Toronto. The elder Service took the manuscript to the unlikeliest of all publishing houses, William Briggs, a firm that specialized exclusively in Methodist hymnbooks but which also did job printing on the side. There, an astonishing thing happened: the firm's own employees went crazy over Service's poems. The composing room foreman noticed it first: he had never seen type set so fast; the printers were actually reciting the verses at their machines. One of the travellers grabbed the first proofs and he, too, began to recite out loud. The Briggs firm scarcely knew what hit them; they received seventeen hundred orders for the book from the galleys alone. On the train west, in January 1907, their traveller, R. B. Bond, let his meal grow cold as he read the proofs, while passengers crowded around to hear him declaim. Briggs hurriedly sent Service's cheque back. The poet was chagrined. Shortly after, however, he received an offer of a ten per cent royalty. When the book actually reached Whitehorse, however, he was embarrassed; his own minister reproached him for writing about bad women. Only when the summer came and the tourists started to demand his autograph did Service and the town begin to comprehend his celebrity.

The book, published in Canada as *Songs of a Sourdough* and in New York by Barse and Hopkins as *The Spell of the Yukon*, ran into seven editions before publication day and twenty-four by 1912. Since that time it has sold close to two million copies. It helped make Service not just the wealthiest poet ever to come out of Canada but also the wealthiest writer of any kind. Within a decade he was hailed by the *New York Times* as one of the two best-known living poets in the English language, the other being Edgar Guest.

The publication of his first book rocked the literary world. Aesthetes such as T. P. O'Connor, the Irish poet, praised it. Shackleton the explorer took it with him to the Antarctic. Others attacked the author as a mere versifier, a writer of doggerel, a poor man's Kipling, pandering to popular taste. Service did not disagree, then or later. "Rhyming has my ruin been," he was to write, "with less deftness I might have produced real poetry." More than thirty years after *Songs of a Sourdough* was published, the author wandered into a lecture room to hear himself reviled in the course of a talk on contemporary poetry. When the lecturer had finished, Service rose from the back and said that he knew the poet in question and that he would be the first to "disclaim the imputation that he was a writer of poetry." Service never used the word poet to describe himself; he was, he said, a rhymer.

In the spring of 1908, to Service's delight, the bank posted him to Dawson. He arrived with the mail, which contained a royalty cheque for one thousand dollars; the resultant welcome by his fellow bank clerks was appropriately Rabelaisian. Dawson, once a city of thirty thousand, had declined to four thousand. Service walked the wooden sidewalks, trying to "summon up the ghosts of the argonauts," and listened endlessly to the yarns of men who had climbed the Chilkoot and prospected on Last Chance. In four months, working from midnight until three in the morning, he finished his second book, *Ballads of a Cheechako*. By the rules of literary success, this obvious sequel should have been a flop; it turned out to another bestseller. First, however, Service became involved in a wrangle with his publishers, who didn't want to distribute the book at all because they thought the material too raw. He compromised and removed one objectionable poem in return for an additional five per cent royalty.

Ballads, which contains such classics as "The Man from Eldorado" and "Clancy of the Mounted," confirmed Service as a superb story-teller in verse. They have everything; the surprise ending, the humorous twist, the raw adventure, and, more than once, a whiff of the supernatural. Some of his openings are marvellously gripping:

> There was Claw-Fingered Kitty and Windy Ike
> living the life of shame
> When unto them in the Long, Long Night came
> the man-who-had-no-name
> Bearing his prize of the black fox pelt, out
> of the Wild he came.

Others, in a single line, caught the essence of the insanity that gripped North America when a ship arrived out of the Arctic with a ton of Klondike gold aboard:

Gold! We leapt from our benches. Gold! We sprang
from our stools
Gold! We wheeled in the furrow, fired by the faith
of fools.

Service was just far enough removed from the manic days of the stampede to stand back and see the romance, the tragedy, the adventure and the folly. His verses sprang out of incidents that were common occurrences in the Dawson of that time: Clancy, the policeman, mushing into the north to bring back a crazed prospector; the Man from Eldorado hitting town, flinging his money away and ending up in the gutter; Hard Luck Henry, who gets a love message in an egg, and tracks down the sender only to find that she has been married for months because Dawson-bound eggs are ripe with age.

This was not fiction, as "Dan McGrew" was. As a boy in Dawson I watched Sergeant Cronkhite of the Mounted Police, his parka sugared with frost, mush into town with a crazy man in a straight jacket lashed to his sled. As a teenager, working on the gold creeks, I saw a prospector on a binge light his cigar with a ten-dollar bill, fling all his loose change in the gutter and lose his year's take in a blackjack game. The eggs we ate, like Hard Luck Henry's, came in over the ice, packed in waterglass, strong as cheese, orange as the setting sun.

After *Ballads*, Service decided to write a novel based on the great stampede. Before he could begin he learned to his horror that the bank was about to promote him to manager of its Whitehorse branch. He did not want the responsibility and he did not want to leave Dawson. After some soul-searching he quit. He rented a hillside log cabin (never realizing that half a century later, the Canadian government would restore it in painstaking detail and at enormous expense) and then began to walk the hills, soaking up atmosphere for the book.

He had no idea of the plot when he began to write. He lifted the name of the heroine, Berna, from the label of a can of condensed milk. He scrawled his story on anything that came to hand – copy books, typing paper, building paper, wrapping paper, wallpaper. After five months he had completed *The Trail of '98*, which immediately became a raging bestseller and was later a blockbuster of a motion picture, employing as many as fifteen thousand extras in a single scene. No one reads the novel today: it is a mawkish and saccharine piece of work. It is hard to believe that Service's New York publishers, Dodd, Mead, thought it too bawdy (a seduction scene had to be cut out) and that it was actually banned in Boston.

Service took the manuscript personally to New York, leaving it twice on park benches where, happily for him, if not for posterity, it was twice retrieved. His publishers were astonished to find their Yukon author looking so tame. "Why didn't you arrive in mukluks and a parka, driving a dog team down Fifth Avenue?" he was asked. "It would have made a great ad."

He did not return to the Yukon for a year. Instead he walked all the way from New York to New Orleans and then took a boat to Cuba, where he lived in luxury and boredom. It is typical of Service that, on reading a magazine article about motherhood one day, he recalled that his own mother, whom he had not seen in thirteen years, was now on the same side of the Atlantic, living on a farm near Edmonton. Back he went to Canada and jingled up to the farmhouse in a hired sleigh. One of his sisters answered the door. Service introduced himself to her as an encyclopaedia salesman. His mother was not deceived: "Why," said she, "if it isn't our Willie!"

That spring he decided to return to the Yukon. Characteristically he took the most difficult but also the most romantically adventurous route – the "all-Canadian route" of the Edmonton Trail of '98. He travelled by stage coach to Athabasca Landing, by canoe to Fort McMurray, by Hudson's Bay barge to Fort Smith, by birchbark canoe to Great Slave Lake and then proceeded on down the Mackenzie by steamer. He crossed the Mackenzie divide by canoe and portage, slipped down the Porcupine to Fort Yukon on the steamer *Tanana* and reached Dawson on August 11, "with a face ambushed in an ebony thicket of three weeks' growth, nose broiled to lobster red, hands a Mongolian shade, trousers shredded," to quote the *Dawson News*.

The durability of Service's work was never better illustrated than by his composition, during this long trek, of a song entitled "When the Iceworms Nest Again." This is, perhaps, the best-known folk song in all the north. It has been quoted in various versions in several anthologies. For years there was speculation about its origin. In 1934, the *Northwest Miner* put it into print and credited it to Anon. In 1938, the Yellowknife *Prospector* published it and attributed it to a riverboat crew in 1919. I heard it sung in Yukon mining camps in the late 1930s, but nobody then knew where it had come from. The song was actually composed by

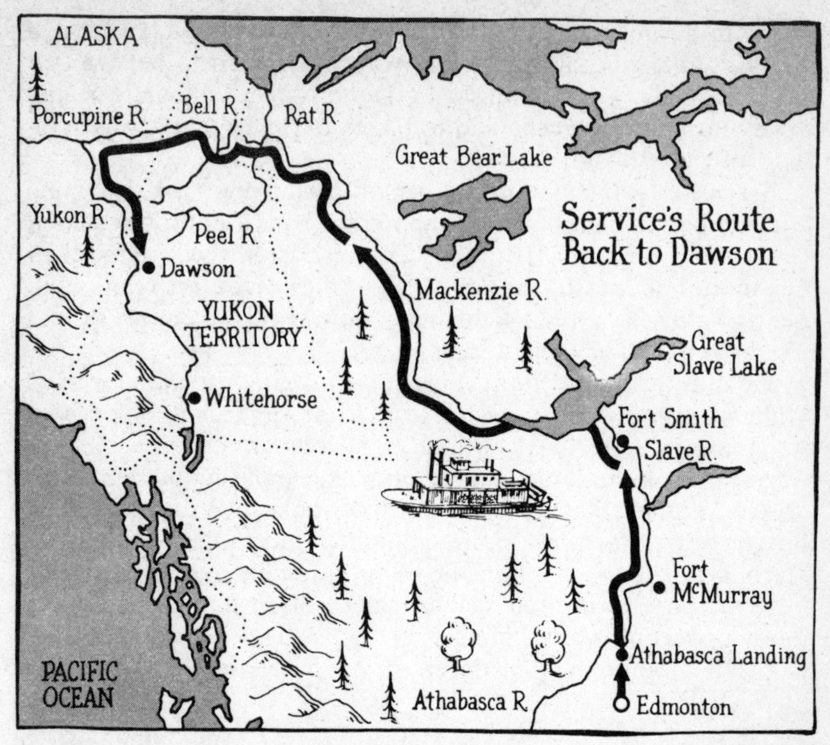

Service and sung to the crew of the *Tanana* in that summer of 1911. In 1939 he published it in a book of songs called *Bath-tub Ballads*, his original version differing considerably from the one handed down orally over three decades.

Back in Dawson, Service settled down once again in the same log cabin, nestling under the hill on Eighth Avenue. Here he began to compose the verse for his third collection, *Rhymes of a Rolling Stone*. Another extraordinary bestseller, it was his Yukon swan song. In *The Spell of the Yukon* he had written: "There's a land – oh, it beckons and beckons. And I want to go back – and I will." But in the autumn of 1912, when the buckbrush on the hilltops had changed to purple, Robert Service took the last steamboat out of Dawson never to return. In the forty-six years that followed he never gave the slightest indication that he ever wanted to see the Yukon again.

By his own account, he continued to lead an adventure-packed life. The *Toronto Star* sent him to cover the Balkan war, where he also served in the Turkish Red Cross. He moved on to Paris, costumed himself in a broad-brimmed hat, a butterfly tie and a velveteen jacket and mingled with artists, models and writers of the order of Gelett Burgess and Jeffery Farnol. Of those days, he was to write: "Like an actor, I was never happy unless I was playing a part. Most people play one character in their lives; I have enacted a dozen and always with my whole heart."

In Paris, Service fitted easily into the role of an impoverished poet. One day in 1913, he rescued a young Frenchwoman from a mob after a streetcar accident. She married him without having the slightest idea who he was, shared his garret on the Boulevard Montparnasse and scrimped for groceries while he wrote his second novel, an autobiographical work aptly named *The Pretender*. She had no idea that her husband was a wealthy man until he took her on a bicycle trip through Brittany, knocked boldly on the door of a luxurious mansion, was welcomed by the concierge who had dinner prepared, and then revealed to her that he had bought the house with the proceeds of his verse.

In the Great War that followed, Service worked as a Red Cross man for the Americans and then as an intelligence officer in the Canadian army. During an illness, he produced another book of verse, *Rhymes of a Red Cross Man*, the most popular collection of war poems to be published in North America. In 1917 and again in 1918, it headed the non-fiction bestseller lists. It also received adulatory reviews from some unexpected sources. Several literary magazines hailed Service as the new Kipling. In *The Dial*, the poet Witter Bynner wrote: "We have been inquiring for the poetry of war. In my judgement, here it is." Service was rapidly attaining a respectability that he had never sought. The Norwegian journalist, Carl J. Hambro, later president of the League of Nations, translated his verse into his native tongue and castigated his countrymen for ignoring the Yukon bard. Louis Untermeyer praised Service in *The Bookman*. "Like Burns," he wrote, "he took the curse off effeminacy in poetry."

By this time, even pale copies of Service's verse was bringing his imitators a modicum of fame. In 1921, *Vanity Fair* published "The Ballad of Yukon Jake, The Hermit of Shark Tooth Shoal." This parody of Service's style by a young Yale graduate was so successful that the magazine republished it in 1926 and again in 1934 and filled requests for thousands of photostatted copies. Eventually the parody appeared in book form and earned its author, Edward E. Paramore, Jr., an invitation to join the Adventurer's Club of Los Angeles, whose board apparently assumed that he was a seasoned Yukon explorer.

When Untermeyer published his *Collected Parodies* in 1926 several of Service's fans complained that he was making sport of a man who couldn't defend himself. By this time it was widely believed that Service was dead. Shortly after the war, *The Times* of London had published an article about writers and artists who had been lost in trenches. The Bard of the Yukon was included. Service did nothing to contradict the assumption; on the contrary, he was amused and a little relieved by it; there was less mail to answer. His French neighbours in Brittany and later in Monte Carlo had no idea who he was and he didn't bother to tell them. Meanwhile, he occupied himself by churning out more novels and books of verse – nine of them between 1920 and 1940, including a curious work on physical fitness – and by travelling the world from Tahiti to the Soviet Union. When he returned to North America in 1940, after fleeing France a few steps ahead of the invading Germans, Service began to encounter people who thought they were seeing a ghost. These included some of his own brothers and sisters. He had, by this time, forgotten how many of them there were (or so he says in his autobiography) and often failed to recognize them when they came up to shake his hand. Two of them, whom he met in hotel lobbies in Canada, opened with the identical salutation: "My God, Bob, I thought you were dead."

Even his two volumes of autobiography, *Ploughman of the Moon*, published in 1945, and *Harper of Heaven*, in 1948, did not entirely dispel the myth of his passing. In the postwar years, Service produced eight more books of verse to an ever-diminishing audience, but his original Yukon poems, anthologized and reanthologized by his publishers under a variety of titles, continued to enjoy a healthy sale. He spent his winters in Monte Carlo and his summers in the same house in Brittany which he had bought years before for his bride. Money had ceased to have any meaning for him; early in the game, the one-time bank teller had sunk all his royalties into annuities. He had no idea what he was worth and he didn't care; his whole idea was to live as long as possible to beat the insurance tables. The health and physical fitness book *Why Not Grow Young*, which he wrote in the 1920s, long before its time, was republished in the 1950s. Among other things, it urged the consumption of vast quantities of potatoes; Service himself claimed to eat twenty-two thousand a year, a statement that even the most devoted follower must have found hard to swallow. None the less, he was a living advertisement for his own theories, a chipper octogenarian, still working daily at his typewriter turning out verse after verse.

I met him, at last, in the spring of 1958, when he had reached the age of eighty-four. The Canadian Broadcasting Corporation asked me to visit him in Monte Carlo and prepare a half-hour filmed interview for television. There was some difficulty in clearing the assignment since several members of the upper echelon were convinced that Service had died years before. A letter from the corpse, however, made it clear that he welcomed the proposal:

Above: *Robert Service in front of his cabin in Dawson City*, c. *1910.*
Below: *The author, left, with Service in Monte Carlo in May 1958.*

For me this will be probably a unique television show as I am now crowding eighty-five, and the ancient carcass will soon cease to function. For that reason I hope you will bring it off successfully. My home here makes a nice setting for an interview which if well planned could be quite attractive.

Patrick Watson and I arrived with a television crew in May. The poet met us at the door of his Villa Aurore, overlooking the warm Mediterranean. He was casually dressed in a sleeveless sweater and slacks, a small, birdlike man with brightly veined cheeks, a sharp nose and a mild, Scottish accent. We started to discuss the interview, but Service held up his hand.

"It's all arranged," he said. "I've spent the week writing it up. Here's your script – I'm afraid you've got the smaller part because, you see, this is *my* show!"

He handed me two sheafs of paper, stapled and folded. "It's in two parts," he said. "We can do the first part after lunch. Now you boys go back to your hotel and *you* (to me) learn your lines. I already know mine, letter perfect. Come back this afternoon and we'll do it."

I looked at Watson. This is not the way spontaneous television interviews are conducted. He gave a kind of helpless shrug and we left.

"What do we do now?" I asked.

"I guess we'd better read what he's written," said Watson.

What Service had written, it turned out, was pretty good – lively, witty, self-effacing, romantic:

I'm crowding eighty-five now (he had written) *and I guess this will be my last show on the screen. Oh, I'm feeling fine though I'm a bit of a cardiac. In middle age I strained my heart trying to walk on my hands. After sixty a man shouldn't try to be an athlete. Only yesterday I was talking politics to a chap in the street. I'm Right and he was Left so we got to shouting, when suddenly I felt the old ticker conk on me, and I had to go home in a taxi, chewing white pills. Say, wouldn't it be a sensation if I croaked in the middle of this interview?*

When we returned Service was easily persuaded to submit to a less formal interview. But whenever one of my questions coincided with one in his script he gave me a letter-perfect answer – even to the line about croaking on television. Service, the actor, managed to make even that sound spontaneous.

We spent three days with Robert Service, his wife and his daughter, filming, in his own words, his own version of his long, checkered life, including, of course, the familiar story of how he wrote "The Shooting of Dan McGrew." In between camera setups, Service and I talked together about the Yukon. He remembered my mother very well and talked about Lousetown, the tenderloin district across the Klondike River. "We used to go down the line every Saturday night," he said, a little wistfully. I asked him why he had never returned to the Yukon. His wife and daughter had made a pilgrimage to the famous cabin during the war years when Service was in Hollywood but the poet himself had stubbornly refused to go. "It would be too sad for me," he said. "I wanted to remember it as it was." My own feeling is that Service just couldn't be bothered. The past did not intrigue him; he lived for the present. He never looked back, never reread any of his work, could not remember any of it. He did not even bother to read the galleys of his books; he paid somebody else to do that because he found them monumentally boring. Only one thing concerned him and that was the work at hand; his greatest poem, to him, was always the one which he was in the act of composing. The Yukon, which had given him fame and of which he had written with so much love and passion, belonged to another era, it seemed, to another man; its spell did not grip Service. "Oh, it's too cold," he told me. "I'm a sun lover."

When the filming was completed, Service, with great ceremony, opened a bottle of champagne which he had been saving for the occasion. All during the filming he had been an enthusiastic interview subject, lively, loquacious, ebullient. "It's made me young again," he said at one point. "I'm just loving it."

Now, as we toasted him, he seemed cast down.

"Is it really over?" he said. "Haven't you got any more questions? I could go on, you know."

But the crew was already packing up the equipment.

"Oh, I do wish we could go on," said Service. "I wish it didn't have to end."

He stood in his dressing gown in the doorway of his villa and the wind, catching the silver of his hair and blowing it over his face, gave him an oddly dishevelled look.

"I wish it could go on forever," said Robert Service, and I caught, briefly, the image of the telegraph operator, running along the riverbank, pleading with us to stay just a little longer.

The interview was shown on the CBC television program *Close-up* in June and was a great success. Almost everybody commented on Service's spontaneous remark about croaking on television. Imagine him saying that! What a character!

It was, indeed, his last performance. That September, in Brittany, Robert Service's heart gave out and he was buried under the sun he loved so well and far, far from those cold snows, which he disliked so heartily, even though they made his fortune.